ENGAGING ECONOMICS

Engaging Economics

New Testament Scenarios
and Early Christian Reception

Edited by

Bruce W. Longenecker *&* Kelly D. Liebengood

WILLIAM B. EERDMANS PUBLISHING COMPANY
GRAND RAPIDS, MICHIGAN / CAMBRIDGE, U.K.

Published 2009 by

Wm. B. Eerdmans Publishing Co.

2140 Oak Industrial Drive N.E., Grand Rapids, Michigan 49505 /

P.O. Box 163, Cambridge CB3 9PU U.K.

Printed in the United States of America

14 13 12 11 10 09   7 6 5 4 3 2 1

Library of Congress Cataloging-in-Publication Data

Engaging economics: New Testament scenarios and early Christian reception /
    edited by Bruce W. Longenecker & Kelly D. Liebengood.
        p.   cm.
    ISBN 978-0-8028-6414-7 (pbk.: alk. paper)
    1. Economics — Religious aspects — Christianity. 2. Economics in the Bible.
    3. Bible. N.T. — Criticism, interpretation, etc.
    I. Longenecker, Bruce W.   II. Liebengood, Kelly D., 1970-

    BR115.E3E63   2009
    261.8'5 — dc22

                                                    2009022382

www.eerdmans.com

Contents

EARLY CHRISTIAN RECEPTION

INTRODUCTORY MATTERS

1. Introduction

Bruce W. Longenecker and Kelly D. Liebengood

1. Economics and the New Testament?

Tertullian once skeptically asked what Athens had to do with Jerusalem.[1] In a similar manner, it might be asked today what Wall Street has to do with Jerusalem. That is, what does economic practice have to do with the seemingly unrelated world of the New Testament?

The view that New Testament interpretation should not be diluted by economic considerations has strong currency today. This was reinforced in an experience that one of the editors of this book had several years ago. When proposing to colleagues that he might teach a course on "Poverty and Wealth in Early Christianity," the response from university colleagues was that it would be better to offer courses dealing with the foundational concerns of the New Testament. This response buys heavily into the assumption that issues of poverty and wealth have little to do with the primary theological interests evident across the spread of the earliest Christian texts — i.e., theology proper, christology, pneumatology, soteriology, ecclesiology, ethics, and the like. Arguably, in light of the magnitude of these overarching interests in New Testament texts, issues of poverty and wealth should be seen as relatively peripheral. In this frame of reference, the long-lasting treasures of New Testament texts are theological insights divorced from any economic interest, since theology should have little to do with economic realities.

As we write these words (December 2008), the western world faces its

---

1. *De Praescriptione Haereticorum* 7.9.

deepest financial crisis since the great depression of the 1930s. Long-established banks and financial institutions are collapsing, countries are going bankrupt, trillions of dollars have suddenly vanished from the stock markets, and governments from opposite sides of the globe are meeting in an attempt to shore up their foundering and intertwined economies. Economics is front and center on the world stage, and so are questions of identity, morality, and ideology.

Who is to say whether the crisis will have subsided long before these words are published? From our current vantage point, it does not look likely that this will be the case. We can only hope that profound lessons will have been learned, or reinforced, in the process. As if it could ever have been doubted previously, the structures of the twenty-first-century world are now shown more clearly than ever to be embedded within a profoundly intertwined and globalized configuration. And at the heart of that globalized interconnectedness lies an economic dimension that shapes and controls the identities of things-that-matter, from whole nations at one end of the spectrum to distinct and diverse individuals at the other end. Quite simply, the current crisis has underscored what many knew already — that economic status is a primary factor in the taxonomy of personal and corporate identity the world over.

If world affairs have recently reminded us of the central role that economics plays in the formation of identity, then hopefully *Engaging Economics* can play a role in demonstrating just how prominently economic responsibility is to be embedded within the formation of Christian identity — at least according to much of the New Testament and its reception in the early centuries of the common era. In essence, the contents of this book go a long way in challenging the view that Wall Street has nothing to do with Jerusalem — that is, if Christian theology in the twenty-first century is to be informed by New Testament texts from the first century.

Engaging Economics joins an already ardent conversation that spans diverse areas of academic interest regarding the economic dimensions of life in the Greco-Roman world during the time of the Roman Empire. Certain sectors within New Testament studies, for instance, evidence a growing interest in economic interpretation of early Christian texts. In the field of Pauline studies, high-water marks include Wayne Meeks's *The First Urban Christians*,[2] Justin

---

2. New Haven: Yale, 1983. The socioeconomic focus of Meeks's second chapter forms something of a spine for the rest of the chapters of his book; see Bruce W. Longenecker, "Socio-Economic Profiling of the First Urban Christians," in *After the First Urban Chris-*

Meggitt's *Paul, Poverty and Survival*,[3] and Steve Friesen's significant article "Poverty in Pauline Studies: Beyond the So-Called New Consensus."[4] While these studies dedicate much of their contents to determining the socioeconomic level of early urban followers of Jesus, often they do so precisely to illuminate the ideological muscle behind the extraordinary rise of the early Christian movement within the Greco-Roman world. And in that regard, economic features are at the forefront of the book entitled *The Jesus Movement: A Social History of Its First Century* by Ekkehardt and Wolfgang Stegemann,[5] along with Douglas Oakman's *Jesus and the Economic Questions of His Day*,[6] or his *Jesus and the Peasants*,[7] or Luise Schottroff and Wolfgang Stegemann's *Jesus and the Hope of the Poor*.[8]

In classical studies, the economic environment of the Greco-Roman world is currently the subject of unprecedented attention, with intense effort being given to determining the identities and significance of various economic drivers in the Greco-Roman world. Since Moses Finley's *The Ancient Economy*,[9] high points in this enterprise would include Peter Garnsey and Richard Saller's *The Roman Empire: Economy, Society, and Culture*,[10] the 1000-page *Cambridge Economic History* (much of which is dedicated to the Greco-Roman world),[11] and William Harris's *The Monetary Systems of the Greeks and Romans*.[12]

With heightened interest in the Greco-Roman economic landscape, church historians are now giving economic features of the early church more attention than ever before. Recent studies of note include Justo Gonzalez, *Faith and Wealth: A History of Early Christian Ideas on the Origin, Significance, and Use of Money*,[13] Peter Brown's *Poverty and Leadership in the Later*

---

tians: The Socio-Historical Study of Pauline Christianity Twenty-Five Years Later, ed. Todd Still and David Horrell (London/New York: Continuum, 2009).

3. Edinburgh: T&T Clark, 1998.

4. *JSNT* 26 (2004): 323-61. For interaction with these and other studies, see Bruce W. Longenecker, *Remember the Poor: Paul, Poverty, and the Greco-Roman World* (Grand Rapids and Cambridge: Eerdmans, forthcoming).

5. ET: Minneapolis: Fortress Press, 1999.

6. Lewiston, NY: Edwin Mellen Press, 1986.

7. Eugene, OR: Cascade Books, 2008.

8. ET: Maryknoll, NY: Orbis, 1986.

9. London: Chatto & Windus, 1974.

10. London: Duckworth Press, 1987.

11. Edited by W. Scheidel, I. Morris, and R. Saller (Cambridge: Cambridge University Press, 2007).

12. Oxford: Oxford University Press, 2008.

13. San Francisco: Harper & Row, 1990; reprinted: Eugene, OR: Wipf & Stock, 2002.

Roman Empire,[14] the Festschrift for Peter Garnsey entitled *Poverty in the Roman World* (half of which studies the early church),[15] Richard Finn's *Almsgiving in the Later Roman Empire: Christian Promotion and Practice 313-450*,[16] and *Wealth and Poverty in Early Church and Society*, edited by Susan R. Holman.[17]

Although necessarily incomplete, this brief survey of recent work on economic history is indicative of the notable interest in the subject area across various sectors of study. But sectors of the academy are not alone in pursuing these interests. Some sectors within contemporary Christianity have been assiduous in probing the relationship of Christian faith and economic practice. Notice, for instance, the on-going popularity of Ronald J. Sider's *Rich Christians in an Age of Hunger*,[18] or the recent best-seller *The Irresistible Revolution* by Shane Claiborne.[19] The fact that these and other influential books address issues of poverty and wealth from often quite different perspectives only underscores the point that questions of economic responsibility and practice are engaging many "ordinary Christians" in a renewed fashion today.

2. Engaging Economics within the Covers of This Book

If economic interpretation of ancient data is currently showing signs of considerable momentum and vitality, there is nonetheless more to be done, not least in two related fields: (1) interpretation of New Testament texts and (2) study of their reception in early Christianity.

In this regard, exploring economic dimensions of New Testament interpretation might be done in any number of ways. It might involve appropriating economic evidence from the ancient world order to understand better a particular text in the New Testament. Or it might involve using New Testament texts as sources from which to gain a better appraisal of the economic realities of first-century life. Or it might involve discerning the economic matrix inherent within the theology of a New Testament text. Or it might involve assessing how interpreters of the New Testament have appropriated its texts to inform their own theologies of economic practice.

14. Hanover, NH: University Press of New England, 2002.
15. Cambridge: Cambridge University Press, 2006.
16. Oxford: Oxford University Press, 2006.
17. Grand Rapids: Baker Academic, 2008.
18. Reprinted repeatedly; most recently, Nashville: Thomas Nelson, 2005.
19. Grand Rapids: Zondervan, 2006.

All of these facets are evident within the covers of this book, as each contributor seeks to address various lacunae in at least one of these various fields. Nonetheless, the predominant interest within *Engaging Economics* is the exploration of the New Testament's theological contribution to issues of economic responsibility, not only for the sake of historical interest but as a contribution to the theo-economic discourse of those whose identity is shaped by the New Testament even today.

Most of the essays presented here have their origins in a rolling program of the Biblical Studies Seminar at the University of St. Andrews between February and April 2008. A "call for papers" resulted in international offers of over thirty essays. Of those, twelve essays were incorporated in the seminar program, where they were presented to and discussed among graduate students and faculty members. Of those essays, ten have found their way into this book, with three of the other offered papers being added to the published lineup.[20]

The articles selected for this book fall into two parts: (1) New Testament Scenarios and (2) Early Christian Reception. Ordered roughly according to canonical sequence, the first part explores the interface between economics and a healthy selection of the New Testament, including Gospel texts and, behind them, the historical Jesus; the Acts of the Apostles; Pauline theology and practice; the letter of James; and 1 Peter. The Johannine Apocalypse, or Revelation, does not go unrepresented, but its treatment falls in the second part of the book, which includes five essays that examine the reception of particular New Testament texts in the patristic age. Those essays highlight ways in which patristic interpretations (a) differed from the current consensus among New Testament scholars, (b) employed hermeneutical sophistication to appropriate New Testament texts in new economic situations, or (c) in one case, generally missed the economic dimension of a New Testament text.

The voices assembled in this book range from younger scholars who are on promising academic trajectories and who offer here the firstfruits of their doctoral research, to the most seasoned biblical interpreters who have spent much of their academic careers writing on the interface between economics and the New Testament. Each voice contributes to the repertoire and advances the discourse within a particular field of study. And when heard together, as a chorus of voices, they demonstrate that economic con-

---

20. The editors wish to thank Patrick Egan for assiduously compiling the indices of this book, and the editorial team at Eerdmans for its careful processing of the manuscript.

siderations feature integrally both in understanding the texts of the New Testament and in understanding the essence of Christian self-definition and moral formation.

*　　　*　　　*

Two points require brief mention. First, among the contributors and editors of this book, no one is receiving royalties or payment for his or her efforts. Instead, all the proceeds from sales of this book are being donated to World Vision, an organization known for its engagement with issues of global poverty in a manner that is sensitive to indigenous concerns.

Second, the editors wish to dedicate this book to Alan Torrance, currently Professor of Systematic Theology at the University of St. Andrews. His keen theological acumen, his probing intellectual curiosity, his effective rhetorical skill, and his sincere concern for his students and colleagues have all helped to foster his much-deserved reputation as a leading figure in the theological disciplines. And regarding his reputation as one who has helped to shape so many lives for the better, the editors themselves are not only eyewitnesses, but beneficiaries.

2. Methodological Issues in Using Economic Evidence in Interpretation of Early Christian Texts

Peter Oakes

1. Economics and Early Christian Texts

When the Good Samaritan left money with the innkeeper for the care of an injured traveler, how long would this have covered the cost of keeping him? Was it enough to make the innkeeper look after him with particular care? In his new book *Jesus and the Peasants*, Douglas Oakman explores "The Buying Power of Two Denarii (Luke 10:35)."[1] Was the Samaritan making a substantial sacrifice, or was it loose change? Understanding the sum of money is a small but significant element in interpreting the type of impact that the story was expected to have.

Elsewhere in the book, Oakman sets up one of the sharpest issues in the interpretation of early Christian texts. What is happening when the acts and sayings of a Galilean peasant (or something close to that) are expressed in written form by members of an urban, literate class?[2] When Luke's Jesus says, "Blessed are you who are poor" (Luke 6:20), should we think of this in the peasant economic context of Galilee, or the Greco-Roman urban context of Luke, or the shadowy world of the scribal transmitters of Luke's sources? In the Gospels, we have a poor teacher and his followers being described by the somewhat wealthier kinds of people who could write.

---

1. Douglas Oakman, *Jesus and the Peasants* (Eugene, OR: Cascade [Wipf and Stock], 2008), pp. 40-45.

2. Oakman, *Jesus and the Peasants*, p. 3. He characterizes Jesus as a "crucified, illiterate peasant."

The use of economics in the study of early Christian texts ranges between these two limits, from elucidation of texts which directly refer to some aspect of the first-century economic system through to use of theories in which the economic situation of writers, readers, or characters in the texts is related to class interests that are seen as shaping every aspect of the text.

Within this very broad and highly contested field, the aims of this article are quite limited. It seeks to do three things. First, it seeks to bring a little extra clarity to work in this area by differentiating fairly sharply three possible relationships between economics and interpretation. Many people, when faced with a book that uses economics in textual interpretation, will tend to mix the three possibilities together, resulting in confusion and, sometimes, an undue nervousness in using anything that relates to economics. Second, the article draws on my own encounters with archaeological material, textual material, and comparative material to make a few comments about how each of these sources can be used as economic evidence and about some difficulties that stand in the way of doing so. Third, the article returns to questions of economic stratification on which I have written briefly before and suggests that a way forward lies in focusing on single economic variables that produce models which, although they only partially reflect social structure, can do so in a way designed to be useful for interpretation of early Christian texts.

This means that this article is not contributing to the ongoing post-Finley debate about the nature of the ancient economy, or lack of one. For recent work on that, see, for example, Bang, Ikeguchi, and Ziche, *Ancient Economies, Modern Methodologies*.[3] Neither is the article about social class *per se*. For some of the complications on that, one can still profitably read Richard Rohrbaugh's 1984 article.[4] We will have to talk about some class issues because class forms the basis of one of the possible relationships between economics and interpretation. However, when we consider stratification in the final section of the paper, our concerns will be specifically economic. The question on which we will focus is that of the extent to which various possible models of society map the distribution of economic resources among various groups in ways that are fruitful for interpretation of

3. Peter F. Bang, Mamoru Ikeguchi, and Hartmut Ziche, *Ancient Economies, Modern Methodologies: Archaeology, Comparative History, Models and Institutions* (Bari: Edipuglia, 2006).

4. Richard Rohrbaugh, "Methodological Considerations in the Debate over the Social Class Status of Early Christians," *Journal of the American Academy of Religion* 52 (1984): 519-46.

early Christian texts. We will not be considering whether any of the models provides a viable concept of class.

Having made these disclaimers, we cannot avoid one theoretical issue at the outset. There is a temptation for modern interpreters to see economics as a free-standing aspect of a society. Economists tend to analyze issues of resource distribution as a system dependent on specifically economic variables such as supply and demand. They tend to avoid getting too far into analysis of other issues, such as politics and religion. (This compartmentalization has actually become rather difficult to maintain recently: many economists increasingly do interact with all sorts of disciplines, including some, such as meteorology, that would have seemed very surprising not long ago.) In studying the first few centuries of the Christian movement, any attempt to isolate economics from other social factors such as politics would be doomed. As Karl Polanyi argues, all ancient economies were "embedded economies."[5] Financial decisions in such economies were rarely taken for financial reasons alone. For example, the nature of patron-client relationships ensured constant distortion of what we might expect to be market interaction. Distribution of resources was dependent much more on power relationships than on the market.

With this in mind, what counts as economic evidence? When, as an undergraduate, I took a course on economics, I remember the lecturer defining it as "the study of the allocation of scarce resources." In one major current textbook, Michael Parkin defines it as "the social science that studies the *choices* that individuals, businesses, governments, and entire societies make as they cope with *scarcity* and the *incentives* that influence those choices."[6] Air is not scarce, so it is generally free. Breathing is not usually an economic issue. Wine is not free. Its production and distribution require land, water, transport, storage, and labor, all of which are scarce resources. We will return to wine production in a little more detail later as a good example of the range of types of economic evidence available. At a couple of points, Parkin's definition sounds a little awkward for an ancient context. The focus on choice is problematic in a society where most economic activities are governed more by custom or compulsion. I suppose it works fairly reasonably as long as one remembers that the choices lie with the powerful

5. Karl Polanyi et al., *Trade and Market in the Early Empires* (Chicago: Henry Regnery, 1971), p. 250. For a useful summary and application to NT studies, see Halvor Moxnes, *The Economy of the Kingdom: Social Conflict and Economic Relations in Luke's Gospel* (Philadelphia: Fortress, 1988), pp. 28-32.

6. Michael Parkin, *Economics,* 7th ed. (Boston: Addison Wesley, 2005), his emphasis.

elite. The stress on incentives might be useful, but only if it is realized that, for most people, they were generally of an "offer you can't refuse" type. There was not the kind of varying levels of inducement that a modern market system might include.

Avoiding this kind of definition entirely, Ekkehard and Wolfgang Stegemann prefer to base their study of economics in the early Christian movement on a definition of economy by cultural anthropologist Marvin Harris as "the sum of all actions that are responsible for the provisioning of a society with goods and services."[7] Although this can clearly fit scenarios in a wide range of cultures, I would rather not use it for first-century society. Much activity that I think we should describe as economic is not centered on provisioning anyone. I prefer the first definition that I offered, "the study of the allocation of scarce resources." Despite being rooted in study of modern economics, this definition can work for ancient embedded economies as well. It does not presuppose whether the resources are allocated by a market or by diktat from the powerful. As well as money, etc., it can cover issues such as labor, including slave labor. It also allows an interface with class issues, because all theories of class have some relation to resource allocation. In line with this definition, we will take economic evidence as being evidence of the patterns of allocation, the processes of allocation, the initiators or recipients of allocation (or intermediaries in the process), and the scarce resources being allocated.

All these categories of evidence could be significant in, for example, a full contextual interpretation of 1 Thess 4:11. There Paul urges his hearers, "Work with your hands." In first-century Thessalonica, which socioeconomic groups "worked with their hands"? Should we infer that all the letter's recipients were among those groups? If not, what would it have meant to give this exhortation to someone from a socioeconomic group that did not usually work with their hands? Had some Thessalonian Christians stopped working? If so, what would be the economic implications? Were first-century craft-working families likely to have savings to live off for a few months? Was there a banking system that extended to the non-elite? Were they likely to own possessions that they could sell and live off for a time? Might some in the church have started supporting others so that they did not need to work? If so, was this a patronage structure? Was Paul's exhorta-

---

7. Ekkehard W. Stegemann and Wolfgang Stegemann, *The Jesus Movement: A Social History of Its First Century*, trans. O. C. Dean Jr. (Minneapolis: Fortress, 1999), p. 16, citing a 1989 German translation of what is now Marvin Harris and Orna Johnson, *Cultural Anthropology*, 5th ed. (Boston: Allyn and Bacon, 2000).

tion aimed at preventing laziness, or debt, or patronage? A full range of economic evidence could usefully be put to work.

2. Possible Relationships between Economics and Interpretation

We need to distinguish between three possible types of link between economics and interpretation. First, economics can provide an *overall analytical framework* for interpretation. Second, the *aim* of the interpretation of a text may be to gather economic evidence. Third, economic evidence may be a *resource* that is used in interpretation.

2.1 Use of an Economic Analytical Framework for Interpretation

"The farmer and the cowman should be friends!" This song sums up the socioeconomic narrative that underlies the musical *Oklahoma*. Rodgers and Hammerstein present the founding of the state as resting on a reconciliation between the interests of cattle ranchers, who wanted wide-open spaces to run cattle, and of agriculturalists, who wanted the land divided into smaller units. The reconciliation rather favors the farmer: Curly the cowboy ends by giving up his saddle, horse, and gun to win the hand of the farmer's daughter.

In that musical, the economic issues are, fairly clearly, a fundamental structural element of the plot. However, many scholars use economics as their key framework for analysis, irrespective of whether the text seems overtly to deal with economic issues. For example, Itumeleng Mosala's reading of the story of Cain and Abel could be summarized as "the pastoralist and the agriculturalist cannot be friends — and God is on the side of the pastoralist!" Mosala (following quite a number of other scholars) locates the production of the story in the social struggle between groups that raised sheep and those that grew crops.[8] Douglas Oakman's analytical framework of considering the potentially competing interests of peasants, represented by Jesus' actual teaching, and scribal groups, responsible for producing that teaching in written form, goes as far as to see some of these scribes as conceivably being opponents of Jesus.[9]

---

8. Itumeleng J. Mosala, *Biblical Hermeneutics and Black Theology in South Africa* (Grand Rapids: Eerdmans, 1989).

9. Oakman, *Jesus and the Peasants*, p. 303. In this he evokes the fictional Andreas from

Interpreters will have various reactions to the idea of using economics to provide the central analytical framework. It will be the prime method if the interpreter sees economic issues as inherently the fundamental ones, as in a Marxist view. Equally, if the aim of the particular piece of interpretation is to draw economic conclusions, such a framework may be suitable. However, some interpreters will worry about what they see as economic reductionism inherent in such a method. When the primary interpretative questions posed to a text are about whose economic interests it serves and how it serves them, then, inevitably, the primary results of the interpretation will be economic and political. Other aspects of the text may not be brought to light. More subtly, there is a risk that, when analyzing the interests of a writer, too much weight is put on class interests rather than individual interests. In the case of Paul, for example, it is probable that the effects of his particular individual combination of background and experiences are more frequently significant than are the effects stemming from his general socioeconomic level.

On the other hand, to some degree these systemic economic questions are inescapable. If we are interpreting Luke's Gospel, with Mary's announcement of the downfall of the mighty (Luke 1:52) and Jesus' announcement of his calling to preach good news to the poor (Luke 4:18), we must consider the socioeconomic location of Luke, his sources, and his expected audience. Moreover, the issue goes beyond the obviously economic passages, to reach even those dealing with apparently the most theological subjects such as sin, forgiveness, and prayer, in which ideas about indebtedness and petition to higher authorities are a vital part of the interpretative mix. What was the role of indebtedness in the lives of Galilean peasants or the Greco-Roman urban non-elite? What would forgiving a debt mean in such contexts? How might that affect its use as an expression relating to sin? Just as some methods may be described, from some viewpoints, as being economically reductionistic, many other methods are anti-economically reductionistic. On either side, the danger is of using a method that fails to bring to light significant aspects of the text.

2.2 Gathering of Economic Data as the Aim of Interpretation

A second possible relationship between economics and interpretation is that the aim of the interpretation is to use the text as a source for gathering eco-

---

Gerd Theissen's *The Shadow of the Galilean: The Quest of the Historical Jesus in Narrative Form,* trans. J. Bowden (Minneapolis: Fortress, 1987).

nomic evidence. This is a major feature of the *People's History of Christianity* project. This has resulted in publication of a series of books under that title and continues in more detailed studies applying the approach to individual texts. In the introductory essay to volume one, Richard Horsley describes the aim of the project as being not interpretation of texts but recovery of history of ordinary people, evidence of whose lives can be gleaned from the texts.[10] The aim is history, especially socioeconomic history. Any interpretation is only a means to that end. This approach is of particular value in questioning past over-reliance on the sweeping narrative schemes produced by writers such as Eusebius and Bede, which tend to focus on church leaders and secular rulers. The use of early Christian texts as a source of economic evidence is a crucial part of the task of correcting and filling out the picture produced by "grand narratives."

Drawing economic evidence from Christian texts is important in any historical study of the period. Many Roman social historians have been forced into the murky waters of interpretation of the Book of Revelation when studying popular responses to the Imperial Cult. Revelation also includes economic evidence, such as a real or imagined (but still interesting) list of Rome's imports:

> gold, silver, jewels and pearls, fine linen, purple, silk and scarlet, all kinds of scented wood, all articles of ivory, all articles of costly wood, bronze, iron, and marble, cinnamon, spice, incense, myrrh, frankincense, wine, olive oil, choice flour and wheat, cattle and sheep, horses and chariots, and bodies and souls of people. (Rev 18:12-13, NRSV, altered)

As long as the historian is careful enough to tackle issues such as the relationship between this text and Ezekiel 27, there are still interesting points to be gleaned from how this late-first- or early-second-century apocalyptic writer from the province of Asia chose to depict economic aspects of the envisaged downfall of Rome.

Early Christian texts are particularly valuable for social history because of the wide economic range of the movement's members. The only other ancient writings that reach as far down the economic scale are fairly brief, functional texts such as non-literary papyri and graffiti. Only early Christian texts offer something such as 1 Thessalonians, a letter from an itinerant preacher to a group of people — maybe mainly craftworking families —

10. Richard A. Horsley, "Unearthing a People's History," in *A People's History of Christianity,* Volume 1: *Christian Origins,* ed. Horsley (Minneapolis: Fortress, 2005), p. 5.

whom he had persuaded, just a few weeks earlier, to abandon their traditional religious practices in favor of giving honor to a crucified Galilean preacher and healer. And this is not just a letter of greetings or recommendation, as we might find among the papyri, but a substantial text, teaching how to live and how to face death: a substantial first-century text, written for a non-elite audience.

2.3 Using Economic Evidence as a Resource for Interpretation

The third possible relationship is where economic evidence is used to contribute to interpretation. The rest of this paper is given to thinking about how this happens. The best place to begin this is by thinking about the nature of the evidence. We will look at various types of evidence and some opportunities and difficulties in using them.

3. The Nature of the Economic Evidence

Let us return to wine. To grow vines requires land ownership or tenancy. Vines need planting and tending. Grapes need harvesting and pressing. Wine needs fermenting, storage in amphorae, transport, marketing, and pouring into cups in bars and homes. There are also collateral economic effects, such as sale of food in bars and the need for someone to pay for damage caused by some of the people who drink the wine. There is *archaeological* evidence of every stage of this story of wine production and distribution. There is also considerable *textual* evidence, which has recently been published fairly exhaustively by John Kloppenborg in his book *The Tenants in the Vineyard*.[11] A third category of evidence to help us understand ancient wine production would be *comparative* evidence drawn from studies of more recent communities that produced wine in traditional ways. We shall take each of these three forms of economic evidence in turn: archaeological, textual, and comparative (although realizing that some types of evidence, such as inscriptions, fall into more than one category).

---

11. John Kloppenborg, *The Tenants in the Vineyard*, WUNT 195 (Tübingen: Mohr Siebeck, 2006), pp. 355-586.

3.1 Archaeological Evidence

The most productive first-century archaeological site, Pompeii, yields a wide range of economically significant evidence. Scholars of early Christianity have tended to ignore it. This is mainly because no Christian texts originated there. It is probably also because access to usable data has been difficult. The first of these reasons is, I will argue, misguided. The second is very reasonable but the situation has been rapidly improving, to the point where there is now undoubtedly evidence that can be put to use.

At a macro level there is the layout of the town. The distribution of housing and businesses, in terms of location and size, suggests various points about the economic organization of society there. Ray Laurence has done valuable work on the geographic patterns.[12] Andrew Wallace-Hadrill has surveyed the range of individual houses.[13] We will return to his work when thinking about economic stratification. Individual blocks also tell us interesting things about socioeconomic structure and development. Roger Ling is currently editing a series describing one block in detail, the *Insula of the Menander*.[14] For almost the first time, through the work of Ling, Penelope Allison, and others, we can see the coordination between various types of evidence in a well-preserved block of houses. For example, the loose finds in house 7 of the block suggest that the inhabitant was something like a cabinet-maker, who maybe also did part-time surgery. The size of the house shows that such a person could afford about eleven or twelve fair-sized rooms. The wall decoration shows that he could also pay someone to come in and paint for him.[15] On an outside wall of the block, there is a set of graffiti that shows that a weaver living nearby was probably literate to some degree. He appears to have read a piece of insulting graffiti about him and to have written a reply (albeit in Latin that is sometimes rather incomprehensible).[16] These kinds of evidence are useful contributions to considering the

12. Ray Laurence, *Roman Pompeii: Space and Society*, 2nd ed. (London: Routledge, 2006).

13. Andrew Wallace-Hadrill, *Houses and Society at Pompeii and Herculaneum* (Princeton: Princeton University Press, 1994).

14. Roger Ling, *The Insula of the Menander at Pompeii*, Volume I: *The Structures* (Oxford: Clarendon, 1997); Volume II: *The Decorations*, by Roger Ling and Lesley Ling (2005); Volume III: *The Finds, a Contextual Study*, by Penelope M. Allison (2006).

15. Ling, *Menander I*, pp. 152-63; Ling and Ling, *Menander II*, pp. 140-47; Allison, *Menander III*, pp. 348-49.

16. M. Della Corte, *Corpus Inscriptionum Latinarum* IV.3.I nos. 8258-59. For one possi-

socioeconomic implications of the description of early Christians as typically being craftworking families. Some craftworkers had money for discretionary spending such as wall decoration — or support of itinerant missionaries. Among poorer craftworkers there could still be functional literacy to permit at least a basic engagement with written texts. There were sufficient social commonalities among Greco-Roman urban centers for this rich Pompeian evidence to be relevant to the debates, despite the town not being the source of Christian texts.[17] As well as the Insula of the Menander, there has recently been an economically interesting publication of some other Pompeian houses, especially with Joanne Berry's work on finds.[18] Some studies also use techniques such as analysis of plant remains and skeletons to draw conclusions about diet and medical care.[19]

Although not as full as at Pompeii, there is economically significant archaeological evidence from sites throughout the areas in which early Christian texts were written and read. At Philippi, the archaeological evidence shows the substantial Hellenistic framework of the city and indicates its early economic base in gold-mining and agriculture. We then see the sharp Roman remodeling of the town after colonization, especially in the Claudian and Antonine forum developments, which testify both to the city's (agricultural) prosperity and to the economic and political domination of the town by Roman colonists. There are also archaeological indications of the continuing existence of a substantial, but economically subordinate, non-Roman population.[20] This provides a context for analysis of topics such as the suf-

---

ble translation, see N. Lewis and M. Reinhold, *Roman Civilisation, Selected Readings,* Volume II: *The Empire,* 3rd ed. (New York: Columbia University Press, 1990), p. 277.

17. For a fuller discussion of the Pompeian evidence and its implications see my *Reading Romans in Pompeii: Paul's Letter at Ground Level* (London: SPCK; Minneapolis: Fortress, forthcoming).

18. For example, J. Berry, "Household Artefacts: Towards a Re-interpretation of Roman Domestic Space," in *Domestic Space in the Roman World: Pompeii and Beyond,* ed. R. Laurence and A. Wallace-Hadrill, Journal of Roman Archaeology Supp. Series 22 (Portsmouth, RI: JRA, 1997), pp. 183-95.

19. For Pompeian plant remains, the classic study is Wilhelmina F. Jashemski, *The Gardens of Pompeii,* 2 vols. (New Rochelle: Caratzas Bros., 1979, 1993). See also Jashemski and Frederick G. Meyer's edited collection, *The Natural History of Pompeii: A Systematic Survey* (Cambridge: Cambridge University Press, 2002). For skeletal evidence, the forthcoming book by Estelle Lazer, *Resurrecting Pompeii* (London: Routledge), looks likely to be of particular interest.

20. For the range of Philippian evidence see especially Peter Pilhofer, *Philippi I: Die erste christliche Gemeinde Europas* (Tübingen: J. C. B. Mohr, 1995).

fering that Paul's letter to the Philippians describes as going on among the largely non-Roman Christians there.[21] Corinth has been the most common focus of debates in NT scholarship on socioeconomic issues. David Horrell and Edward Adams's edited collection, *Christianity at Corinth,* reprints and discusses many of the classic studies.[22] Daniel Schowalter and Steven Friesen have recently edited a useful interdisciplinary collection of work on the city.[23] The debate in which the links between archaeology, economics, and interpretation have been most direct has been over whether the aedile Erastus, who donated a pavement to the city,[24] is Erastus, ὁ οἰκονόμος τῆς πόλεως ("the steward of the city"), from whom greetings are brought in Romans 16:23.[25] A further interpretative debate fueled by archaeology and economics centers on Corinthian eating practices. We will return to this below. Rome is another site that has, of course, received particular attention, most notably in Peter Lampe's monumental work, which draws eclectically on archaeological and textual evidence to trace the socioeconomic development of early Christianity there.[26] There has also been considerable economic analysis of archaeological remains from Galilee and Judea. Major studies include those by Sean Freyne, by Oakman and K. C. Hanson, and by Jonathan Reed.[27]

There are many obstacles to good use of archaeological economic evidence. First, archaeology is an entire discipline in its own right, with a range of theories and methods. Moreover, as Kevin Greene argues, its use in rela-

21. Peter Oakes, *Philippians: From People to Letter,* SNTSMS 110 (Cambridge: Cambridge University Press, 2001).

22. David G. Horrell and Edward Adams, eds., *Christianity at Corinth: The Quest for the Pauline Church* (Louisville: Westminster John Knox, 2004).

23. Daniel Schowalter and Steven J. Friesen, eds., *Urban Religion in Roman Corinth: Interdisciplinary Approaches* (Cambridge, MA: Harvard University Press, 2005).

24. Erastus appears in this section because of his link to a particular structure in Corinth, but he could just as well have appeared in the "textual evidence" section.

25. For arguments in favor see, e.g., Andrew D. Clarke, *Secular and Christian Leadership in Corinth: A Socio-Historical and Exegetical Study of 1 Corinthians 1–6* (Leiden: Brill, 1993), pp. 46-56. For those against see, e.g., Justin J. Meggitt, *Paul, Poverty and Survival* (Edinburgh: T&T Clark, 1998), pp. 135-41.

26. Peter Lampe, *From Paul to Valentinus: Christians at Rome in the First Two Centuries,* trans. M. Steinhauser, ed. M. D. Johnson (Minneapolis: Fortress; London: T&T Clark, 2003).

27. Sean Freyne, *Galilee from Alexander the Great to Hadrian, 323 BCE to 135 CE* (Wilmington, DE: Michael Glazier, 1980); K. C. Hanson and Douglas E. Oakman, *Palestine in the Time of Jesus: Social Structures and Social Conflicts,* 2nd ed. (Minneapolis: Fortress Press, 2008 [1998]); Jonathan Reed, *Archaeology and the Galilean Jesus* (Harrisburg: Trinity Press, 2000).

tion to economics is particularly likely to be best served by several methods.[28] Even the archaeology of a single site can be a major subdiscipline. Use of Pompeian evidence, for example, requires careful attention to issues relating both to disrupted circumstances in the decades prior to the eruption and to removal of artifacts in the centuries afterwards. Having basically understood the archaeological reports on an artifact or site of interest, we then usually need to move on to study aspects of the social history of the period if we are to understand the economic significance of the evidence. Furthermore, to gather worthwhile economic evidence, we often need to use a survey of a sizeable set of data. This brings in the complication of more or less sophisticated mathematics. We can rarely jump from one archaeological example to the interpretation of a particular point in a text.

All this constitutes a fascinating challenge for a specialist study. The process, archaeology understood in relation to social history and interpretation of text, can be very fruitful. There is also one more stage in this process, one that takes us from the text to the archaeology in the first place. This can vary from a simple observation (e.g., the NT name Erastus appearing at a certain place on the site at Corinth) to a complex theory. Oakman, for example, draws on a range of social-scientific theories that take him from the text to particular kinds of evidence and then inform the process by which he moves from the evidence back to textual interpretation.

Help is available in handling the interdisciplinary complexity. Many archaeologists and ancient historians have put considerable effort into gathering and drawing together economic evidence. Kevin Greene has already been mentioned.[29] Both Richard Duncan-Jones and Peter Garnsey present material in ways that are particularly usable.[30] An important current way into the scholarship is the volume of the *Cambridge Economic History* edited by Scheidel, Morris, and Saller.[31] One of the most practical imperatives produced by the complexity that we have been looking at is the need for interdisciplinary interaction, both in seminars and one-to-one. A recent high

28. Kevin Greene, "Archaeological Data and Economic Interpretation," in Bang, Ikeguchi, and Ziche, *Ancient Economies,* pp. 109-36.

29. Kevin Greene, *The Archaeology of the Roman Economy* (London: Batsford, 1986).

30. For example, R. Duncan-Jones, *The Economy of the Roman Empire: Quantitative Studies,* 2nd ed. (Cambridge: Cambridge University Press, 1982); Peter Garnsey, *Cities, Peasants and Food in Classical Antiquity: Essays in Social and Economic History,* ed. with addenda by Walter Scheidel (Cambridge: Cambridge University Press, 1998).

31. Walter Scheidel, Ian Morris, and Richard Saller, eds., *The Cambridge Economic History of the Greco-Roman World* (Cambridge: Cambridge University Press, 2007).

quality example of this is the volume on early Christian families edited by David Balch and Carolyn Osiek.[32]

3.2 Textual Evidence

Textual evidence comes from papyri, ostraca, inscriptions, graffiti, and literary texts, including early Christian ones. As with archaeological evidence, textual evidence can be drawn on either by looking at specific cases in detail or, more frequently for economic issues, by surveying a range of instances of a type of evidence. A crucial area of evidence is the study of papyri of Egyptian census returns. The classic presentation is Bagnall and Frier's *The Demography of Roman Egypt*,[33] which has been subject to critique by scholars such as Tim Parkin and April Pudsey.[34] The surveys are the main source of frequently quoted results, such as the "average family size" of four. In fact, the results are more specific. In urban settings, the average family size is 4.04, and the average household size is 5.31. The corresponding figures for rural villages are 4.46 and 4.82.[35] For some Egyptian Christian texts, the production context is very close to that of the censuses. For other texts, the sharpest critical issue is how far the Egyptian evidence is specific to its locality and how far it is typical. As with the Pompeian evidence, the Egyptian censuses provide such unparalleled detail that, if used with caution, they are bound to be a factor in debates about households elsewhere in the empire. Another economically interesting example of evidence on papyri and ostraca is the collection of bills and receipts from the Roman fort of *mons claudianus* in Eastern Egypt.[36] Graffiti at Pompeii and Herculaneum also yield evidence for prices by advertising the cost of wine and prostitutes.[37]

---

32. David Balch and Carolyn Osiek, eds., *Early Christian Families in Context: An Interdisciplinary Dialogue* (Grand Rapids: Eerdmans, 2003).

33. Roger S. Bagnall and Bruce W. Frier, *The Demography of Roman Egypt* (Cambridge: Cambridge University Press, 1994).

34. Tim G. Parkin, *Demography and Roman Society* (Baltimore: Johns Hopkins University Press, 1992); April Pudsey, *Sex, Statistics and Soldiers: New Approaches to the Demography of Roman Egypt, 28 BC–259 AD* (Manchester: University of Manchester Press, 2007).

35. Bagnall and Frier, *Demography of Roman Egypt*, p. 68, table 3.3.

36. Published in reports by Jean Bingen, Adam Bülow-Jacobsen, and others. The texts are available in the Duke Databank of Documentary Papyri, accessible via the Perseus website, http://www.perseus.tufts.edu.

37. For a convenient collection, see the relevant sections of Jo-Ann Shelton, *As the Romans Did: A Sourcebook in Roman Social History,* 2nd ed. (Oxford: Oxford University Press, 1998).

Among inscriptions, those of associations are of particular socio-economic interest. For example, the inscriptions listing the *cultores* of Sylvanus at Philippi include people of a range of social statuses, from Orinus *coloniae*, who was presumably a civic slave, to P. Hostilius Philadelphus, who appears both in the list of members and at the top of the inscription as the dedicant and so was probably of high status and wealth.[38] One effect of this and similar association inscriptions is to induce caution in arguing that early Christian communities were distinguished from Greco-Roman associations by the wide socioeconomic spread of church membership. The churches' socioeconomic patterns do indeed differ from those of associations but the differences are subtler than was once thought.[39]

Another key group of inscriptions are funerary ones. A classic survey of these is Pertti Huttunen's study of social strata represented in epitaphs from Rome.[40] Funerary inscriptions can also yield evidence about trades and family relationships. As always, there are methodological complications. Valerie Hope, for example, has shown how representation of family relations is not simple documentation but includes projection of how the dedicant wished to be seen.[41]

Literary texts, and other texts that are substantial although not clearly literary (such as astronomical texts and many early Christian texts), yield both general and specific economic evidence. At a systemic level they give evidence of interests and aims of various groups who produce texts. If we are considering, say, someone of scribal class producing the Gospel of Matthew, or someone of Augustine's background producing *The City of God*, analysis of works by other writers of similar socioeconomic level should give some control to speculation about what the relevant interests are. In terms of more specific economic evidence, even elite texts can give good evidence of wider economic life. Seneca's description of apartment living and Pliny the

---

38. Peter Pilhofer, *Philippi II: Katalog der Inschriften von Philippi*, WUNT 119 (Tübingen: J. C. B. Mohr, 2000), pp. 163-66.

39. As well as being experts on wine production, John Kloppenborg and his research team at Toronto have led the field in gathering and analyzing the evidence for associations (John S. Kloppenborg and Stephen G. Wilson, eds., *Voluntary Associations in the Graeco-Roman World* [London: Routledge, 1996], followed by publications from Richard Ascough, Philip Harland, and Alicia Batten).

40. Pertti Huttunen, *The Social Strata in the Imperial City of Rome: A Quantitative Study of the Social Representation in the Epitaphs Published in the Corpus Inscriptionum Latinarum Volumen VI* (Oulu: University of Oulu, 1974).

41. Valerie Hope, "A Roof over the Dead: Communal Tombs and Family Structure," in Laurence and Wallace-Hadrill, eds. *Domestic Space*, pp. 69-88.

Younger's comments on conditions in Bithynia are of considerable value. And not all Greco-Roman writers are wholly elite. Even some Roman writers who ended up close to imperial circles came from non-elite backgrounds. Horace's father was a freedman (albeit wealthy), and Horace occupied various status levels in his life. We do need to exercise caution in drawing economic evidence from Greco-Roman writers. They often have an economically foreshortened view of society, lumping the poor together. There can also be questions of genre that make economic inference complex. The satirical form of Juvenal's works, in particular, is often problematically neglected by social historians who use him as a source. However, Greco-Roman writers remain a vast reservoir of material relating to socioeconomic realities.

3.3 Comparative Evidence

When C. R. Whittaker wanted possible figures for the proportion of Rome's population that were poor, he looked further afield. He writes, "One method of getting some idea of Rome's population is by a comparative view of what life looked like in better documented ages."[42] He draws on thirteenth-century Florence, where 70 percent of households had needs that exceeded incomes, and fifteenth- to eighteenth-century Norwich, Lyon, Toledo, and Rome. In these cities, fairly consistently, 4-8 percent could not earn a living, a further 20 percent were permanently in crisis, and 30-40 percent faced periodic crises.[43]

On a broader level, anthropologists such as Julian Pitt-Rivers and historians such as Horden and Purcell speak of a pre-industrial Mediterranean cultural area, which has certain economic features, such as being an advanced agrarian economy with olive production, and some other features with economic implications, such as the common prioritizing of concerns of family honor above creation of conditions for open markets.[44] This conceptual framework made its greatest impact on early Christian studies through the Context Group for Biblical Research, especially Bruce Malina, whose

---

42. C. R. Whittaker, "The Poor in the City of Rome," in *Land, City and Trade in the Roman Empire,* Variorum (Aldershot: Ashgate, 1993), p. 4.

43. Whittaker, "The Poor," p. 4.

44. Julian Pitt-Rivers, *The Fate of Shechem or the Politics of Sex: Essays in the Anthropology of the Mediterranean* (Cambridge: Cambridge University Press, 1977); Peregrine Horden and Nicholas Purcell, *The Corrupting Sea: A Study of Mediterranean History* (Oxford: Blackwell, 2000).

textbook, *The New Testament World: Insights from Cultural Anthropology,* has run to several editions.[45]

To what extent should we draw economic evidence from contexts that differ geographically, temporally, or socially from the setting of the text that we are interpreting? How can we control the accuracy of use of such comparative evidence? This actually affects our archaeological and textual evidence as well. To what extent is Pompeii relevant for Ephesus, or Seneca relevant for Thessalonian craftworkers? This issue affects all fields, not just economics, but, as in the Whittaker example, it has been a central methodological issue for economic questions. Let us look at some examples.

In 1 Corinthians 11, Paul criticizes the behavior of the Christians when they meet for communal meals. David Horrell has recently challenged Jerome Murphy-O'Connor on his use of the Anaploga villa at Corinth as a typical setting that illuminates the issues that could arise if wealthier and poorer people ate together in substantial numbers in a Roman house. Horrell argues that Murphy-O'Connor incorrectly dates the key dining room that he uses. Horrell also suggests a large upstairs hall in an area of housing east of the theater in Corinth as a more likely type of setting for such a meal.[46]

Both Murphy-O'Connor's and Horrell's studies are valuable for interpretation of 1 Corinthians 11. Murphy-O'Connor moves consideration of the issues into a concrete Greco-Roman context, making effective use of archaeological evidence about the economic disparities in dining and the ways in which Roman architecture enshrined them. Horrell has corrected some errors in Murphy-O'Connor's work and has moved the debate forward by describing a type of space for dining that was likely to be more accessible to the Corinthian Christian community. However, a key methodological question is, How far should they be focusing on specifically Corinthian housing to provide the socioeconomic evidence for interpreting the text?

A reasonable first step in contextual study of 1 Corinthians 11 is to use Paul's letters to Corinth, and archaeological and textual evidence about Corinth, to reflect on the probable social make-up of the Corinthian church. We can then think about types of housing the church's members were likely to

45. The most recent being Bruce Malina, *The New Testament World: Insights from Cultural Anthropology,* 3rd rev. ed. (Louisville: Westminster John Knox, 2001).

46. David Horrell, "Domestic Space and Christian Meetings at Corinth: Imagining New Contexts and the Buildings East of the Theatre," *New Testament Studies* 50 (2004): 349-69, responding to Jerome Murphy-O'Connor, *St. Paul's Corinth: Texts and Archaeology* (Collegeville: Liturgical Press, 1990).

live in, especially wealthier members, who were most likely to host meals. However, this second step could be done with reference to Greco-Roman housing as a whole, with a particular focus on well-preserved housing. Remains of housing at Corinth would come into this process as a guiding factor. For example, if they suggested a prevalence of apartment blocks, we might focus on examples of such blocks in Rome and Herculaneum. However, in general we should consider a substantial set of possible houses or apartments, a number of which could then be used in reconstructing possible scenarios for 1 Corinthians 11. Although exclusive use of mid-first-century Corinthian housing avoids some methodological difficulties, this advantage is outweighed by the fact that doing so excludes the vast majority of the best-preserved relevant evidence. Murphy-O'Connor does actually use some evidence from elsewhere, to show that the Anaploga villa is typical. However, I would suggest that, in principle, both he and Horrell have *over-localized* the issue. I think this is especially so in Horrell's criticism of Murphy-O'Connor on the dating of the dining room. Since the aim of the exercise is imaginative interpretation by use of a typical setting, it is beside the point to worry about the structure of the rooms at particular dates, unless one could argue that the changes were ones that affected most dining rooms of a relevant type across Corinth as a whole.

Peter Lampe's work on Rome shows the value of localizing a study. Its strength comes from being a well-analyzed collection of evidence that is specifically related to early Christians at Rome. Even so, the analysis would have benefited from more use of comparative material to contextualize the evidence from Rome. For example, when he discusses whether "the external image" of the house-churches might have involved comparison with associations, he could usefully have compared aspects of the Roman house-churches with aspects of associations elsewhere in the empire.[47] Some of his arguments are also over-localized in a social sense. A key element of his discussion of the economic level of the early Christians is consideration of which parts of the city of Rome the Christians lived in. As part of this, he looks at burial practices, taking the locations of early Christian catacombs and tracing back into Rome along main roads to find likely locations for Christians who used them.[48] However, by restricting his discussion to Christian evidence he has over-localized it socially. He needs to consider evidence from other social groups. The method really requires study of all the early

47. Lampe, *From Paul to Valentinus*, ch. 38.
48. Lampe, *From Paul to Valentinus*, pp. 23-38.

burial places, non-Christian as well as Christian. Only by thinking, for the population as a whole, about how burial locations related to where people lived can useful conclusions be drawn about how Christian burial places related to where Christians lived.

Do Whittaker and, even more so, Malina go too far in the other direction and under-localize their studies of aspects of the first-century world? Sometimes this does happen. The significance of slavery in Roman society poses some sharp questions both for use of data from medieval Florence and for Malina's general models of pre-industrial urban populations, which try to cover both slave-based and non-slave-based economies.[49] However, although Florence and Norwich are not Rome, there is clearly some analytical value in finding out what proportion of urban dwellers tend to be poor in such contexts. Similarly, many of Malina's main economic characteristics of the Mediterranean world, such as a peasant concept of limited good,[50] are clearly relevant to the early Christian period.

For interpreters, the ideal solution to the localization issue must be to keep in mind all levels from the most local to the most general. A practical way forward may be to work with three levels: pre-industrial Mediterranean, Roman Empire, and immediately local to the text. For example, to reflect on possible socioeconomic ideas in a text from Rome about petitionary prayer, we might want to think in general about relationships involving dependency and petition in pre-industrial Mediterranean societies; we might go on to think about the Roman patronage system; and we might end by thinking about how tenants in a first-century apartment block in Rome would go about trying to gain a favor from someone more powerful.[51]

Keeping these three levels in view seems a practical way of trying to maximize fruitful use of economic evidence. It also provides something of a control for occasions when ideas proposed at one of the levels may not fit well with those relating to one of the others. For example, to help interpret Paul's response to the Philippians' financial gift, we could bring in Seneca's essay *On Benefits*, which handles gift-giving and proper responses. This is a useful "Roman Empire level" resource. However, we ought to control its use by analysis of the local socioeconomic situation in the Philippian church,

49. Oakes, *Philippians*, pp. 40-46, responding to Malina, *New Testament World*, pp. 72-73 (1983 ed.).

50. Malina, *New Testament World*, pp. 81, 94, etc. (2001 ed.).

51. For an actual study of prayer in relation to patronage, see Jerome Neyrey, *Render to God: New Testament Understandings of the Divine* (Minneapolis: Fortress, 2004), pp. 21-25, etc.

which might limit the relevance of the formal patronage and friendship interchanges that Seneca discusses.

4. Stratification Models

A methodological issue that has pervasive effects on interpretation of early Christian texts in relation to economic matters is that of how to handle social stratification. No model of social structure can successfully be all things to all people. The question here is about what forms of social-structure modeling can handle economic issues in ways that are as helpful as possible for the interpretation of early Christian texts.

Many scholars of early Christianity make use of Alföldy's classic diagram of first-century social stratification. His triangular diagram divides its upper part into seven horizontal bands, representing levels within the 1 percent of the population who form the elite. Below that, in the other 99 percent of the population, there is no differentiation in social level as such. However, there is differentiation, at the same social level, between urban and rural and between free-born, freed, and slave.[52] In systemic terms, Alföldy's structure represents a society in which a very small hierarchical elite rules a non-elite that is weakened as a class by division into mutually distrustful categories: urban-rural, free-slave. This is very much in line with E. Gellner's model of the "agro-literate state," in which the hierarchical elite rule "laterally insulated communities of agricultural producers."[53]

The chief difficulty in using Alföldy's structure if we are studying early Christian texts is that our interest is almost entirely in the non-elite and he has no differentiation of social level within the non-elite. If our interests are economic, then a further problem is that Alföldy's structure is based on the official Roman status levels, the *ordines*. Even though admission to various upper levels of the *ordines* was based on property qualifications, the *ordines* do not correspond directly to an economic structure. For example, many equestrians were richer than some senators. Alföldy tries to handle some of the anomalies in his system by inserting a small dotted triangle, straddling the elite and non-elite, to represent slaves and freedmen of the imperial

52. Geza Alföldy, *The Social History of Rome* (Totowa, NJ: Barnes & Noble, 1985), p. 146.

53. E. Gellner, *Nations and Nationalism,* 2nd ed. (Oxford: Blackwell, 2006), pp. 9-10, fig. 1, discussed in Ian Morris, "The Early Polis as City and State," in *City and Country in the Ancient World,* ed. John Rich and Andrew Wallace-Hadrill (London: Routledge, 1991), pp. 46-47 and fig. 6.

household and rich freedmen in general. However, the essential basis of his structure is not economic.

Gerhard Lenski provides another model used by scholars of early Christianity. Whereas Alföldy's is a structure for Roman society, Lenski's is for advanced agrarian economies in general. One way in which the diagram of Lenski's model differs from that of Alföldy is that it rises to a tall narrow point, representing the small numbers of the elite and the wide range of their levels of wealth. Lenski also includes a class of retainers: people just below the socioeconomic level of the elite and dependent on them.[54] This affects studies of early Christian texts because most scribal groups would often be regarded as part of the retainer class. This gives them a close relationship with the elite, which makes the status of texts rather ambiguous. Should they be regarded as non-elite productions if their writers, as a class, are inevitably quite closely identified with the interests of the elite? This must remain a sharp question, especially for texts such as Luke and Acts that are offered to a patron. On the other hand, for study of the socioeconomic make-up of the early churches, Lenski's model is rather too generalized. As with Alföldy, there is not enough differentiation among the non-elite, once our interests move to people below the retainer class.

The view of social structure in Justin Meggitt's *Paul, Poverty and Survival* is rather like Alföldy's in that Meggitt does not see significant stratification among the non-elite. This is because he is seeking to correct Gerd Theissen and others by arguing that "the non-elite, over 99% of the Empire's population, could expect little more from life than abject poverty."[55] He argues that all first-century Christians fell into this category, so Theissen is wrong to think that there were some elite among the Christians and that some tensions within churches were due to sharp differences of social level. There are many strengths in Meggitt's handling of an impressive range of economic evidence, and his book has acted as a focus for a great deal of discussion, which we will not revisit here. However, one methodological difficulty is frequently also a problem for other scholars who handle economic issues. It relates to the laws of probability. Meggitt constructs a long series of arguments about individuals mentioned in Pauline texts. The basic form of each argument is "although some scholars have said that such-and-such a

---

54. Gerhard Lenski, *Power and Privilege: A Theory of Social Stratification* (New York: McGraw-Hill, 1966), p. 82. For use in NT interpretation, see Dennis C. Duling, "Matthew as Marginal Scribe in an Advanced Agrarian Society," *Hervormde Teologiese Studies* 58, no. 2 (2002): 520-75.

55. Justin J. Meggitt, *Paul, Poverty and Survival* (Edinburgh: T&T Clark, 1998), p. 50.

piece of evidence shows that person X is affluent, that is not necessarily the case." He then concludes that none of the Christians in the Pauline churches were affluent. A problem with this is that, roughly speaking, he needs to multiply together the probabilities of each person not being affluent to get the probability that not a single one of them is affluent. This is bound to end up as a very low probability.[56] No one handling economic issues (or, ultimately, any issues) can avoid the fact that their arguments need to be combined in accordance with the laws of probability. In Meggitt's case this seriously weakens his argument. One further difficulty in Meggitt's book is over exactly what should be counted as affluence. We will return to this shortly.

Ekkehard and Wolfgang Stegemann somewhat combine Alföldy and Lenski. Their triangular diagram starts from the top with aristocracy and then retainers. They introduce differentiation of social level among the non-elite by dividing them into "relatively poor, relatively prosperous," "minimum existence," and "absolutely poor." They calculate minimum existence by use of calorific intake, converted into a minimum necessary wage or a minimum necessary size of farm.[57] This threefold division of the non-elite is a substantial step forward. Some information can be gleaned from early Christian texts about wage levels for the people depicted in them — most prominently in the case of day-laborers in Jesus' parables. These can be related to the model. However, the differentiation among the non-elite is still fairly limited and there are questions about whether "minimum existence" is the best criterion for delineating poverty.

This takes us to Stephen Friesen's influential 2004 article, "Poverty in Pauline Studies."[58] Friesen constructs what he calls a "poverty scale for the Roman empire" (see p. 30).[59] In my article responding to Friesen, my main concern was with what constituted a poverty scale and how to define poverty. I took current sociological work on poverty in places such as Britain

---

56. For example, if one out of every three long-distance travelers in the Roman empire were "affluent," it would be true to say that any given traveler was not necessarily affluent. However, if you had ten random travelers, the probability that none of them was affluent would be two-thirds times two-thirds times two-thirds . . . and so on, ten times. The result of that multiplication is less than one-fiftieth — i.e., there is more than a forty-nine in fifty chance that at least one of them is affluent.

57. Stegemann and Stegemann, *The Jesus Movement*, pp. 53-88, esp. Social Pyramid I, p. 72.

58. Steven J. Friesen, "Poverty in Pauline Studies: Beyond the So-called New Consensus," *JSNT* 26 (2004): 323-61.

59. Adapted from Friesen, "Poverty," pp. 337-47, esp. figs. 1 and 3.

PS1	Imperial elites	0.04%	Includes a few retainers and local royalty.
PS2	Regional or provincial elites	1%	
PS3	Municipal elites	1.76%	Includes some merchants.
PS4	Moderate surplus resources	7%?	Includes some merchants, some traders, some freedpersons, some artisans (esp. those employing others), and military veterans.
PS5	Stable near subsistence (with reasonable hope of remaining above min. to sustain life)	22%?	Includes many merchants and traders, regular wage earners, artisans, large shop owners, freedpersons, and some farm families.
PS6	At subsistence level (and often below minimum to sustain life)	40%	Includes small farmers, laborers, artisans (esp. employed), wage earners, most merchants/traders, and small shop owners.
PS7	Below subsistence level	28%	Includes some farm families, unattached widows, orphans, beggars, disabled, unskilled day laborers, and prisoners.

and India and argued that it is best defined in terms of deprivation, that is, the economically enforced inability to participate in the normal activities of society. The onset of poverty comes quite a way above subsistence level. An effective poverty scale would measure the extent of a person's inability to participate in normal activities.[60] I also had questions about Friesen's figures. At the lower end, he is dependent on Whittaker, so there are the issues about use of evidence from medieval Florence. At the upper end, Friesen, like Alföldy, uses the *ordines* — senator, equestrian, and decurion — as his basic organizing framework. This can particularly be seen in his calculations (some of which use really hair-raising combinations of disparate types of scholarly study). If we are trying to produce an economic model of social

60. Peter Oakes, "Constructing Poverty Scales for Graeco-Roman Society: A Response to Steven Friesen's 'Poverty in Pauline Studies,'" *JSNT* 26 (2004): 367-71.

structure, the criteria for stratification must be economic. Again, we cannot use the *ordines* as a short-cut to avoid economic analysis. A useful example of why this is so can be seen in John R. Clarke's recent work on the House of the Vettii at Pompeii. He sees the house as an instance of art among the non-elite.[61] This is reasonable if the *ordines* form the boundary of the elite. The Vettius brothers are freedmen and thus not part of the elite *ordines*. However, anyone who has seen their opulent house will know that, if we are using an economic social scale, Clarke's point is far from true. In economic terms, the Vettii are certainly to be numbered among the elite. Social historians and scholars of early Christianity have tended to blur these distinctions.

Given these difficulties, how can we make progress in creating models of economic stratification that are useful for study of early Christian texts? Probably the answer is to think practically. Our aim is not to produce a perfect economic model of society. We only need something that functions well for handling particular texts. We can work with selected, accessible economic indicators, without worrying that we are not depicting every aspect of society.

Each of the following could be a usable economic indicator and is accessible through archaeological work: house size, quality of wall and floor decoration, quantity of loose finds of types relating to discretionary expenditure, frequency of access to expensive medical care as indicated in skeletal remains, degree of variety in diet as indicated by study of food remains, and estimated expense of funerary monument.

Each of these could yield an economic scale. Some scales would cover more aspects of society than others. Each scale could incorporate some description of "elite"/"affluent" and "poor." For example, an economic scale based on variety of diet could, say, take elite households to be those whose diet included a number of high-value imported foods, and could take households to be poor if their diet consisted almost exclusively of one or two low-cost staples. Such a diet-based economic scale would be unable to distinguish social structure within households. It would also only cover households that dumped food remains in certain archaeologically recoverable ways. On the other hand, an economic scale based on the medical condition of skeletal remains would work well at relating to individuals rather than just households. However, there would clearly also be all sorts of difficulties with this scale because of issues such as those relating to general standards of health in various groups.

---

61. John R. Clarke, *Art in the Lives of Ordinary Romans: Visual Representation and Non-elite Viewers in Italy, 100 BC–AD 315* (Berkeley: University of California Press, 2003), p. 98.

In research for *Reading Romans in Pompeii*, I used control of urban space, measured by house-plan size, as the economic variable for construction of a social scale. Viable samples of this are obtainable at various sites. I used evidence from Andrew Wallace-Hadrill's survey of houses in Pompeii and Herculaneum[62] and followed him in dividing the house-plan sizes into bands of 100 square meters, giving the percentage of houses in each band. At one end of the scale, 34 percent of householders had houses of less than 100 square meters in ground-floor area; 22 percent had between 100 and 200 square meters, and so on. At the other end of the scale, 0.7 percent had houses between 800 and 1000 square meters and 5 percent had houses of more than 1000 square meters (ranging up to 2800 square meters).[63]

This produced a model that achieved the key functional objective of differentiating strongly between non-elite households in a first-century context, dividing them into ten economic bands (taking 1000 square meters as the top: see below), with percentages for each. The model also offers an interesting economic definition of "elite." The percentage of houses in each 100 square meters band decreases fairly steadily until about 1000 square meters. There is then a small bulge above that size. This suggests that a wealthy group are monopolizing more resources than you would expect in a random distribution of wealth. In that circumstance, I think we can talk about there being an economic elite in that society. My definition of an economic elite would be that they are a wealthy group that monopolizes an undue proportion of scarce resources, as represented in this case by house-plan size. Elite householders, in this model, are those with houses covering an area larger than about 1000 square meters. The model is not so good at offering a definition of "poor." House-plan sizes go down fairly steadily until some minimum size units which, in any case, tend to be shops, although typically with some accommodation. We might pick a certain small house size as marking a limit of poverty, but that would be a fairly arbitrary decision.

Many limitations of the model are clear. It represents only ground floor area. If we were to factor in space upstairs, the strongest effect would be to increase average size at the bottom end of the scale, because most inhabited one-room dwellings had a mezzanine upper floor. The model does not distinguish among types of space or location. A vegetable garden comes up

---

62. Wallace-Hadrill, *Houses and Society,* appendix 1.

63. These are draft figures as of June 2008. They may be subject to correction by the time of the publication of *Reading Romans in Pompeii.* The percentages are based on the average of Wallace-Hadrill's three samples, slightly adjusted to reflect different decisions on the inclusion of certain buildings.

looking like a fair-sized house. However, this still represents control of an amount of the rather limited urban space. The model does not represent ownership. Most householders were tenants. However, again, these householders were exercising control over space, whether they paid rent or a purchase price. Most significantly, the model only represents householders. This is a limited fraction of the population. A substantial further group would be members of the householders' immediate families. The rest of the population (maybe about half) would be living as dependents or slaves in other people's houses, or would be homeless or living in marginal structures. Dependents varied widely in wealth. The model does not show up that aspect of social structure.

Given all its limitations, and given that it is based on Pompeii, how can this model of social structure be functionally worthwhile for interpreting early Christian texts? It is of value because the Pompeian evidence keys into the kind of economic evidence that many early Christian texts give about their writers, expected audience, or characters in narratives. For example, early Christian texts often give clues about people's occupations. In many instances, Pompeian house contents indicate the occupations of the house's inhabitants. Since we know the size of each house, we can then map some instances of various occupations onto the model of social structure based on house floor-plan size.

Having done this, the model, despite its limitations, begins making exegetically interesting points. Priscilla and Aquila (Acts 18:2; Rom. 16:3; etc.) are well-traveled craft-workers who employed Paul in Corinth and hosted a house-church. If we put them at a similar social level to the cabinet-maker of House 7 of the Insula of the Menander, that would give them, at Pompeii, a house of 310 square meters.[64] This would be a larger house than 70 percent of householders — a fair way up the scale of householder wealth, and even further up the scale than we would get if we included non-householders. In this craftworker's house they would not have very large rooms, but they

---

64. Peter Lampe (*From Paul to Valentinus*, pp. 187-95) would put Priscilla and Aquila at a lower economic level, in a workshop of about 27 square meters, with maybe a mezzanine sleeping area above. I agree with his skepticism about scholars who picture them as major entrepreneurs. However, he probably over-compresses the social range of ordinary craftworkers. Within that range, Priscilla and Aquila are likely to have been towards the upper end. For example, although, as he argues, the total cost of their journeys may not have been above about 1000 *sestertii*, this had to be paid out of their surplus, not their basic income. A craftworker at the poorer end of the scale would surely have had great difficulty in generating such a surplus.

would have a garden, a small colonnade, and a couple of rear-facing dining rooms that, altogether, could probably host a meeting of a few dozen. They could, if they wanted, afford a couple of nice Greek mythological paintings on the wall, but they could not run to expensive decoration in every room. Overall, they would have about six times as much housing space as the average person among the bottom 34 percent of householders. Pompeii is not Rome or Ephesus, where we know of Priscilla and Aquila acting as house-church hosts. However, it is interesting, and potentially fruitful for interpretation, to think about the house and culture of a person of Priscilla and Aquila's kind of economic level, even one living at Pompeii.

5. Conclusions

I have argued that a number of methodological points should be borne in mind when handling economics and early Christian texts. First, it needs doing. As well as the texts that obviously raise economic questions, about tax-collecting, etc., there are economic issues inherent in many (some would say, all) other texts, either because the socioeconomic location of author, audience, or patron is significant for interpretation, or because the theology of the text is expressed in ideas relating to everyday life and hence, often, to economics. Second, we need to distinguish clearly three possible relationships between economics and the text: economics as an analytical framework, gathering of economic evidence as the aim of interpretation, and economic evidence as a resource for interpretation. Third, we can use archaeological, textual, and comparative sources for gathering economic evidence. Each has much to offer but has its own methodological challenges. Finally, there are many models of socioeconomic stratification that have proven valuable, and will continue to do so, for interpretation of early Christian texts. However, there could be scope for further progress by use of models that focus on single economic indicators, chosen because they relate in potentially fruitful ways to texts under consideration.[65]

---

65. I would like to thank Dennis Duling and Douglas Oakman for their kind comments on a draft of this essay.

NEW TESTAMENT SCENARIOS

3. Money Matters: Economic Relations and the Transformation of Value in Early Christianity

Stephen C. Barton

Among the numerous titles or roles ascribed to Paul by exegetes and historians of early Christianity (e.g., apostle, missionary, pastor, prophet), the title "Paul the accountant" is not often heard. Yet, in Paul's remarkable autobiographical statement in Philippians 3, the language of accounting, of gains and losses, is pronounced. Having listed first his impressive assets "in the flesh," he proceeds to an astonishing confession: what he regarded previously as his assets, he regards now as losses, perhaps even liabilities — a radical *re-valuation* made necessary by a personal alliance that has turned Paul's value system upside down.[1] So Phil 3:7-9 reads:

> But whatever gain [κέρδη] I had, I counted as loss [ζημίαν] for the sake of Christ. Indeed I count everything as loss [ζημίαν] because of the surpassing worth of knowing Christ Jesus my Lord. For his sake I have suffered the loss of all things [τὰ πάντα ἐζημιώθην], and count them as refuse, in order that I may gain Christ [Χριστὸν κερδήσω] and be found in him.

What we have here is one of the most profound articulations of the *transformation of value,* and therefore also of *identity,* that comes to us from the period of Christians origins. And the leverage for this transformation is Paul's acceptance that he has been taken possession of by Christ (cf. Phil

1. This is noticed also by Markus Bockmuehl, *The Epistle to the Philippians* (London: A & C Black, 1997), pp. 204-5. At p. 204, he says: "This financial imagery should be noted very carefully. Paul's wholesale rejection applies not to the qualities and achievements listed but the *value* he had attached to them."

3:12), heavenly broker and benefactor *sans pareil,* knowledge of whom and identification with whom open the way to membership of a heavenly "commonwealth" (πολίτευμα) and hope of resurrection from the dead (cf. Phil 3:20-21).[2]

Against this backdrop, the aim of this essay is to offer a historically informed account of some of the transformations in value-making and value-marking in Christianity in its originating socioeconomic contexts that opened the way for new ways of ordering patterns of relationship and exchange, production and consumption, in human society. What I want to show, by close attention to several key texts and authors, is how economic attitudes and practices contributed to *early Christian social formation and self-definition* in the context of the social and religious plurality of ancient society. On the constructive side, and in the light of the testimony of the sources to (what we may call) *the economy of the kingdom of God* (that is, to the economy of redemption and new creation revealed in Christ as gift of God), I will draw out also possible moral-theological strands of normative value from the period of Christian origins about how human economic relations are to be interpreted and practiced today.

As will become apparent, I am indebted in what follows to a growing body of scholarly literature on both economic aspects of early Christianity[3] and on theological interpretations of economics.[4] In addition, a recent monograph by Catherine M. Murphy, entitled *Wealth in the Dead Sea Scrolls and in the Qumran Community,*[5] merits special mention for the insightful way it offers an analysis of economic matters and meanings in their complex interconnection with sociological and ideological factors. In this regard, the final words of her methodological reflection are worth quoting:

2. For a thorough study of economic and related matters in Philippians, see G. W. Peterman, *Paul's Gift from Philippi: Conventions of Gift-Exchange and Christian Giving* (Cambridge: Cambridge University Press, 1997).

3. See, for example, Martin Hengel's early study, *Property and Riches in the Early Church* (ET, London: SCM, 1974); and more recently, Douglas E. Oakman, "Money in the Moral Universe of the New Testament," in *The Social Setting of Jesus and the Gospels,* ed. Wolfgang Stegemann et al. (Minneapolis: Fortress, 2002), pp. 335-48.

4. See, for example, M. Douglas Meeks, *God the Economist: The Doctrine of God and Political Economy* (Minneapolis: Fortress, 1989); William Schweiker and Charles Mathewes, eds., *Having: Property and Possession in Religious and Social Life* (Grand Rapids: Eerdmans, 2004); and Kathryn Tanner, *Economy of Grace* (Minneapolis: Fortress, 2005).

5. Catherine M. Murphy, *Wealth in the Dead Sea Scrolls and in the Qumran Community* (Leiden: Brill, 2002).

[My] goal will not be simply to count the coins at the site and to define the economic terminology of the scrolls, but rather to reconstruct in some measure the symbolic world in and against which the sectarian economy functioned. . . . [T]his symbolic world was governed by the commitment to radical covenant fidelity. Economic transactions will provide community members with so many occasions to apply the Torah commands to love God with their whole strength and to love their neighbors. This symbolic system of covenant fidelity allows several other frameworks of meaning to be integrated with a radical Torah ethic, including the wilderness experience of Israel's past, the cultic context of sacrificial acts, and the eschatological ideals of a restored Temple and an economy turned on its head.[6]

Murphy's interpretation of economic matters as expressing and sustaining the beliefs, values and practices of the Qumran sectaries (especially their commitment to "radical covenant fidelity") over against those of alternative groups and peoples in the world at large offers a valuable parallel to the interpretation of economic matters in early Christianity.

1. A Rich Legacy: Property and Possessions in Torah

First, however, it is vital to set early Christian economic practice in the wider context of its inherited traditions, the most important of which is the Torah. As Patrick Miller has shown, the moral space opened up by the Ten Commandments (Exod 20:2-17; Deut 5:6-21) and their effective history is a trajectory where wisdom about property and possessions plays a very significant part.[7] In fact, the contours of life with God and neighbor are delineated in the Commandments *more in relation to wealth and property matters than any other issue.* This is remarkable. It shows how vital are economic goods, signs, values, and practices for creating and sustaining the cultures of Israel, and subsequently Judaism, as life-giving.

Thus, the "second table" of the Commandments has prohibitions that all bear in one way or another on what threatens the fabric of personal, house-

---

6. Murphy, *Wealth*, p. 24.

7. For what follows, see Patrick D. Miller, "Property and Possession in Light of the Ten Commandments," in Schweiker and Mathewes, eds., *Having*, pp. 17-50. Also valuable is Carl E. Braaten and Christopher R. Seitz, eds., *I Am the Lord Your God: Christian Reflections on the Ten Commandments* (Grand Rapids: Eerdmans, 2005).

hold and communal flourishing. Murder, as the unjust taking of a neighbor's life, irreparably diminishes the shape, productivity, and viability of a household — that social institution which the preceding positive commandment ("Honor your father and your mother") aims to preserve. Similarly, adultery, as the taking of a neighbor's sexual property, undermines the stability of his marriage, as well as the economic and social prospects of his family. Stealing, as either the taking of persons to sell them into slavery or the taking of the neighbor's material property, destroys the other's economic viability and life prospects. Bearing false witness (or lying), often in order to gain material advantage in matters of dispute whether in or out of court, destroys a neighbor's reputation as well as his material and social capital. Coveting, as the misdirected desire that seeks to augment one's own life and wealth at the cost of what properly belongs to one's neighbor, undermines the trust that underpins the social fabric. Nor is it coincidental that the prohibition against covetousness comes last and is elaborated at the greatest length (Exod 20:17; Deut 5:21). Unlike the other commandments of the second table, but taking us full circle back to the first, it addresses the fundamental matter of *the orientation of the heart.* Coveting is that orientation of the heart toward possessing what is not one's own that contributes to every other false "taking": murder, adultery, stealing, and bearing false witness. Insofar as it represents the attempt, in the act of taking, to advance (or "save") one's life independently of God and at the neighbor's expense, it is a departure from the obligation set out in the second commandment to have "no other gods."

Overall, the Torah's delineation of life with God and neighbor in terms of property and possessions takes many overlapping and intersecting forms. There are commands both positive ("Remember the Sabbath day, to keep it holy") and negative ("You shall not steal"). The kinds of action covered include the one-off (lying against a neighbor) and the on-going (stripping fields or vineyards, leaving the destitute with nothing to glean), as well as actions governed calendrically (the seventh-year release from debt and the Jubilee) and actions governed sacerdotally (the giving of firstborn sheep and oxen to the Lord). External acts are put in the spotlight (theft, swearing an oath falsely), but so are internal dispositions (coveting what belongs to the neighbor). And finally, warrants for good neighborliness in economic matters are of a kind that resonates deeply with the people's history and identity. The point is that to be true to who they are, as liberated slaves they will not seek in their economic practices to enslave others, and as people of the covenant they will display in their common life the beneficence and justice that God has bestowed on them. Thus, the warrants for good neighborliness include a conception of God as one who in his divine compassion hears the cry of the poor — typically, the widow, orphan, and stranger (cf. Deuteronomy 10). There is also the warrant of sacred remembrance ("You shall remember that you were a slave in the land of Egypt"). Such warrants are conveyed and represented variously along an extensive trajectory — through legislation, story, prophecy, and song. Out of all this, considerable insight into the nature of wealth and its place in protecting, sustaining, and valuing life (especially the life of the poor and vulnerable) is seen to develop.[8]

2. God and Mammon: Wealth as a Symbol of the Moral Life according to Matthew

Another way of articulating the above-mentioned connection in the Commandments between the prohibitions of coveting and the worship of "other gods" is the pithy wisdom statement of Jesus in the Sermon on the Mount: "You cannot serve God and mammon" (Matt 6:24; cf. Luke 16:13). In other words, there is a fundamental continuity between Torah and Jesus (or between Old Testament and New) on wealth as a symbol of the moral life — on wealth as a marker of what it means to be the people whom God has called from slavery to freedom and from death to life. This is not least the case with the Gospel of Matthew.

The extent to which the nature of the moral life, or what constitutes "righteousness" is displayed in economic terms in the Gospel of Matthew is remarkable. This fits with Matthew's emphasis (in a theology shaped by the covenantal theology of Deuteronomy reinterpreted christologically) on desires of the heart rightly ordered — in particular, the demand for total, undivided love of God and love of neighbor (cf. Matt 5:43-48; 19:19b; 22:35-39). It also fits with Matthew's emphasis on right practice, on not just hearing what Jesus says but doing it (cf. 5:21-27), and on the imperative of bearing good fruit (cf. 7:15-20), especially in works of mercy (cf. 5:7; 23:23; 25:31-46).[9] This is the way the church as the true Israel orders and sustains its common life, in faithful fulfillment of the covenant. This is the way also that the church

8. As Miller puts it ("Property and Possession," pp. 49-50): "the very character of property and possessions is seen to be complex and inclusive of material and nonmaterial goods, land and the means of living, honor and reputation, familial relationships and the nurturing of a way of life."

9. See further, Stephen C. Barton, *The Spirituality of the Gospels* (London: SPCK, 1992), pp. 18-28.

distinguishes itself from inferior, failing, and idolatrous alternatives. In other words, economic matters are ways of talking about the *lines of value and social relation* that run through the community of the elect in the Last Days, as well as being ways of representing the boundary lines that separate the community from outsiders.

Christology and community are mutually reinforcing in this respect. Taking christology first, we note that, from the outset, the narrative presents Jesus as the embodiment of a new, eschatological economy, his covenant loyalty the antitype of old Israel's repeated disloyalty. The temptation narrative, for example, has the character of a haggadic tale arising out of reflection on Deuteronomy 6–8, from which Jesus quotes three times.[10] In resisting the three temptations, Jesus shows true covenant obedience, namely, that, in the words of the Shema (Deut 6:4-5), there is one Lord and that he loves the Lord God threefold — with all his heart, with all his soul, and with all his might.[11] Thus, in refusing (in the first test) to use his power to satisfy his personal need for food and instead placing his existence under the word and will of God, Jesus shows that he loves God with all his heart. Significantly, when he does use his power to make bread, it is to meet the needs of others, the hungry crowds (14:13-21; 15:29-38). And in the third and climactic test, the offer of "all the kingdoms of the world and their glory," but at the cost of exclusive covenant loyalty to the one true God, Jesus shows that he loves God with all his might (or wealth): "Begone, Satan! for it is written, 'You shall worship the Lord your God and him only shall you serve'" (4:10). Such examples could be multiplied. They present a Messiah embodying in humility and obedience (cf. 11:25-30) the values of the divine economy of the kingdom of heaven over against demonic alternatives, and receiving in the resurrection his due reward — "*all* authority in heaven and on earth" (28:18).

As for the Messiah, so also for his followers. We see this in the Sermon on the Mount.[12] What the Matthean Jesus sets out in this first and program-

---

10. Deut 8:2-3 will have been particularly influential: "And you shall remember all the way which the Lord your God has led you these *forty* years in the *wilderness,* that he might humble you, *testing* you to know what was in your heart, whether you would keep his commandments, or not. And he humbled you and let you *hunger.*"

11. See further, Birger Gerhardsson, *The Testing of God's Son* (Lund: Gleerup, 1966); but note, with regard to the possible influence of the Shema, the reservations of W. D. Davies and Dale C. Allison, *The Gospel according to Saint Matthew,* vol. 1 (Edinburgh: T&T Clark, 1988), p. 353.

12. For a very lucid exposition, see Dale C. Allison, *The Sermon on the Mount: Inspiring the Moral Imagination* (New York: Crossroad, 1999).

matic extended discourse is a kind of divine constitution, reminiscent of the Mosaic constitution but intensifying and radicalizing it in terms appropriate to the dawn of a new era (cf. 5:17-20). Noteworthy, for our purpose, are the opening words, those of the First Beatitude: "Blessed are the poor in spirit [οἱ πτωχοὶ τῷ πνεύματι], for theirs is the kingdom of heaven" (5:3). The concern for a certain kind of interior disposition is striking. The new constitution is built on a right ordering of the spirit or heart, in particular one which, in acknowledgement of its poverty or lack, is *able to receive*. The overriding ethic is one of humility, that displacement of self that opens one to God — in the Matthean circumlocution, to the "kingdom of heaven." Likewise the parallel Third Beatitude, again with its socioeconomic imagery: "Blessed are the meek, for they shall inherit the earth [or 'land'; κληρονομήσουσιν τὴν γῆν]" (5:5). The language of present and future blessing or reward or gift is explicit here as in the rest of the Beatitudes. Such language serves as eschatological promise and consolation. This allows for the element of exacting obligation in the Sermon as a whole to be predicated on divine sovereignty and present and future blessing. The use of economic imagery allows for the articulation of the surprising *reversals of value* attendant upon the coming of the Messiah and the inauguration of a new constitution.

Alongside the reversals of value comes wisdom about *practice*. Particularly interesting for our purposes is the teaching on wealth in Matt 6:19-34. This has two main parts: vv. 19-24 are a warning about becoming a slave of money (or mammon), and vv. 25-34 are a corresponding assurance about the heavenly Father's providential care. Verses 19-24 may be divided further into three parts. The first (vv. 19-21) has two commands in antithetical parallelism, followed by a warrant: "Do not lay up for yourselves treasures on earth . . . but lay up for yourselves treasures in heaven. . . . For where your treasure is, there will your heart be also." The rhetorically powerful contrast is between goods liable to corruption and good works (like almsgiving; cf. vv. 2-4) with no such liability, between earthly capital and heavenly capital. The anthropological underpinning is that one's heart or affections will follow what one treasures most.

Anthropological reflection about the heart leads by association to anthropological reflection on the eye and the body, in 6:22-23. Contrary to the modern notion that the eye lets light *in*, the basic point in the context of antique physiological and philosophical speculation[13] is that the eye lets *out* what is going on inside — hence, "The eye is the lamp of the body" (v. 22a).

13. On this, see Allison, *The Sermon on the Mount*, pp. 142-45.

A body full of light will be reflected in bright, healthy eyes; a body full of darkness in dull, unhealthy eyes (vv. 22b-23a). Only this makes sense of the concluding statement: "If then the light in you is darkness, how great is the darkness!" (v. 23b). In the immediate context, the point appears to be that a righteous person will be predisposed toward generosity, whereas an evil person will be predisposed toward selfishness. Once again, and reminiscent of the Beatitudes, attention is drawn to interior affections, dispositions, and motivations. The moral concern is for *integrity:* for a unity of inner and outer life — and for an inner and outer life in unity with the will of God (cf. also 7:15-20; 12:34-35; etc.).

The alternative to the person of integrity is the person divided. Linked back in to the theme of the practice of wealth, this is the subject of the third and final part of this section. Once more, it follows a pattern of opening assertion, followed by statements in parallel, followed by a conclusion: "No one can serve two masters; for either he will hate the one and love the other, or he will be devoted to the one and despise the other. You cannot serve God and mammon" (6:24). Here, in perfect consistency with the account of Jesus' wholehearted devotion to the one God in the temptations and in line with the Gospel's concern for personal and communal integrity, a stark contrast is drawn between service of God and service of mammon. Why the unusual, Semitic loanword "mammon" (μαμωνᾶς)? Perhaps because it suggests the name of an idol. That is to say, so serious is the threat to the health of the individual and the community posed by money and the kinds of attachments it invites that it merits a warning sign: "Beware idolatry!"[14]

Corresponding to this teaching about the threat of wealth to wholehearted devotion is the teaching that follows aimed at countering anxiety about material sustenance (6:25-34). On this, it must suffice to observe that arguments drawn from sapiental traditions about divine providence in nature are piled one upon another in a rhetorically powerful way to overcome anxiety and stimulate faith[15] — all this in preparation for the climactic imperative, "But strive first for the kingdom of God and his righteousness, and all these things will be given to you as well" (v. 33).

In sum, economic matters are used in Matthew to offer the reader a stark moral-theological choice between two kinds of people, those who

14. Cf. Allison, *The Sermon on the Mount,* p. 145: "'Mammon' is a Semitic loanword meaning 'money' or 'possessions.' Whether or not it already had pejorative connotations in Jesus' time is unclear. But perhaps the tradition transliterated instead of translating because it functioned like the name of an idol."

15. Note that the challenge is addressed to those "of little faith" in 6:30.

show their love of God and neighbor by their deployment of money and power, and others (typified by the Pharisees) who show their lack of integrity and failure in love by their idolatrous pride and self-interest. According to Matthew's apocalyptic theology, these two kinds of people follow one of two ways, one leading to life, the other to destruction (cf. 7:13-14, 24-27; 25:31-46). In a likely historical context of the parting of the ways between church and synagogue in the time after A.D. 70,[16] when searching questions of self-definition are being asked against a backdrop of polemic and mutual vilification (cf. Matthew 23), Matthew's Gospel represents the claim that true covenant fidelity belongs with those who, in poverty of spirit, follow Jesus and deploy their wealth in accordance with the "greater righteousness" Jesus reveals.

3. Detachment from Wealth as a Symbol of Eschatological Faith according to Mark

One of the most striking socioeconomic practices displayed in the Gospels is that of *detachment from wealth* and related matters such as occupation, marriage, and family ties. As is now more widely recognized, Jesus and his disciple group constituted a radical reform movement in Judaism, participation in which demanded a discipline appropriate to its eschatological ethos and goals.[17] Expressive of this discipline of detachment is the tradition preserved in both Matthew and Luke of the two would-be disciples:

> And a scribe came up and said to him, "Teacher, I will follow you wherever you go." And Jesus said to him, "Foxes have holes, and birds of the air have nests; but the Son of Man has nowhere to lay his head." Another of the disciples said to him, "Lord, let me first go and bury my father." But Jesus said to him, "Follow me, and leave the dead to bury their own dead." (Matt 8:19-22; Luke 9:57-60)

---

16. See further, Donald A. Hagner, "The *Sitz im Leben* of the Gospel of Matthew," in *Treasures New and Old: Recent Contributions to Matthean Studies,* ed. David R. Bauer et al. (Atlanta: Scholars Press, 1996), pp. 27-68.

17. On one particular aspect of this, Jesus' practice of "prophetic celibacy," see Geza Vermes, *Jesus the Jew: A Historian's Reading of the Gospels* (London: Collins, 1973), pp. 99-102. Cf. also Dale C. Allison on Jesus as "millenarian ascetic" in his *Jesus of Nazareth: Millenarian Prophet* (Minneapolis: Fortress, 1998), pp. 172-216.

What we have in sayings like these is not some kind of principled hostility to family ties and filial duties (as some think), but something other: the *call rhetoric* of a prophetic movement for the renewal of the whole people of Israel in light of a Spirit-inspired conviction of the imminent in-breaking of the rule of God.[18] This detachment had a prudential aspect, no doubt: it allowed Jesus and the disciple band to travel light and to get on with the business that now had a higher priority — taking the gospel to the people and calling them to repentance and renewed holiness (cf. Matt 10:5-14). But it had a symbolic aspect also. In ways analogous at some points perhaps with the "anti-social" behavior of itinerant Cynic philosophers,[19] at other points, with the holy war tradition of the desert community at Qumran,[20] detachment from settled, domestic economic patterns was an eschatological, prophetic act (cf. 1 Kgs 19:19-21) that disrupted and challenged normal social and economic life and *created a space* for the practice of an economy of a different kind.[21] In this economy, "the poor" (however defined) are brought from the social and symbolic margins to the centre by benefactions of attention, forgiveness, healing, and hospitality.

Jesus' practice of eschatological detachment is given special attention in the Gospel of Mark. At the very beginning, in one paradigmatic story after another, Jesus is represented as summoning disciples to leave their settled family life and occupations to follow him in faith and engage with him in itinerant mission: "Follow me and I will make you become fishers of people!" (Mark 1:16-20; cf. also 2:14; 10:28-30).

But the theme receives greatest attention in the story, set in the wider context of teaching about true discipleship (8:27–10:45), of the seeker after eternal life whose attachment to his "many possessions" (κτήματα πολλά) deters him from becoming Jesus' follower (10:17-31 and par.).[22] Remarkably, this is the only time in Mark's Gospel when Jesus' call to follow is refused.

18. See further, Stephen C. Barton, *Discipleship and Family Ties in Mark and Matthew* (Cambridge: Cambridge University Press, 1994). For a different view, see Dale B. Martin, *Sex and the Single Savior* (Louisville: Westminster John Knox, 2006), pp. 103-24, esp. 104-9 and 226 n. 16, for a critique of my 1994 study.

19. Cf. F. Gerald Downing, *Jesus and the Threat of Freedom* (London: SCM, 1987).

20. Cf. Otto Betz, "Jesu Heiliger Krieg," *NovT* 2 (1957-58): 116-37.

21. For a recent, innovative study of the spatial impact of the Jesus movement, see Halvor Moxnes, *Putting Jesus in His Place: A Radical Vision of Household and Kingdom* (Louisville: Westminster John Knox, 2003).

22. For a sensitive analysis, see Sondra Ely Wheeler, *Wealth as Peril and Obligation: The New Testament on Possessions* (Grand Rapids: Eerdmans, 1995), pp. 39-56. On Mark 10:28-31 in particular, see Barton, *Discipleship and Family Ties,* pp. 96-107.

That Mark devotes so much space to the episode is indicative of its importance. The carefully constructed three-part story, with the encounter with the inquirer (10:17-22) followed by two intensive exchanges with the disciple group (10:23-27, 28-31), returns again and again to the matter of attachment to wealth as a stumbling-block to eternal life. Notably, what Jesus says meets with shock and astonishment each time (10:22, 24, 26). The shock and astonishment are rhetorical ways of dramatizing the resistance to the counterintuitive and countercultural (i.e., resistance to a world being turned upside down) in what Jesus says and does.

The first part of the story comes to a climax with Jesus' word of prophetic and empathetic insight into the crucial "one thing": "You lack one thing; go, sell what you have, and give to the poor, and you will have treasure in heaven; and come, follow me" (10:21). In the light of the coming of the kingdom of God, the will of God asks more of the faithful than before. Torah observance is intensified, not least in matters of the economy of the household, which is the thread that joins together all the material from 10:1 to 10:31. Just as divorce (itself in part an economic practice) is ruled out now as contrary to the eschatological will of God revealed at creation (10:1-12), and just as children are to be welcomed in ways that challenge socioeconomic assumptions about power and hierarchy (10:13-16; cf. 9:33-37), so also the social and material obligations of household and neighborhood economy encoded in the second table of the Decalogue (cf. 10:19) are taken to a new, more rigorous, level: "You lack one thing."

The second part, with Jesus pictured taking the initiative by "looking around" on his disciples, begins with one of Jesus' "hard sayings": "How hard it will be for those who have riches to enter the kingdom of God!" Then, to overcome their resistance and reinforce the point, the teaching is repeated and elaborated, beginning in the same way and repeating the fundamental theological motif of the kingdom of God, "Children, how hard it is to enter the kingdom of God! It is easier for a camel to go through the eye of a needle than for a rich man to enter the kingdom of God" (10:24b-25). The disciples' shocked response, "Then who can be saved?" may be heard as a response representative of that deeply rooted biblical and sapiental tradition according to which wealth is a sign of divine blessing.[23] But the commentary Jesus offers in reply represents, perhaps, wisdom of a more apocalyptic

23. Cf. Thomas E. Schmidt, *Hostility to Wealth in the Synoptic Gospels* (Sheffield: JSOT Press, 1987), p. 60: "The OT declares that wealth is a confirmation of God's covenant with his people, a reward for keeping the terms of his covenant."

strain, wisdom reinterpreted by eschatological faith. According to this wisdom, entry into the life-giving realm of God requires radical self-dispossession. In the imagery of the immediately preceding pericope, it is a matter of becoming "like a little child" (10:15). Participation in "eternal life" is *not a matter of what one has but of where one's trust is placed, where one's heart is.* And on this point the teaching of Jesus is radically theocentric: "With humankind it is impossible, but not with God; for God all things are possible" (10:27).

Peter, representative of the twelve in ways Mark shows to be sometimes praiseworthy, sometimes blameworthy (cf. 8:27-33), now intervenes with testimony which both harks back to the paradigmatic call stories in 1:16-20 and, in the present context, contrasts with the departed inquirer's refusal: "Behold, we have left everything [ἡμεῖς ἀφήκαμεν πάντα] and followed you" (10:28). Jesus' response is one of affirmation; but it also universalizes and intensifies the ethic of self-dispossession in words that are remarkable for the rhetorical force of their repetition and hyperbole:

> Truly, I tell you, there is no one who has left house or brothers or sisters or mother or father or children or fields for my sake and for the gospel who will not receive a hundredfold now in this time, houses and brothers and sisters and mothers and children and lands, with persecutions, and in the age to come eternal life. But many that are first will be last, and the last first. (10:29-31)

The promise of eternal life in 10:30 brings the narrative wheel full-circle. What the inquirer sought (10:17) but was offered at a price he was unwilling to pay is promised now for "the age to come" to those who are willing to pay the price. Significantly also, and poignantly for the man who has left the scene, there is a substantial advance: for "in this age," what has been left behind for the sake of Jesus and the gospel will be compensated "one hundredfold" (ἑκατονταπλασίονα)[24] in both material and fictive kinship terms, even if (and here we get a possible insight into the Markan *Sitz im Leben*) such compensation comes with the ominous disclaimer "with persecutions" (μετὰ διωγμῶν, 10:30; cf. 4:17).

What we have in this powerful story is a narrative exploration of earlier material, including the first and most important of the Markan parables, the Parable of the Sower, where the third type of seed that fails is identified as

---

24. One is reminded here of the Parable of the Sower, in 4:1-9, with the hundredfold (ἐν ἑκατόν) yield from seed sown in the good soil.

seed sown among thorns, themselves identified as "the cares of the world, the delight in riches, and the desire for other things" (4:18-19). But the story is also an elaboration of the teaching on discipleship that follows the first passion prediction at the heart of Mark's Gospel (8:31-38). Here, notably, economic language is used to reinforce the call to radical self-denial: "For what does it profit [ὠφελεῖ] a man to gain [κερδῆσαι] the whole world and forfeit [ζημιωθῆναι] his life? For what can a man give [δοῖ] in return [ἀντάλλαγμα] for his life?" (8:36-37). And other Markan stories invite comparison and contrast. One thinks, for example, of the blind beggar Bartimaeus, who throws off what belongs to him, his cloak, and follows Jesus "on the way" (10:46-52); the poor widow who puts into the Temple treasury two copper coins, described as "her whole living" (12:41-44); and the anonymous woman who, operating according to an economy unintelligible to the disciples, anoints Jesus' head with the "very costly" ointment in the leper's house (14:3-9).

In sum, we may say that economic matters serve Mark in multiple ways. On the one hand, they are a profound way of representing the crisis in human affairs and the challenge to social and spiritual values entailed in the revelation of the "mystery" (cf. 4:11) of the kingdom of God in Jesus, his death and resurrection. On the other, they are important as signifiers of a social world in the making for people of a new, eschatological covenant (cf. 14:22-25), participation in which requires detachment, letting go, accepting loss — after the manner of the messiah.

4. Economic Relations as a Symbol of Salvation and Judgment according to Luke

Of all the Gospels, it is arguably the case that money matters and economic relations bulk largest in the Gospel of Luke, and these interests carry over into his second volume, as we shall see.[25] Their meanings in Luke are multiple, as we would expect. But perhaps most characteristic in this Gospel is the way economic relations are a practical and symbolic medium for displaying and enacting Luke's central message of the dawning of a new age of salvation for Israel and the nations with the coming of Jesus the Messiah.

---

25. Especially relevant is Halvor Moxnes, *The Economy of the Kingdom: Social Conflict and Economic Relations in Luke's Gospel* (Philadelphia: Fortress, 1988); also, Jerome H. Neyrey, ed., *The Social World of Luke-Acts* (Peabody, MA: Hendrickson, 1991).

The main aspects are as follows. First, Jesus' message of "good news to the poor" and "release to the captives" represents the claim that God's promise to Israel of salvation is being fulfilled, that with the coming of Jesus the time of eschatological Jubilee has arrived (4:18-19; cf. Leviticus 25; Isa 61:1-2a). Second, the universal scope of salvation and the magnitude of divine grace are represented in Jesus' boundary-crossing table-fellowship with the socially and economically marginalized, and his acts of indiscriminate healing irrespective of wealth, class, age, race, or gender. Third, the condemnation of the complacent rich who by their greed oppress the poor expresses both divine judgment on socioeconomic injustice and the reversal of values and practices that the economy of the kingdom of God entails. Fourth, as the Zacchaeus story shows (19:1-10), transformed economic relations (including almsgiving and the restitution of unjust gain) display what is involved in repentance and conversion. Fifth, and related to this, practices of generosity and self-dispossession, such as hospitality and almsgiving, show the qualities of character appropriate to life in the new age. They constitute also a significant public witness. Sixth, the characteristic joy and rejoicing that accompany the welcome and restitution of the poor and the lost express the ethos of the divine economy of open-handed prodigality. Seventh, and drawing the threads together, wealth-related matters represent not only the crossing or transgressing of social and communal boundaries but also the marking out of new boundaries — boundaries that mark and maintain a new order of things, as also a new order of persons.

One extraordinary text that exemplifies a number of these facets is Luke 14:12-14:

> [Jesus] said to the man who had invited him, "When you give a dinner or a banquet, do not invite your friends or your brothers or your kinsmen or rich neighbors, lest they also invite you in return, and you be repaid. But when you give a feast, invite the poor, the maimed, the lame, the blind, and you will be blessed, because they cannot repay you. You will be repaid at the resurrection of the just."[26]

The setting is a typical Lukan meal, the context so often of discourse and action pertaining to the new order of things and the new order of persons. It is the Sabbath, and the host is a member of the local elite from among the sect of the Pharisees (14:1). We know from elsewhere in Luke that the Pharisees

---

26. For what follows, I am drawing especially on Moxnes, *Economy of the Kingdom*, pp. 127-38.

represent the old order (cf. 11:37-54), their resistance to the new characterized (uniquely among the Gospels) by their attitude to money: they are "lovers of money" (φιλάργυροι, 16:14)! So the hearer or reader expects not socia-
bility at the meal, but challenge and riposte.

Two mini-episodes have taken place already. In the first (14:2-6), the appearance from among the assembly of a man suffering from dropsy (i.e., one
of Luke's "poor") offers Jesus the opportunity to challenge his host and the
host's Pharisee friends on a point of Sabbath *halakah:* if the law allows the rescue of an ass or ox on the Sabbath, why not also the deliverance of a sick man?
Interestingly, there is no riposte to the challenge (14:6). In the second episode
(14:7-11), the proclivity of the guests to choose "the places of honor" presents
Jesus with the opportunity, via a barely disguised "parable" of a wedding feast,
to challenge the taken-for-granted norms of status and practices of honor-
seeking. In the eschatological wedding feast which Jesus' mission is inaugurat-
ing, such taken-for-granted norms and practices are appropriate no longer.

Then comes our text as the third episode, and the challenge this time is
not about who sits where, but about who is invited in the first place. A clear
contrast between two guest lists is drawn. The first consists of members of
the host's own circle, determined by friendship, kinship, and social status
marked by wealth. This list is characterized negatively: "do not invite your
friends or your brothers or your kinsmen or rich neighbors." The second list
consists of members outside the host's own circle on account of their low social status and ritual impurity. Subversively, this list is characterized positively: "invite the poor, the maimed, the lame, the blind."[27] The contrasting
guest lists correspond to contrasting ideas and expectations of reciprocity:
the expectation of "repayment" in the form of an invitation in return (what
anthropologists term "generalized reciprocity") on one side, over against an
expectation of reciprocity deferred to the eschatological future and from the
hand of a (divine) third party, on the other, rendering the act, in effect, one
of sheer gratuity, analogous to almsgiving (cf. 11:41).

In sum, what Jesus' teaching here represents is *a challenge to the ordering
of things, persons, and patterns of exchange* represented by "the Pharisees," in
favor of a different ordering, one expressive of the new economy of salvation
understood as "good news to the poor." Here, those on the margins are wel-

---

27. On the exclusion of precisely such as these from the Qumran community on account of their "impurity," see J. D. G. Dunn, "Jesus, Table Fellowship, and Qumran," in *Jesus
and the Dead Sea Scrolls,* ed. James H. Charlesworth (New York: Doubleday, 1992), pp. 254-
72, esp. 261-68.

comed without calculation of reciprocal favors. This corresponds precisely with the teaching in the Sermon on the Plain: "Lend, expecting nothing in return; and your reward will be great, and you will be sons of the Most High" (6:35). The implications of this for the socioeconomic relations of antiquity are well captured by Moxnes: "Compared to Hellenistic and later Christian texts, it is remarkable that there is no expectation of reciprocity, not even in the form of gratitude from the poor. . . . This is the end of a patron-client relationship in a traditional sense."[28]

5. Wealth Practices as a Symbol of Unity in the Holy Spirit according to Acts

The economic matters and meanings introduced by Luke in his Gospel are taken up and developed in the Acts of the Apostles. In his account of the beginnings of Christianity, matters of an economic kind are, once again, all-pervasive.[29] Particularly noteworthy, and what I want to explore in this section, is how wealth and related matters (especially, of course, the voluntary sharing of resources and holding of goods in common) offer the symbols and practices of Spirit-inspired unity and self-definition both within the community of believers and at its boundaries. Once again, lines running through the community and lines running around the community are articulated and given value by means of economic symbols. In this particular case, it is community characterized in terms of *unity in the Spirit*, where the value is concentrated.

What Luke narrates in Acts 2, for example, displays a profound association between the manifestation of the Holy Spirit, the apostolic preaching of the resurrection, repentance, and baptism in the name of Jesus Christ, and a consequent *change of life* — both material and spiritual. Central to this change of life is all that goes to make up the foundations of a holy society: new authority figures (the apostles), a new sociality, practices of commen-

28. Moxnes, *Economy of the Kingdom,* p. 133.

29. For a recent recognition of this and an attempt to explain it in social-anthropological terms, see Douglas J. Davies, "Purity, Spirit and Reciprocity in the Acts of the Apostles," in *Anthropological and Biblical Studies: Avenues of Approach,* ed. Louise J. Lawrence and Mario I. Aguilar (Leiden: Deo, 2004), pp. 259-80. In general, for what follows I am indebted to Brian Capper, "The Palestinian Cultural Context of Earliest Christian Community of Goods," in *The Book of Acts in Its Palestinian Setting,* ed. Richard Bauckham (Grand Rapids: Eerdmans, 1995), pp. 323-56.

salism ("the breaking of bread"), and practices of piety (the prayers) (2:42). Luke continues:

> And fear came upon every [πάσῃ] soul; and many wonders and signs were done through the apostles. And all [πάντες] who believed were together [ἐπὶ τὸ αὐτό] and had all things in common [ἅπαντα κοινά]; and they sold their possessions and goods and distributed them to all [πᾶσιν], as any had need. And day by day, attending the temple together [ὁμοθυμαδόν], and breaking bread in their homes, they partook of food with glad and generous hearts, praising God and having favor with all the people. And the Lord added to their number day by day those who were being saved. (2:43-47)

The unity of the newly baptized as a characteristic of their change of life is pronounced. It is conveyed rhetorically through the emphatic repetition of words like "every/all" (πᾶς, 2:43, 44 [2x], 45), "common" (the κοιν- word group, 2:42, 44) and "together" (ἐπὶ τὸ αὐτό, 2:44; ὁμοθυμαδόν, 2.46).[30] The narrator points also to a shared ethos (i.e., that of φόβος, "awe" or "fear," 2:43) in response to the apostles' display of charismatic power. This ethos gives rise to (as well as is reinforced by) a strong ethic of solidarity.

The solidarity has economic aspects, both "horizontal" and "vertical." On the vertical plane, it takes the form of an economy of devotion embodied in particular deployments of time, space, and voice: that is to say, "daily" attendance at the Temple and the witness of praise to God (2:46-47). On the horizontal plane it takes the form of a distributive economy of gift, of "all things in common" (ἅπαντα κοινά, 2:44), the material lack of the poor being met by the sale of property and the distribution of the proceeds on the basis of need, all this reinforced by the social and material practice of eating together κατ᾽ οἶκον ("in their homes" or "from house to house"), and doing so in a spirit of effervescent generosity (ἐν ἀγαλλιάσει καὶ ἀφελότητι καρδίας, 2:46), itself indicative of a pronounced lack of calculation. The "payback" is that of blessing which takes place also on horizontal and vertical planes. On the horizontal plane, the new community is the recipient of "favor" (χάρις) from "the whole people"; on the vertical plane, their membership is augmented "daily" by the risen Lord (2:47).

30. On ἐπὶ τὸ αὐτό, see Max Wilcox, *The Semitisms of Acts* (Oxford: Oxford University Press, 1965), pp. 93-100; on ὁμοθυμαδόν, see S. Walton, "῾Ομοθυμαδόν in Acts: Co-location, Common Action or 'Of One Heart and Mind'?" in *The New Testament in Its First Century Setting,* ed. P. J. Williams et al. (Grand Rapids: Eerdmans, 2004), pp. 89-105.

As is well known, the pattern set in Acts 2 is repeated (with minor differ-ences) in Acts 4:32-37. Pentecost-like, there is another earth-shattering mani-festation of the Holy Spirit (4:31), following which (and the sequence is im-portant) the narrator offers a cameo of the believers' common life. Once again, emphatic attention is drawn to their unity and, once again, that unity is both displayed in economic terms and effected by economic means. The opening makes this clear: "Now the company of those who believed were of one heart and soul [καρδία καὶ ψυχὴ μία], and no one [οὐδὲ εἷς] said that any of the things which he possessed was his own, but they had everything in common [ἄπαντα κοινά]" (4:32). Here, to be "of one heart and soul" is not (or not only) a matter of inner disposition or will, a meeting of minds, as it were; it is a matter also of sharing material goods — indeed, pooling assets[31] and placing them at the disposal of a unitary authority, that of the apostles, for the sake of redistribution on the basis of need.

In short, the presence of the Spirit as the benefaction of the risen and as-cended Lord issues in a new society whose economic relations, in the Lukan perspective, are *supernatural.* Not coincidental is Luke's placing of the state-ment of divine empowerment at the heart of his account: "And with great power [δυνάμει μεγάλη] the apostles gave their testimony to the resurrec-tion of the Lord Jesus, and great grace [χάρις . . . μεγάλη] was upon them all" (4:33). The point is that the believers' pattern of social and economic rela-tions is of an order so remarkable that it is inexplicable in human terms — it is a manifestation of "great grace" and a response that grace makes possible.

That the economic order portrayed here is (what may appropriately be called) a pneumatic or charismatic or supernatural order is reinforced by the two contrasting episodes that follow. The first, much briefer, and entirely positive cameo (4:36-37) tells of Joseph, soon to become a leading figure (cf. 9:27), who voluntarily sells a field and hands the proceeds over to the apos-tles for their disposal. That he is identified in advance here as honored by the apostles with the surname Barnabas, "which means son of encouragement,"

31. As discussed below, given the example of Barnabas (in 4:36-37), I take it that Luke intends the reader to understand that it is primarily *disposable* assets that are involved. Nev-ertheless, the utopian aspect of Luke's rhetoric of solidarity here leaves open the possibility of more radical interpretations — of the kinds debated and actualized in subsequent peri-ods of Christian history. As one example, take the debates over "evangelical poverty" in Franciscan and Wycliffite circles in the thirteenth and fourteenth centuries: on which see Joan Lockwood O'Donovan, "The Poverty of Christ and Non-Proprietary Community," in *The Doctrine of God and Theological Ethics,* ed. Alan J. Torrance and Michael Banner (Lon-don: T&T Clark International, 2006), pp. 191-200.

is hardly surprising, for what he does is a model, an encouragement, for others in the community to follow.

Over against this is the extended, and entirely negative, story of Ananias and Sapphira (5:1-11) which, as a story of satanic invasion (cf. 5:3) and divine judgment, serves as a striking counterpoint. The account is told vividly by means of rhetorical doubling, as first the man and then his wife are judged, punished with death, and carried out for burial. In this way, the structured story is a warning against the calculated misrepresentation of one's level of material commitment (itself a symbol of one's level of communal *trust*) and the associated threat such misrepresentation poses to the unity of heart and soul of the community. In terms of Torah, discussed above, it constitutes a form of "bearing false witness" that is inimical to covenantal community. Similarly, at Qumran, lying about wealth — including the property one is depositing with the community on joining — is forbidden and punishable (cf. CD 14:20-21; 1QS 6:24-25).[32] In sociological terms, wealth practices function, in Acts as in these other examples, to *define and patrol the community's boundaries.* What Ananias and Sapphira do in lying to the Holy Spirit (spoken of also, with emphatic repetition, as lying to God and putting the Spirit to the test, 5:3, 4, 9) places them outside the sphere of grace and the communal circle of salvation and into the sphere of Satan. Their instant death, removal, and burial (5:5-6, 10) constitute a graphic purity statement involving both boundary marking and boundary preservation. In the end, the unity of the community, far from being undermined, is strengthened, reinforced by the recurrence of the ethos of "fear" (φόβος) arising from the supernatural drama unfolding in the community's midst (5:5, 11; cf. 2:43; 3:10; etc).

Overall, Luke's portrayal of early Christian community in matters both material and spiritual is powerful rhetorically and theologically. We may imagine that it is intended to have a persuasive force on both believers and unbelievers among its readers (or hearers). Rhetorically, the portrayal allows Luke to associate the early church positively with utopian ideals and practices of community past and present in the wider world. Thus, on the one hand, Luke's portrayal fits well with Greek and Hellenistic philosophical traditions relating to friendship and the ideal society, going back at least as far as to Plato and Aristotle and popular among the Stoics.[33] On the other hand,

32. Murphy, *Wealth*, pp. 52-54, 101, 144-45, etc.

33. See further, Capper, "Community of Goods," pp. 324-25. Cf. also Hengel, *Property and Riches*, pp. 3-11. On p. 5, Hengel cites Strabo's account (in *Geography* 7.3.9) of the Scythians, as follows: "They are frugal in their ways of living and not money-getters, they not only are orderly towards one another, because they have all things in common, their

it fits well with biblical and early Jewish (especially Qumran) traditions depicting the people of the one true God as themselves a "oneness."[34] But more important than the rhetorical dimension is the theological. Theologically, Luke's portrayal allows him to represent the church as "fulfilling" and even surpassing all precedents and current alternatives. For Luke, the church is *the* eschatological society whose wealth practices reflect the *purity, spontaneity, intensity, and universal appeal* of a supernatural common life made possible by the power of the Risen Christ through the Spirit.

Conclusion

By way of conclusion, I offer the following general reflections. First, economic practices are not at all marginal to Christianity either in its originating moments or subsequently.[35] They are not some kind of secondary, material epiphenomenon of something more fundamentally "spiritual." On the contrary, they are at the heart of early Christian self-definition, moral formation, and sociality. We see this in Jesus' prophetic detachment from household ties and adoption of a life of itinerant, "charismatic poverty" for the sake of the kingdom. We see it in the Gospel of Luke in Jesus' identification with the poor, the sick, and the oppressed and in his practice of open table fellowship; we see it also in the Acts of the Apostles in the believers' practice of "all things in common." If we ask *why* economic practices bulk so large, the answer must be that, as cultural mechanisms or symbols of value, connection and exchange, they function in the movement inaugurated by Jesus to allow communication both of *what really counts* and of *how to attain* it.

Second, and related, in its literary deposit and common life, early Christianity represents a *re-narration* of what really counts and how to attain it. Building upon biblical wisdom about just sociality and good neighborliness, this re-narration itself takes a variety of forms and expressions, shorthand versions of which include "the kingdom of God," "the new covenant," "dying

---

wives, children, the whole of their kin and everything, but also remain invincible and unconquered by others, because they have nothing to be enslaved for."

34. See further, Capper, "Community of Goods," pp. 335-37.

35. On the patristic period and subsequently, see Peter C. Phan, *Message of the Fathers of the Church: Social Thought* (Wilmington: Michael Glazier, 1984); Boniface Ramsey, *Beginning to Read the Church Fathers* (London: Darton, Longman and Todd, 1986), pp. 182-96; and the recent historical study of Peter Brown, *Poverty and Leadership in the Later Roman Empire* (Hanover, NH: University Press of New England, 2002).

and rising with Christ," and "freedom in the Spirit." But at its heart is an eschatological story of *amazing grace*, of God's overflowing beneficence as One
who is "rich in mercy," of redemption from slavery, of having been "bought
with a price," of heavenly gifts imparted without respect to race, class, status,
or gender.

This story (or "gospel"), thirdly, *radicalizes, intensifies, confounds, and
disrupts* culturally dominant notions of what really counts and how to attain
it. It does so as the power of God revealed in divine self-dispossession or self-
giving for the sake of the other. In the words of Paul to the Corinthians: "For
you know the grace of our Lord Jesus Christ, that though he was rich, yet for
your sake he became poor, so that by his poverty you might become rich"
(2 Cor 8:9). In its *pure gratuity* (i.e., the gratuity of love), this divine self-
dispossession has a *transgressive* quality. It crosses boundaries and challenges
paradigms, and in so doing opens a space and a time for new (and renewed)
ways of being human-in-relation, that is, for a new ordering of things and
persons, a new economy.

This means, fourth, that there are both continuity and discontinuity
with other economies, other patterns of value and exchange, in early Christianity's past and present. What is good and life-giving in the wisdom, utopi-
anism, and "oikonomic" practices of paganism can be taken over and modified. We see this in early Christian co-option of widely held values of good
citizenship[36] and in the Christianizing of household codes (i.e., the
οἰκονομία) of ancient provenance.[37] Even more, however, is this the case for
what is good and life-giving in Torah and the socioeconomic institutions of
Israel and Judaism. Witness, on the critical side, the "two ways" tradition in
Matthew and elsewhere, with its stark choice between God and mammon, or
the ongoing Christian critique of greed as idolatry in the Pauline tradition
(cf. Col 3:5; Eph 5:5).[38] On the constructive side, witness the ethos of
"Jubilary" debt-release in Jesus' mission statement in Luke of "good news to
the poor . . . [and] release to the captives" (Luke 4:18-19). Witness also the
Christian co-option of practices of almsgiving and collecting for the poor,
practices rooted in the biblical ethic of neighborly love and Jewish Temple
piety. But decisive now (i.e., what provides the narrative hermeneutic and

36. Relevant here is Bruce Winter, *Seek the Welfare of the City* (Grand Rapids:
Eerdmans, 1994).

37. See further, David L. Balch, *Let Wives Be Submissive: The Domestic Code in 1 Peter*
(Atlanta: Scholars Press, 1981).

38. On the latter, see Brian S. Rosner, *Greed as Idolatry: The Origin and Meaning of a
Pauline Metaphor* (Grand Rapids: Eerdmans, 2007).

the "norming norm") is the eschatological, transgressive, "new creation" economy of the kingdom of God and life in Christ through the Spirit.

The implications of all this for Christian identity, formation, and sociality today are as profound and far-reaching as they have ever been, not least because economic matters are matters of life and death, and money, in its fluidity and mystifying power, touches everything. Here, I make just one point. It would be possible, in the context of the rampant materialism and consumerism of the modern world, to respond in one of two ways: either to accommodate or to separate, to model the church on the market and "baptize" wealth accumulation as the calling of the Christian and sign of divine blessing, or to repudiate economic life and money-making to go in quest of an essentially disembodied, "authentic spirituality."[39] Neither response is a truly Christian performance of Scripture, however. The one makes the church a counterfeit of its true self in which the distinction between God and mammon becomes blurred or collapses altogether. The other is a kind of "Manichean" separation of the spiritual and the material and, as such, a radical departure from incarnational Christianity and from the true nature of creaturely life under God in the world.

For a better guide to a truly Christian performance of Scripture in the sphere of economic relations,[40] I would turn in two directions, although the possibilities are multiple. First, I would turn to the lives of the saints. Insofar as the saints "body forth" Christ in the world, they signify what really matters: the economy of grace and holy self-dispossession for the sake of the other, which is the economy of life in God. Furthermore, in so far as they "body forth" Christ in ways recognizably extreme, parodic, or transgressive in relation to the norms of the day, they *create a space* (at either the center or the periphery) where the value of things and people can be seen and practiced in new ways. Think, then, of Saint Anthony and the desert fathers,[41] whose adoption of the ascetic way and relocation to the wilderness meant exchanging the economy of the earthly city for that of the heavenly city and

39. Cf. L. Gregory Jones, "A Thirst for God or Consumer Spirituality? Cultivating Disciplined Practices of Being Engaged by God," *Modern Theology* 13 (1997): 3-28; also, Brian Rosner, "Soul Idolatry: Greed as Idolatry in the Bible," *Ex Auditu* 15 (1999): 72-86, esp. 81-84.

40. On the metaphor of "performance," see most recently A. K. M. Adam, "Poaching on Zion: Biblical Theology as Signifying Practice," in A. K. M. Adam et al., *Reading Scripture with the Church: Toward a Hermeneutic for Theological Interpretation* (Grand Rapids: Baker Academic, 2006), pp. 17-34.

41. See further, Andrew Louth, *The Wilderness of God* (London: Darton, Longman and Todd, 1991), pp. 43-61.

the angelic life and paved the way for a new kind of sociality, that of the monastery. Think also of Saint Francis.[42] Like Saint Anthony, taking the Gospel narratives of Christ literally as the script for his own life, he renounced his wealth (in obedience to the dominical command in Matt 10:9-10), adopted a life of poverty, and founded a religious order dedicated to the imitation of Christ through self-denial and the service of the poor. Such examples could be multiplied many times over.[43] In their very particular ways of mediating Christ, inviting imitation and creating community, saints and martyrs are the standard of a different scale of values, *the agents of a different, eschatological order of things and people.*

Second, and to conclude, I turn to Christian worship — in particular, to the liturgy of the Eucharist and, within that, the curious phenomenon of *the taking up of a collection,* itself a part of the offertory.[44] This intrusion of money-matters into the service of worship at its profoundest moment, this juxtaposition of money with the central, solemn symbols of the sacrifice of Christ, as they (bread, wine, and money) are brought up to the altar in procession, is remarkable. What it represents is "a mundane means of participating in grace, of imitating Christ, and of joining in the life of Christ."[45] Here, money and economic matters are placed in their rightful context. They become part of a larger interpretative narrative and social-symbolic practice, at the heart of which are divine grace and call. The grace is the revelation of God's own *uncalculating and incalculable self-giving in Christ* for the sake of the world. The call is to the constitution of a community of the Spirit to witness to that grace through the life-imparting ordering of people and things that God's self-giving makes possible.

42. See further, James C. Howell, "Christ Was like Saint Francis," in *The Art of Reading Scripture,* ed. Ellen F. Davis and Richard B. Hays (Grand Rapids: Eerdmans, 2003), pp. 89-108.

43. See further, David Matzko McCarthy, "The Gospels Embodied: The Lives of Saints and Martyrs," in *The Cambridge Companion to the Gospels,* ed. Stephen C. Barton (Cambridge: Cambridge University Press, 2006), pp. 224-44.

44. See further, D. Stephen Long and Tripp York, "Remembering: Offering Our Gifts," in *The Blackwell Companion to Christian Ethics,* ed. Stanley Hauerwas and Samuel Wells (Oxford: Blackwell, 2004), pp. 332-45.

45. Timothy Jenkins, "Giving," in *An Experiment in Providence* (London: SPCK, 2006), pp. 57-60, at 60.

4. Jesus, Virtuoso Religion, and the Community of Goods

Brian J. Capper

Jesus sometimes appears to have condemned wealth and possessions absolutely. He proclaimed that the service of God and Mammon are mutually exclusive (Matt 6:24). He told a rich man to sell all that he owned, distribute the proceeds to the poor and, bereft of wealth, to follow as a traveling disciple. When the man turned away, Jesus told his disciples, who had left all to follow him, that it is harder for a camel to pass through the eye of a needle than for a rich man to enter the kingdom of God (Mark 10:21, 23, 25). He instructed his traveling group of disciples to sell their possessions, making alms of the proceeds (Luke 12:33). One of his sayings explained: "Whoever does not give up all that he has cannot be my disciple" (Luke 14:33). He uttered blessings upon the presently suffering poor while cursing the satisfied rich of this age (Luke 6:20-25).

Such phenomena are among the harsher sayings of Jesus about wealth and possessions found in the Synoptic Gospels. Jesus himself carried no purse but lived communally with his twelve traveling disciples from a purse in which their wealth was pooled, administered by the disciple Judas (John 12:6; 13:29). Early in Acts we hear that the first community of post-Easter believers in Jesus apparently held their property in common, and frequently liquidated possessions for the common good (Acts 2:42-47; 4:32–5:11; cf. 6:1-6). This account is almost universally read with suspicion and regarded as both idealized and barely historical.[1] It is often treated with frank skepticism

---

1. See, for example, Richard S. Ascough, "Benefaction Gone Wrong: The Sin of Ananias and Sapphira in Context," in *Text and Artefact in the Religions of Mediterranean Antiquity:*

despite the immediately prior precedent for community of property found in the common purse of Jesus' traveling party, from which Jesus lived with his especially chosen twelve disciples, who had left all to follow him (Mark 10:28).[2]

Thus, while Jesus' concern for the poor is enthusiastically received by his modern interpreters, his occasional theme of renunciation of property and his sometimes seemingly absolute condemnation of wealth often seem both mysterious and rather unpalatable. Many modern western interpreters experience these more inaccessible aspects of Jesus' legacy concerning wealth and possessions as from another, strange world, incapable of sympathetic reading or imitation.[3]

As will be outlined in the course of this paper, much progress has been made in recent decades in understanding Jesus' general approach to wealth and poverty by examining his teaching from the perspective of a social-scientific understanding of the pre-industrial, agrarian society which was his context. The specific purpose of this paper is to develop this socio-historical approach through a supplementary socio-religious and macroeconomic explanation of Jesus' more unpalatable theme of renunciation of property and his actual, practiced community of goods, to which the Gospels bear historical witness. This paper will also extend this method of explanation to the Acts account of the apparent community of goods of the first Jerusalem

---

Essays in Honour of Peter Richardson, ed. Stephen G. Wilson and Michel Desjardins (Waterloo, ON: Wilfrid Laurier Press, 2000), pp. 91-110, who gives a useful bibliography that includes my earlier pieces on this theme. He largely follows the usual skeptical view. Against Ascough's turn to Greco-Roman practice external of Palestine for understanding these practices of the early Jerusalem church, I would set my elaboration of the case for their origins in the Judean economic and cultural context offered in my "The Church as New Covenant of Effective Economics: The Social Origins of Mutually Supportive Christian Community," *International Journal for the Study of the Christian Church* 2 (2002): 83-102; "Two Types of Discipleship in Early Christianity," *JTS* 52 (2001): 105-23; "The Holy Congregation in Jerusalem," in *Encyclopedia of the Dead Sea Scrolls,* ed. Lawrence H. Schiffman and James C. VanderKam (New York: Oxford University Press, 2000), vol. 1, pp. 369-70; "'With the Oldest Monks . . .': Light from Essene History on the Career of the Beloved Disciple?" *JTS* 49 (1998): 1-55.

2. Joachim Jeremias, *Jerusalem in the Time of Jesus* (London: SCM, 1969), p. 130.

3. F. Scott Spencer comments on the harsher words about possessions attributed to Jesus: "By all accounts, Jesus offers little comfort to merchants and financiers. To put it mildly, his words would find little welcome on modern Wall Street; indeed, they would be repudiated." *What Did Jesus Do? Gospel Profiles of Jesus' Personal Conduct* (Harrisburg, PA: Trinity Press International, 2003), p. 129.

post-Easter believers in Jesus. The social-scientific model advanced will be that of *virtuoso religion.*

1. Virtuoso Religion

In order to understand the notion of virtuoso religion, it is best to put the concept of social elites front and center. In sociological perspective, groupings of people are usually led by elites.[4] The elite may be sociologically defined in two ways. From one perspective, the elite are those who *de jure* occupy the positions of highest authority within a social grouping or organization. Yet from a different perspective, the elite may be understood as those who have attained the highest levels in the group's most respected and valued activities. What might be termed the "institutional elite" carry the greatest formal authority, while those who might be called the "skill-and-achievement-elite" or the *virtuoso* elite exemplify the group's highest values and may represent important *de facto* authority for many in the group and sometimes inconvenient competition for its formal leadership.[5]

The notion of the virtuoso religious elite easily applies to Jesus and his first followers. When Jesus called his accompanying group of disciples to be "fishers of people" (Mark 1:16-20), he called them to leave all and to accompany him so that they might be trained to exercise the specialist religious task, *mission,* in which he would have them become expert. Their special *apostolic* task carried with it a call to renounce worldly connections and to share among themselves, a call to a distinctive, *apostolic* mode of life. This mode of life allowed them constantly to be *with* Jesus and thereby to receive teaching both in content and intensity markedly beyond that which Jesus made available to the crowds who heard him and even to his other, locally based disciples (Mark 3:9-19). Jesus' specialist group (his *virtuoso* group of twelve) would find themselves, with him, in conflict with both Pharisees and especially with the Jerusalem-based Sadducees, the elite who held institutional power and preferred, as it were, to retain full control over the fish-stock and to control all angling rights, whatever mas-

---

4. Non-hierarchical social groups are rare, if they truly occur at all.

5. Cf. T. B. Bottomore, *Elites and Society* (London: C. A. Watts, 1964), pp. 1-3; Anthony Giddens, *The Class Structure of Advanced Society* (London: Hutchinson, 1973), pp. 119-20, as used and modified by Stephen Sharot, *A Comparative Sociology of World Religions: Virtuosos, Priests and Popular Religion* (New York and London: New York University Press, 2001), pp. 11 and 264 n. 21.

tery in the religious realm the ordinary mass of the population ascribed to Jesus and the Twelve.

It should be stressed that not all religious virtuosi are ascetics (e.g., monks, nuns, etc.), though ascetic and non-ascetic virtuosi share loyalty to their religious tradition's core values. The accusation that Jesus was a "glutton and a drunkard" shows the surprise of his opponents that someone taking the role he did of an independent, self-assertive religious virtuoso was not markedly temperate, if not definitely ascetic (Matt 11:19; Luke 7:34; cf. Deut 21:20). However, that Jesus parried the accusation by pointing to their mocking of John the Baptist's distinctly rigorous asceticism does not prove that there were no ascetic aspects to Jesus' practice. That Jesus did not inculcate fasting according to the calendar of fasts (Mark 2:18-22) likewise is not evidence of a complete absence of asceticism in his practice.[6]

Although not all religious virtuosi are rigorist ascetics, virtuoso religion always implies a disciplined application of method. The most expert and useful current typology of virtuoso religion is that offered by Ilana Silber, which may be summarized as follows:

1. Virtuoso religion is a matter of individual choice.
2. Virtuoso religion involves an intensification of personal commitment over normal compulsory religious routine, norms, and behavior.
3. Virtuoso religion involves the seeking of perfection, an extreme urge to go beyond everyday life and average religious achievement.
4. The seeking of perfection involved in virtuoso religion is sustained in a disciplined, systematic fashion through a defined rule or method.
5. Virtuoso religion implies a normative double standard; its rigor is not only not necessary for all, but it is also impossible for all.
6. Virtuoso religion is based in achievement and non-ascriptive criteria, and is in principle an option for all, although in practice only achieved by a "heroic" minority.[7]

As may be seen from these features, the religious virtuoso is intensely preoccupied with ultimate concerns and values. Within the wider religious com-

6. See the discussion of Dale C. Allison, "Jesus as Millenarian Ascetic: Deleting a Consensus," chapter 3 of his *Jesus of Nazareth: Millenarian Prophet* (Minneapolis: Augsburg Fortress, 1998), pp. 172-216.

7. Ilana Silber, *Virtuosity, Charisma, and Social Order: A Comparative Sociological Study of Monasticism in Theravada Buddhism and Mediaeval Catholicism* (Cambridge: Cambridge University Press, 1995), pp. 190-94.

munity, religious virtuosi are perhaps most distinguishable by their intense seeking to express ultimate values and concerns through the employment of discipline and method (point 4 above), by which their religious focus becomes comprehensive, embracing very visibly all life and activity.

Moreover, Silber regards virtuoso religion as operating as a part of the wider religious community and tends to distinguish it from sectarianism. "Virtuosi represent something that is considered potentially disruptive, yet has a place in the collective set of values."[8] Points 5 and 6 above assume this connection to and acceptance within the wider religious community. Thus virtuoso religion is able to sustain liminal social structures; virtuoso groups, while retaining a connection with the wider religious community, have a distinctive inner life. The internal economic and social life of communities of religious virtuosi may even represent a reverse image of the values and normal behavior of the surrounding religious community. Monks and nuns, for example, usually limit contact with surrounding society, emphasize personal possessionlessness and operate an entirely communal economy. Their daily routine usually differs markedly from surrounding society, with a pronounced focus on worship and spiritual disciplines. Silber makes use of Victor Turner's social concepts of "structure" and "antistructure" and argues that religious virtuosity has the capacity to create permanent antistructure, entailing elements such as egalitarianism and status leveling which are not found in society outside the group.[9]

This observation appears highly relevant for the study of Jesus' traveling disciple group, which seems to have captured in its social pattern ideals of mutual service, personal possessionlessness, and the reversal of the norms of hierarchy which pertained in the world outside the group. So, for instance, Jesus taught that his senior disciples must be servants and the most senior a slave of all (Matt 20:26-27; Mark 9:35; 10:43-44; Luke 22:26; cf. 14:11; 18:14b).

Virtuoso religion does not demand a complete separation from the surrounding world, but exists, as noted, in a liminal social position. Indeed, while sometimes appearing separate from wider society, religious virtuosi may exercise disproportionate and considerable influence upon their surrounding religious community and social world. Max Weber noted that be-

8. Silber, *Virtuosity,* p. 44.

9. Silber, *Virtuosity,* pp. 40-41, 53; Victor Turner, *Dramas, Fields and Metaphors: Symbolic Action in Human Society* (Ithaca, NY: Cornell University Press, 1974), especially the chapter titled "Metaphors of Anti-Structure in Religious Culture," pp. 272-300; Timothy Ling, *The Judaean Poor and the Fourth Gospel* (Cambridge: Cambridge University Press, 2006), pp. 70-74.

cause of its peculiar and highly concrete forms, the religiosity of virtuosi has often been

> of decisive importance for the development of the way of life of the masses. This virtuoso religiosity has therefore also often been important for the economic ethic of the respective religion. The religion of the virtuoso has been the genuinely "exemplary" and practical religion.

Weber pointed out that laypersons could be subject to a certain ethical regulation by virtuoso religion because the virtuoso was often the layperson's "spiritual adviser" and spiritual director. "Hence, the virtuoso frequently exercises a powerful influence over the religiously 'unmusical.'"[10] Such influence may extend not merely to the ordinary mass of the population, but as far as the political elite and, within monarchic social organization, even to the ruler.[11]

If space permitted, I would demonstrate that religious virtuosi in first-century Palestine (1) developed precedents offered by ancient forms of virtuoso religion in Israelite and Jewish history and (2) created virtuoso patterns out of other traditional social forms. In particular, Jesus developed the mode of virtuoso peripatetic prophecy; the Essenes, on the other hand, constructed a new pattern of virtuoso religion based primarily on a reinterpretation of priestly holiness. Both of these forms of virtuoso religion adapted their differing precedents to express (1) symbolic value statements in opposition to those of the reigning, exploitative form of agrarian economy and (2) practical modes of economic sharing. The distinctive social forms and exhortation of these differing religious virtuosi both precipitated and facilitated actual economic redistribution in the wider Jewish religious community.

The virtuoso piety of the Essenes and, I believe, Jesus and his followers expressed the reaction of many of the pious toward the greed, land accumulation, and luxury of the political elite. In virtuoso piety, it becomes *holy* and *honorable* to express the opposite of acquisitive elite behavior by espousing poverty and even celibacy. This reversal of external values within the first-century Jewish virtuoso group allowed it to consider itself the true elite of

---

10. Max Weber, "Social Psychology of the World's Religions," in *From Max Weber: Essays in Sociology*, ed. H. H. Gerth and C. Wright Mills (London: Routledge and Kegan Paul, 1948), pp. 267-301, at 289.

11. From 1905 to 1916 Rasputin was close to the family of the last Russian Tsar, Nicholas II. Two of the most powerful world leaders of the early twenty-first century, George W. Bush and Tony Blair, both acknowledged their recourse to expert spiritual counsel.

the nation and to compete before the populace for reputation and power over against the institutional hierarchy of the Jerusalem Temple. Along these lines, Jesus and his followers will be the primary focus of this investigation.

2. Jesus' Critique of Wealth and Poverty

Against the backdrop of the typical social pattern of agrarian society, much in Jesus' teaching about possessions becomes accessible.[12] Jesus' view was framed within the simple contrast of "rich" versus "poor" (cf. Luke 6:20-26). This reflects the typical agrarian social bifurcation between unjust rich and struggling poor which had already characterized strands of Jewish apocalyptic, in which terrible judgment awaited the land-grabbing and luxuriously living wealth-elite who had forfeited their place within God's covenant by their wicked exploitation of the Jewish peasantry (cf. *1 Enoch* 91–92; 95:7; 96:3-8; 97:1-2; 98:11-15; 100:6-7; 107). Similarly, Jesus spoke of "unrighteous mammon" (Luke 16:9, 11) and of the punishment in fiery *She'ol* of an owner of great estates who has indulged himself in the fine garments and rich feasting of the elite while neglecting a poor sick man who had languished at his courtyard's gate (Luke 16:19-31; cf. *1 Enoch* 21-22; 63:10). So also Jesus framed a parable around a disloyal, dishonest estate steward losing his status as one of the narrow, trusted retainer class and contemplating his looming, rapid descent to poverty below the level of subsistence laborers, begging among the underclass (Luke 16:1-15).

Jesus expressed his concern for those desperately seeking subsistence, illustrated God's graciousness, and encouraged landowners to similar graciousness, by speaking of a vineyard owner who generously assisted some impoverished day laborers. These had walked the rural roads in search of work for much of the day, finding only little, yet he gave them a full day's pay

---

12. For further background on the comparisons in this section see Brian J. Capper, "Wealth," in *Jesus in History, Culture and Thought: An Encyclopedia,* ed. Leslie J. Houlden (Santa Barbara, Denver, and Oxford: ABC Clio, 2003), vol. 2, pp. 864-69, and "The Church as New Covenant of Effective Economics"; Ekkehard W. Stegemann and Wolfgang Stegemann, *The Jesus Movement: A Social History of Its First Century* (Edinburgh: T. & T. Clark, 1999); William Herzog, *Parables as Subversive Speech* (Louisville: Westminster John Knox, 1994); R. David Kaylor, *Jesus the Prophet: His Vision of the Kingdom on Earth* (Louisville: Westminster John Knox, 1994); Richard A. Horsley, *Jesus and the Spiral of Violence* (San Francisco: Harper and Row, 1987; Minneapolis: Fortress, 1993); Donald E. Oakman, *Jesus and the Economic Questions of His Day* (Lewiston, NY: Edwin Mellen, 1986).

so that both they and their families could eat that evening (Matt 20:1-15). Within the clearly stressed Galilean subsistence economy, Jesus taught his disciples a prayer that included a prominent petition for a "daily ration of bread" sufficient for survival (Matt 6:11; Luke 11:3). He was remembered for his striking willingness to dine with prostitutes — i.e., brutalized women of the Galilean underclass (Matt 9:9-13; cf. 21:31-32; Mark 2:13-17; Luke 5:27-32; cf. 7:36-50).[13] Through his parable of the rich fool he urged the well-off to refrain from hoarding and to share with the poor (Luke 12:16-21; cf. *Gospel of Thomas* 63). He counseled the rich to generous meal fellowship with those who could not reciprocate their generosity (Luke 14:12-14) and urged all to generous and unostentatious, honor-forsaking almsgiving (Matt 6:2-4). He seems to have urged generous release of the hopelessly indebted (Matt 6:12 and 18:21-35). In Jerusalem he overturned the tables of the Temple's money-changers and drove out sacrificial animals, apparently in protest against the avarice of the Temple hierarchy, which demanded payment of the Temple tax in pagan, Tyrian coinage of exceptionally high silver content and profiteered from the monopolistic Temple trade in sacrifices.[14] To understand more fully, however, Jesus' theme of renunciation of property and the community of property of his group of traveling disciples, we must assess his practice from the point of view of virtuoso religion.

3. Jesus' Traveling Disciples as a Prophetic Virtuoso Group

If we ask what was the precedent in Old Testament and Jewish tradition for the formation of virtuoso religious groups, we find a model which clearly gave both John the Baptist and Jesus scriptural precedent for forming the virtuoso circles of assistant-disciples with whom they seem to have lived in permanent close fellowship of life. In Israelite tradition, the prophets were religious virtuosi who regularly stood in opposition to the hierocrats of ritualistic religion and the political elite's tendency to accumulate all land and resources. The early Israelite prophets formed guilds which may fairly be termed virtuoso religious groups; their religious practice was different from

13. Cf. K. E. Corley, "Prostitute," in *Dictionary of Jesus and the Gospels,* ed. Joel B. Green et al. (Downers Grove, IL: InterVarsity Press, 1992), p. 643.

14. Cf. Richard J. Bauckham, "Jesus' Demonstration in the Temple," in *Law and Religion: Essays on the Place of the Law in Israel and Early Christianity,* ed. Barnabas Lindars (Cambridge: James Clarke, 1988), pp. 72-89 and 171-76; Marcus Borg, *Jesus in Contemporary Scholarship* (Valley Forge: Trinity Press International, 1994), pp. 112-16.

that normal for the populace and, though they did not hold institutional religious office, they functioned as an accepted part of the wider religious
community on account of their acknowledged, experimentally demonstra-
ble spiritual giftings.

The early bands of prophets used musical instruments and probably
dance techniques to enter the prophetic mode (1 Sam 10:1-13; 19:18-24). In
this we see a demonstration of the intensity of practice and perceived spiritual giftings that give religious virtuosi reputation in the eyes of their popular audience. Elisha too used music to induce prophecy (2 Kgs 3:13-20). What
is significant for our present purpose is that these incidents of virtuoso religious practice were presented as legitimate in received Scripture.[15] Around
the time of Jesus and John the Baptist there were attempts within Jewish
pietist groups to imitate the model of the prophetic guilds offered by Scripture, especially the groups around the powerful peripatetic "sign prophets"
Elijah and Elisha, which seem to have offered models for both John the Baptist and the traveling disciple group of Jesus himself. Jesus' group seems to
have sought intensely to imitate the charismatic practice of Elijah and
Elisha.

I would suggest that a primary purpose of the intense fellowship of life
Jesus created in his traveling party was intensive training in the virtue and
understanding he thought necessary for the development of spiritual powers
like those of the Old Testament sign prophets. Jesus intended his trained disciples to perform the works of power that characterized his own activity, and
he sent them out to do such works once trained. Their training was served by
separation from secular work, renunciation of personal property, and an intense fellowship of life which extended from common prayer, worship, and
teaching to common meals arising from the sharing of property in a common purse. Jesus' well-remembered focus on wealth and poverty strongly
suggests that he intended the practices of renunciation and sharing to serve
the ideological purpose of emphasizing the need for selfless sharing and economic redistribution.

Jesus' calling of his disciples, an important locus of his call to renunciation, is closely modeled on Elijah's call of Elisha. Just as Elijah called Elisha

15. While some biblical scholars will accept the view of the text that such techniques
genuinely brought on the activity of the God's Spirit, others will side with the more anti-
supernaturalist stance of the translators of the New Revised Standard Version, who understand the verb "prophesy" in these early texts to indicate a self-induced psychological state
of "prophetic frenzy" (1 Sam 10:5-6, 10, 13; 19:20-21, 23-24). There may of course be truth in
both positions.

from his secular work and forbad him to return to it, so Jesus called disciples away from their previous work as fishermen or collectors of tolls. Occasionally there was hesitation on the part of some. The possibility of refusal shows that the choice of the virtuoso lifestyle is in all cases voluntary (Mark 1:16-20; 2:13-14; 10:17-31; cf. 1 Kgs 19:19-21; Matt 8:19-22; Luke 9:59-62; John 1:35-51). As with Elijah's call of Elisha, the bond between caller and called in the Gospels is lifelong and itinerant, unlike the association of discipleship in Rabbinic Judaism, which was temporary and located in the stable abode of the house of study.[16]

Like Elijah and Elisha, the disciples whom Jesus sent out to preach, heal, and exorcise demons were to operate as peripatetics dependent on the hospitality of others (Mark 6:6b-13; Matthew 10; Luke 9:1-6, 10; 10:1-20; cf. 1 Kgs 17:9). The disciples Jesus sent out on mission were certainly conscious of the model in Scripture of the early peripatetic sign prophets. This is most clearly apparent in the question James and John put to Jesus when some Samaritans rejected his message. They believed that Jesus had so completely equipped them in the exercise of miraculous spiritual power that they could, at Jesus' command, imitate Elijah's most spectacular and powerful sign, the calling down of destructive fire from heaven (Luke 9:51-56; cf. 1 Kgs 18:20-40; 2 Kgs 1:9-14).

The activities of Elijah and Elisha provided extensive, wider legitimating background in Scripture for the formation of first-century virtuoso prophetic groups. Elijah, Elisha, John the Baptist, and Jesus were all celibates. Both Jesus (Matt 16:14, 21:11, 46; Mark 6:15; 8:28; Luke 7:16) and John the Baptist (Matt 21:26; Mark 11:32) were identified by their popular audiences as prophets because of their personal charisma. Jesus' miraculous powers confirmed him as a prophet in popular understanding. John the Baptist's use of Elijah symbolism in his garb was accepted by his audience (Mark 1:6; cf. 2 Kgs 1:8; Zech 13:4); Jesus identified John as a prophet (Matt 11:7-10) and compared him with Elijah (Matt 11:14; cf. Mal 4:5). Neither possessed high official status; both found themselves in opposition to institutional religious and political power. While John and his group apparently did no miracles (John 10:41), Jesus compared himself, on account of his works of power, with the great Old Testament sign prophets Elijah and Elisha (Luke 4:24-27). The range of miracles performed by Elijah and Elisha forms a close analogy to

16. Martin Hengel, *The Charismatic Leader and His Followers* (Edinburgh: T.& T. Clark, 1981), pp. 4-5, 16-18, 31-32, 42-57; cf. Gerd Theissen and Annette Merz, *The Historical Jesus: A Comprehensive Guide* (London: SCM, 1998), pp. 213-17.

the range of Jesus' attested miraculous powers, which included supernatural knowledge at a distance (Mark 2:5; Luke 9:47; John 2:24-25; cf. 2 Kgs 5:26; 6:8-12), prophecy of future events (cf. 2 Kgs 7:1-20), numerous miracles including healings (cf. 2 Kings 5), multiplication of food (Mark 8:1-10; cf. 1 Kings 17:13-16), power over nature (Mark 4:35-41; 6:45-52; John 6:16-25; cf. 1 Kgs 18:36-39; 2 Kgs 1:8-15), and raisings from the dead (Mark 5:35-43; Luke 7:11-17; cf. 1 Kgs 17:17-24; 2 Kgs 4:8-21; also Matt 27:52; cf. 2 Kgs 13:21) and apparently visionary experience, ecstasy and hearing God's voice (Mark 3:10-11; 9:1-13; Luke 10:17-21; cf. 1 Kgs 19:7-18; 21:17; 22:19-24; 2 Kgs 1:3-4, 15; 2 Kgs 6:13-17). Jesus identified himself as a prophet (Matt 13:57; Mark 6:4; Luke 4:24), and his disciples set out on mission as his prophetic servants (Matt 10:40-42), whose precursors were the persecuted ancient prophets (Matt 5:12). He instructed those he sent out to greet no one on the road, as Elisha had bade his servant Gehazi when on an urgent mission (Luke 10:4; cf. 2 Kgs 4:29).

We know little about the inner operation of the "sons of the prophets" of the time of Elijah and Elisha, but there are at least two hints of communal economy. According to 2 Kgs 6:1-2, a group of "sons of the prophets" lived in a common house under the charge of Elisha. At Gilgal, Elisha commanded the guild who sat under his charge to "Put the large pot on, and make some stew for the sons of the prophets" (2 Kgs 4:38-41). Elijah and Elisha appear not to have depended on personal property, but to have lived by the generous patronage of their supporters (1 Kgs 17:8-24; 2 Kgs 4:8-37). Jesus may have developed this scriptural model, resulting in his gathering of a peripatetic prophetic group around him that embodied an alternative society. Jesus' disciples James and John reveal the challenge of virtuoso religion to hierocracy in their request to Jesus that they might occupy the best thrones next to his when Jesus established his kingdom in Jerusalem (Mark 10:35-37). This question shows that the Twelve understood themselves as an elite who paralleled the phylarchs.[17] Jesus deliberately chose twelve disciples in order to press an eschatological claim to address the twelve tribes[18] and to set a picture of perfect relations in matters of property at the heart of his vision for the renewed nation. In this the pattern of his group goes beyond the scriptural model of prophecy and complements the absolute claim he makes for himself in other ways over against the sequence of mere prophets (cf.

17. Cf. William Horbury, "The Twelve and the Phylarchs," in his *Messianism amongst Jews and Christians* (London/New York: Continuum, 2003), pp. 157-88.

18. Cf. John P. Meier, *A Marginal Jew: Rethinking the Historical Jesus,* vol. 3, *Companions and Competitors* (New York: Doubleday, 2001), pp. 125-97.

Mark 12:1-12).[19] Renunciation of property and practical community of goods figure more prominently in the depiction of his traveling party than in the scriptural presentation of the similar practice of the early Israelite prophetic group. These differences show the adaptation of the scriptural model to Jesus' own purposes and to the needs of the age and the prominence of the issues of poverty and wealth among those needs. Jesus pressed his points about wealth, possessions, and poverty upon his audience with a lived, ideal alternative in the distinctive social pattern of his traveling group, an antistructural utopia which served as an observable critique of greed.

4. The Jesus Movement's Bipartite Mode of Practice with Respect to Property

Jesus proclaimed in a memorable saying: "You cannot serve God and mammon" (Luke 16:13; Matt 6:24). Martin Hengel has suggested that "Jesus attacks mammon with the utmost severity where it has captured men's hearts, because this gives it demonic character by which it blinds men's eyes to God's will — in concrete terms, to their neighbour's needs." Hengel emphasizes the preservation of the Aramaic *mammon* in the Greek sayings tradition: "Perhaps the early church left this Semitic loan-word untranslated because they regarded it as the name of an idol: the service of Mammon is idolatry."[20] We may compare how Paul calls greed "idolatry" (Col 3:5).[21] Possessions may seduce human beings away from the exclusive worship of which only God is worthy. Jesus emphasized that the "deceitfulness of wealth" (Mark 4:19) might choke his word of repentance. However, while renunciation of property was definitely a part of the movement Jesus began, he did not require renunciation of property of all who believed in him. Only those he chose for the spiritual calling of teaching, healing, and wielding authority over the demonic world were to renounce property. Such disciples were to give up all that they had, selling their possessions and giving away the proceeds to the poor (Luke 12:32-34; 14:33). They left all to follow him (Mark 1:16-20; 2:13-17; Luke 5:1-11). Like Jesus on his preaching tours, their

19. Cf. Martin Hengel, "Das Gleichnis von den Weingärtnern Mc. 12, 1-12 im Lichte der Zenonpapyri und der rabbinischen Gleichnisse," *ZNW* 59 (1986): 1-39.

20. Martin Hengel, *Property and Riches in the Early Church* (London: SCM, 1974), pp. 24 and 30.

21. Cf. Brian S. Rosner, *Greed as Idolatry: The Origin and Meaning of a Pauline Metaphor* (Grand Rapids: Eerdmans, 2007).

connections with the ordinary world were in effect to be severed (Matt 8:19-22; Luke 9:57-62).

The Essene movement also incorporated a bipartite social structure, comprising both marrying groups and the "upper echelon" of male celibates who renounced property. These, as the *Rule of the Community* shows, were more intensely involved with study and prayer.[22] Josephus tells us that the celibate male Essenes when traveling from one place to another would be welcomed and offered complete hospitality by the community of celibates they found at their destination. He explains that *in consequence* of the certain provision that awaited them they carried "nothing whatever with them on their journeys, except arms as a protection against brigands" and goes on to emphasize the frugality of these celibate males in changing neither garments nor shoes until they were worn with age.[23]

Josephus's description of the male celibate Essenes' mode of travel and frugal dress is a very close analogue to the "mission charge" passages of the Gospels. Jesus forbade those who preached his message to carry food, money, wallet, or changes of garments and shoes.[24] Nothing in Jesus' instructions definitely suggests that he desired onlookers to note any distinction between the mode of travel of those who proclaimed his message and traveling celibate male Essenes.[25] We may fairly conclude that Jesus' instructions concerning possessionless travel for the purpose of preaching expressed largely the same values with respect to property as the possessionless travel of Essene renouncers, perhaps practiced by other Jewish virtuosi too, and may have imitated such Jewish models rather than the Cynic mode of travel, as is currently often claimed.[26]

Among Jesus' first followers, those who were not called to wield spiritual

22. Cf. 1QS 6:6-8.

23. Josephus, *Jewish War*, 2.8.4 §§124-27.

24. Mark 6:8-9; Luke 9:3; 10:4; 22:35; Matt 10:9-10.

25. Josephus says the celibate male Essenes always wore white (*Jewish War* 2.8.2 §123 and 2.8.7 §137; we do not know if Jesus' disciples always wore white when on mission. At Matt 10:10 and Luke 9:3 Jesus' missionaries are not to travel with a staff, while at Mark 6:8 they are allowed a staff. It is likely that Mark's earlier version is correct, the staff being carried as protection against attack. As noted above, Josephus explains that the traveling male celibate Essenes carried arms for protection. At Luke 22:38 members of Jesus' traveling group show him two swords they evidently carried for protection.

26. Comparison is often made between the wandering Cynic philosopher and Jesus' mission charge. It is worth noting that several descriptions of the Cynics' garb include mention of the wallet, into which alms begged of hearers would be placed. Cf. Arrian, Epictetus, 3.22 §10. The traveling rabbi took bag, staff, and cloak, *pYeb.* 16.7, *bBaba Bathra* 133b.

authority were allowed to retain private property. Such supporters were to be generous and unostentatious in their almsgiving, and to lend willingly to those who asked (Matt 5:42; 6:2-4). Implicit in the Gospel narratives are local supporters who offered hospitality to Jesus and his traveling party and whose houses often became the venue for teaching. Such local figures of good standing (Matt 10:11; cf. Mark 6:10) also hosted those disciples sent out by Jesus in pairs (Mark 6:7; Luke 10:1) to preach, heal, and exorcise demons.

According to Luke, Jesus was supported on his own preaching tours by the patronage of women of means who comprised part of his traveling party. These included Joanna the wife of Chuza, senior steward of the estates of Herod Antipas, ruler of Galilee (Luke 8:1-3). Jesus demanded that those with wealth generously assist the destitute and undernourished. Since Jesus and the Twelve were religious virtuosi who practiced renunciation of property and community of goods, when they exhorted "the haves" to share with those who had not, their exhortations would have carried a certain moral and strategic legitimacy. We see this in the story of Zacchaeus, who, gladdened by Jesus' presence in his house, both repented of his misdealings as a senior tax collector and made restitution; he also gave half his wealth to the poor (Luke 19:1-10). As one who practiced renunciation and community of goods, Jesus was able to employ the sharpest devices in his exhortation of the wealthy without fear of rebuke. Though engaged in full-time religious activity, supported by wealthy patrons and no longer practising his craft as a *tekton*, Jesus was never accused of hypocrisy, except perhaps on the occasion of the "glutton and drunkard" accusation, perhaps meant to accuse him of the despised luxury of the wealthy with whom he sometimes associated. This accusation was easily parried and never stuck (Matt 11:19; Luke 7:34). Jesus successfully maintained his honorable reputation as a religious virtuoso of impeccable character. Hence he was able to rebuke powerfully with his parable of the rich fool the greed of a farmer who selfishly hoarded surplus grain and other goods, looking forward to a life of easy luxury (Luke 12:16-21; cf. *Gospel of Thomas* 63). From justified moral high ground, he threatened owners of great estates who indulged themselves in fine garments and rich feasting with his parable of the rich man and Lazarus (Luke 16:19-31). Despite the strictures of the Law and the Prophets, the parable tells of a rich man who ignored the needs and appeals of a poor sick man who has languished at his gate. He is condemned to unmitigated torment, while awaiting resurrection and final judgement, in a fiery corner of the place of the dead (cf. *1 Enoch* 21–22).

Such firm teaching means that, as we see the transition from Jesus' travelling party in the Gospels to the settled church of Acts, we should expect to find a continuation of virtuoso practice, including renunciation of property, community of goods, and generosity from the wealthy patrons around Jesus' growing group, which is precisely what we find in Acts 2:44-45 and 4:32-36.[27]

We have noted that the disciple Judas administered the common purse of Jesus' traveling group of disciples (John 12:6; 13:29). We may assume that the monetary support of wealthy and high status women patrons (Luke 8:1-3) was received into this purse. Disbursements for the poor appear to have been made from this common purse during Jesus' ministry. According to Mark, some present at Jesus' anointing at Bethany imagined that the costly perfumed oil poured over Jesus might have been sold and the proceeds donated to the poor, probably through the auspices of Judas as the group's treasurer (14:4-5). Matthew tells us these detractors were disciples (26:8-9), while John identifies Judas as the lone, or perhaps principal, scolding voice (12:4). John tells us that at Jesus' Last Supper some of his disciples, after Judas's departure following Jesus' cryptic words to him, thought Jesus had instructed Judas to make purchases for the group's needs at the feast, or to give alms to the poor (13:29). This suggests a pattern of both common expenditure on the virtuoso group's behalf and disbursements for the poor from the common purse. When Jesus asked Philip where bread might be purchased to feed a large crowd near Passover, Philip exclaimed that two hundred *denarii* would not suffice. Jesus' question was intended to test Philip (John 6:5-7), perhaps because it was not usually beyond the financial resources of the common purse to aid the needy in Jesus' audience.

We may assume that Jesus frequently sanctioned expenditures for the needy outside his immediate group from his group's common purse. Very substantial benefactions would have been within the means of Jesus' wealthy elite women patrons. He often appears dining and teaching at meals; the existence of the common purse suggests that his traveling party did not always dine at the expense of local hosts. I would take the view, rather, that the needy probably received assistance at open meals financed from the traveling group's purse, though certain meals were private to Jesus and his traveling group. We may assume that Jesus was able to offer more assistance to the needy than food alone, through the resources of the common purse, and that he was often influential enough to precipitate generosity from local (and perhaps distant) benefactors when resources proved too little to meet

27. For an analysis of the community of goods of the early Jerusalem church from the point of view of patronage, see Ascough, "Benefaction Gone Wrong."

all legitimate needs. The complete consecration to service in God's kingdom of Jesus' mobile party of disciples was expressed, in part, by their possessionless travel and generous common life.

The Essene movement also embraced both religious virtuosi and many who both married and retained property. Josephus called these a "second order" of Essenes.[28] Their way of life was regulated by the *Code of Damascus* (CD) or *Damascus Rule.* The two orders of Essenes together comprised the Essene *covenant,* which was termed in the *Damascus Rule* the "new covenant."[29] According to the *Rule of the Community,* the "instructor" was to "welcome into the covenant of kindness all those who freely volunteer to carry out God's decrees."[30] The marrying members of the wider Essene covenant accepted mutual economic responsibility for each other, to which aim they contributed substantial sums to a central fund regularly:

> And this is the rule of the Many, to provide for all their needs: the wages of at least two days each month they shall place into the hands of the Overseer and of the judges. From it they shall give to the injured and with it they shall strengthen the hand of the needy and the poor, and the elder who is bowed down, and to the sick and to the prisoner of a foreign people, and to the girl who has no redeemer, and to the youth who has no teacher, and for all the works of the community, and the house of the community shall not be deprived of its means. (CD 14:12-17)

This section of the Essene *Damascus Rule* bears remarkable similarity to a passage from the second-century Christian apologist Aristides, who emphasizes the mutual economic support among Christians:

> Kindliness is their nature. There is no falsehood among them. They love one another. They do not neglect widows. Orphans they rescue from those who are cruel to them. Every one of them who has anything gives ungrudgingly to the one who has nothing. If they see a travelling stranger they bring him under their roof. They rejoice over him as a real brother, for they do not call one another brothers after the flesh, but they know

---

28. Josephus, *Jewish War,* 2.8.13 §§ 160-61.

29. CD 6:19; cf. 8:21; 19:33-34; 20:10-12.

30. 1QS 1:7-8. The theme of covenant reappears several times in column 1; columns 1-3 legislate a covenant renewal ceremony; cf. also 4Q255-257, 4Q262, and 5Q11. The version of the Rule reflected by 2Q258 does not include the covenant renewal ceremony. Cf. James C. VanderKam, "Covenant," in Schiffman and VanderKam, eds., *Encyclopedia of the Dead Sea Scrolls,* vol. 1, pp. 151-55, esp. 153.

they are brothers in the Spirit and in God. If one of them sees that one of their poor must leave this world, he provides for his burial as well as he can. And if they hear that one of them is imprisoned or oppressed by their opponents for the sake of their Christ's name, all of them take care of all his needs. If possible they set him free. If anyone among them is poor or comes into want while they themselves have nothing to spare, they fast two or three days for him. In this way they can supply the poor man with the food he needs. (Aristides, *Apology* 15)

We may note that those whose high degree of mutual economic commitment Aristides describes in such remarkable terms understood themselves to be fellow members of a *new covenant*. Paul emphasized, when horrified that some drank while others went hungry at the Christian meal in Corinth, that all were members of a covenant, sealed with Jesus' own blood.[31] We would be incorrect to divorce entirely the high degree of mutual economic commitment which emerged among the early Christians from the covenanted, communitarian form of Judaism we know of as Essenism, with its bipartite socioeconomic pattern. Local Christian congregations too formed only a part of the total social structure of early Christianity through its first century or more. They were served by peripatetic missionaries who appear to have renounced all for the sake of preaching the message of Jesus and were the founders and spiritual authorities over the local congregations, capable of successfully exhorting local wealthy figures, such as these misdemeanants in Corinth, to generosity toward the poor.

5. Community of Property in Acts

The Gospels, then, bear witness to receipts from wealthy patrons into the common purse of Jesus' disciple-group, and probably to disbursements for the needs of both Jesus' traveling party and the needy outside this group. We probably find, early in Acts, a continuation of this pattern. All who believed and joined the expanding group of Jesus' disciples "had all things in common." Believers sold their possessions; distributions were made to meet the needs of all (2:44-45). We learn that "as many as owned lands or houses sold them," laying the proceeds at the apostles' feet (4:34-35). The Levite Barnabas

---

31. 1 Cor 11:20-34; cf. especially Luke 22:14-20 (v. 20 also "new covenant"); also Mark 14:22-25 and Matt 26:26-29.

sold some land (4:36-37). These events occurred only weeks after Jesus' death and resurrection. Since these accounts appear in Acts, it is easy to conceive them primarily as part of "church history," and to look forward to the later chapters of Acts and the letters of Paul for analogies to help us understand their pattern, rather than to look back to the ministry of Jesus in order to find their direct root in the practice of his traveling party. During the period between Jesus' last Passover and the subsequent Pentecost feast, his disciple-group, according to Luke-Acts, settled in Jerusalem and followed a life of intense, continuous prayer and worship. The group of Jesus' followers, gathered from Galilee and planted in Jerusalem, were somehow billeted together in the guest premises of "the room upstairs where they were staying." There, they lived a communal life together, "constantly devoting themselves to prayer," and so continued the communal sharing initiated by Jesus, their now heavenly master (Acts 1:13-14; cf. Luke 24:49-52; Acts 1:1-5). Their economic pattern of life — based around a common purse into which large donations were received from wealthy patrons, from which the group lived, and from which the needy might receive support — was not a *novum*. This economic way of life bore the stamp of Jesus' authority and practice and expressed the continued consecration to him of those who proclaimed him as heavenly Lord. It was also analogous to the economic sharing of many respected Judean religious virtuosi.

The skeptical view of the "community of goods" of Acts 2–6 has found various difficulties with the Acts account, which I have dealt with at length in other publications and can only overview here.[32]

1. "Utopian" stylizing of these passages in phrases such as holding "all things common" and calling "nothing one's own" is clearly present, but it does not undermine the historical value of the accounts. Philo and Josephus stylize their accounts of Essene virtuosi with a wide variety of motifs drawn from philosophical reflection on the ideal society, but since the discovery of the *Rule of the Community* from Qumran, such stylizing is no longer taken as a sound argument against the existence of Essene communities which fully shared their property. In Acts too, stylizing after the model of high Greek ideals of sharing cannot disprove the essential historicity of the original formal community of goods of the earliest post-Easter followers of Jesus in Jerusalem.

---

32. For these arguments see especially Brian J. Capper, "Community of Goods in the Early Jerusalem Church," in *Aufstieg und Niedergang der Römischen Welt,* ed. H. Temporini and W. Haase, series II, volume 26, part 2 (Berlin: De Gruyter, 1995), pp. 1730-74, and "The Palestinian Cultural Context of the Earliest Christian Community of Goods."

2. Peter's challenge to Ananias and Sapphira emphasizes that their property donation was voluntary (Acts 5:3-4). This is often taken as an argument that there was no universally practiced community of property within the group. Despite the extraordinarily frequent repetition of this argument, it is fallacious. Community of goods, when practiced by virtuoso religious groups, is always undertaken on a voluntary basis. However, those who voluntarily choose to join a "common life" are obliged fully to follow whatever rule and range of obligations are the norm. Moreover, in Peter's emphasis on Ananias's property belonging to him equally in two successive stages ("before it was sold it was yours, and after it was sold it was in your power"), there is an echo of the multi-stage procedures which are typical of groups that practice community of property. The Essene novice surrendered his property to the community in the penultimate stage of his entry in the community, but it still belonged to him until his final examination and permission to enter the community fully (cf. 1QS 6:13-23). That we find reflected in Acts such a procedure from the immediate local, cultural environment is a very strong argument that there was a formal property-sharing structure in the earliest community of Jesus' followers in Jerusalem. In my view, community of goods was the universal or intended universal practice of the first believers in Jerusalem for perhaps the first year of the group's life, perhaps becoming the practice of only an "inner group" within the community at the time of, and as a result of, the dreadful punishment of Ananias and Sapphira.[33]

3. In Acts 6:1-6, a problem of care for a group of widows emerged "when the disciples were increasing in number." This has been taken as an argument that there was no community of goods extending across the whole community, but only charity to underprivileged groups. I would argue, however, that at this point we witness the spread of the gospel of Jesus to new types of groups in Jerusalem, those called "Hellenists" (Acts 6:1). These were groups growing within the Greek-speaking synagogues of Jerusalem (6:9). The Hellenist widows were not incorporated into the central property-sharing group; the leaders of the Hellenist Christians appear, rather, to have been encouraged to administer almsgiving arrangements within their own communities. Although believers among the Hellenists are called "disciples," they did not practice renunciation of property. At the beginning of the Jesus movement, it appears that only the traveling group of twelve disciples, and

---

33. Cf. Brian J. Capper, "Holy Community of Life and Property amongst the Poor: A Response to Steve Walton," *Evangelical Quarterly* 80, no. 2 (April 2008): 113-27.

Jesus himself, practiced renunciation, while local adherents to Jesus did not. There emerged a pattern of two types of discipleship — those who practiced renunciation and those who did not (such as Mnason, perhaps, who is said in Acts 21:16 to be among the earliest of the Jerusalem disciples of Jesus and yet still retained his house).[34]

In light of these three reinterpretations of its evidence, the Acts account of the community of property of Jesus' earliest followers in Jerusalem may be taken as a good historical report.

The cultural and economic context of the community of goods practiced by Jesus' traveling party and the earliest group of his followers in Jerusalem was part of the wider response of Jewish pietist groups to the economic problems of the age. The difficulties of providing a subsistence diet for all may lead to the ideal of a "virtuoso" or "holy" life, where many of the poor may find a place in community with those who serve the poor.[35] Virtuosity may find expression in personal possessionlessness and communal devotion to study, prayer, preaching and charitable works, community of property, and even an ideal of frugal consumption. Those most vulnerable in the outer economic world, especially the children of poor families, are often drawn into this life of devotion. While those who become religious virtuosi may forgo the pleasures and status of heads of families, they gain great honor as the preservers, interpreters, and ideal practitioners of holy tradition. According to the religious worldview generated, the poor who become religious virtuosi are no longer the "offscourings of the earth" but those of greatest status. The material has been "traded" for the spiritual in their lived, respected, reversed image of the social and economic relations of the wider world. Moreover, in view of the high honor paid to the religious renouncer by the whole of society, such figures and communities are not only able to encourage the rich to be generous toward the poor, but are also trusted to administer such redistribution wisely and without self-interest. It would appear that the Jerusalem church began as such a "holy community of property and life." Over time we may assume that the property-sharing practice of the first group became reduced to that of an inner group, which continued to operate as a base for "apostolic operations," a place to which the peripatetics might retire when not on active mission. Perhaps this central group of the Jerusalem church drew in and provided both nourishment and

---

34. Cf. Capper, "Two Types of Discipleship in Early Christianity."

35. This is especially the case when the social world is dominated by ideals of holiness and belief in the perfectibility of human beings. Cf. Ling, *Judaean Poor*, p. 75.

training in the Jesus tradition for many children of the poor of Judea. Some of these may have become the next generation of missionary apostles, while others probably married and became ardent supporters of the missionaries and their central base, and of its continued work among the poor.

The "community of goods" of Acts 2–6 does not offer scriptural legitimation for those who would extend community of property across the whole of the Christian congregation, or across the state. The Reformation rejection of the "apostolic life" of religious orders has, however, denied to readers of biblical scholarship a pointer to its true application in the life of voluntary virtuoso religious communities. The renunciation of property by Jesus, his traveling disciples, and early believers in him in Jerusalem offers precedent for voluntary groups within the Christian church who renounce property and practice community of goods, a model especially suited for mission among the poor. This may not sound like an exciting conclusion to those eager to press a political case concerning world poverty or to encourage Christians to generosity. However, the significance of the actual model of the common purse of Jesus and his traveling party, and of their first social project in Jerusalem, teaches much. In the most difficult situations of poverty, groups achieve a great deal who together share property and channel resources to the most needy in the context of their whole witness and community life. Such groups act for the wider church and can be richly supported by it; their mode of life demonstrates a real identification with the plight of the poor.

5. The Spirit and the "Other," Satan and the "Self": Economic Ethics as a Consequence of Identity Transformation in Luke-Acts

Aaron J. Kuecker

Scholarly enquiry into Luke's treatment of the economic ethos of the early Christian community has, for the past several decades, focused on contemporary (and not-so-near contemporary) socioeconomic parallels. Scholars have posited many sources for the inspiration undergirding the "utopian ideals" of the Jerusalem community primarily described in Acts 2:42-47 and 4:32–5:16. Was Luke patterning his description upon Essene (or, even more radically, Qumran) ideals, descriptions of the Pythagoreans and the Golden Age imported from Greek culture, Greco-Roman friendship ideals, a narrative description of an idealized Israel answering God with one accord at the base of Sinai, the intragroup relations of Greco-Roman voluntary associations, or simply kinship structures?[1] The quest for phenomenological parallels has been fruitful to a point. Luke's description of the earliest groups

1. Four positions are especially noteworthy. Brian J. Capper draws parallels with Essene/Qumran communities of goods ("The Palestinian Cultural Context of Earliest Christian Community of Goods," in *The Book of Acts in Its Palestinian Setting,* ed. Richard Bauckham (Grand Rapids: Eerdmans; Carlisle: Paternoster, 1995), pp. 323-56). Allan C. Mitchell sees a parallel and critique of the Greek philosophic friendship ideals ("The Social Function of Friendship in Acts 2:44-47 and 4:32-37," *JBL* 111, no. 2 [1992]: 255-72). James C. VanderKam sees a parallel with Israelite "ideal community" as expressed in national unity at Sinai ("Covenant and Pentecost," *Calvin Theological Journal* 37, no. 2 [2002]: 239-54). S. Scott Bartchy argues for the historicity of the community of goods based on the presence of contextual precedents, while allowing the Acts community to be socially unique ("Community of Goods in Acts: Idealization or Social Reality?" in *The Future of Early Christianity: Essays in Honor of Helmut Koester,* ed. Birger A. Pearson, A. Thomas Krabel, George W. E. Nickelsburg, and Norman R. Petersen [Minneapolis: Fortress Press, 1991], pp. 309-18).

of Jesus followers must be contextually situated and there is no reason to believe that the ethos of the community was fashioned out of whole cloth. Of all of the Gospel writers, Luke is arguably the most culturally savvy, displaying a good knowledge of both Jewish and non-Jewish ethnic particularities, linguistic differences, and intergroup relations. However, I wish to argue in this essay that the quest for contextual parallels has also distracted interpreters from appreciating what should be taken as a unique and important Lukan contribution to early Christian economic ideologies. For Luke, the economic ethos of the early Jerusalem community (and of other Jesus followers later in Acts) is not simply a matter of mimicking alternative socioeconomic practices; it is the result of a pneumatologically transformed identity.

Stated succinctly, the Spirit transforms and reorients human identity in a manner that has implications for the way groups and individuals conceive of those who can be categorized as "other," whether those "others" are inside or outside the group.[2] The radical nature of Luke's description of human identity is highlighted when viewed against typical human identity-forming processes. Social identity theory, a sub-discipline of social psychology, consistently has demonstrated that one important aspect of human identity (especially in collectivistic societies) is formed by participation in the groups to which humans belong.[3] Groups, in turn, maintain a positive personal and social sense of identity by contrasting themselves with a less positively (or negatively) evaluated "other." The textual data in Luke demonstrates that the Spirit reorients identity processes in a way that results in positive identity existing simultaneously with a favorable disposition toward the "other." This is a subversion of normal identity processes. *One of the primary effects of this identity transformation is a radically reoriented economic praxis that privileges the "other" over the self in economic exchange.* For Luke, and contrary to those who have worked to demonstrate that Luke is imitating proximate socioeconomic phenomena within his context, the economic praxis of the early community is not a product of the imitation of any "utopian ideal." Economic

---

2. In this essay, "other" is simply a broad reference to someone other than the self. The impulse toward the "other" is a correction of what Luke appears to view as inherent tendency of humans to be highly self-centered.

3. Social identity theory has generated a vast body of literature. A convenient overview of the theory and its utility in understanding the role of groups in the formation of identity can be found in Rupert Brown, "Agenda 2000 — Social Identity Theory: Past Achievements, Current Problems, and Future Challenges," *European Journal of Social Psychology* 30, no. 6 (2000): 745-78.

praxis is a reflection of a pneumatological reality within the lives of individuals and groups. Luke sets his pneumatological economics as one pole of a duality formed by contrasting the transformational impact of the Spirit with the transformational impact of Satan. While the Spirit predisposes individuals to privilege the "other," Satan predisposes individuals to privilege the self. Regularly, for Luke, those influenced by Satan demonstrate an economic ethos that inherently privileges the self at the expense of the "other." It is this self-centered economic system that, in Luke's description, characterizes the economy of the Empire. Thus, the ideal Luke describes is in fundamental contrast with Greco-Roman economic ideals. Yet it must again be stated that Luke is not simply proposing an alternate economic system. Luke's economic descriptions are an epiphenomenon upon transformed human identity. Thus, it is actually not enough to claim simply that Luke takes issue with the Roman economic system. Luke aims much higher — to the heart of human identity, an admittedly etic concept that accounts for a broad spectrum of human activity in social contexts.[4]

My argument in this essay will proceed in three parts. I will first examine Luke's conception of "ownership" by investigating his use of the adjective ἴδιος. This investigation will demonstrate that ἴδιος is a boundary-marking word used by Luke in certain instances to make claims about human identity and its orientation toward the "other." I will then discuss the most prevalent usage of ἴδιος in Greco-Roman public space in order to demonstrate Luke's contextual distinctiveness. With this background information in hand, I will turn to Luke's treatment of Barnabas, Ananias, and Sapphira. This narrative forms the epicenter of Luke's pneumatological economics as it draws together motifs of Spirit/Satan influence, social identity, and economic praxis as it impinges upon the "other." Proceeding from this narrative I will demonstrate the consistency with which Luke presents the fact that transformed economic praxis is only available via the transformation of human identities through the power of the Spirit, who alone can overcome the malformed

---

4. *Etic* refers to the categorical perspective of the outside observer, while *emic* refers to the point of view, concepts, and language used by insiders that reflect an inside point of view. Luke may have never claimed to be concerned with identity. Clearly, however, Luke was concerned with the relations between people groups, and the question "Who are my people?" is an orienting question for Luke's work. Because membership in a social group and identity are inseparable, identity is a valid and fruitful etic concept through which to read Luke-Acts. For a discussion of the necessary correspondence between etic and emic conceptualities, see Philip F. Esler, *Conflict and Identity in Romans* (Minneapolis: Fortress, 2003), p. 8.

identities (and hence, the malformed economic praxes) of those influenced by Satan.

1. ἴδιος as a Lukan Boundary-Marking Word

A good deal of the scholarly reflection upon Luke's economic ethos has centered upon the second of Luke's so-called "community summaries" in Acts 4:32-35. There, Luke claims that the early community shared an impressive level of communal solidarity (they were "of one heart and soul" [4:32]). One of the results of this solidarity was that no community member claimed "that any of the things which he possessed was his own" (οὐδὲ εἷς τι τῶν ὑπαρχόντων αὐτῷ ἔλεγεν ἴδιον εἶναι [4:32]). Instead, Luke claims that the community members held "everything in common" (4:32). It seems relatively clear from the following material that Luke is not describing a proto-communism in which goods were held in a common trust. Instead, it is more accurate to say that Luke describes a community of *unconditional availability* in which relationships with group members are privileged over relationships to personal possessions. This posture, which I will argue is a *symptom* of a transformed identity by virtue of the work of the Spirit, is expressed by the periodic and need-based liquidation of possessions for the sake of needy persons in the community. "There was not a needy person among them, for as many as were possessors of lands or houses sold them, and brought the proceeds of what was sold and laid it at the apostles' feet; and distribution was made to each as any had need" (4:34-35). While scholars have been keen to uncover what, precisely, Luke envisioned when he made the claim that "no one said that any of the things which he possessed was his own [ἴδιος]" (4:32), I have yet to discover an interpreter that has examined Luke's use of the adjective ἴδιος.[5] Yet it is this adjective that functions within Luke's wider narrative as a part of a strategy that positions economic praxis as a reflection of a more fundamental human reality.

5. Important treatments on the mechanics of the communal praxis described by Luke include: Luke Timothy Johnson, *The Literary Function of Possessions in Luke-Acts,* Dissertation Series, Society of Biblical Literature, no. 39 (Missoula, MT: Scholars Press, 1977); David Seccombe, *Possessions and the Poor in Luke-Acts* (Linz: Fuchs, 1983); Brian J. Capper, "The Interpretation of Acts 5:4," *JSNT* 19 (1983): 117-31; Capper, "Palestinian Cultural Context"; John Gillmand, *Possessions and the Life of Faith: A Reading of Luke-Acts* (Collegeville, MN: Liturgical Press, 1991); Halvor Moxnes, "Patron-Client Relations and the New Community in Luke-Acts," in *The Social World of Luke-Acts,* ed. Jerome H. Neyrey (Peabody, MA: Hendrickson, 1998), pp. 241-68.

In its adjectival form, ἴδιος has the basic meaning "one's own," "peculiar to," or "belonging to an individual," and as a possessive pronoun it often has an emphatic sense.[6] ἴδιος is common in the New Testament, appearing 114 times with a relatively even spread and meaning across the documents.[7] While the adjective can carry great theological freight in the Pauline corpus (e.g., Rom 8:32) or John (e.g., John 10:3, 4, 12; 15:19), the importance of the word within the Lukan corpus has not yet been appreciated. Luke uses ἴδιος 6 times in the Gospel and 17 times in Acts. His usages carry two primary senses: (1) to describe personal possession (a mule as the private possession [ἴδιος] of a Samaritan) or (2) to describe sequestered privacy (Jesus explains a parable to his disciples *in private* [ἴδιος]).[8] Inherent in these meanings is the implication that a relationship exists between the person/group and the object/space that can be classified as one's "own" (ἴδιος). The fact that the adjective signals relationship (usually possession) is a primary clue that the word can function to mark social and physical boundaries. To claim that something is your "own" (ἴδιος) is to claim a relationship of exclusive influence, control, or power over such an object. By definition, this claim marks a boundary of exclusivity. Usually, the claim that something is the possession (ἴδιος) of a group or person implies quite directly that it is *not* the possession (ἴδιος) of another person or group. Thus, claims to hold something as one's "own" (ἴδιος) help to configure the socioeconomic world, marking possession and access to goods, resources, and social spaces.

Strikingly prominent in Luke's writings is the insistence that how one handles one's possessions (ἴδιος) is a fundamental clue to one's orientation toward Jesus, the Jesus community, or the "other." Those who cling to their "own" (ἴδιος) erect a boundary that functions to sequester them away from Jesus and the community that follows him. In this way, for Luke, the claim to exclusive ownership/possession (ἴδιος) can be more than a boundary — it can be a primary *barrier* to the life of the faithful. This is evident initially in the fact that Peter equates the relinquishment of all claims of possession (ἴδιος) with definitive proof of complete identification with Jesus: "behold, we have left our possessions and we have followed you" (ἰδοὺ ἡμεῖς ἀφέντες τὰ ἴδια ἠκολουθήσαμέν σοι, Luke 18:28). Conversely, ἴδιος renders the boundary established by Judas in his betrayal of his own group. Peter claims

6. Horst Balz and Gerhard Schneider, eds., *Exegetical Dictionary of the New Testament*, vol. 2 (Grand Rapids: Eerdmans, 1993), p. 171.

7. E.g., John 13:1; Rom 14:5; 1 Tim 5:8; 1 Pet 3:1; Jude 6.

8. Luke 6:41, 44; 9:10; 10:23, 34; 18:28; Acts 1:7, 19, 25; 2:6, 8; 3:12; 4:23, 32; 13:36; 20:28; 21:6; 23:19; 24:23; 25:19; 28:30.

that Judas left his portion of the apostleship established by Jesus to "go to his own place" (Acts 1:25, εἰς τὸν τόπον ἴδιον). In this case, Judas's decision to privilege his own (ἴδιος) place results in his separation from, and opposition to, the community of Jesus followers.

At Pentecost, the Spirit (by empowering proclamation in the Diaspora languages of Jews who had resettled in Jerusalem) ensures that neither the Galilean regional identity of the apostles (a central identity ascribed to the apostles in Acts 1:11; 2:7) nor ethnolinguistic identity would become normative for the identity of Jesus followers.[9] The proliferation of Diaspora languages at Pentecost affirmed linguistic plurality rather than particularity, a move that ensured that nothing the Galilean apostles claimed as their "own" (ἴδιος, whether linguistic or regional identity) could form a boundary keeping those who were in some way "other" from full identification with the Jesus group.[10] Luke marks this pluralization of language with our adjective of interest (Acts 2:8: "in their own language" [τῇ ἰδίᾳ διαλέκτῳ]; cf. 2:6).

We can hone in more closely on Luke's unique conception of the proper role of one's possessions (ἴδιος) within the early community when we move our focus to two deployments of the term in quick succession in Acts 4:23 and 4:32. This section of Acts, I suggest, forms the epicenter from which Luke's pneumatological economics radiate bidirectionally. Obscured by modern English translations that depict Peter and John leaving their accusers in the Sanhedrin and returning to their "friends" (NIV) or to the "other believers" (NLT) is the fact that Luke portrays Peter and John returning to "their own": πρὸς τοὺς ἰδίους (Acts 4:23). Luke describes a social reality in which the early believers considered other community members to be, quite

9. There appears to have been a tradition that anticipated a return to the universal use of Hebrew in Israel's eschatological future. This tradition intensifies after 70 CE, but it was clearly extant prior to the destruction of the Temple. The tradition builds on Zeph 3:9 and is evident in both 4Q464 and *Jubilees* 12:25-27. For the post-70 commodification of the Hebrew language, see Seth Schwartz, "Language, Power and Identity in Ancient Palestine," *Past and Present* 148 (1995): 3-47, esp. 4. Cf. *y. Megillah* 71a; *Midrash Tanhuma* 28; *Testament of Judah* 25:1-3. *Targum Pseudo-Jonathan* and *Targum Neophyti I* on Gen 11:1 insert "holy tongue" and "language of the sanctuary" as descriptions of the global human language pre-Babel. *3 Enoch* 1:11-13 implies Hebrew is the angelic language. Cf. the possibility of "angelic language" as a status symbol in 1 Corinthians 12–14.

10. Herodotus, *Histories* 4.18, 22 refers to the Scythians as an "ethnic group unto themselves" (ἔθνος ἐὸν ἴδιον) and an "ethnic group many and separate" (ἔθνος πολλὸν καὶ ἴδιον). Social identities (in this case, ethnic identity), when held tightly as a possession (ἴδιος), function as social boundaries that can limit the extent of human community.

literally, their possession.[11] This statement gives significant insight into the social identity of the early community. In the midst of their Jerusalem context, Peter and John consider the community of Jesus followers to be, in some way, their "own" — their ἴδιος.[12]

Acts 4:23 stands in stark contrast with the claim in Acts 4:32 that the believers did not consider any of their possessions to be their own (καὶ οὐδὲ εἷς τι τῶν ὑπαρχόντων αὐτῷ ἔλεγεν ἴδιον εἶναι). The quick contrast of 4:23 and 4:32 functions to demonstrate that the members of the early community did not consider their possessions to be their own, but they did consider their fellow community members to be their own. Pressed one step further, believers did not identify (in a relationship of possession) with their belongings, but they did identify with the members of their community. Thus the possessions that could rightly be claimed as one's "own" (ἴδιος) are not allowed, in Luke's description, to establish a boundary between those who have and those who do not have. Instead, such a boundary is overcome by the realization that it is people, and not possessions, to which one has a fundamental and orienting relationship.

Essential to comprehending the more fundamental reality described by Luke's assertion that no person claimed anything to be his or her "own" is the fact that the contrasting possession/ownership/relationship claims in 4:23 and 4:32 are separated by the second major Spirit-filling described in Acts. The flow of the narrative makes it apparent that one of the effects of the renewed influence of the Spirit upon the community (4:31) was the willingness to relinquish the claims to possession in a way that profoundly benefited those who potentially could have been configured as "other," even the socioeconomically deprived "other" within one's own Jesus commu-

11. Luke Timothy Johnson, *Sharing Possessions: Mandate and Symbol of Faith* (Philadelphia: Fortress, 1981), p. 193, thinks that ἴδιος in 4:23 refers only to the apostles, not the whole community (cf. Luke Timothy Johnson, *The Acts of the Apostles*, Sacra Pagina, ed. Daniel J. Harrington [Collegeville, MN: Liturgical Press, 1992], p. 83). However, the narrative suggests otherwise: there is no indication that the activities described in 4:24-31 are restricted to a segment of the community. 4:31 states that they were *all* filled with the Spirit and leads directly into a summary of the life of the entire community, not just the apostles.

12. Cf. Acts 24:23, where the believers who tend to Paul while imprisoned in Herod's headquarters are designated Paul's ἰδίων. See also 1 Tim 5:8 which distinguishes one's "own" (ἴδιος) from one's οἰκεῖος ("household members"). Hearers of this epistle are told that anyone who fails to care for these two categories of social relation (apparently, those related by blood and those related through faith in Jesus) has "disowned the faith and is worse than an unbeliever." In NT usage, οἰκεῖος is qualified with an adjective if it is intended to refer to those related by circumstance or by faith, rather than by kinship (see Gal 6:10; Eph 2:19).

nity.[13] The unwillingness to use one's "own" (ἴδιος) in a way that excludes the benefit of the other is described paradigmatically in Acts 20:28 in relation to a christological model of self-giving. There, in his speech to the Ephesian elders, Paul proclaims:

> Take heed to yourselves and to all the flock, of which the Holy Spirit has made you overseers, to care for the church of God which he obtained with his own blood [διὰ τοῦ αἵματος τοῦ ἰδίου].

Regardless of the syntactical object of the construction, the point is clear. The possessions and position of God (i.e., his ἴδιος) have not been leveraged only to God's advantage, but instead have been poured out *for the sake of the "other."*

We can conclude this section on Luke's use of ἴδιος by restating 5 salient points. (1) ἴδιος, for Luke, is a boundary-marking word that denotes a relationship of influence or power with the object (whether physical or social) so designated. (2) According to Luke, what one claims as one's "own" (ἴδιος) can have a significant impact on that person's relationship to Jesus and the Jesus group. (3) Luke portrays the early community members as claiming the community itself as their possession (ἴδιος), a move which, through the influence of the Spirit, appears to be related to the unwillingness to designate physical possessions as one's 'own' (ἴδιος). (4) The paradigmatic use of one's possessions (ἴδιος) appears to be modeled by none other than God who gave up his "own" to obtain the church (Acts 20:28). (5) Through this lens, we can begin to see that the privileging of the community, rather than possessions, as one's ἴδιος in Acts 4 is a Spirit-enabled reality that results in an economic ethos in which possessions are set free to be used on behalf of the "other."

2. ἴδιος in Context: A Marker of Benefaction

We will return momentarily to examine Luke's use of Barnabas, Ananias, and Sapphira to illustrate the core of his pneumatological economics, espe-

---

13. We know without question from texts like 1 Cor 11:18-34 and Jas 2:1-9 that socioeconomic distinctions could create in-groups and out-groups within the early Jesus movement. More proximate to our concerns, Luke shows this to be a live issue in the Jerusalem community in Acts 6:1-7. It should be noted that in Luke's description of the widow controversy it is those who are notably "full of the Spirit" (Acts 6:3) who are most equipped to solve a problem revolving around economic possessions and the once specific (ethnolinguistic) category of "other."

cially as it relates to the conditions leading to the proper conceptualization and use of possessions. First, however, it is important briefly to discuss arguably the most common use of ἴδιος in Greco-Roman public space — honorary inscriptions. The Packard Humanities Institute inscription database includes 1,654 occurrences of the phrase ἐκ τῶν ἰδιῶν, "from their own."[14] The phrase is extant in 54 inscriptions from Greater Syria and functions as a marker of benefaction. The common formula commemorates a certain gift that certain people have given "from their own."[15] This can be amply demonstrated by a passage from Josephus.

> He [King Cyrus of Persia] also permitted them to offer their appointed sacrifices, and that whatever the high priest and the priests needed, and those sacred garments wherein they used to worship God, should be made at his own charges [ἐκ τῶν ἰδιῶν]; and that the musical instruments which the Levites used in singing hymns to God should be given to them. (*Antiquities* 11:62)

BDAG suggests that the phrase ἐκ τῶν ἰδίων is "commonly associated with the gifts of generous officials."[16] This is certainly the case for Josephus, who records the benefaction of, among others, the high priest (generically), King Hezekiah, Nehemiah, the Oniads, Hyrcanus, and Herod with the benefaction phrase ἐκ τῶν ἰδίων.[17]

Benefaction reflects a rather ambiguous relationship between the benefactor and the receiving community. In one way, the effort to give something from one's own (ἐκ τῶν ἰδίων) to a community, group, or association indicates a certain level of identification with that social entity.[18] However, the function of benefaction inscriptions in the procurement of social honor en-

---

14. http://epigraphy.packhum.org/inscriptions/ (accessed April 25, 2008). See, for example, SIG 547, 37; 1068, 18; CIJ nos 548, 746.

15. Gerd Theissen, *The Social Setting of Early Christianity: Essays on Corinth* (Edinburgh: T&T Clark, 1982), p. 148.

16. BDAG, 467.

17. *Antiquities* 3:242, 257; 9:273; 11:62, 181; 12:158; 14:276, 485; *War* 1:356.

18. It is worth noting the existence of the *Idios Logos,* who functioned within the *fiscus* to investigate "the properties that are without owners and ought to fall to Caesar" (Strabo 797; cf. P.Oxy. 1188). The existence of this office, likely adopted from the Ptolemies, is evidence that the chief "benefactor," Caesar, made extensive claims to hold portions of the empire as his "own" (ἴδιος). See Fergus Millar, *Rome, the Greek World and the East,* vol. 2: *Government, Society and Culture in the Roman Empire,* ed. Hannah M. Cotton and Guy M. Rogers (Chapel Hill and London: University of North Carolina Press, 2002), p. 59.

sured that (1) the relationship between the benefactor and the goods given was actually perpetuated and (2) while initially looking like magnanimity, the claim to have given something from one's own (ἐκ τῶν ἰδίων) actually elevated the benefactor *above* the receiving community at least with regard to socioeconomic status. The use of one's possessions (ἴδιος) in conjunction with Greco-Roman benefactory norms again serves to create a boundary that reveals a fair amount about the identity of the giver in question.[19]

It is probable that, in conjunction with the abandonment of possession/ownership (ἴδιος) claims, the practice of laying gifts at the "feet of the apostles" served to separate the givers of those gifts from benefaction claims (Acts 4:36-38).[20] Instead of affixing a donor's name to the good given ἐκ τῶν ἰδῶν, the Acts community subverted reciprocity obligations by distributing goods through someone other than the giver. The truly remarkable thing about the generosity of the early community is that their giving occurred *without* expected reciprocity — whether that reciprocity was in the form of goods or honor.[21] This is not because Luke is unaware of normal patron-client reciprocity or benefaction (Luke 7:1-5; Acts 10:22; 12:12). Indeed, given the other evidence of human benefaction in Luke-Acts, it seems in Acts 4:32-37 Luke is at pains to depict an economic ethic that stands in contrast with the convention of benefaction and the honor claims so pervasively implied both in the benefactory act itself and in its public recognition. In this way, the giving of the early community was clearly countercultural. But this, for Luke, goes well beyond an altruistic impulse or the replication of some utopian system of ancient or contemporary parallel. Neither is this simply a rejection of a defective practice. Rather, the "economics" described in Acts 4:32-37 are intimately connected to human identity, and the economic praxis is an immediate and primary outworking of a fundamental pneumatological reality that results in the transformation of human identity. This is

19. See Bruce W. Winter, "The Public Honoring of Christian Benefactors: Romans 13:3-4 and 1 Peter 2:14-15," *JSNT* 34 (1988): 87-103, on the promise of public recognition for benefactors. Winter suggests some New Testament documents encourage public benefaction as a means to secure approval of local authorities (e.g., Rom 13:3-4; 1 Pet 2:14-15). This would set Peter and Paul at odds with Luke on this issue.

20. *Pace* Johnson, *Acts*, p. 91, who interprets the gesture as submission to apostolic authority. Chrysostom (*Homilies on the Acts of the Apostles* 11 [PNF 1 14:455]) was aware that apostolic distribution of goods eliminated the reciprocity ethic: "To them [the apostles] they left it to be the dispensers, and made them the owners that thenceforth all should be defrayed as from common, not from private, property. *This was also a help to them against vainglory.*" For Greco-Roman reciprocity, see Moxnes, "Patron-Client."

21. See Mitchell, "Social Function," p. 266.

clear at several points throughout Luke-Acts, but it finds its center in Acts 4:32–5:11, the description of the early community and its positive and negative exemplars, Barnabas, Ananias, and Sapphira.

3. Barnabas: Exemplar of a New Identity

We turn our attention now from a contextual examination of Luke's usage of the boundary-marking word ἴδιος to a discussion of the identity formed by participation in the Jesus community. It is at the junction of social identity and possessions that Luke's uniquely pneumatological economics are most evident. It is no coincidence that we are introduced to Barnabas, Ananias, and Sapphira directly on the heels of the description of the community's economic practice. Within social groups, individuals that represent in themselves the prototypical characteristics of the group's own self-definition function as exemplars.[22] Exemplars play an important role in the shaping of community identity, serving as figures whose characteristics are to be imitated and who are, themselves, the essence of the group.[23] There can be no question that Luke establishes Barnabas as an exemplar of the early community in Acts 4:36-37. Immediately after proclaiming that the members of the group did not claim their possessions as their own (ἴδιος) but sold their property when there was need and allowed the apostles to distribute the proceeds, Luke associates Barnabas with that very community-defining act. Barnabas "sold a field which belonged to him, and brought the money and laid it at the apostles' feet" (Acts 4:37). Barnabas thus embodies in his person and character the best that the community has to offer. But there is more to be said about Luke's treatment of this often underappreciated player in the spread of the early Jesus movement.

22. See D. L. Medin, M. W. Altom, and T. D. Murphy, "Given Versus Induced Category Representations: Use of Prototype and Exemplar Information in Classification," *Journal of Experimental Psychology: Learning, Memory, and Cognition* 10 (1984): 333-52; E. R. Smith and M. A. Zarate, "Exemplar-Based Model of Social Judgment," *Psychological Review* 99 (1992): 3-21.

23. G. V. N. Bodenhausen, N. Schwarz, H. Bless, and M. Wanke, "Effects of Atypical Exemplars on Racial Beliefs: Enlightened Racism or Generalized Appraisals?" *Journal of Experimental Social Psychology* 31 (1995): 48-63, at 60. Cf. J. C. Turner: "Common category characteristics are inferred from the available exemplars of the category [social group], including oneself, and then automatically assigned, along with long-term criterial traits, to all members, again including oneself" (J. C. Turner, "Towards a Cognitive Redefinition of the Social Group," in *Social Identity and Intergroup Relations,* ed. Henri Tajfel [Cambridge and New York: Cambridge University Press, 1982], p. 29).

Luke gives abundant identity-related information about Joseph Barnabas, who, not insignificantly, is the first newly introduced character in Acts who is neither an apostle nor a member of Jesus' biological family.[24] He is a native of Cyprus and a Levite, thus a Cypriot Israelite with an important ethnic heritage.[25] His Cypriot identity indicates that Greek was likely the language of his birth, a tantalizing possibility given the linguistic tensions that arise in Acts 6. Luke's introduction tells hearers that Joseph Barnabas has several honorable nested social identities from which to draw.[26] But after giving us this biographical information (which must not in any case be considered extraneous to Luke's purposes), Luke introduces Joseph with his new name — Barnabas.

Two factors must be kept in tension at this point: (1) nicknames were common among Jews in the Greco-Roman world and (2) naming is extremely significant to the formation of identity. R. Bauckham's research on Jewish naming practices has demonstrated the prevalence of nicknames in ancient Judea.[27] There appears to have been a relatively small cohort of common names in use from 330 BCE to 200 CE. Fully 15.6 percent of named males from the period possessed one of the two most popular names, Simon or Joseph.[28] The large number of men with common names required strategies for differentiation, one of which was the adoption of a nickname.[29] At this

24. Joseph Barsabbas is also named in Acts 1:23, but only in the context of his consideration for apostleship. James D. G. Dunn, *The Acts of the Apostles* (Peterborough, UK: Epworth Press, 1996), pp. 59-60, notes that Barnabas is "an absolutely crucial figure in the early expansion of Christianity beyond Israel and out to the Gentiles."

25. Levites were not permitted to own property (Josh 14:4), but the practice must have either fallen out of use by this time or must not have been practiced in Barnabas's native Cyprus.

26. "Ethnic self-identification has usually been conceptualized in the literature as an option between two identities; in other words, an either/or phenomenon, tending not to accommodate the possibility of bi-cultural identification. . . . This dichotomous model is simplistic. People may consider themselves to be members of two or more groups, in which case a single identity label would be insufficient" (A. Saeed, N. Blain, and D. Forbes, "New Ethnic and National Questions in Scotland: Post-British Identities among Glasgow Pakistani Teenagers," *Ethnic and Racial Studies* 22, no. 5 [1999]: 824-25). Cf. Daniel Burdsey, "One of the Lads? Dual Ethnicity and Assimilated Ethnicities in the Careers of British-Asian Professional Footballers," *Ethnic and Racial Studies* 27, no. 5 (1999): 757-79.

27. Richard J. Bauckham, *Jesus and the Eyewitnesses: The Gospels and Eyewitness Testimony* (Grand Rapids: Eerdmans, 2006), pp. 67-92. Cf. Tal Ilan, *Lexicon of Jewish Names in Antiquity: Part I, Palestine 330 BCE–200 CE* (Tübingen: Mohr Siebeck, 2002).

28. Bauckham, *Jesus and the Eyewitnesses*, p. 71.

29. Bauckham, *Jesus and the Eyewitnesses*, p. 81. Cf. Joseph Barsabbas (Acts 1:23) and Simon Peter (Luke 6:14).

level it is unsurprising that a Joseph (one of several in the early community, cf. Acts 1:23) would adopt a nickname.

The commonness of nicknames does not, however, preclude the importance of Luke's decision to introduce Barnabas by the name indicative of his identity *as a member of the community*. According to Philo, Old Testament name changes were often a reflection of the true identity or virtue of the person receiving the new name.[30] Proselytes often changed their name to reflect their new "Israelite" identity, a phenomenon marked on ossuary inscriptions in Judea.[31] New Roman citizens and freedmen received either the name of their former master or the benefactor through whom they received their citizenship, and the *tria nomina* was a sure sign of Roman identity.[32] In short, new names locate people within a reconfigured social context. This is the case for Barnabas, whose name was given to him by the apostles for his identification *within the community of believers*.[33]

The lexical meaning of Barnabas's name has proved somewhat perplexing to scholars. Barrett sets forth the three main interpretive options, which include: (1) "son of *a prophet*" (from Hebrew נביא), (2) "son of *comfort*" (from Syriac *br + nby'*), and (3) "son of *consolation*" (from Hebrew נוחא).[34] Given the association of the Jerusalem assembly with Hebrew/Aramaic (Acts 6:1-6), options (1) and (3) appear most viable. In my view, option (1) is preferable, but only when understood in relation to the *practice* implied by the prophetic vocation — that is, exhortation.[35] This would suggest

---

30. *De mutatione nominum* 70-71, 121.

31. Craig S. Keener, *The Spirit in the Gospels and Acts: Divine Purity and Power* (Peabody, MA: Hendrickson, 1997), p. 64. See also Shaye J. D. Cohen, *The Beginnings of Jewishness: Boundaries, Varieties, Uncertainties* (Berkeley and Los Angeles: University of California Press, 1999), chap. 5.

32. Janet Huskinson, *Experiencing Rome: Culture, Identity and Power in the Roman Empire* (New York and London: Routledge, 2000), pp. 131-32.

33. Similarly, Simon's nickname (Peter) reflects his emerging role in the community, a fact made most explicit in Matt 16:18. See Bauckham, *Jesus and the Eyewitnesses*, pp. 103-4.

34. See C. K. Barrett, *The Acts of the Apostles*, vol. 1, International Critical Commentary (London and New York: T & T Clark, 1994), p. 259.

35. Luke's use of παράκλησις and παρακαλέω are instructive here. Luke uses the verb παρακαλέω 28 times and the noun παράκλησις 6 times, often using the word group to refer to insistent persuasion (see esp. Luke 8:41; Acts 13:42). But when the word group is used by a follower of Jesus in public speech within the Jesus-following community, it usually carries overtones of urging/exhorting hearers to remain faithful to the gospel message (see Acts 2:40; 11:23; 14:22; 15:32; 16:40; 20:1; 28:20). This links the word closely with prophecy. But παράκλησις can also carry meanings closely related both to exhortation and to consolation/encouragement (see Luke 16:25; cf. Acts 15:31) — that is, to prophecy and encourage-

that the best way to understand the lexical meaning of "Barnabas" is "son of prophecy/exhortation." Luke's typical usage of παρακαλέω/παράκλησις within the community of believers makes it fairly clear that the driving point Luke is making with Barnabas's intra-communal name is the fact that Barnabas is one who regularly exhorts the community (in word and in deed) to remain unflinchingly true to the implications of the gospel. At several key points in Acts, Barnabas's exhortation serves the life of the community, calling it to gospel faithfulness and often helping abrogate social boundaries.[36] In other words, Barnabas's new name describes his identity within the context of his social group.[37] He is a Levite and a Cypriot, but primarily he is Barnabas, a son of exhortation within the emerging Jesus group.[38]

At this point we must recall the fact that Barnabas is an exemplar of a community that has experienced the filling of the Holy Spirit (Acts 4:31). While some interpreters have argued that "not one syllable" of the community summaries implies the direct influence of the Spirit, the narrative progression leading to both Acts 2:42-47 and 4:32-37 makes it rather apparent that Luke intentionally placed the descriptions of the community on the heels of the first two major Spirit episodes.[39] It is only by a disjointed,

---

ment (Barrett's first and third options). Luke ascribes the practice of exhorting/urging (παρακαλέω) to those he specifically names as prophets, specifically John the Baptizer (cf. Luke 3:18) and Judas and Silas (Acts 15:32). In this way Luke connects the task of exhortation/urging, at least when practiced within the community of believers, to the vocation of prophets.

36. Acts 9:27; 11:22; 13:2; 15:12; 37. In the last instance, Barnabas's exhortation causes sharp dispute with Paul. Johnson, *Acts,* p. 87, attributes to Barnabas a "mediatorial" role in the community.

37. Robert W. Wall, *The Acts of the Apostles,* The New Interpreter's Bible, vol. X, ed. Leander E. Keck (Nashville: Abingdon Press, 2002), p. 97, notes that names often change with "vocational changes."

38. It should be noted that option (3) — "son of consolation" — remains a viable and plausible way to conceive Barnabas's role in the community. "Son of exhortation," however, better captures the active sense of παρακαλέω and the active sense of Barnabas's activities with his property, his former enemies (Paul), and the ethnic "other" (in Antioch and at the Jerusalem Council).

39. Quote from Hermann Gunkel, *Die Wirkungen des Heiligen Geistes* (Göttingen: Vandenhoeck & Ruprecht, 1899), p. 10. Cf. Robert P. Menzies, *The Development of Early Christian Pneumatology with Special Reference to Luke-Acts* (Sheffield: Sheffield Academic, 1991), pp. 96-97. Y. Cho sees at best an indirect influence of the Spirit only through the communal response to Spirit-inspired prophetic speech (Youngmo Cho, *Spirit and Kingdom in the Writings of Luke and Paul: An Attempt to Reconcile These Concepts* [Waynesboro, GA: Paternoster, 2005], p. 133).

particularistic reading of the text that one can avoid this implication. More-over, the proper function of the community in Acts is regularly related to the influence of the Holy Spirit or to specifically Spirit-marked individuals. This is true in the widow controversy (Acts 6:1-7), after the incorporation of Saul into the community (Acts 9:31), in Antioch (Acts 11:24) and at the Jerusalem Council (Acts 15:7-11, 28). In each of these instances, those filled with the Spirit express a concern for those who would erstwhile be categorized as "other." In Acts 6:1-7 the Spirit-empowered seven repair an injustice done to those who, on the basis of ethnolinguistic identity, were aprototypical. In Acts 11:24, Barnabas — who again is specifically said to be full of the Holy Spirit — is the chief agent responsible for the incorporation of the non-Jewish Antiochene believers into the community of Jesus followers. In Acts 15, it is Peter's and James's awareness of the testimony of the Spirit that leads, decisively, to the full incorporation of non-Jews *as non-Jews* into the Jesus group. In other words, what is indicated initially in Acts 4:31-37 appears to be paradigmatic throughout Acts. The Spirit prompts both strong identifica-tion with the community *and a concern for the incorporation and well-being of the "other."* I note again that this love for the group coupled with simulta-neous love for the other is a rather rare phenomenon in intergroup relations.

Barnabas's Spirit-formed identity, an identity underscored by his new name, is expressed by his voluntary handling of possessions.[40] His behavior is a practical expression of the refusal to name any*thing* as one's "own" (ἴδιος). He sells a field and delivers the proceeds to the apostles for distribu-tion with no hint of either reciprocity or complete divestiture.[41] Rather, his goods are *unconditionally available* for the mitigation of poverty in the com-munity.[42] Barnabas, a Spirit-filled member of the group (Acts 4:31; 11:24), uses possessions in a manner indicative of his disposition toward — or full identification with — the new group. He values his people as his "own" (ἴδιος) but holds his possessions loosely and makes them available to others.

40. On the voluntary nature of Barnabas's act, see Ben Witherington III, *The Acts of the Apostles: A Socio-Rhetorical Commentary* (Grand Rapids: Eerdmans, 1998), pp. 207-8; I. Howard Marshall, *The Acts of the Apostles: An Introduction and Commentary* (Grand Rapids: Eerdmans, 1980), p. 84; French L. Arrington, *The Acts of the Apostles* (Peabody, MA: Hendrickson, 1988), p. 35. *Pace* Capper, "Palestinian Cultural Context" (who claims to favor "voluntary donation" but whose proto-monastic scheme leaves little room for choice be-yond a certain point); Wall, *Acts*, p. 73.

41. See 1QS 6:19-20 for a practice implying full divestiture.

42. Berd Kollmann, *Joseph Barnabas: His Life and Legacy* (Collegeville, MN: Liturgical Press, 2003), p. 12.

He turns his whole self toward the community, embodies the community in his person, and is a pattern to be imitated.[43] Thus, the economic ethic displayed by Barnabas is, in Luke's description, a symptom of a deeper pneumatological identity transformation.[44]

3.1 Ananias and Sapphira: Intragroup Threat and the Community of the Spirit

If Barnabas exemplifies the emerging social identity formed by Luke's new group, Ananias and Sapphira are anti-exemplars, or villains.[45] Fitzmyer distills six approaches that modern scholars have taken toward the difficult story of Ananias and Sapphira.[46]

1. An etiological reading based upon 1 Thess 4:13-17: divine judgment explains the death of Christians before the parousia.[47]
2. A Qumran reading comparing the couple's punishment with that of the Qumran initiate who deceives by concealing property.[48]
3. A typological interpretation based on Achan in Joshua 7.[49]
4. An institutional reading which interprets the episode as an excommunication from the church.[50]

---

43. Barnabas's significance for early Christian identity is evident in other ancient writings. See *Epistle of Barnabas; Gospel of Barnabas; Acts of Barnabas by John Mark; Acta Bartholomaei et Barnabae;* and *Laudatio Barnabae.* Tertullian attributed Hebrews to Barnabas (*De Pudicitia* 20). M. Öhler studies the "historical Barnabas" (Markus Öhler, *Barnabas: die historische Person und ihre Rezeption in der Apostelgeschichte* [Tübingen: Mohr Siebeck, 2003]).

44. Bede finds an interesting connection between the Spirit as "Paraclete"/*paraclesis* (cf. John 14:16) and Barnabas's name (*Commentary on the Acts of the Apostles* 4:36b; CS 117:53).

45. O. W. Allen (*The Death of Herod: The Narrative and Theological Function of Retribution in Luke-Acts* [Atlanta: Scholars Press, 1997], p. 124) treats the punishment of villains in Luke-Acts.

46. Joseph A. Fitzmyer, *The Acts of the Apostles: A New Translation with Introduction and Commentary,* Anchor Bible Commentary (New York: Doubleday, 1998), pp. 318-19. Fitzmyer (317) thinks the narrative casts doubt on the historicity of Acts, but he asserts this less emphatically than Hans Conzelmann, *Acts of the Apostles,* Hermeneia, ed. Eldon J. Epp and Christopher R. Matthews (Philadelphia: Fortress Press, 1987), p. 37.

47. Barrett, *Acts,* pp. 263-64.

48. Capper, "Interpretation"; "Palestinian Cultural Context."

49. Johnson, *Acts;* Cho, *Spirit and Kingdom.*

50. G. Shille, *Apostelgeschichte* (Berlin: Evangelische Verlag, 1983), p. 151.

5. A history of salvation reading which views the incident as an obstacle to the Acts 1:8 commission.[51]

6. An "original sin" reading that reads the episode as an example of sin at the beginning of the community's existence and hence in relationship to other accounts of sin at "beginnings" (e.g., Adam and Eve, sons of God and daughters of men [Genesis 6], the golden calf, David and Uriah).[52]

While these approaches contain valuable insights, each of them neglects the intricate connections between Spirit, identity, and possessions as well as the relationship between this couple and Barnabas.[53]

Anti-exemplars (i.e., villains) have an important role in the formation of social identity, helping to establish boundaries for communities.[54] The memories of villains help a society to define itself, largely by serving as model of behavior to be avoided.[55] For Luke, Ananias and Sapphira's attitude toward possessions arises as a result of their decision to self-sequester into a sort of *anti-group*.[56] This is established already in their introduction: "*Ananias, with his wife Sapphira,* sold a piece of property" and "*with his wife's knowledge* he kept back some of the proceeds" (5:1-2). Similarly, Peter asks Sapphira, "How is it that you have agreed *together* to tempt the Spirit of the Lord?" (5:9). The furtive actions of the couple imply the emergence of a subgroup that takes precedence over the group of believers. They are, as it were, counterfeit community members.[57] Unlike Barnabas, they have re-

---

51. P. B. Brown. "The Meaning and Function of Acts 5.1-11 in the Purpose of Luke-Acts," Dissertation, Boston University, 1969.

52. Daniel Marguerat, "La mort d'Ananias et Saphira (Ac 5:1-11) dans la stratégie narrative de Luc," *NTS* 39 (1993).

53. Marguerat's reading, in which the sin of the couple is a retreat from the Edenic character of the community toward the individualism implicated in the "fall," is attractive because it understands that the identity of the community and community members is in play.

54. Gary Allen Fine, *Difficult Reputations: Collective Memories of the Evil, Inept, and Controversial* (Chicago: University of Chicago Press, 2001), p. 8.

55. Fine, *Difficult Reputations,* p. 11.

56. Seccombe, *Possessions,* p. 211, agrees that it is not as a "negative aspect of the sharing of goods" that the couple has importance. He suggests they function to illustrate the fear surrounding the community and its holiness. These factors are important but subsidiary and subsequent to the role of Ananias and Sapphira in the narration of the community's identification with the Spirit.

57. Bartchy, "Community of Goods," p. 316: "By lying in order to achieve an honor they had not earned, Ananias and Sapphira not only dishonored and shamed themselves as patrons *but also revealed themselves to be outsiders, non-kin*" (emphasis mine).

tained possessions, but not community members, as their "own" (ἴδιος). Though the Spirit turns people toward community and outward toward the "other," Ananias and Sapphira have turned inward and away.[58]

We must be emphatic that their misuse of possessions is not the *cause* but the *symptom* of a more fundamental disposition which reveals Luke's uniquely Spirit-focused understanding of identity, the "other," and possessions.[59]

> Ananias, why has *Satan filled your heart* to lie to the Holy Spirit. . . ? How is it that *you have contrived this deed in your heart?* You have not lied to men but to God. . . . How is it that you have agreed together to tempt the Spirit of the Lord? (5:3, 4, 9)

Ananias and Sapphira, in their deception, have (1) "lied to" or "falsified" (ψεύδομαι) the Holy Spirit (5:3), (2) lied to God (5:4), and (3) tempted the Spirit of the Lord (5:9).[60] It is best to take Peter's accusations not as differentiated infractions but as a series set in parallel. Hence, the lies are the result both of Satan's filling of Ananias's heart (5:3) and of Ananias's and Sapphira's (5:9) own contrivance (5:3-4).

Ananias is not the first person in Luke's narrative to be "filled" by Satan. Judas, the narrative's most infamous villain, was filled by Satan (Luke 22:3: "Then Satan entered Judas called Iscariot") *before betraying the Jesus group.* While there are several parallels between Judas and Ananias and Sapphira, most striking is the fact that in both narratives *the influence of Satan causes the creation of an anti-group through an act of self-sequestering that ultimately leads to community betrayal expressed in part through the misuse of possessions.*[61] This is emphasized by Peter in Acts 1:25, who notes that Judas self-

---

58. This connection between the use of one's possessions (ἴδιος), the Spirit, and the "other" appears in the *Epistle of Barnabas* 19:7-8 and the *Didache* 4:8-10. In *Barnabas,* one should share everything with his neighbor and not claim anything to be his "own" (ἴδιος) because the Spirit comes without regard for "reputation." The *Didache* teaches its hearers to share with brothers and sisters in need and not claim that anything is your "own" (ἴδιος) (4:8). The basis for this sharing is the common identity produced by the Spirit, who overcomes status distinctions (4:11).

59. Suggestions for the actual "sin" of the couple include misuse of possessions (Johnson, *Sharing Possessions,* p. 206; cf. *Acts,* p. 91); deception (Dunn, *Acts,* p. 63) and "trifling" with the apostles (Barrett, *Acts,* p. 262).

60. The most proximate occurrence of "Lord" refers to Jesus (Acts 4:33).

61. Another parallel includes the role of money in relation to property (Ananias sells a field, Judas buys one).

sequestered by leaving the apostles to "go to his own [ἴδιος] place." The stories of these prominent villains give heightened attention to the relationship between Satan and anti-groups, yet it is not only villains who are susceptible to satanic influence. Jesus warned Peter that Satan sought to "sift" him (Luke 22:31), but that Peter, afterward, should instead *strengthen his brothers* (Luke 22:32). Even Jesus himself (Luke 4:1-13) was tempted by Satan to turn inward and away from his true identity and mission. Satan, opposing the community of God, seeks to divide and isolate, while God, through his Spirit, seeks to unite and build up Jesus-centered community.[62] At this point, Ananias and Sapphira are acting in line with benefaction norms — appearing to identify with the community but doing so only out of self-interest. There is a misuse of the things that were given from one's own (ἐκ τῶν ἰδίων).

The ramifications of the Satan/self and Spirit/other dynamic (expressed in Acts 4 and 5 by the way one handles possessions) are clarified by reading Ananias and Sapphira in light of Peter's speech in Acts 3. There we learned that improper response to Jesus leads to separation from the community and self-exclusion from the times of "refreshing" (Acts 3:19: ἀνάψυξις) given to those who repent and are included in the community. Ananias and Sapphira, filled by Satan, form an anti-group that tragically leads to their destruction from the people. Their destruction is described with the verbal opposite of ἀναψύχω ("to refresh"), ἐκψύχω ("to die"; Acts 5:5, 10).[63] For Luke,

---

62. Bruce W. Longenecker ("Until Christ Is Formed in You: Suprahuman Forces and Moral Character in Galatians," *CBQ* 61 [1999]: 92-108) sees a similar relationship between spiritual influence, identity, and behavior in Galatians.

63. The unmediated nature of Ananias and Sapphira's fate separates it from other "judgment miracles" in a way that elevates the necessity of community membership. A certain divine agency must be assumed in Acts 5:1-11, though note that Peter does not call down punishment upon the couple nor does Luke narrate direct divine punishment. This is in clear contrast with explicit judgment miracles in Acts 12:20-23 ("an angel of the Lord smote him [Herod]") and 13:9-11 ("The hand of the Lord is against you [Elymas] and you will be blind . . ."). By contrast, Peter's words in Acts 5:1-11 are more "explanatory than condemnatory" (Robert F. O'Toole, "You Did Not Lie to Us (Human Beings) but to God (Acts 5.4c)," *Biblica* 76, no. 2 [1995]: 194). Although Peter's words are often read as conveying stern rebuke or anger, they can as easily be read with a sense of disappointment, sadness, or regret over something gone horribly wrong. This accords with Peter's frequent willingness to give second chances (evident in Acts 3:17-26 and 8:22) and is likely the result of his own rehabilitation back into the community (see the discussion of Peter's characterization in Bauckham, *Jesus and the Eyewitnesses*, pp. 174-79). It is not Peter's decisive judgment (in fact, Peter gives Sapphira a chance to repent) but something that is apparently an inherently natural consequence of self-separation from the community. Allen (*Death of Herod*, pp. 202-5) suggests that divine retribution functions to "legitimate the story of . . . people who find themselves

the community inhabited by Spirit-filled people is the *place of life*. To be cut off from the community is to find death. This is true both temporally (based upon the immediate fate of the couple) and eschatologically (based upon the cosmic dualism evoked by the Spirit/God vs. Satan imagery).[64]

3.2 Forging an Identification Between the Spirit and the Community

Peter's initial question ("Why has Satan filled your heart to lie [ψεύδομαι] to the Holy Spirit?") can be taken in one of two ways, either of which highlights the identity of the community. ψεύδομαι + accusative object can mean "lie to," but it can also mean "falsify."[65] If "lie to" is the intended sense, Peter's question equates a lie to the community with a lie to the Spirit. If "falsify" is the intended sense (a judgment that can only tentatively be made), the implication is that by valuing possessions over people Ananias and Sapphira have "falsified" the work of the Spirit in the community. The deceit of Ananias and Sapphira stands in contrast to the allocentric identity of which the community is a collective expression, and thus has shined an unfavorable light upon (falsified) what the Spirit has been doing. Hence, Peter notes that they are filled by Satan rather than the Spirit.[66] The dichotomy between Satan-influence and Spirit-influence gives us the definitive clue to the identity of the community. A lie to the community is a lie to the Spirit (5:3)/God (5:4)/Spirit of the Lord (5:9). The new community is *the community of the Spirit*, who comes to empower and mark those who are identified with Jesus.

It is at this auspicious moment that Luke introduces the term ἐκκλησία for the group. For Israelites, the name evokes the LXX designation of the "Hebrews wandering in the desert, the assembly of returned exiles, or the cultic assembly of Israel."[67] In the broader Roman Empire, the name evokes Greco-Roman civic assemblies. Returning to the beginning of this section,

---

in a context somewhat different than that in which the story of their origins took place" and that "nobody can destroy what God has intended."

64. Max Turner, *Power from on High: The Spirit as Israel's Restoration and Witness in Luke-Acts* (Sheffield: Sheffield Academic, 1996), p. 406, suggests this cosmic dualism.

65. Johnson, *Acts*, p. 88. Mikeal C. Parsons and Martin M. Culy, *Acts: A Handbook on the Greek Text* (Waco, TX: Baylor University Press, 2003), p. 86, note that when that context includes an actual lie, the emphasis could be "on the consequences or implications of lying."

66. Dunn, *Acts*, p. 64.

67. Fitzmyer, *Acts*, p. 325. Cf. F. F. Bruce, *Commentary on the Book of Acts*, 2nd ed. (Leicester, UK: Marshall, Morgan and Scott, 1954), p. 136.

we are reminded that a social group is defined by self-ascription and ascription by others.[68] The naming of the community after this first incident of intragroup conflict highlights the fact that the community, in Luke's view, has a definite social status. The reality of this new identity is evident in the response to the incident from others in Jerusalem toward the community at large.[69]

> None of the rest dared join them, but the people held them in high honor. And more than ever believers were added to the Lord, multitudes both of men and women. (Acts 5:13-14)

The conflation of fear over the prospect of violating the community and eagerness to be assimilated into the community is a reflection of the numinous awe elicited by the community itself and demonstrates a perception of something dangerously generative about this group.

3.3 Barnabas, Ananias, and Sapphira: Summary

For Luke, a clear relationship exists between influence by the Spirit or by Satan, human identity as it impinges upon relationships with the "other," and the use of earthly goods. Possession of/by the Holy Spirit explicitly turns people away from the self and *outward* toward the broader community and the "other." The outcome of this allocentric identity is that people, and not possessions, become valued as one's "own" (ἴδιος). Spirit-influence thus leads to the use of possessions freely for the "other," as is exemplified by Barnabas. In clear contrast, the influence of Satan turns people away from the broader community and the "other" and *inward* toward the self. The outcome of this egocentric identity is that possessions, and not people, become valued as one's "own" (ἴδιος). Satan-influence thus leads to the use of possessions solely for the self, as exemplified by Ananias and Sapphira. *Satan prompts a treacherous turn away from the community and leads to destruction* (ἐκψύχω: Acts 5:5, 10).[70] *The Spirit prompts a turn toward the community and*

---

68. Turner, "Cognitive Redefinition," pp. 15-16.

69. *Pace* Johnson, *Acts,* p. 95. Johnson thinks that only the apostles are intended in the final summary. To arrive at this, he must posit that 4:23 implies only the apostles to the exclusion of the broader community. I have demonstrated the difficulty of this position above.

70. Cf. Peter's rebuke of Simon the Samaritan's self-centered pneumatic interests in Acts 8:18-25 and Paul's rebuke of Elymas in Acts 13:8-11.

leads to restored relationships and times of refreshing (ἀναψύχω: Acts 3:19). The descriptions of Barnabas, Ananias, and Sapphira serve powerfully to solidify the social identity commensurate with membership in the Jesus community. Their portrayal highlights Luke's conviction that the influence of the Spirit forms an allocentric identity that turns outward toward the "other" and that is often expressed by refusal to claim possessions as one's own.

The early economic ethos of the Jerusalem community cannot be taken as mere replication. For Luke, this precisely misses the point. The ethic advanced in the community is unattainable through mimicry and can occur only through a profound transformation of human identity empowered by the work of the Spirit. In this treatment, Luke does not set his community up as the recapitulation of other "communities of goods"; instead, he sets his community as a loud contrast against the prevailing economic ethos of the Greco-Roman world. Yet the contrast, for Luke, goes far deeper than praxis or practicality. The contrast, for Luke, is thoroughly spiritual and is fueled by Luke's vision of competing kingdoms — the kingdom of God, of which the Spirit now exists as the executive power of the exalted Jesus, and the kingdom of Satan, whose pervasive grasp on systems and persons results in the corruption of human community (and, as a result, the corruption of human economic relations) via an egocentric impact upon those affected by the dark kingdom.

4. Ecclesial and Economic Implications

If I am correct, this reading poses a challenge, in the form of a pneumatological corrective, for many sectors of the contemporary Christian church. The challenge is especially acute in the affluent North Atlantic world (and perhaps particularly within my own American context). This challenge arises on two levels. First, given the widespread acknowledgment that certain sectors of the church have neatly separated the "gospel" from the (less significant, in their eyes) "social gospel," this reading of Luke highlights the ongoing need of the church to more fully submit to the reign of the exalted Jesus through the power and presence of the Spirit in order more faithfully to bridge the spurious "gospel"–"social gospel" dichotomy. Luke anticipates that the filling of the Spirit will lead to a renewed relationship with the "other," expressed to a large degree by the transformed use of all that one can rightfully claim as one's "own." Hence, the proclamation of Jesus' lordship, manifest through the presence of the Spirit, can (perhaps ironically) never remain purely "spiritual." The social gospel versus spiritual gospel dichotomy must not only disappear, it must be recognized as a truncated expression of the inaugurated new creation that is the hallmark of the reign of God and that, for Luke, is available only through the power of the Spirit.

Second, this reading of Luke's pneumatological economics poses yet another challenge to the purveyors of "health and wealth" ideology. This movement, which has generated the most traction in ecclesial traditions that emphasize the role of the Spirit in the life of the believer, contends that the increased presence of the Spirit (resulting from greater personal faith) is correlated with an increase in personal economic benefit. The primary evidence of the Spirit-led life of faith, as articulated by this ideology, is the acquisition of more objects that one can claim as one's "own" (ἴδιος). This is diametrically opposed to Luke's supposition, in which the presence of the Spirit frees people from attachment to their possessions (ἴδιος) so that they can use them to reflect a renewed posture toward the "other." That the purveyors of "health and wealth" ideology have taken their movement to the developing world and seduced many with the promise that faith and the Spirit bring economic self-benefit is more than scandalous or even anti-Lukan; it is a fundamental misrepresentation of the Christian gospel.

6. Agrarian Discourse and the Sayings of Jesus: "Measure for Measure" in Gospel Traditions and Agricultural Practices

John S. Kloppenborg

In current research on the discourse of the early Jesus tradition, in particular parabolic discourse, there are several competing approaches. Few nowadays would defend the proposition that Jesus was an allegorist, speaking in one discursive realm but in fact intending to evoke other discursive realms — for example, salvation history or the care of the soul. Of course, it is clear that allegorical meanings were soon imputed to the parables. Matthew took parabolic discourse in this direction, turning the story of the Great Supper into an allegory of the fate of Jerusalem. Much later Origen read the Good Samaritan as an account of salvation history from Adam to Christ.

Some argue that Jesus told stories that deliberately evoked certain cultural codes found in ancient Judean literature, such that his parables functioned as oblique commentary on current events. Parables that featured vineyards thus evoked the trope of Israel as God's vineyard and served to comment on the current standing of Israel in covenantal relationship to God.[1] Parables

---

1. E.g., Klyne R. Snodgrass, *The Parable of the Wicked Tenants,* WUNT, vol. 7 (Tübingen: J. C. B. Mohr [Paul Siebeck], 1983) and those authors discussed in John S. Kloppenborg, *The Tenants in the Vineyard: Ideology, Economics, and Agrarian Conflict in Jewish Palestine,* WUNT, vol. 195 (Tübingen: J. C. B. Mohr [Paul Siebeck], 2006), chap. 4.

This paper was written with the support of the Social Sciences and Humanities Research Council of Canada. It uses the standard abbreviations for papyri found in John F. Oates, Roger S. Bagnall, and William H. Willis, *Checklist of Editions of Greek Papyri and Ostraca,* 5th ed., BASP Supplements 9 (Oakville, CT: American Society of Papyrologists, 2001), online: http://scriptorium.lib.duke.edu/papyrus/texts/clist.html.

about shepherds might be seen to evoke the various shepherds of the Hebrew Bible (e.g., David, Cyrus, or the incompetent shepherds of Jeremiah and Ezekiel) and thus might be thought to offer a commentary on current leadership. Without rejecting such approaches outright, this essay begins with the methodological insistence that the most basic meanings of the images in question need to be properly established before moving to abstract, symbolic, or allegorical meanings. It is also important to consider the possibility that, in some cases, a vineyard or a shepherd in a parable of Jesus is just a vineyard or a shepherd.

What is routinely neglected in discussions of the sayings of Jesus, or given only fleeting consideration, is an understanding of the social and economic *realia* invoked in Jesus' sayings and parables. Exegetes are often satisfied to assume on the basis of contemporary cultural knowledge that they understand how vineyards were operated and why tenants might revolt or economic and social aspects of transhumance, without significant inquiry into what ancient sources can tell us. They assume, wrongly as it turns out, that ancient vineyards operated pretty much in the same way that modern vineyards do (except of course for the lack of mechanization) and that contemporary practices of shepherding can be assumed. Consequently, they miss key aspects of ancient viticulture and especially social aspects of shepherding.[2] The result is often anachronistic and ethnocentric readings of the sayings of Jesus.[3]

In this essay I wish to explore a single instance of agrarian discourse, Q 6:38c//Mark 4:24, and track how this expression of balanced reciprocity is employed at various levels of the Jesus tradition. In this I am concerned with both *verbal continuity* and *ideological discontinuity* and to account for the ideologically freighted reshaping of agrarian discourse in the literature of the later Jesus movement.

2. See especially Brent D. Shaw, "Bandits in the Roman Empire," *P&P* 105 (1984): 5-52; Thomas Grünewald, *Räuber, Rebellen, Rivalen, Rücher: Studien zu Latrones im römischen Reich,* Forschungen zur Antiken Sklaverei, vol. 31 (Stuttgart: Franz Steiner Verlag, 1999). The transition from shepherd to bandit and back again was sufficiently common that the identification of shepherds with *latrones* was common. An inscription from Caria orders local officials to "flog shepherds who commit their accustomed acts of banditry" (*MAMA* IV 297). The porous boundary between banditry and shepherding can still be seen. See Gabriela Vargas-Cetina, "Our Patrons Are Our Clients: A Shepherds Cooperative in Bardia, Sardinia," *Dialectical Anthropology* 18, no. 3-4 (1993): 337-62.

3. See Kloppenborg, *Tenants,* for an outline and analysis of the history of exegesis of Mark 12:1-12, showing how anachronistic and ideologically guided assumptions have distorted the reading of the parable.

The particular kind of exchange under investigation involves reciprocity, a characteristic of agrarian societies. It is now common to invoke the typology of reciprocity advocated by Marshall Sahlins. *General reciprocity* is an open exchange typical of the relationships between close kin and friends. Exchange generates general obligations for reciprocation, but reciprocation is left indefinite both in terms of its timing and its quality. *Balanced reciprocity*, by contrast, is a *quid pro quo* exchange that aims at equivalence and timeliness. Market exchange is a form of balanced reciprocity that involves strict equivalence of exchange.[4] In other forms of balanced reciprocity, patron-client relationships for example, the exchange is not goods for goods or goods for currency, but rather public displays of gratitude and loyalty in exchange for various benefits. The expectation of reciprocity, nonetheless, is not left diffuse and its timing is not left entirely open. Whereas in general reciprocity exchange serves to cement social relationships, in balanced reciprocity there is a greater concern to secure self-interest. The supplying of goods or benefits generates the expectation of an equivalent return, normally within a limited temporal framework. *Negative reciprocity* is fundamentally exploitive, "the attempt to get something for nothing with impunity, the several forms of appropriation, transactions opened and conducted toward net utilitarian advantage."[5]

These are not air-tight categories but exist on a spectrum of social exchanges. All three types of exchange may exist within a single social group, and certain exchanges may straddle general and balanced reciprocity. The degree to which overt self-interest is at stake in exchange also varies, especially since certain forms of balanced reciprocity (patron-client relationships) and negative reciprocity often presented themselves in the language of friendship or kinship (general reciprocity) in order to mask the fundamentally unbalanced and exploitative nature of the exchange.

To anticipate the conclusion of this essay, appeals to principles of reciprocity were commonplace in ancient society and constituted the basic logic of social exchange. While *quid pro quo* forms of exchange might be regarded nowadays as too mercantile in structure to rise to the level of genuine moral action, ancient morality was deeply rooted in reciprocity. In this essay I shall

---

4. On the relationship between Sahlins's model of reciprocity and Karl Polanyi's distinctions between reciprocity, redistribution, and market exchange, see Alan Kirk, "Karl Polanyi, Marshall Sahlins, and the Study of Ancient Social Relations," *JBL* 126, no. 1 (2007): 182-91.

5. Marshall D. Sahlins, *Stone Age Economics* (New York: Aldine, 1972), chap. 5, here p. 191.

argue that a classical expression of balanced reciprocity was employed in the early Jesus tradition as the anchor for the articulation of a more adventuresome ethic.

1. The Measure-for-Measure Aphorism of Q 6:38c//Mark 4:24b

The measure-for-measure aphorism, which is part of Mark's cluster of sayings concerning the revelation of the kingdom (Mark 4:21-25), and which in Q and *1 Clement* 13 serves to buttress admonitions against judging and in support of kindness (Q 6:37-38a; *1 Clem.* 13.2), is not often treated as an authentic saying of Jesus. It is not that it is routinely rejected as inauthentic; more often than not it is simply not discussed at all.[6]

In one of the few substantial treatments of the saying, Michael Steinhauser concluded that as a bit of conventional wisdom, Mark 4:24b-25 contributes little to our understanding of the historical Jesus.[7] The Jesus Seminar argued that Mark 4:24b was common wisdom, though giving it a "gray" rather than "black" rating. The Seminar argued that "without some modification the saying appears inimical to Jesus' fundamental announcement of God's unlimited love and expansive mercy."[8] That is, the saying expressed *quid pro quo* logic. Members of the Seminar assumed both (1) that the saying was in the first place about values such as mercy and (2) that characteristic of Jesus' authentic sayings was an articulation of God's unlimited mercy. Consequently, the Jesus Seminar decided that a *quid pro quo* statement about mercy was fundamentally unworthy of Jesus' discourse. Beyond that, few others even comment on the saying and its possible authenticity.

As long as sayings such as Q 6:38c//Mark 4:24b are treated atomistically, and as long as the criterion of dissimilarity implicitly or explicitly controls the discussion of the historicity of sayings ascribed to Jesus, it is easy to see why Q 6:38c//Mark 4:24b is not ranked highly among authentic sayings. Examples abound of maxims that express a symmetry between action and reaction, whether that relation is deemed to be a matter of natural law, of hu-

---

6. John Dominic Crossan, *The Historical Jesus: The Life of a Mediterranean Jewish Peasant* (San Francisco: Harper & Row, 1991), p. 438, inventories the saying as a triply attested saying at the "first stratum of tradition" but does not discuss it further.

7. Michael G. Steinhauser, "The Sayings of Jesus in Mark 4:21-22, 24b-25," *Forum* 6, no. 3-4 (1990): 197-217.

8. Robert W. Funk and Roy W. Hoover, *The Five Gospels: What Did Jesus Really Say?* (San Francisco: HarperSanFrancisco, 1993), p. 57, cf. 297.

man justice, or of divine recompense. Both Proverbs and Hesiod state that evil deeds produce their own punishment.[9] So Prov 22:8 reads: "Who sows injustice will harvest calamity." In Hesiod (frag. 286), the saying appears as: "If one sows evils, let him also reap evils; if he suffers what he did, true justice may occur." Other formulations articulate principles of human or divine justice, the *lex talionis:* "As one does, so let it be done to him" (Lev 24:19). Still other sayings turn the "law" of human action into an admonition, as in Publilius Syrus (*Sententiae* 2): "Expect from another what you have done to him." The same is true for Q 6:31: "As you wish that people to do you, do also to them." On the principle of dissimilarity, the form of the saying found in Q 6:38c//Mark 4:24b scarcely rises above common wisdom and fails to meet the bar of distinctiveness routinely expected of Jesus.

If one privileges not dissimilarity, however, but multiple attestation, the case for the authenticity of Q 6:38c//Mark 4:24 improves. There are at least three independent attestations of the admonition:

Q 6:37-38 (see also Matt 7:2; Luke 6:37-38):
"Do not judge. . . . You will not be judged. . . . By the measure that you measure, it will be measured back to you [ἐν ᾧ μέτρῳ μετρεῖτε μετρηθήσεται ὑμῖν]."

Mark 4:24:
And he said to them, "Pay attention to what you hear; the measure you give will be the measure you get [ἐν ᾧ μέτρῳ μετρεῖτε μετρηθήσεται ὑμῖν], and still more will be given you."

1 Clem. 13:2:
For He said this: "Show mercy, that you may receive mercy; forgive, that you may be forgiven. As you do, so shall it be done to you. As you give, so shall it be given to you. As you judge, so shall you be judged. As you show kindness, so shall kindness be shown to you. With the measure you use, it will be measured to you [ᾧ μέτρῳ μετρεῖτε, ἐν αὐτῷ μετρηθήσεται ὑμῖν]."[10]

---

9. For more examples, see John Pairman Brown, "From Hesiod to Jesus: Laws of Human Nature in the Ancient World," *NovT* 35, no. 4 (1993): 330-43.

10. *Apostolic Fathers: English Translation,* ed. and rev. Michael W. Holmes (Grand Rapids: Baker Books, 1992/1999).

To this might be added Polycarp, *Philippians* 2.3:

> . . . but instead remembering what the Lord said as he taught: "Do not judge, that you may not be judged; forgive, and you will be forgiven; show mercy, that you may be shown mercy; with the measure you use, it will be measured back to you [ᾧ μέτρῳ μετρεῖτε, ἀντιμετρηθήσεται ὑμῖν]" and "blessed are the poor and those who are persecuted for righteousness' sake, for theirs is the kingdom of God."

Polycarp's version of the saying, however, is so close to Clement's that it seems likely that Polycarp is dependent upon *1 Clement*, perhaps with some influence of Matthew's (or Q's) "do not judge, in order that you might not be judged" (μὴ κρίνετε, ἵνα μὴ κριθῆτε).[11] In the case of *1 Clem.* 13.2, however, the consensus, as confirmed most recently by Andrew Gregory, is that Clement "refers there to a collection of sayings that is independent of and earlier than the broadly similar sayings of Jesus that are preserved also in Matthew and/or Luke."[12]

Assuming, then, that Mark is not dependent on Q — Mark's usage of the maxim is completely different from Q's — and that *1 Clement* is not directly dependent upon Q, we have three independent attestations of the measure-for-measure saying. This datum should at least provide a caution against too quick a dismissal of Q 6:38c from potentially authentic sayings of Jesus.

---

11. Michael W. Holmes, "Polycarp's *Letter to the Philippians* and the Writings That Later Formed the New Testament," in *The Reception of the New Testament in the Apostolic Fathers,* ed. Andrew Gregory and Christopher M. Tuckett (Oxford: Oxford University Press, 2005), pp. 191-92, considered various possibilities — direct dependence of Polycarp on *1 Clement,* dependence on *1 Clement* corrected against Matthew or Luke, citation of *1 Clement* from memory with the influence of Matthew and/or Luke, dependence on a catechism influenced by Matthew that formed a source for *1 Clement,* use of Q or a similar document, and dependence on oral tradition — but concludes that there is insufficient grounds for deciding.

12. Andrew Gregory, "*1 Clement* and the Writings That Later Formed the New Testament," in *The Reception of the New Testament in the Apostolic Fathers,* p. 134, referring to A. J. Carlyle's contributions to *The New Testament in the Apostolic Fathers* (Oxford: Clarendon, 1905), pp. 59-61, and Donald A. Hagner, *The Use of the Old and New Testaments in Clement of Rome,* NovTSup, vol. 34 (Leiden: E. J. Brill, 1973), p. 151.

2. The Measure-for-Measure Aphorism in Judean and Mediterranean Context

It is usual in discussing Q 6:38c//Mark 4:24b to quote Mishnaic and Targumic parallels.[13] For instance, *m. Sota* 1:7 cites the principle "in the measure with which a man measures, they measure it to him" (במדה שאדם מודד בה מודדין לו) in the context of a discussion of the particular punishments appropriate to an adulteress.[14] Similarly *Tg. Neophyti* I to Gen 38:25 cites the same principle in an expansion of the story of the imminent execution of Tamar on the charge of harlotry. As she was being taken away she declared that the things Judah had given her would serve as witnesses and cause Judah to exonerate her. When she produced these articles Judah indeed understood that it was he who had slept with Tamar and declares:

> I beg you brothers and men of my father's house, listen to me: it is better for me to burn in this world with extinguishable fire, that I may not be burned in the world to come whose fire is inextinguishable. It is better for me to blush in this world that is a passing world, that I may not blush before my just fathers in the world to come. And listen to me, my brothers and house of my father: in the measure in which a man measures it shall be measured to him, whether it be a good measure or a bad measure במכלותא דאינש מיכל בה מיתכל ליה בין מכלותא טבא בין מכלותא [בישא].[15]

In later discussions the principle is simply abbreviated as "the rule of measure for measure" (מדה כנגד מדה).[16]

While the rabbinic *talion* principle remains a possible context for the interpretation of Q 6:38c//Mark 4:24b//*1 Clem.* 13.2, there is another interpretive clue supplied by papyri that can be dated much earlier than the third century CE. As B. Couroyer pointed out nearly forty years ago, grain loans from Ptolemaic and early Roman Egypt regularly used a formula that required the borrower to repay the loan using the same measuring vessel

---

13. This has been extensively discussed by Hans Peter Rüger, "'Mit welchem Mass ihr meßt, wird euch gemessen werden,'" *ZNW* 60 (1969): 174-82.

14. On this, see *m. Sota* 1:7; *b. Sota* 8b.

15. Alejandro Díez Macho, *Neophyti 1. Targum Palestinense MS de la Bibliotheca Vaticana. Tomo 1: Genesis* (Madrid and Barcelona: Consejo superior de investigaciones científicas, 1968), p. 225; ET: Martin McNamara, *Targum Neofiti 1: Genesis*, The Aramaic Bible, vol. 1A (Collegeville, MN: Liturgical Press, 1992), p. 177.

16. Cf. *Gen. Rab.* 9.11.

(μέτρον) that had been used to dispense the loan in the first place.[17] This practice was natural: in the absence of standardized weights and measures, it was the obvious way to ensure fairness in borrowing practices. Couroyer's case, which was based on a few second-century BCE Greek and Demotic papyri, can now be supplemented with a wealth of papyri from both earlier and later periods.

This point is crucial since, as will become clear, the logic of Q 6:38c//Mark 4:24b rests not on an abstract principle of moral exchange (mercy, judgment, etc.) but on the very concrete practice of economic exchange. The word μέτρον in the first instance means "measuring vessel" or "measuring scoop." If one loses sight of the fact that Q 6:38c begins as a *metaphor* that invokes an ordinary practice of exchange, the rhetorical force of the saying is lost.

3. Μέτρον as a Measuring Vessel

From well before the common era, loans of seed grain regularly acknowledged the amount of grain loaned and contained an undertaking that the borrower would repay the loan at a specified time, normally following the next harvest, using the same grain vessel that had been used to dispense the loan. For example, *P.Amh.* II 46 from 113 BCE stipulates:

> In the month of Pachon of the fifth year the borrower Thaësis shall repay to Naosesis what has been loaned, clean, fresh grain, delivered to her at her house at her [i.e., Thaësis's] own expense, by means of the measure by which she also had received it [μέτρῳ ᾧ καὶ παρείληφεν].

The same formula can be found in a series of Demotic and Greek papyri dating from the third century BCE to the early first century BCE.[18]

---

17. Bernard Couroyer, "De la measure dont vous mesurez il vous sera mesuré," *RB* 77 (1970): 366-70.

18. *BGU* III 1005.6 (III BCE); *P.Adl.* G15.14 (100 BCE); *P.Amh.* II 47.9-10 (113 BCE): μέ(τρῳ) ᾧ καὶ παρείληφεν; *P.Grenf.* I 10.14 (174 BCE); *P.Grenf.* I 18.18 (131 BCE); *P.Grenf.* I 23.13-14 (118 BCE); *P.Grenf.* I 28 (108 BCE); *P.Lond.* II 218.8 (111 BCE); *P.Lond.* II 225.10-11 (118 BCE). The same formula is attested in Demotic agreements: "And I will give you your wheat 45 artabae of wheat . . . by your measure whereby you have measured it to me" (Field Papyrus, ll. 9, 12-13; see N. J. Reich, "The Field Museum Papyrus [A Promissory Note of the Year 109/8 B.C.]," *Mizraim* 2 [1936]: 35-51 + 1 plate); *P.Adl.* D3.5 (116/15 BCE): "by the measure with which you measured it to me"; *P.Adl.* D5.11-12(108-7 BCE): "by the measure with which you measured it to me." Cf. also *P.Adl.* D6.10 (107 BCE); *P.Adl.* D11.10 (100-99 BCE).

By the early Imperial period we find a slightly different formula, but the sense remained the same. So *P.Berl.Möller* 4 (13 CE) records a loan of barley of the brand of Hermophantos, stipulating that it be repaid with the same brand and using the same measuring container that had been used for the initial loan:

> . . . paying it back in new unadulterated barley of the brand of Hermophantos, measuring it out to the representative of Herakles, by the fourth measure of the merchants [μέτρῳ τετάρτῳ (ἐ)νπόρων τῷ τοῦ Ἡρακλέ(ους)], with fair measure and strickle, at the village granary, paying the granary fee himself.

Similar formulae are attested well into the third century CE.[19] In some instances both the granary to which repayment was to be made and the precise grain vessel (μέτρον) were stipulated, as in *P.Mich.* XII 634.12-15 (25/26 CE):

> . . . the entire forty artabae of wheat measured by the four-choinix measure (μέτρον) of the granary of Julia Augusta and the children of Germanicus Caesar.

That Luke understood Q 6:38c to refer to the measurement of agricultural products is indicated by his expansion of Q. Luke prefaces his measure-for-measure saying with "give and it will be given to you, a good measure (μέτρον καλόν), pressed down, shaken together, running over, will be put into your lap." The phrase "a good measure" is probably an equivalent for the phrase "with a just measure," encountered frequently in provisions for repaying loans or paying rent.[20] The remainder of Luke's expansion refers to the pressing and shaking of grain in the measuring container to ensure the

---

19. See *BGU* II 538.13 (100 CE); *BGU* XI 2033.14 (94 CE); *BGU* XIII 2330.14 (89 CE); *BGU* XIII 2331.12 (91 CE); *P.Athens* 14.14, 25 (22 CE); *P.Dubl.* 7.5 (I/II CE); *P.Fay.* 89.15 (9 CE); *P.Lond.* II 216.15 (94 CE); *P.Mert.* 6.21 (77 BCE); *P.Oxy.* XVIII 2118.8 (107 CE); 2189.39 (220 CE); *P.Oxy.* XXXVIII 2874.29 (108 CE); *P.Oxy.* XLVII 3352.2 (68 CE); *PSI* I 31.13 (164 CE); *PSI* VIII 921.10 (143/4 CE).

20. *BGU* VI 1268.16 (III BCE); *BGU* X 1951.4 (221-203 BCE); *P.Amh.* II 43.9 (173 BCE); *P.Lille* I 24 Fr. 4.9 (III BCE); *P.Tebt.* III/1 824.16 (171 BCE); *P.Yale* I 51 B.23 (184 BCE); etc. In rabbinic texts the "perfect and just measure" appears in the context of a discussion of the regulation of shopkeepers: *b. B.B.* 88b, 89a: "A perfect and just measure [you shall have]," citing Deut 25:15. The terms "good measure" and "bad measure" appear in *Deut. Rab.* 11.9 in a complaint against the divine: "In all your acts [one sees] measure for measure; [then why do you repay me] a bad measure for a good measure, a short measure for a full measure, a grudging measure for an ample measure?"

fullest measure possible (a practice that benefits the lender), and Luke even adds "overflowing," even though this does not accord with the principle of the equality of exchange, which is the ostensible point in the measure-for-measure maxim.

Indeed, each of the Gospel performances of the measure-for-measure aphorism suggests that what is in view is the ordinary agricultural practice of repaying loans with the same vessel used to dispense them.[21] The context in Q is a series of admonitions concerning love of enemies (6:27-28), non-retaliation (6:29), lending without expectation of return (6:30), and treating persons in ways that one also would wish to be treated (6:31), so as to "become sons of your Father, for he raises his sun on bad and good and rains on the just and unjust" (Q 6:35). The smaller unit of which Q 6:38c is part features a binary contrast between the admonition to be merciful ([γίν]εσθε οἰκτίρμονες ὡς ὁ πατὴρ ὑμῶν οἰκτίρμων ἐστίν, 6:36) and the contrasting prohibition of judging.[22] In such a context the buttressing measure-for-measure aphorism probably does not appeal to the *lex talionis,* since the majority of the imperatives concern the encouraging of *positive* practices which spark reciprocal treatment, rather than avoiding certain proscribed behaviors. The well-known agrarian practice of equality of exchange was a perfectly appropriate way to buttress these admonitions.

In *1 Clem.* 13.2 it is even clearer that the argument is not based on the principle of *lex talionis,* since the measure-for-measure admonition is pref-

---

21. Couroyer, "La measure," 370: "Il ne s'agit pas de talion, encore que, dans les deux cas, on retrouve la stricte égalité: 'mesure pour mesure' comme 'oeil pour oeil'. Le logion de Jésus, sous le forme où nous le livrent les synoptiques, pouvait déjà avoir cours de son temps comme, s'il en est l'auteur, il a pu le formuler en s'inspirant de stipulations juridiques dont la stabilité est proverbiale. Prêteurs et emprunteurs de grains devaient avoir, de son temps, les mêmes exigences que celles qu'on retrouve dans les contrats cités plus haut. L'interdiction de juger était au mieux justifiée par le rappel de cette loi des échanges. C'était non une menace, mais une mise en garde par le rappel d'une coutume bien connue."

22. While Matthew uses Q 6:36 as the conclusion to Matt 5:43-48 (ἔσεσθε οὖν ὑμεῖς τέλειοι) and introduces Q 6:37 without a connecting particle (Matt 7:1: μὴ κρίνετε . . .), Luke uses anacoluthon to introduce Luke 6:36 (γίνεσθε οἰκτίρμονες), indicating the beginning of a new unit, and continues v. 37 with καί. The IQP follows Luke by constructing Q as [γ]ίνεσθε οἰκτίρμονες . . . (Q 6:36) and [ ] μὴ κρίνετε . . . (Q 6:37), where the open bracket indicates agreement with Luke's καί, though at a {D} level of certainty, since it is possible to imagine some other connective between v. 36 and 37. See James M. Robinson, Paul Hoffmann, and John S. Kloppenborg, eds., *The Critical Edition of Q: A Synopsis, Including the Gospels of Matthew and Luke, Mark and Thomas, with English, German and French Translations of Q and Thomas,* Hermeneia Supplements (Leuven: Uitgeverij Peeters; Minneapolis: Fortress Press, 2000), p. 74.

aced by the entirely positive admonition: "as you show kindness, thus kindness will be shown to you" (ὡς χρηστεύεσθε, οὕτως χρηστευθήσεται ὑμῖν).

The "fit" of the measure-for-measure aphorism with the logic of Mark's unit is not especially good, since Mark's next aphorism, "for whoever has, to him will be given; and from the one who lacks, even what he has will be taken away," stresses not *equality* of exchange but the privilege afforded to those who "have" and the perils of those who do not. Nevertheless, Mark's point in 4:24b appears to be that cultivation of a positive response to Jesus and his proclamation of the kingdom will be repaid in kind by further divine revelation. Mark's supplementation of the basic form with "and more will be added to you" moves the logic beyond one of strict equality of exchange to one of divine beneficence. Still, it is not the *lex talionis* that best accounts for the logic of Mark 4:24b, but the agricultural practice of measuring out and repaying loans with the same vessel.

Considerations of dissimilarity notwithstanding, Q 6:38c//Mark 4:24b// *1 Clem.* 13.2 presents a reasonable case for authenticity, based on (1) multiple attestation and (2) contextual plausibility. For its imagery and compelling rhetoric, the saying is dependent on an agrarian practice that we know to have been a contemporary practice of lending in late Ptolemaic and early Imperial Egypt. We have every reason to suppose that similar practices were in use in Jewish Palestine. Palestine, after all, was in the third century BCE under the control of Egypt, which introduced various economic and political practices that were simply taken over by the Seleucids and eventually by the Hasmoneans and Herodians. At those points where we are in a position to examine specific economic practices connected with leases and loans, Jewish documents imitate the forms more fully known from Egypt.[23] Other

---

23. Three things need to be noted here. (1) The form of leases in Jewish Palestine correspond to the forms of those in use in Egypt; see Johannes Herrmann, *Studien zur Bodenpacht im Recht der graeco-ägyptischen Papyri,* MBPAR 41 (Munich: C. H. Beck, 1958); and John S. Kloppenborg, "The Growth and Impact of Agricultural Tenancy in Jewish Palestine (III BCE–I CE)," *JESHO* 51, no. 1 (2008): 33-66. (2) The details of the leases from Murabbaʿat bear many resemblances to Greco-Egyptian loan contracts, requiring that the rent be paid in "good quality and uncontaminated wheat" and "measured out at the top of the granary" (see *P. Mur.* 24C.17). (3) The use of a "leveler" (מחוק, מחוק), equivalent to the Greek σκυτάλη, points to common practices. See *t. Šabb.* 1:7 "R. Eliezer says, 'On that day they overfilled the *seʾah* measure'. R. Joshua says, 'On that day they leveled (מחקו) the *seʾah* measure. For so long as the measure is full and one puts more into it, in the end it will give up part of what [already] is in it.'" See further, Ben-Zion Rosenfeld and Joseph Menirav, *Markets and Marketing in Roman Palestine,* trans. Chava Cassel, JSJS vol. 99 (Leiden and Boston: E. J. Brill, 2005), pp. 79-81.

sayings and parables ascribed to Jesus take for granted a wide range of ordinary practices in agrarian society, for example: owners' worries about being defrauded by their estate managers, hiring practices at harvest time, absenteeism as a standard feature of large-scale viticulture, and the practice of communicating with tenants via slave-agents.[24] We presume that such images were ready-to-hand because Jesus and the earliest Jesus movement in Galilee were thoroughly embedded in the agrarian economy of village and small town life.

4. Point of View: Borrower or Lender?

At this point it is important to inquire more deeply into the logic and the perspective of the measure-for-measure admonition. All three performances of the aphorism agree in putting it as a second-person plural, in contrast to the usual framing of the *lex talionis* in the third person. We also find a second-person formulation of an admonition concerning "measuring" along with the use of both the verb "measure" (μετρεῖσθαι) and the noun "measuring vessel" (μέτρον) in Hesiod (*Opera et Dies* 349-51):[25]

> Take fair measure [μετρεῖσθαι] from your neighbor, and pay him back [ἀποδοῦναι] fully by the same measure [αὐτῷ τῷ μέτρῳ], or more, if you are able; so that when you are in need you will find him someone to rely on.

Hesiod's phrase "by the same measure" appears to refer to the same practice later described in documentary papyri as paying back loans with the same measuring vessel. What should be noted in Hesiod's formulation is that it is framed from the point of view of the borrower. It recommends a borrowing practice designed to ensure easy access to loans in the future. Borrowing "fairly" (i.e., by means of an accurate measure) and returning the loan in the same way will assure the lender of the borrower's absolute honesty and will, Hesiod believes, encourage future generosity on the part of the lender. Hesiod implicitly assumes a social practice where borrower and lender are more or less of the same status and that the care in measurement and the equivalence of borrowing and repayment are voluntary rather than being

---

24. See Kloppenborg, *Tenants,* chap. 9.
25. See M. L. West, *Hesiod: Works and Days* (Oxford: Clarendon Press, 1978), p. 244.

imposed by the specific terms of the debt instrument. This will not be the case with the documents to which we now turn.

5. The Uses of "Measure" in Legal Documents

In Greco-Egyptian documentary papyri, the verb "measure" and the noun "measuring vessel" are found (sometimes in combination) in several specific contexts. First, in *sitologoi* receipts, the *sitologos* acknowledges receipt of grain in payment of rent or taxes.[26] For example *BGU* XIII 2299 (ll. 4-8; Tebtynis, 162 CE):[27]

> We, [names indiscernable], partners and *sitologoi* of the village of Tebtynis, have had measured out (μεμετρή[μεθα]) to us, by the smoothed public measure (μέτ[ρ]ῳ δη[μοσίῳ] ξυστ[ῷ]) of wheat, from the produce of the same year, to the credit of Paopis son of Psoiphis, by Apia, 17 artabae of wheat for the rent (of public land); for transportation, 1 artaba of wheat, making 18 artabae.

In such receipts the verb "measure" is typically a first-person perfect passive (μεμέτρημαι or μεμετρήμεθα) and sometimes found in abbreviated form (μεμετρη). It was the *sitologos* who measured the grain, or at least the *sitologos* supervised the measuring.

Orders issued to *sitologoi* or other officials instructing them to make payments to certain persons provide us with a second type of document in which "measure" frequently appears. Such orders normally use the imperative μέτρησον, "measure out." When a superior official made such an order it was probably not necessary to stipulate the type of measure to be used, since it would automatically be assumed that some standard measure was in use. For example, in *P.Lond.* III 1213 (65-66 CE), a superior orders a *sitologos* to measure out a four-month ration of grain for a fellow slave, without any indication of the measure to be used.[28] In the case of orders from a scribe to a

26. A *sitologos* was an official in charge of a local granary, being responsible for receiving and documenting revenues and for various disbursements.

27. For similar papyri, see *BGU* XIII 2300-2303; *P.Fay.* 81 (115 CE), 82 (145 CE), 83 (163 CE), 84 (163 CE) and those cited in *BGU* XIII 2299.

28. In *P.Hib.* I 74 (250 BCE), however, an official commands his agent to measure out olyra to two minor officials, stipulating the measures to be used, probably because two different measures were in use at the time. See B. P. Grenfell, A. S. Hunt, and Eric G. Turner, eds., *The Hibeh Papyri,* Egypt Exploration Fund: Graeco-Roman Memoirs, vol. 7 (London:

sitologos to transfer a rental payment to the account of the lessor or owner, however, the measure is given, presumably as a way to ensure that the lessor is receiving her or his full share of the produce. This can be seen in *P.Fay.* 16 (Arsinoites; first century BCE):[29]

> Ptolemaios the scribe, to Ptolemaios the *sitologos* of Autodike, greetings. Measure out [μέτρησον] to Posidonios son of Didymos, against the account of Herakleides son of Zenobios, the rent on Posidonios' plot which he (Herakleides) has cultivated in the vicinity of Kerkeësis in the division of Polemon, 45 artabae by the dromos measure [δρό(μῳ) με . . .]; total: 45 (artabae) drom. Year 1 Pauni 19.

A third type of document where "measure" typically occurs is the lease agreement. In such documents it is usual to stipulate not only that the lessee is obliged to pay a certain quantity of rent (in kind), but also to pay it using a specific measure. For example, a lease from Oxyrhynchus (*P.Amst.* I 42.7-13; III-IV CE) states:

> Let the lessee pay each year in the month of Pauni at the threshing floor in the farmstead of the lessee in the vicinity of the same Mermertha wheat that is clean, unadulterated, unmixed with barley, new, sifted, with the measure that is customary [μέτρῳ τῷ συνήθει] in the lands of the lessor P[. . .], *the measurement* [τῆς μετρήσεως] *being made by her* [i.e., the lessor's] *agents* without delay, from which the lessee shall measure out [μετρήσει] the public charges in grain at his own expense . . .

Here, and in other leases, the lessor's agents supervise and even perform the measuring.[30]

P.Athens 14 (22 CE) involves both a lease of agricultural land and a loan of seed grain. The contract stipulates that the seed grain be measured out to the lessee by the one-quarter artaba measure and the rent (including the loan) had to be returned by the same measure:

> . . . as a rent, including the 4¾ artabae of seed grain that the lessee has received from Kastor each year, in all, for the first year 53 artabae, the second

---

Egypt Exploration Society, 1906-55), 1:227-30. The papyrus mentions both the δοχικόν measure and the ἀνηλωτικόν measure, the ratio between the two being approximately 1 art. δοχ. = 1.05 art. ἀνηλ.

29. See also *P.Fay.* 18a, 18b (first century BCE).

30. See also *P.Athens* 19.13 (154 CE).

year, 43 artabae, and the last year [of the lease] 25 artabae, all by the one-quarter [artaba] measure [πάσας δὲ μέτρῳ τε(τάρ)τῳ] . . . [the lessee] repaying it with new wheat, free of all contaminants and unadulterated, by the [same] measure indicated [earlier] [μέτρῳ τῷ προκειμένῳ] . . .

Finally, it is in *loans* for wheat, barley and other agricultural products that the most attention is paid to the repayment provisions. For example, in *P.Mert.* I 14 (Oxyrhynchus, 103 CE) the precise measure is not stipulated, but the borrower was required to repay the loan at the local public granary where the loan had originally been made. One must assume that the lender knew the measuring system:

> I acknowledge that I have received and have had measured out (to me) by you one hundred seventy artabae of wheat, making 170, which I shall measure (back) [μετρήσω] to your account to the public granary and will deliver this to you on deposit, free of all expenses in the month of Pauni of the present 7th year of Trajan, Caesar and Lord, without any excuse; but if I should not measure out (this grain) I shall pay in addition the added half, and you shall have the right of execution on both me and all my possessions, as if by a judicial judgment . . .

The first-person acknowledgement formula is customary in such loans: "I acknowledge that I have received and have had measured out by you" (ὁμολογῶ ἔχειν καὶ [παρα]μεμετρῆσθαι παρὰ σοῦ). Also customary is a statement concerning the way in which the loan is to be repaid. A slight variation on this formula appears in *P.Sarap.* 16 (Hermopolis; 105-6 CE) where the verb "receive" (ἔχειν) alone appears in the *homologia* portion, and the verb "measure" (μετρήσω) is used in the declaration of repayment:

> Achilleus son of Anoubion to Sarapion son of Eutychides greetings. I acknowledge [(ὁ)μ(ο)λογῶ] that I have received [ἐσχηκένα(ι)] from you a loan of wheat with interest, of twenty artabae, making with interest 20 artabae, which I shall also measure back to you [μετρήσω σοι] in the month of Epeiph of the current 9th year of Trajan, Caesar the Lord, by the Athenian one-sixth measure [μέτρῳ], transporting (the wheat) to Hermopolis to you at your house, without postponement or excuses.

In this case a specific measuring vessel is stipulated by the contract.

The same practice is attested in *P.Lond.* III 975 (Oxyrhynchus, 314 CE), a loan of chickling from one woman to another:

I acknowledge that I have had measured out (to me) by you [ὁμολογῶ (μ)εμετρῆ(σθ)αι παρὰ σοῦ], by a direct payment from your house an interest-bearing loan, for a total, with interest: three artabae of chickling and 1½ artabae of choice [chickling]. . . . I have had measured out both types at the same time, 4½ artabae. I shall measure back (to you) by your measuring vessel [σ(οι μετ)ρ(ήσω) μέτρῳ] in the month of Epeiph . . .

P.Oxy. VI 910 (Oxyrhynchus, 197 CE) combines a lease and a loan agreement from the end of the second century CE. It repeats the same formula that had been used in much earlier loan agreements, such as *P.Amh.* II 46 cited above: "by the measuring vessel by which he had received it." *P.Oxy.* VI 910 involves a standard lease of agricultural land in which the lessor also advances seed grain to the tenant. The lease is framed not as a first-person declaration, but in the third person:

The lessee acknowledges that he has received and has had measured out (παραμεμετρῆσθαι) here by the farmer, as an advance payment for seed grain, for the land of the single current year, seven artabae of wheat, the same amount which he [the lessee] shall necessarily pay back to him together with the rent of the land, in the mouth of Pauni of the same current year, by the measuring vessel with which he received it (μέτρῳ ᾧ παρείληφεν), free of all risks . . .

The final clause, with the details of the rental payment, is then elaborated:

. . . by the four-choinix measure brought by the farmer, with the measuring being done by his agents [μέτρῳ τετραχοινίκῳ παραλημπτικῷ τοῦ γεούχου, τῆς μετρήσεως γ(ε)ινομένης ὑπ(ὸ τῶν) παρ' αὐτοῦ].

Of all the documents compounding the verb "to measure" and the noun "measure," it is Greco-Egyptian agricultural loans that offer the closest conceptual and verbal parallels to the measure-for-measure aphorism of the Jesus tradition. There is, nevertheless, a crucial difference between the loan documents just examined and Q 6:38c//Mark 4:24b. The loan documents are typically framed as first- or third-person *homologiae* of the borrower: "I have had *x* measured out to me, and I will measure it back . . ." Hesiod's advice is likewise framed from the borrower's perspective. The measure-for-measure aphorism of the Jesus tradition, however, is framed with the *lender* in view — the one who "measures out" (μετρεῖτε) and to whom the loan is "measured back" (μετρηθήσεται ὑμῖν). Had the aphorism wished to take the perspective of the borrower, one would expect the following formulation: "with the measure that you have received, with the same measure measure (it) back" (ἐν ᾧ μέτρῳ εἰλήφητε, ἐν τῷ αὐτῷ μέτρῳ μέτρησον). Instead, consistently in the Jesus tradition the measure-for-measure aphorism is distinctive in addressing the lender, not the borrower.

6. The Measure-for-Measure Aphorism in the Jesus Tradition

As an independent aphorism there are two possible applications for a saying that addresses the topic of borrowing with the *lender's* actions in view. The first possibility is that it is a subtle threat: taking "it shall be measured out (to you)" (μετρηθήσεται) as a *passivum divinum* the saying might warn the wealthy (i.e., those in a position to make loans) that their lending practices are under divine scrutiny and, consequently, they are in danger of divine judgment. Crossan treats Mark 4:24b//Q 6:38c as an "isolated apocalyptic sanction" (what Käsemann called a "sentence of holy law"),[31] where the agent of apocalyptic sanction (God) is implied by the passive voice.[32] For Crossan Mark 4:24b is a version of the *lex talionis* whereby "earthly act begets eschatological reaction." Although Crossan does not appreciate the concrete agrarian context of the saying or speculate on the discursive situation in which such an aphorism might be effective, it would appear that the saying might be voiced in circumstances where there was a perceived disparity between what privileged persons gave and what they expected back in return. The problem of dishonest weights and measures was a common one in the marketplace;[33] but the saying might be used metaphorically of other

---

31. Ernst Käsemann, "Sentences of Holy Law in the New Testament," in his *New Testament Questions of Today*, trans. W. J. Montague (London: SCM Press, 1969), pp. 66-81, esp. 77-78.

32. John Dominic Crossan, *In Fragments: The Aphorisms of Jesus* (San Francisco: Harper & Row, 1983), pp. 175-76.

33. See, e.g., *P.Tebt.* I 5.85-92 (Tebtynis; 118 BCE): "And since it sometimes happens that the *sitologoi* and *antigrapheis* use larger measures than the correct bronze measures appointed . . . in estimating dues to the state, and in consequence the cultivators are made to pay [more than the proper number of choinikes?], they have decreed that the *strategoi* and the overseers of the revenues and the *basilikoi grammateis* shall test the measures in the most thorough manner possible in the presence of those concerned in the revenues of . . . and the priests and the clerics and other owners of land . . . , and the measures must not exceed [the government measure] by more than the two . . . allowed for errors. Those who disobey this decree are punishable with death." (I owe this reference to Dr. Giovanni Bazzana.) For rabbinic concerns about weights and measures, see Rosenfeld and Menirav, *Markets and Marketing*, pp. 76-80.

kinds of reciprocal exchange where hypocrisy or double standards threatened the integrity of exchange.

There are at least two potential difficulties with the interpretation of Mark 4:24b//Q 6:38c//*1 Clem.* 13.2 as a threat. In the first place, agrarian discourse as evidenced by the contracts and other documents cited above already overwhelmingly favored the interests of the wealthy, the lender, the creditor, the landowner. This is the case even when weights and measures were not distorted in the lender and lessor's favor, since we typically encounter the insistence on sifting, pressing, and leveling grain when *repaying* the loan, not when dispensing it in the first place. Moreover, the lender typically "measured out" the loan and his agents "measured it back," thus controlling the process. Contracts typically contained provisions against default, permitting execution on the borrower's person and property. Virtually all the mechanisms of law functioned to sustain and protect the interests of the propertied and monied sectors against the interests of those dependent on those classes. The way in which the measure-for-measure principle was applied in contract law, moreover, reinforced the belief (whether or not it was a distortion of what actually happened) that the system of economic exchange aimed at strict equity and fairness. Loan and lease contracts were written in such a way to suppose that if there were any breach of the terms, it would not be on the part of the lender or lessor; it would be on the part of the borrower or the tenant, who might default on a loan, fail to deliver the rent, abandon the lease, pilfer the crop, or otherwise defraud the lessor/lender.[34] The persistent rhetoric of lease and loan contracts constructed the lender and lessor as honest and fair, and the borrower and the lessee as persons whose desires and actions required supervision, surveillance, and the discipline of law to keep in check. This, of course, does not reflect reality as much as it reflects the power arrangements of the ancient world. But for precisely this reason, to use the measure-for-measure aphorism as a subtle threat against the monied and propertied sectors would likely be ineffectual, since they *already* believed themselves to be abiding strictly by principles of equity in exchange. The fact that they also benefited hugely by "compliance" with those principles would probably have gone unnoticed.

In the second place, it is worth noting that none of the earliest independent attestations of the saying in Mark nor Q nor *1 Clement* understood the measure-for-measure saying as a threat to the elite. It is not impossible, of

---

34. *P.Cair.Zen* V 59851 (Philadelphia; mid 3rd century BCE) is a fascinating account of iron tools lent to a cultivator, some of which were broken and replaced with lighter, cheaper implements. For a discussion, see Kloppenborg, *Tenants*, pp. 439-42.

course, that all three have textualized the saying in a way other than the way it had functioned in earlier oral Jesus tradition. But on the other hand, compelling reasons would have to be found to read the aphorism differently from its earliest three interpreters. To do otherwise would be to make the criterion of dissimilarity not only a historiographical criterion, but an exegetical one!

A second way in which to read the measure-for-measure aphorism is the way in which Q and *1 Clement* have read it. As indicated above, Q deploys the maxim in the second panel of a unit (Q 6:27-35), which, as Alan Kirk has shown, extends the conventional Greek and Roman ethic of helping friends/ harming enemies and lending to those who will repay, to benefiting enemies, the indigent, and the morally unworthy. For conventional Greek and Roman ethics, the Greek word χάρις epitomizes the notion of reciprocal exchange, denoting both the "benefaction" offered to another and the "gratitude" that the recipient was expected to show. As is clear from Q 6:27-35, this double-barreled notion of χάρις is not abandoned in the Jesus tradition, but the framework within which reciprocal exchange occurs is redefined. Χάρις is no longer limited to exchange among those who can reciprocate. Rather than abandoning reciprocity, "the passage [6:27-35] rejects the adequacy of the conventional reciprocity ethic by subjecting its core concept, χάρις, to reevaluation and urging the abandonment of the evaluative framework that normally accompanies it."[35] The golden rule (6:31) with its articulation of balanced reciprocity has often been viewed as incompatible with the ethic enunciated by Q 6:27-30, 32-35. It has been understood as an articulation of *quid pro quo* unworthy of the sayings which surround it. But, Kirk argues, far from being inconsistent with or expressive of a "lower form" of morality than the love of enemies admonition, reciprocity is the engine that lifts love of enemies from empty sentimentality to become a definite social vision. It is

> a "starting mechanism" that stimulates the kind of interaction necessary to bring into existence the envisioned social relations. Without the reciprocity motif [of Q 6:31] the command to love enemies remains orphaned from a social context; it is just an emotive slogan, not the inaugural note of a comprehensive social vision.[36]

The principle of balanced reciprocal exchange in Q 6:31 is the mechanism which helps the addressee to imagine *how* love of enemies and giving without

35. Alan Kirk, "'Love Your Enemies,' the Golden Rule, and Ancient Reciprocity (Luke 6:27-35)," *JBL* 122, no. 4 (2003): 684.

36. Kirk, "Love Your Enemies," p. 686.

expectation of return might work: to engage in such practices, *by the very logic of Q 6:31*, will generate a new mode of social exchange that moves dramatically beyond the limits of conventional ethics. If principles of balanced exchange sustain the conventional ethic of helping friends and benefiting those within a narrow social circle, then the principle of balanced exchange will *also* sustain a broader, more socially adventuresome ethic of helping enemies and acting as benefactor to outsiders, precisely because benefaction creates the obligation of reciprocity. It is important to note that, like Q 6:38c, Q 6:31 is framed from the point of view of the one who *initiates* action: it invites one to imagine largesse by the other, but directs the subject to engage in just this action, thus initiating a cycle of reciprocity. Q 6:25-35 imagines a very different world from the world of conventional, limited exchange, and Q 6:31 is key to its logic.

The unit that follows Q 6:27-35 works on a similar logic. It begins with a call to imitate God's mercy ("be merciful just as your Father is merciful," 6:36),[37] perhaps developing the *imitatio Dei* motif that was already in the conclusion of the first unit (Q 6:35). This general admonition is then illustrated by an admonition against judging (6:37), and the two are buttressed by the measure-for-measure aphorism (6:38b). The measure-for-measure maxim, far from expressing a conventional morality, functions as does Q 6:31, to underscore the "payoff." Should one engage in the socially adventuresome behavior of imitating divine mercy or refusing to judge peers, one can also expect a commensurate benefit, precisely on the logic of ordinary agrarian exchange. "The measure you measure out will be measured back." The focus is on the one who *initiates* action, not on the one who reacts. Acting with supererogatory mercy and withholding judgment will, by the logic of Q 6:38c, redound to the subject's benefit. Just as Kirk has observed *a propos* of Q 6:27-35, Q 6:36-38 also calls for a reevaluation of conventional exchange, and it uses the logic of agrarian lending practices to persuade that socially audacious ventures will be repaid in kind.

The logic of *1 Clem.* 13.2 is similar. It is even clearer that what is being proposed is a socially adventuresome posture, but one that is supported by an appeal to the conventionality of reciprocity expectations. Specific appeals to mercy and forgiveness are buttressed by a general *quid pro quo* aphorism, "as you do, so also it will be done to you." Then, using the structure of this aphorism, three further specific appeals are made — to generosity, to careful judgment, and to kindness, all three being buttressed by the measure-for-measure aphorism.

---

37. On Q 6:36 as the beginning of the text unit, see above, footnote 22.

Specific admonitions:

    a Show mercy, that you may receive mercy.

    b Forgive, that you may be forgiven.

Appeal to reciprocity:

    c As you do, so shall it be done to you.

Specific admonitions:

    d As you give, so shall it be given to you.

    e As you judge, so shall you be judged.

    f As you show kindness, so shall kindness be shown to you.

Appeal to reciprocity:

    g With the measure you use, it will be measured to you
      (ᾧ μέτρῳ μετρεῖτε, ἐν αὐτῷ μετρηθήσεται ὑμῖν).

As with Q 6:36-38, there is a strong appeal to self-interest. *1 Clement* 13.2 is not framed by a general admonition to imitate the divine, but the logic of the two expressions of general reciprocity (c and g above) implies that the greater the expression of mercy, generosity, and kindness, the greater will be the reciprocation. The saying thus allows one to imagine an escalating practice of benefaction and kindness.

Although it is precarious to claim that either Q 6:36-38 or *1 Clem.* 13.2 goes back to Jesus in these forms, it is nonetheless striking that both deploy the measure-for-measure maxim to help the auditor imagine how generosity, kindness, forgiveness, and mercy could be instantiated as a social practice. The social vision of Q 6:36-38 (and 6:27-35) is not unlike that articulated by other sayings regularly ascribed to Jesus, such as Q 11:4, "remit us our debts *as we remit the debts of those who owe us*," and Q 14:14-26, the parable of the Great Supper, where the host abandons the norms of balanced reciprocity to play host to those who could not repay him. All of these sayings focus on how agency that ventures to move beyond conventional modes of exchange will, in the end, bring benefit. One might even endorse the interesting suggestion of Douglas Oakman that these sayings, which focus on agency of the lender, the lessor, and the host, reflect Jesus' appeal to retainers such as tax collectors and the middling wealthy to imagine an alternate social praxis aimed at overall debt reduction, a praxis which, on Q's logic, would also redound to the honor of those agents.[38]

---

38. Douglas E. Oakman, *Jesus and the Peasants;* Matrix: The Bible in Mediterranean Context (Eugene, OR: Cascade Books, 2008), pp. 280-97.

7. Later Developments of the Measure-for-Measure Aphorism

Although Mark's formulation of the maxim is virtually identical to Q's in wording, his deployment of the aphorism no longer concerns the inauguration of a counter-ethic, but rather articulates a "rule" to define a counter-society. It is a society based on the reception of special revelation. Mark is not satisfied with the principle of equity enunciated by the measure-for-measure maxim and so adds "and still more will be given you" (καὶ προστεθήσεται ὑμῖν, Mark 4:24). It is at this point that we see the aphorism being lifted from its original context and re-framed. Mark no longer appeals to the principle of equality of exchange that is fundamental to Q and *1 Clement*. Now, those who give a little get much more in return — a fantasy (and perhaps a reality) of the monied and propertied class, but a "text of terror" for the non-elite.[39] The following saying continues this train: those who have will get more, and those who lack will have what they possess taken away. Mark can reframe the saying in this way, probably because he is wholly uninterested in the original agrarian context and logic of the measure-for-measure saying. For Mark, the equality of economic exchange is irrelevant; rather, it is "poverty" and "wealth" in respect of revelation that interests him, and hence he can celebrate the *incommensurability* of initial investment and final outcome. Mark thus relocates the measure-for-measure aphorism into another discursive realm, where it appeals not to reciprocity but to *acquisitiveness*, at least as far as revelation and knowledge are concerned. An aphorism that originally served to encourage those with resources (moral and material) to dispense them on the calculable promise of equivalent return has now become focused on the fantasy of unforeseen gain.[40]

Luke too is concerned not with the absolute equality of exchange but with surplus. Unlike Mark, however, his interest is much closer to the original use of the aphorism. Luke's expansion of Q 6:37-38 focuses on generosity and puts the emphasis not on refraining from certain actions ("Do not judge, and you will not be judged; do not condemn, and you will not be condemned," probably taken or adapted from Q); instead, the culminating emphasis rests on positive actions: "Forgive, and you will be forgiven; give, and

39. See Richard L. Rohrbaugh, "A Peasant Reading of the Parable of the Talents/Pounds: A Text of Terror?" *BTB* 23, no. 1 (1993): 32-39.

40. A similar shift in the social register of discourse can be seen in Mark's treatment of the parable of the Tenants (Mark 12:1-12; *Gospel of Thomas* 65-66), where Mark's editing and apocalypticizing of the parable have made it much more compatible with dominant class interests than is the case with Thomas's version. See Kloppenborg, *Tenants*, chaps. 1-2, 9.

it will be given to you."[41] Luke anticipates the measure-for-measure saying in 6:38b ("A good measure [μέτρον καλόν], pressed down, shaken together, running over [ὑπερεκχυννόμενον], will be put into your lap"), clearly indicating that he understands the agrarian origins of the measure-for-measure aphorism in Luke 6:38c. But his promise of the good measure "running over" (ὑπερεκχυννόμενον) is probably aimed at encouraging benefaction (as he does elsewhere).[42] Loan and lease contracts are normally at pains to stipulate that measuring is done "with fair strickle" (σκυτάλῃ δικαίᾳ) as a way to guarantee strict equivalence of loan and repayment.[43] Luke's promise of *extra* return suggests that he has already lifted the aphorism out of its original context and applied it to another discursive domain, where one could imagine benefactions being repaid with even greater rewards.

It is Matthew who has moved the unit most strongly in the direction of the *lex talionis*. First, he added to the measure-for-measure maxim another phrase, formulated on the model of the measure-for-measure aphorism: "For with the judgment you make you will be judged" (Matt 7:2). Second, by relocating Q 6:39-40 to points later in his Gospel, Matthew brought forward the warning about correcting a "brother" (Q 6:41-42 = Matt 7:3-5). The elaboration of 7:2 and the juxtaposition of 7:1-2 with 7:3-5 thus emphasize the forensic aspect of the sayings, and shift the focus from agricultural practice to the realm of law and punishment. Matthew's deployment of Q 6:38c moves the saying in the direction of the later rabbinic principle "in the measure with which a man measures, they measure it to him."[44] Naturally, Matthew had no need for Mark's expansion "and still more will be given you," nor would Luke's idea of surplus have served his purposes.

41. François Bovon, *Luke 1: A Commentary on the Gospel of Luke 1:1–9:50,* Hermeneia (Minneapolis: Fortress Press, 2002), pp. 241-42.

42. Halvor Moxnes, "Patron-Client Relations and the New Community in Luke-Acts," in *The Social World of Luke-Acts: Models for Interpretation,* ed. Jerome H. Neyrey (Peabody, MA: Hendrickson Publishers, 1991), pp. 241-68.

43. E.g., *BGU* IV 1142.7 (25/24 BCE); *BGU* VI 1271.6 (180-145 BCE); *BGU* VIII 1742.12 (64/63 BCE); *BGU* XIV 2390.33 (160/59 BCE); 2391.9 (250 BCE); 2392.7 (250 BCE); *P.Amh.* II 43.10 (173 BCE); *P.Dion.* 17.24 (108 BCE); 19.18 (105 BCE); 20.20 (105 BCE); P.Freib. III 34.37 (174/3 BCE); P.Heid. VI 369.15 (197 BCE); *P.Hib.* I 98.19 (252 BCE); *P.Lille* I 21.26 (155-144 BCE); I 23.25 (155-144 BCE); I 24.iv.9 (III BCE); *P.Tebt.* 3/1 815.iii.2.13 (228-221 BCE); 823.25 (185 BCE); 824.16 (171 BCE); *SB* V 8754.12 (49/48 BCE). For similar formulations, see also *P.Cair.Isid.* 32.5-7 (279 CE); *BGU* XI 2025.7 (144 BCE); XV 2556.15 (202 CE); *P.Amh.* II 120.14 (204 CE); *P.Fay.* 84.7 (163 CE).

44. Robert H. Gundry, *Matthew: A Commentary on His Literary and Theological Art* (Grand Rapids: Eerdmans, 1982), p. 121.

Conclusion

On the basis of multiple attestation and contextual plausibility, the measure-for-measure aphorism offers a good case for authenticity. It invokes the standard and widespread practice of agricultural marketplaces in which loans are repaid using the same measuring vessel with which they were originally dispensed. The peculiarity of the formulation of Q 6:38c//Mark 4:24b// *1 Clem.* 13.2 is that it is framed not from the point of view of the borrower but from that of the lender — surprising, perhaps, if one were to suppose that Jesus' audience was restricted to the non-elite. This framing suggests that the aphorism was employed to encourage those with resources to distribute them more widely, on the understanding that the more they gave, the more they would recoup — an adventuresome though not wholly unrealistic expectation. This social strategy is consistent with a series of other sayings and admonitions that, on the one hand, counsel against hoarding (Q 12:16-21), and on the other, encourage forgiveness (including debt forgiveness) on the understanding that this will redound to the agent's benefit (Mark 11:25; Q 11:4).

Insofar as the "measure-for-measure" principle was integral to the operation of the economy of Jewish Palestine, there is little problem in imagining that Jesus might have employed it (and in fact, shifted its point of view) in order to appeal to those who were in a position to lend. By citing the very principle of market exchange by which they benefited in loans and lease agreements, Jesus could suggest that other forms of exchange could be conceived along the same lines: generous actions, mercy, forgiveness would *also* redound to their benefit. Of course one did not need to be a lender to understand how the application of this market principle might work in forms of human action.

As the aphorism was deployed in the literature of the early Jesus movement, we can see both continuities and discontinuities. Both 1 *Clement* and Q use the aphorism to encourage the reevaluation of conventional expectations of social exchange, nudging the hearer to imagine social experimentation in the interaction with enemies, debtors, and fellows and the creation of a new ethos of reciprocity. Luke's deployment continues this usage, but has in view the cultivation of benefactors with promises of surplus gain.

But the aphorism was also shifted in two other ways and made to serve different social interests. On the one hand, Mark evidences a process of *abstraction* whereby the original agrarian exchange is eclipsed and its register is shifted from simple agricultural exchange to the acquisition of knowledge, where the importance of surplus and accumulation replaces the principle of equity of exchange. The other transformation is that of Matthew, where the aphorism has been relocated to another discursive realm, that of law and retribution, where the aphorism through verbal imitation is assimilated to the *lex talionis*.

In the history of deployment of the measure-for-measure aphorism verbal continuity is strong. At the level of the discourse of Jesus — best represented I think by Q and *1 Clement* — the aphorism strongly reflects the realities of agrarian exchange in Jewish Palestine, even if Jesus shifted the point of view of the principle from that of the borrower to that of the lender. But the witness of Luke, Mark, and Matthew indicates how a single saying was serviceable in other discursive situations and was refashioned to serve very different conceptual and ideological interests.

7. Is God Paul's Patron? The Economy of Patronage in Pauline Theology

David J. Downs

The cities of the Roman Empire in which the congregations of the Pauline mission took root were deeply influenced by the Roman social institution known as *patrocinium,* or "patronage," as this word is rendered in English. Patronage was a prominent form of social exchange, not only in the Roman colonies that hosted Pauline churches like Corinth and Philippi but also in the Hellenistic cities of the eastern provinces where the Latin loanword πάτρων *(patrōn)* is abundantly attested in the epigraphical record as an honorific designation for Roman supporters of these localities.[1] A first-century BCE Greek inscription from Ephesus, for example, honors the legate Marcus Messala Corvinus as "patron and benefactor" (πάτρων καὶ εὐεργέτης) of the temple of Artemis and of the city (*SEG* 43.775).

In recent years, the phenomenon of patronage has received significant attention among scholars interested in the sociocultural context of earliest Christianity. Beginning in the 1980s, and benefiting from a burgeoning interest in the sociology of patronage among classicists, a number of New Testament researchers, particularly those who developed the use of socio-scientific methods for the interpretation of the Bible, drew attention to the ways in which the social relationships among the earliest followers of Jesus often reflected patterns of patronage and clientism.[2] Studies of the Pauline

---

1. The inscriptional evidence is catalogued and discussed in Claude Eilers, *Roman Patrons of Greek Cities* (Oxford: Oxford University Press, 2002), esp. pp. 191-268.

2. An earlier leader in the study of patronage and the Pauline churches, whose work became foundational for much that followed, was E. A. Judge. A number of Judge's most important essays have recently been republished in *Social Distinctives of the Christians in the*

congregations, in particular, benefited from these new perspectives. John Chow's book *Patronage and Power: A Study of Social Networks in Corinth,* for instance, demonstrates that patron-client relations were an important way in which social ties were structured in the city of Corinth and, not surprisingly, also in the Corinthian house churches.[3] These sociological dynamics, Chow shows, influenced much of the dissension *within* the Corinthian congregation and also factored prominently in the conflict between the church and its apostle (e.g., 1 Cor 9:1-27).

Yet it has become increasingly commonplace for Pauline interpreters to apply a model of patronage not merely to the study of the relational dynamics within the Pauline communities but also to the very structure of Paul's theology itself. According to this perspective, the phenomenon of patronage reveals the following framework for divine-human interaction within Paul's theological worldview: God is the patron, Christ is the broker, and human beings are the clients.[4] Sometimes this position is maintained with reference to the New Testament's representation of God in general, with the Pauline epistles serving as a notable example. For instance, Jerome Neyrey's recent monograph *Render to God* applies a model of patron-client relationships to a variety of New Testament writings. Neyrey claims that "in considering God as patron and benefactor, we must also examine divine benefaction first to Jesus-the-broker and then to God's clients through Jesus."[5] This model is then spelled out with chapters on eight specific New Testament documents, including Romans, 1 Corinthians, and Galatians. With even more direct reference to Paul's theology, in the *Social-Science*

First Century: Pivotal Essays by E. A. Judge, ed. David M. Scholer (Peabody, MA: Hendrickson, 2008). For other early studies of patronage in the New Testament, see J. H. Elliott, "Patronage and Clientism in Early Christian Society: A Short Reading Guide," *Forum* 3 (1987): 39-48; Bruce Malina, "Patron and Client: The Analogy Behind Synoptic Theology," *Forum* 4 (1988): 2-32; Halvor Moxnes, "Patron-Client Relations and the New Community in Luke-Acts," in *The Social World of Luke-Acts: Models for Interpretation,* ed. Jerome H. Neyrey (Peabody, MA: Hendrickson, 1991), pp. 241-68.

3. John K. Chow, *Patronage and Power: A Study of Social Networks in Corinth,* JSNTSup 75 (Sheffield: Sheffield Academic Press, 1992).

4. This perspective is seen in the following works, among others: Jerome H. Neyrey, *Render to God: New Testament Understanding of the Divine* (Minneapolis: Fortress, 2004); idem, "God, Benefactor and Patron: The Major Cultural Model for Interpreting the Deity in Greco-Roman Antiquity," *JSNT* 27 (2005): 465-92; David A. deSilva, *Honor, Patronage, Kinship and Purity: Unlocking New Testament Culture* (Downers Grove, IL: InterVarsity, 2000); Zeba A. Crook, "The Divine Benefactions of Paul the Client," *JCRCJ* 2 (2001-2005): 9-26.

5. Neyrey, *Render to God,* p. 255.

Commentary on the Letters of Paul by Bruce J. Malina and John J. Pilch, readers are told:

> God is the ultimate patron whose resources are graciously given. By proclaiming the gospel of God about the God of Israel raising Jesus from the dead with a view to an emerging kingdom of God, Paul in effect is announcing a forthcoming theocracy for Israel along with the ready presence of divine patronage. In Paul's proclamation, Jesus is broker or mediator of God's patronage and proceeds to broker the favor of God through the Spirit of God.[6]

To cite one final example, in Peter Lampe's chapter on "Paul, Patrons, and Clients" in the recently published handbook *Paul in the Greco-Roman World*, Lampe writes:

> An analogy can be drawn between the patron-client model and the relationship that Christ has with Christians. Christ is their Lord (e.g., Rom 1:4; 10:9, 12; 14:6-9, 14; 1 Cor 1:3). They are joined to him (Rom 7:4; cf. 1 Cor 3:23). They live for him and not for themselves (Rom 14:7-8; 2 Cor 5:15). Christ intercedes for the Christians before God (Rom 8:34; cf. 8:27), as a patron seeks the advance of his client in forensic and other social contexts.[7]

Lampe goes on to list Paul's statements about Christ as a corporate representative for humanity, such as those found in 1 Cor 15:20-22 and Rom 5:12-19, as well as the faithfulness and loyalty implied in the πίστις Χριστοῦ construction, as aspects of the patron-client relationship between Christ and the people of God. He concludes, "Last but not least, God's role as it is pictured in Romans 1–5 can be interpreted in analogy to the patron-client model, although Paul himself does not use these technical terms."[8]

This final line raises precisely the question with which the present essay is concerned. If Paul does not call God patron (that is, if "Paul himself does not use these technical terms"), does this mean that God is not, in fact, Paul's patron? Those who would apply a model of patron-broker-client relations in the attempt to explain the interaction between God, Christ, and humanity in

---

6. Bruce J. Malina and John J. Pilch, *Social-Science Commentary on the Letters of Paul* (Minneapolis: Fortress, 2006), pp. 384-85.

7. Lampe, "Paul, Patrons, and Clients," in *Paul in the Greco-Roman World*, ed. J. Paul Sampley (Harrisburg, PA: Trinity Press International, 2003), pp. 505-6.

8. Lampe, "Paul, Patrons, and Clients," pp. 505-6.

the Pauline epistles would undoubtedly respond with a negative answer to this question. The very fact that these interpreters are employing a *model* serves as an indication that we need not find specific language of patrons and clients in order to describe the reality behind the rhetoric: the absence of the terminology does not necessarily indicate the absence of the conceptualization. As with any socio-scientific or anthropological model, therefore, the value of the patronage model is found in its ability to move beyond the explicit *language* used by an ancient author in the attempt to describe the socio-cultural and/or theological dynamics within and behind the rhetoric of an ancient text.[9]

This essay has two aims. First, in assessing the model of patronage used by those who contend that God is patron in the Pauline epistles, I shall argue that patronage is an unsuitable framework when it is applied to Paul's understanding of divine-human relations because appropriations of this model misconstrue some important things both about patronage and about Pauline theology. Second, and more positively, I shall highlight the extent to which Paul tends to avoid the terminology of patronage in his discussions of both human and divine activity. Paul's primary metaphor for God is not "patron" — a term he never applies to God — but "father." While we should not assume that patronage and kinship are always mutually exclusive, I shall suggest that Paul's consistent identification of "God our Father" (Rom 1:7; 1 Cor 1:3; 2 Cor 1:2; Gal 1:3; Phil 1:2; Phlm 3) functions to frame the identity and character of God outside the Greco-Roman patronage system.

---

9. Even those who work with a model of patronage are not always careful to maintain this precise distinction, however. For example, Neyrey's *Render to God,* which self-consciously employs a model of patronage taken from the social sciences, regularly slips into a pattern of ascribing patron-client terminology to the apostle Paul. We read, for example, that in 1 Corinthians "God acts and *is described as* Benefactor/Patron to the church" (p. 145), that "*Paul primarily explains* God's relationship with the Corinthians *in terms of* the common social pattern of patronage" (p. 145), that "*Paul employs* this model of social interaction" (p. 146), that "there is in *Paul's articulation* of the patron-client relationship between God and himself a special nuance that God reverses worldly values and expectation" (pp. 147-48), and finally that "*Paul's understanding* of his client-Patron relationship has relevance to the lively issues of disunity and conflict in the community" (p. 148; emphasis added). All of these statements fail to account for the fact that nowhere in the Corinthian correspondence is God described with terminology taken from the realm of the Roman patronage system.

1. Definitions of Patronage: Sociological and Institutional

Biblical scholars and classicists who employ the concept of patronage to study the literature and practices of Greco-Roman antiquity typically utilize models of patronage developed in the social sciences. In the field of Classics, for example, perhaps no work has had as profound an impact upon the study of patronage in Roman society as Richard Saller's pioneering monograph *Personal Patronage under the Early Empire.* In his attempt to define patronage, Saller draws upon the work of anthropologist Jeremy Boissevain to define patronage in the following way:

> First, [patronage] involves the *reciprocal* exchange of goods and services. Secondly, to distinguish it from a commercial transaction in the marketplace, the relationship must be a personal one of some duration. Thirdly, it must be asymmetrical, in the sense that the two parties are of unequal status and offer different kinds of goods and services in the exchange — a quality which sets patronage off from friendship between equals.[10]

Saller's broad definition, which has been quite influential in the development of the scholarly discussion, certainly includes the kind of relationship that Romans expected *patronus* (patron) and *cliens* (client) to share with one another. As Saller is keen to point out, the absence in source material of what is often considered the technical terminology of *patronus, cliens,* and *patrocinium* (patronage) does not necessarily imply that a relationship of patronage was not present, for Roman patrons typically called their clients "friends" *(amici).*[11] Due to its ability to cover a broad range of social in-

---

10. Richard P. Saller, *Personal Patronage under the Early Empire* (Cambridge: Cambridge University Press, 1982), p. 1; cf. Jeremy Boissevain, "Patronage in Sicily," *Man* 1 (1966): 8-33. Saller himself is quite clear that this definition is crafted in light of modern anthropological studies.

11. In a later essay, Saller ("Patronage and Friendship in Early Imperial Rome," in *Patronage in Ancient Society,* ed. Andrew Wallace-Hadrill, Leicester-Nottingham Studies in Ancient Society 1 [London and New York: Routledge, 1989], pp. 50-62) contests the claim that there was a technical view of the terms *patronus* and *cliens* in ancient Rome. According to Saller, "[T]he Romans applied the language of patronage to a range of relationships, with both humble dependants and their junior aristocratic colleagues labeled *clientes:* usage was more fluid than usually supposed, and the connotations of *amicus, cliens* and *patronus* were subtly and variously manipulated in different circumstances" (p. 57). David Konstan ("Patrons and Friends," *Classical Philology* 90 [1995]: 328-42), on the other hand, argues that there was a sharp distinction between patronage and friendship.

teractions, a sociological model of patronage offers the possibility of genuine cross-cultural comparison, not only between the Roman and Greek cultures of the ancient world, but also between the societies of Mediterranean antiquity and other contexts in which patronage functions as a form of social organization.[12]

The trouble with a broad sociological definition of patronage, however, is that it also runs the risk of covering far too many forms of social interaction, and in more than a few instances it includes relationships that the Romans would never have recognized as examples of *patrocinium*. Except when it involves relationships between equals, all friendship would be considered "patronage," according to the sociological definition offered by Saller. In the Greco-Roman world, marriage and slavery were also long-lasting relationships of reciprocal exchange based on asymmetrical distributions of status. Should these relationships be considered patronage? As Claude Eilers points out, "Definitions are valuable not only for what they include, but also for what they exclude. The above definition disallows almost nothing."[13] I would also suggest that sociological definitions of patronage tend to reflect relatively undeveloped and static notions of status. Patronal relationships, we are told, must be "asymmetrical, in the sense that the two parties are of unequal status and offer different kinds of goods and services in the exchange." Yet this definition fails to recognize that status is notoriously difficult to define. The implicit assumption seems to be that status is defined primarily in socioeconomic or material terms — that is, in terms of access to goods and services.[14] Yet, as Wayne Meeks reminded us long ago, status comes in all shapes and sizes. One's status might include such variables as power, professional prestige, financial resources, education, age, ethnicity, gender, family lineage, marital status, and/or religious esteem.[15] With respect to the Pauline communities, we are lucky if we have as many as two or three status markers for any members of Paul's churches. Even in the few cases in which such information might be available, however, there is no way

12. See, e.g., S. N. Eisenstadt and L. Roniger, *Patrons, Clients and Friends: Interpersonal Relations and the Structure of Trust in Society* (Cambridge: Cambridge University Press, 1984).

13. Eilers, *Roman Patrons of Greek Cities*, pp. 6-7.

14. For an excellent analysis of the economic impact of patronage in the Roman world, see Koenraad Verboven, *The Economy of Friends: Economic Aspects of Amicitia and Patronage in the Late Republic*, Collection Latomus 269 (Brussels: Éditions Latomus, 2002).

15. See Wayne Meeks, *The First Urban Christians: The Social World of the Apostle Paul*, 2nd ed. (New Haven: Yale University Press, 2003), pp. 53-55.

to measure the relative weight ascribed to each of these indications of status. When Paul wrote to Philemon while the apostle was "a prisoner of Christ Jesus" (v. 1), surely Paul possessed fewer material goods and services than the wealthier recipient of his epistle. That does not mean, however, that Paul was of lower "status" than Philemon; still less does it mean that Paul was Philemon's client. Indeed, when read in light of a sociological definition of patronage, much of the letter turns on the question, "Who is the patron of whom?"

In contrast to a sociological definition, another option for describing patronage in the Greco-Roman world would be to define patronage more narrowly as the official, institutional relationship that obtained between *patroni* and *clientes*. *Patrocinium*, as the Romans called it, was a social institution characterized by a more or less formal set of duties for patrons and clients.[16] Clients, on the one hand, were expected to attend the customary morning *salutatio* at the home of their patrons, to accompany their patrons each day on the trip from home to the Forum, and to vote and canvas for their patrons during political elections. Patrons, on the other hand, were obliged to provide clients with business assistance, legal advice, and representation in court; sometimes patrons would also offer their clients dinner invitations or *sportulae*.[17] Patronage was not only an institution characterized by relationships between individuals, however. Formal relationships between patrons and clients were also established between members of the Roman senatorial elite and various municipalities throughout Italy and in the Greek-speaking eastern parts of the Empire, where a number of inscriptions identify wealthy and powerful Romans as πάτρωνες of Greek cites.[18]

Such an institutional approach to patronage, too, is not without its problems. In focusing on one specific relationship that the Romans understood as *patrocinium*, the evidence for this social institution is partly ob-

16. That such a formal relationship existed among *patroni* and *clientes* in the Roman imperial period has sometimes been denied (see Andrew Wallace-Hadrill, "Introduction," in Wallace-Hadrill, ed., *Patronage in Ancient Society*, pp. 9-10). References to *patroni* and *clientes* in Roman legal texts, however, make sense only if it was possible to determine, based on some shared understanding, who was a patron and who was a client (cf. *Dig.* 47.2.90; 49.15.7; Plutarch, *Mar.* 5.4).

17. See Jo-Ann Shelton, *As the Romans Did: A Sourcebook in Roman Social History* (New York and Oxford: Oxford University Press, 1998), pp. 11-15.

18. See the inscriptions listed in Eilers's appendix (*Roman Patrons of Greek Cities*, pp. 191-268). Patronage of cities in Italy is the subject of the collection of essays in Kathryn Long and Tim Cornell, eds., *'Bread and Circuses': Euergetism and Municipal Patronage in Roman Italy* (New York and London: Routledge, 2003).

scured by the fact that the Roman writers who describe the practices of patronage typically refrain from using terms such as *patronus* and *cliens*. Instead, authors prefer to characterize patronage as "friendship" *(amicitia)*, even when the parties involved were hardly equals in terms of "status" and wealth. This is true of both individual and international partnerships. The Romans only very rarely referred to their relationships with so-called "client states" with the term *clientela;* instead, Romans designated subservient states with the more polite title "friends."[19] Does absence of the terminology of "patrons" and "clients" mean that Rome's conquered territories were not "clients"? In this context, we are reminded of sociologist Paul Veyne's light-hearted critique of the "philological convention . . . of seeking to interpret the realities of an epoch solely through the concepts and symbols of that epoch"; in that form of historiography, "one is not allowed to assert that the sky over Rome was blue and that the Romans had two arms and two legs, if chance has it that these facts are not mentioned in any of the ancient writings which have survived."[20]

The point of this brief review of the difficulty of defining patronage among those who specialize in the study of Roman antiquity is not to argue for one definition of patronage over the other. Both approaches have their strengths and their weaknesses, and both can helpfully illuminate the literature and practices of the Greco-Roman world. In point of fact, New Testament scholars are almost compelled to work with a sociological model of patronage when studying social relations within nascent Christianity, given the paucity of references in the extant writings of the earliest followers of Jesus to the terminology and rituals of Roman *patrocinium*. Many New Testament scholars might avoid some confusion, however, if they were more explicit about the model of patronage that informs their study.[21]

19. See John Rich, "Patronage and Interstate Relations in the Roman Republic," in Wallace-Hadrill, ed., *Patronage in Ancient Society,* pp. 117-35. In 1 Maccabees, for example, the Hasmoneans are frequently called "friends and allies" (φίλοι καὶ σύμμαχοι) of the Romans (1 Macc 8:20, 31; 14:40; 15:17).

20. *Bread and Circuses: Historical Sociology and Political Pluralism,* trans. Brian Pearce (London and New York: Penguin, 1990), p. 346; translation of *Le Pain et le cirque* (Paris: Éditions du Seuil, 1976).

21. A good example of this confusion may be found in Alicia Batten's otherwise instructive article "God in the Letter of James: Patron or Benefactor?" *NTS* 50 (2004): 257-72. Batten begins her review of patronage by stating that "evidence for patronage is found in many sites, including Gaul, Syria, and Palestine, including Galilee" (p. 258). She then alludes to Saller's work: "Saller states that ancient patronage consisted of three chief characteristics . . ." (p. 258). Saller does not, however, begin with a definition of "ancient patronage." He

I am not, therefore, objecting to the use of social-science models for the study of New Testament texts.[22] I am, however, raising questions about the efficacy of employing a particular model of patronage developed from the social-sciences in the attempt to describe the structure of Paul's theology. I would like to challenge the utility of this particular perspective on the framework of divine-human interaction in the Pauline epistles by exploring two aspects of patronage that are often neglected by those who claim that, for the apostle Paul, God is patron, Christ is broker, and human beings are clients. These two aspects are (1) the unbalanced and potentially exploitative nature of patron-client relationships and (2) the distinction between patronage as a social *relationship* and patronage as a social *system*.

1.1 Patronage and Exploitation

Given the fact that patronage is defined, according to the sociological model, as an asymmetrical relationship involving reciprocal exchange between parties of unequal status, there is an inherent potential for patron-client relations to become exploitative. Patron-client relations are not necessarily exploitative but, in Peter Garnsey's words, patronage is "a potentially unstable relationship which, because of the unequal bargaining position of the two parties, can easily slide into overt exploitation."[23]

Of course, the mythology of Roman patronage, as recounted in Dionysius of Halicarnassus's *Roman Antiquities,* emphasized the beneficent origins of the institution. Dionysius's comments about the establishment of patronage by Romulus are instructive, not so much for what they reveal about the historical origins of the institution, but for what they imply about the view of patronage among one member of the wealthy elite in the early first century BCE:

---

opens with a definition of patronage taken from the social sciences and then uses that definition to explore relationships among the Roman imperial elite in North Africa.

22. For two very different perspectives on the usefulness of models from the social sciences for the interpretation of NT texts, see the exchange between David G. Horrell, "Models and Methods in Social-Scientific Interpretation: A Response to Philip Esler," *JSNT* 78 (2000): 83-105; and Philip F. Esler, "Models in New Testament Interpretation: A Reply to David Horrell," *JSNT* 78 (2000): 107-13.

23. Peter Garnsey, *Famine and Food Supply in the Graeco-Roman World: Responses to Risk and Crisis* (Cambridge: Cambridge University Press, 1988), p. 58.

The purpose of this arrangement [i.e., πατρωνεία] was to avoid the dissension that arises in other cities through the abuse inflicted on the weak by their superiors. [Romulus] also entrusted the plebeians to the care of the patricians, allowing each of the common people to have a protector of his choice. In this he improved on an old Greek custom which the Thessalians long continued to observe, as initially did the Athenians. For they treated their dependants arrogantly, imposing on them duties that did not befit free men, whipping them for any failure to carry out their orders and generally maltreating them like bought slaves. . . . In contrast, Romulus not only selected a genial term to enhance the relationship by calling the protection of the poor and humble "patronage," but he also assigned each party obligations that were beneficial, organising the ties between them on a humane basis and one appropriate to citizens of the same community. . . . [It] is remarkable how intensely both parties competed with each other in their demonstrations of goodwill, each anxious to inconvenience their clients as little as possible, and accepted no gifts of money — a testimony to the self-discipline of their conduct with respect to any kind of pleasure and to their use of virtue, not fortune as the measure of happiness. (2.9.1-3; 10.4)

Dionysius's exalted etiology of patronage is a siren that has often tempted historians to evaluate patron-client relationships more positively than the reality behind the rhetoric would indicate. There is much to suggest that Roman and Greek authors were well aware of the manipulative nature of many patron-client relationships. In his study of patronage (or the lack thereof) in classical Athens, for example, Paul Millett contends that "patron-client relationships, inasmuch as they are generated by inequality and are a constraint on an individual's freedom, are inappropriate to democracy."[24] The Athenian *polis* appears to have developed numerous alternatives to patronage, including frequent financial disbursements from the state to citizens (in the form of payment for jury service, compensation for holding public office, recompense for attending assemblies, etc.) and "the maintenance of an equilibrium through reciprocal exchanges between people of similar status," such as friends and family members.[25]

Athens, of course, may have been anomalous in this regard, as it was in so many other ways. More significantly, the orators, playwrights, and satirists of Rome made great use of the shame associated with the role of the cli-

24. Millett, "Patronage and Its Avoidance," in Wallace-Hadrill, ed., *Patronage in Ancient Society*, p. 25.
25. Millett, "Patronage and Its Avoidance," p. 43.

ent.[26] Patrons were notorious for treating their clients rudely. Seneca, for instance, chastises patrons for the practice of shaming clients by failing to appear at the morning *salutatio:*

> How many patrons are there who drive away their clients by staying in bed when they call, or ignoring their presence, or being rude? How many are there who rush off on a pretense of urgent business after keeping the poor client waiting for a long time? How many avoid going through an atrium packed with clients and escape through a secret back door, as if it were not ruder to avoid a client than to turn him away? How many, still hung-over and half-asleep from last night's drinking, will yawn disdainfully at men who have interrupted their own sleep in order to wait upon his awakening, and will mumble a greeting through half-open lips, and will need to be reminded a thousand times of a client's name? (*Brev. vit.,* 14.4)

In a similar vein from a later time period, Pliny the Younger remarks on the impoliteness shown by a dinner host who serves fine wine and food to himself and a few guests but pitiable fare to his clients and freedmen (*Ep.,* 2.6.1-2; cf. Plutarch, *Quaest. conv.* 2.10.1). The sting of clientism is felt most strongly, however, in the writings of the satirists. No doubt the situations described by writers like Horace, Martial, and Juvenal are exaggerated for comedic effect; nevertheless, the genre of satire requires that the skewering of the behavior of patrons and clients have some basis in historical reality.[27] Here Gilbert Highet's memorable summation of the life of a client, perhaps sharpened by a cynicism that can only come from an intense reading of Juvenal's poems, captures well the demeaning existence experienced by many Roman clients:

> The life of a "client" was horrible: without self-respect, without hope of independence unless after long servitude, without any real leisure, and without any real work — a lifetime of standing in waiting-rooms and loitering in corridors and bowing to blind eyes and begging for petty favours, the friend of a man who was neither your equal nor your companion, the dependant of a man who treated you as a useless ornament, the flatterer of a man whom you hated and who usually knew it.[28]

---

26. On this, see Cynthia Damon, *The Mask of the Parasite: A Pathology of Roman Patronage* (Ann Arbor: University of Michigan Press, 1998).

27. See Damon, *The Mask of the Parasite,* pp. 190-91.

28. Gilbert Highet, *Juvenal the Satirist: A Study* (Oxford: Oxford University Press, 1961), p. 7.

For these reasons, a number of authors prefer to distinguish between Roman patronage and Greek benefaction as two different forms of social exchange. Stephan Joubert, in particular, has argued for a clear distinction between patronage and benefaction (or "euergetism") as two different but related forms of social exchange.[29] Joubert advocates such a differentiation in part because of terminological differences between *patrocinium* and εὐεργεσία and in part because of his claim that the former was inherently more unbalanced than the latter. Joubert writes:

> Regarding its *social nature,* Roman patronage also differed from benefaction, particularly in terms of the status differentials between patrons and clients, which were emphasised further by social exchanges. Patrons remained in the superior position, even if they failed to reciprocate their clients' public bestowals of loyalty and honour. Return gifts from clients did not place patrons in a submissive position.[30]

Because of his heavy reliance upon Seneca's *De Beneficiis* to frame his conceptual categories, Joubert may be guilty of idealizing Greek benefaction in order to establish a sharp contrast between euergetism and patronage.[31] Moreover, Joubert is also not always clear in maintaining the distinction for which he argues. For example, in describing Pliny the Younger's patronage of cities, Joubert writes, "Informally, a number of *benefactors* who did not possess the status of *patron,* nevertheless, conferred *benefactions* on communities, thus unofficially acting out the role of *patrons.*"[32] The confusion of this sentence results, I would suggest, from a lack of clarity about whether patronage is to be defined sociologically or institutionally. Not every bene-

---

29. Joubert, "One Form of Social Exchange or Two? 'Euergetism,' Patronage, and Testament Studies," *BTB* 31 (2001): 17-25; so also Batten, "God in the Letter of James," pp. 257-72.

30. Joubert, *Paul as Benefactor: Reciprocity, Strategy, and Theological Reflection in Paul's Collection,* WUNT II/124 (Tübingen: Mohr Siebeck, 2000), p. 67. It is unclear, however, that "benefactors" were placed in a "submissive position" upon receiving acclaim for their gifts. This flawed assumption stands at the heart of Joubert's larger argument that Paul was placed in the debt of the Jerusalem church because of Jerusalem's acknowledgement of Paul's Torah-free mission to the Gentiles.

31. Seneca, after all, writes in Latin, so it is not entirely clear that he is not describing Roman patronage. So Zeba A. Crook, *Reconceptualising Conversion: Patronage, Loyalty, and Conversion in the Religions of the Ancient Mediterranean,* BZNW 130 (Berlin and New York: Walter de Gruyter, 2004), p. 62.

32. Joubert, *Paul as Benefactor,* p. 71; for this critique, see also Crook, *Reconceptualising Conversion,* p. 64.

faction bestowed upon a municipality or an individual is an example of *patrocinium;* while every patron was in some sense a benefactor, not every benefactor was a patron. I am inclined, therefore, to agree with Zeba Crook's correction that Greek benefaction and Roman patronage were slightly different but essentially overlapping forms of "general reciprocity."[33] Nevertheless, Joubert's point that Roman patronage could easily become a means of social control (or worse) is well-taken. Given the potentially exploitative nature of many patron-client relationships in the Greco-Roman world, we should pause before too readily utilizing patronage as a model for Pauline theology, even if patronage is defined in sociological terms.[34]

1.2 *Patronage as a Social System*

I turn now to a second question regarding the usefulness of applying a model of patron-broker-client relations to Paul's understanding of God, Christ, and humanity — namely, the distinction between patronage as a relation and patronage as a system. Too often neglected in the application of the sociology of patronage to the Pauline epistles is an important contribution to the discussion of patronage made by Terry Johnson and Chris Dandeker. These authors penned an essay that punctuates the collection of articles published in *Patronage in Ancient Society* — a volume given entirely to the work of classicists, with the singular exception being the concluding piece by sociologists Johnson and Dandeker.[35]

Most studies of patronage in the Greco-Roman world focus rather narrowly on relations between individuals. Yet when patronage is defined

---

33. Crook, *Reconceptualising Conversion,* pp. 60-66. Joubert is also incorrect when he states, "Greeks in general did not understand the Roman rule over them as patrocinium (as the Romans did)." The epigraphical evidence catalogued by Eilers *(Roman Patrons of Greek Cities)* calls this claim into question.

34. I am not suggesting that Paul *could not* have employed a model of patronage for divine-human relations simply because human patronal relations were potentially exploitative. Slavery was often a far more abusive and demeaning social relation in Greco-Roman antiquity than patronage, yet that did not stop Paul from identifying himself as "slave of Jesus Christ" (Rom 1:1; Gal 1:10) or the members of his churches as "slaves" of Christ (1 Cor 7:22). I am simply suggesting that we ought to consider the potentially exploitative nature of patronal relations before we apply that model to divine-human relations in Paul, given other problems with this model that I will address below.

35. "Patronage: Relation and System," in Wallace-Hadrill, ed., *Patronage in Ancient Society,* pp. 219-41.

as a dyadic, vertical relationship of reciprocal exchange, any number of social interactions can be described through this particular model. This overly broad definition may be seen in the brief description of patronage offered by anthropologist Anton Blok: "Patronage is a model or analytic construct which the social scientist applies in order to understand and explain a range of different social relationships: father-son, God-man, saint-devotee, godfather-godchild, lord-vassal, landlord-tenant, politician-voter, professor-assistant, and so forth."[36] As is seen in the difficulties of defining patronage in sociological terms, this approach is potentially far too broad to provide useful descriptive categories. Highlighting the divide between sociological and institutional definitions of patronage, Johnson and Dandeker draw a distinction between studies of patronage that work on a relational level and those that understand patronage as a larger network of such relations:

> The origins of this divide, between those who see patronage as a universal phenomenon and those who identify it as an historically specific structure, can be found . . . in a common failure to distinguish between two levels of the analysis of patronage. . . . The distinction to which we draw attention is that between patronage, defined as *a particular kind of relationship* and patronage as a *system of relationships*. Patronage, it is suggested, can be understood as either a *social relationship* or a *social system*. In the first and most common case, patronage is defined as an elementary or cell structure of social life with discrete, yet universal, characteristics. In the second, patronage is identified as a system of such relations, constituting a social mechanism which functions strategically in the reproduction of the major social institutions of power.[37]

This is an important and often overlooked distinction. New Testament scholars who apply a socio-scientific model of patron-client-broker relations to describe divine-human interaction in the Pauline epistles invariably understand patronage as a relationship. God functions as patron, Christ as broker, and humanity as the clients in this triadic relationship. Such analysis, however, fails sufficiently to probe the historical and theological implications of the claim that God is Paul's patron. First, viewing patronage in the Pauline epistles solely as a relation not only employs a concept of patronage

---

36. Anton Blok, "Variations in Patronage," *Sociologische Gids* 16 (1969): 366; cited in Neyrey, *Render to God*, 249.

37. Johnson and Dandeker, "Patronage: Relation and System," pp. 220-21.

that is too general to offer useful descriptive categories. This approach also, ironically, serves to dehistoricize the study of social and theological relationships within the Pauline epistles. As Johnson and Dandeker point out, "The relational concept of patronage has the effect of tearing the cell-relationship of patron-client out of its historical and social conditions of existence, depriving the analyst of any possibility of answering the most important questions."[38] Thus, scholars who apply a model of patronage to Paul's theology with the hope of understanding that theology within its socio-cultural context actually achieve the opposite result: a transcultural model of patronage is applied to the structure of divine-human interaction in the Pauline epistle in such a way that those relational dynamics are necessarily abstracted from their socio-cultural environment.

More importantly, however, it becomes readily apparent that Johnson and Dandeker's call for understanding patronage as a *social system* renders the patron-broker-client model problematic when it is applied to the God-Christ-humanity relationship in the Pauline epistles. Given the elastic nature of sociological definitions of patronage (which potentially cover interactions as diverse as *patrocinium,* marriage, tenancy, and schooling), patronage should be understood not as a type of relationship but as "a complex and hierarchically organised series of chains of such relationships."[39] A system of patronage implies competition for the distribution of resources among numerous patrons, brokers, and clients. From a historical viewpoint, Johnson and Dandeker note the following:

> [O]nce we recognise that a complex network of [patron-client relations] can function as the prime mechanism in the allocation of scarce resources and the dominant means of legitimising the social order, then we can also understand that there have existed societies in which such a system has played a strategic role in the maintenance and reproduction of power relations.[40]

Such a system clearly existed in the Roman Empire, which is partly why patronage has been such a useful tool for studying socioeconomic relationships within the Pauline churches, particularly at Corinth. Yet when this patronage model is abstracted from its socio-historical context and applied as a framework for Paul's theology, at least two serious problems arise.

38. Johnson and Dandeker, "Patronage: Relation and System," p. 222.
39. Johnson and Dandeker, "Patronage: Relation and System," p. 223.
40. Johnson and Dandeker, "Patronage: Relation and System," p. 223.

First, for the apostle Paul, believers do not compete with one another or outsiders for resources distributed by any number of divine patrons, for "there is one God, the Father, from whom are all things and for whom we exist, and one Lord, Jesus Christ, through whom are all things and through whom we exist" (1 Cor 8:6). The God who commissioned Paul as apostle to the Gentiles, the God to whom Paul prays, the God who raised Jesus from the dead, the faithful God who calls believers "into the fellowship of his Son, Jesus Christ our Lord" (1 Cor 1:9) — this God and the actions of this God are axiomatic for Paul's mission and theology.[41] That this God is one is a fundamental assumption that figures prominently in Paul's discussions of meat offered to idols in 1 Cor 8:1–11:1 and in Paul's articulation, in the opening chapters of Romans, of a gospel that reveals the righteousness of God for all humanity, both Jews and Gentiles, on the same basis of faith (Rom 1:17–3:31; cf. Gal 3:20). Even where the oneness of God is not directly invoked to warrant theological claims, it is an assumption that grounds Paul's entire theological framework.[42] While Paul may acknowledge the existence of other "so-called" gods and lords (1 Cor 8:4-5), including beings such as Satan, demons (1 Cor 10:20-21), and perhaps the powers and rulers of this age (Rom 8:38-39; 1 Cor 2:6-8; cf. Col 1:16; 2:15) who stand in opposition to God's purposes for the cosmos, these anti-God forces certainly do not function as "patrons" within Paul's apocalyptic worldview. Indeed, exactly the opposite is the case. Satan, for example, is involved in the destruction of the flesh (1 Cor 5:5), the temptation and outwitting of believers (1 Cor 7:5; 2 Cor 2:11; 11:4), the frustration of Paul's missionary ventures (1 Thess 2:18), and the personal torment that Paul himself faces through his "thorn in the flesh" (2 Cor 12:7). Even when compared with the exploitation experienced by many human clients at the hands of their human patrons, these cosmic anti-God forces hardly qualify as patrons from whom humans may seek resources: an adversary is not a patron by any definition. Thus, Paul's christological monotheism means that patronage, if it is applied to the structure of divine-human interaction in the Pauline epistles, cannot be understood as part of a system of social rela-

41. See James D. G. Dunn, *The Theology of Paul the Apostle* (Grand Rapids: Eerdmans, 1997), pp. 28-50.

42. On monotheism in Paul and in the ancient world, see Loren T. Stuckenbruck and Wendy E. S. North, eds., *Early Jewish and Christian Monotheism,* ECC (London and New York: T&T Clark, 2004); and Carey C. Newman, James R. Davila, and Gladys S. Lewis, eds., *The Jewish Roots of Christological Monotheism: Papers from the St. Andrews Conference on the Historical Origins of the Worship of Jesus,* JSJSup 63 (Leiden: Brill, 1999).

tions in which God functions as one patron among many.[43] For Paul, God is one and there is no other.

A second reason that this perspective on patronage as a *social system* renders the patron-broker-client model problematic when it is applied to God-Christ-humanity in the Pauline epistles is that patronage as a *social system* depends upon competition for a limited number of goods. As Andrew Wallace-Hadrill points out in a discussion of how a Roman patron might have delivered subsidies to numerous clients:

> [The] power of the patron may not derive from the ability to secure benefits for all who ask, but from the sheer impossibility of securing them for any but a minority. The secret of the game is the manipulation of scarce resources: where all need resources that are in short supply, it is easier for the patrons to secure control of the routes of access, so rendering access impossible except through a patron.[44]

The patron establishes power because of his or her ability to secure and distribute resources in an economy of limited good. Clients may be drawn to patrons for any number of reasons, but chief among them is the potential to gain from patrons access to these scarce resources, sometimes at the expense of, and in competition with, other (potential) clients. In a society like the Roman Empire, where patronage functioned as an important social institution, the system of patronage itself competed with other social institutions in the allocation of resources through networks of relationships based on power (including, at times, the state and the household). Indeed, in this system of patronage, competition is a crucial factor. "Where client loyalty is voluntary, patronage remains a highly fluid structure, adapted to change, driven by the twin motors of patron competition and client choice."[45] Cli-

43. In a very different context, John Rich makes a similar suggestion with respect to the tendency of the Romans to avoid calling subservient states "clients": "I would suggest that the terminology [of patronage] may have been avoided because it was only felt appropriate in a world where there could be a multiplicity of patrons. This was the case within the state, where a patron might help his clients against other patrons or in their dealings with the government, and in an international community like that of the Gallic tribes, but *if Rome was the patron there could be no other*. The states under the hegemony were formally known as their friends and allies. When Romans spoke of political realities, they used the language of empire" ("Patronage and Interstate Relations," p. 127; emphasis added).

44. Wallace-Hadrill, "Patronage in Roman Society: From Republic to Empire," in Wallace-Hadrill, ed., *Patronage in Ancient Society*, p. 73.

45. Johnson and Dandeker, "Patronage: Relation and System," p. 228.

ents themselves served as resources to be acquired, redistributed, and perhaps discarded by brokers and patrons who sought the honor and acclaim associated with developing a large retinue of followers.

From this it should be clear that patronage as a social system is a model that cannot fit the framework of Paul's theology, for Paul does not conceive of the economy of God as an economy of limited good. To cite with slightly different accent the creedal affirmation mentioned above: "there is one God, the Father, *from whom are all things* and for whom we exist, and one Lord, Jesus Christ, *through whom are all things* and through whom we exist" (1 Cor 8:6). Similarly, when Paul reaches the climax of his complex reflection on God's faithfulness to God's promises in spite of Israel's rejection of the gospel in Romans 9–11, the apostle simply declaims, "Oh, the depth of the wealth and the wisdom and the knowledge of God. . . . For from him and through him and to him are *all things*" (Rom 11:33, 36). There is no end to the benefits and resources available from God, for God is the origin and the giver of all things. This point is so axiomatic for the apostle Paul that it hardly needs demonstrating. While the economy of patronage is characterized by the attempt to deal with a scarcity of resources, the economy of God abounds (περισσεύω) with grace (Rom 5:15), hope (Rom 15:13), love (1 Thess 3:12), consolation (2 Cor 1:5), and thanksgiving — all to the glory of God (2 Cor 4:15).

Thus, claims that God serves as patron, Christ as broker, and human beings as clients in the Pauline epistles not only ignore the fact that God does not, from Paul's perspective, compete with other patrons for the accumulation of honor. These claims also fail to recognize that God's economy is an economy of abundance and blessing, rather than an economy of limited good. Applications of a patron-broker-client model to the structure of Paul's theology, therefore, are more problematic than helpful. A sociological definition of patronage is particularly useful when it is possible to identify an intricate network of power relationships based on the distribution of scarce resources. Yet this model simply does not fit Paul's understanding of God.[46]

---

46. The present essay focuses on Paul's own theologizing. An interesting investigation, although one far beyond the scope of the present essay, would focus on questions of if and to what extent Paul's theological discourse was read with reference to patronage by his earliest interpreters. I suspect we would find a similar reticence to speak as God as "patron" among the Apostolic Fathers, although perhaps for different reasons.

2. Paul's Opposition to Patronage in the Corinthian Correspondence

In this final section of the essay, I would like to highlight the extent to which Paul tends to avoid the terminology and structure of patronal relationships in his discussions of both human and divine activity. "Patron" (πάτρων), "client" (πελάτης), and "patronage" (πατρωνεία) were all words readily available in Paul's own cultural context, and these are terms that he might have applied metaphorically to describe the relationship between God and the people of God.[47] Yet Paul does not avail himself of this metaphor. With the exception of Paul's reference to Phoebe as προστάτις in Rom 16:2, the language of patronage is absent from the Pauline epistles.[48] This fact alone should be taken into account when considering patronage as a potential model for Paul's theology. While socio-scientific methods can be valuable in the study of ancient texts, these methods should be tested against the evidence of the ancient texts themselves. Even if patronage is defined broadly in terms borrowed from the social-sciences, it is still surprising that the terminology of the Roman patronage system does not figure at all in Paul's de-

47. Along with Dionysius of Halicarnassus, Plutarch also provides an indication that, while *patrocinium*/πατρωνεία may have been a distinctively Roman social institution, the Greeks knew of it; see *Fort. Rom.*, 323: καὶ πελάτης τις εἶχεν αὐτήν, οὓς κλιέντης ʿΡωμαῖοι καλοῦσιν ("and a certain πελάτης, whom the Romans call *clientes,* had her [as a wife])"; cf. *Quaest. conv.* 649; *Rom.* 13.8.

48. I cannot accept Steven Friesen's claim that προστάτις in Rom 16:2 cannot mean "patron" or "benefactor" because "προστάτις is not the normal term for a benefactor, and Paul asks the Romans to help her when she arrives, which would be inappropriate for a client (Paul) to do on behalf of his benefactor" ("Poverty in Pauline Studies: Beyond the So-called New Consensus," *JSNT* 26 [2004]: 355). First, the masculine προστάτης is used as a term for a benefactor (see LSJ 1526; *IG* II² 1369, 4747; *IGR* 1.5.1172). Plutarch himself points out that those whom the foreigners call προστάτης the Romans call Πάτρωνά (*Rom.* 13.3-4). Second, I am not aware of any evidence to suggest it would be inappropriate for a "client" to ask for a favor on behalf of a patron, let alone a "benefactor." Indeed, according to Dionysius of Halicarnassus's account of the origins of patronage, clients were regularly expected to perform services on behalf of their patrons, including paying for dowries for the marriages of the daughters of patrons, paying ransom if someone in the patron's family was kidnapped, and paying public fines incurred by their patrons. Perhaps the best explanation for the use of this unusual term from the Roman patronage system in this context is Peter Lampe's: "I am able to interpret this in no other way than to say that Paul, who was a Jew for the Jews and a Greek for the Greek, now becomes a Roman for the Romans" (*From Paul to Valentinus: Christians at Rome in the First Two Centuries,* trans. Michael Steinhauser [Minneapolis: Fortress, 2003], p. 164). One wonders also if Paul endorses Phoebe in such strong terms because her gender would have diminished her status from the perspective of some members of the Roman churches.

scriptions of God's identity and activity, particularly given the availability of the metaphor in Paul's cultural context.[49] Paul's primary metaphor for God is not "patron" but "father." While we should not assume that patronage and kinship are always mutually exclusive, I would like to conclude by suggesting that Paul's consistent identification of "God our Father" (Rom 1:7; 1 Cor 1:3; 2 Cor 1:2; Gal 1:3; Phil 1:2; Phlm 3) functions to frame the identity and character of God outside the Greco-Roman patronage system.[50]

It has often been noted that vertical relationships of patronage, defined sociologically, stand in tension with, and perhaps undermine, other forms of horizontal communal organization, such as the family, the village, and the (democratic) state.[51] The power of patronage is found in the ability of the system to distribute goods and services to some but not all, and the vertical ties created between patrons and clients subvert the potential for solidarity between those of low status. As Peter Garnsey and Greg Woolf state, "Patronage provides an alternative or a supplement to reciprocity within kinship groups between status equals."[52]

In Paul's discussions of the pecuniary practices of the churches of his mission, the apostle consistently, and sometimes emphatically, discourages the establishment of "patronage relationships." As a heuristic example, let us

49. That said, I am not aware of a single instance in the literature of the Greco-Roman world where a god is called *patronus* or πάτρων. No texts of this sort, for example, are cited in Neyrey, "God, Benefactor and Patron," pp. 465-92.

50. According to the ideology of patronage, *patroni* could function as "fathers" for their clients. Indeed, the Latin words *patron* and *patrician* are derived from the same root as the word *pater*. Dionysius of Halicarnassus points out that Roman patricians were supposed to do for their plebeians what "fathers do for their sons with regard both to money and to the contracts that are related to money" (*Rom. Ant.* 2.10.1). In the inscriptional record, too, kinship and patronage are occasionally connected (cf. *Syll*³ 776, where Marcus Agrippa is called συγγενὴς καὶ πάτρων τῆς πόλεως). However, using the metaphor of God as father would not necessarily evoke God as patron, particularly given the absence of other contextual clues and the prominence of fatherhood imagery for God in the Old Testament, which more readily accounts for Paul's terminology. One place where there might be an interesting connection between patronal and paternal identity would be the image of the emperor; see, e.g., Meret Strothmann, *Augustus — Vater der res publica: Zur Funktion der drei Begriffe* restitutio, saeculum, pater patriae *im augusteischen Principat* (Stuttgart: Franz Steiner, 2000), pp. 72-90, 191-99; Beth Severy, *Augustus and the Family at the Birth of the Roman Empire* (New York: Routledge, 2003), pp. 158-86.

51. Eisenstadt and Roniger, *Patrons, Clients, and Friends,* p. 50; Peter Garnsey and Greg Woolf, "Patronage of the Rural Poor in the Roman World," in Wallace-Hadrill, ed., *Patronage in Ancient Society,* pp. 155-66.

52. Garnsey and Woolf, "Patronage of the Rural Poor," p. 157.

briefly examine some issues from the Corinthian correspondence that illustrate this point. These letters are instructive for at least two reasons: first, because, as inhabitants of a Roman colony, the members of the Corinthian house churches might have been more familiar with the social institution known as *patrocinium;* and second, because economic matters figure prominently in Paul's exchanges with the Corinthians.

2.1 Paul's Apostolic Monetary Policy

Paul was the founder of the Corinthian congregation — their "father through the Gospel," as he describes himself in 1 Cor 4:15. Yet in 1 Cor 9:1-23, in the context of a longer discussion about the propriety of eating meat sacrificed to idols (1 Cor 8:1–11:1), Paul provides a defense (ἀπολογία, 9:3) of his decision to refuse financial support from the Corinthians for his apostolic service. It appears that other apostles were taking advantage of their right (ἐξουσία) to receive provisions from the church (9:12), possibly appealing to a dominical tradition that "those who proclaim the gospel should receive their living from the gospel" (9:14; cf. Matt 10:9-10; Luke 10:7). Paul acknowledges that he, too, possesses this "right," yet he refuses to accept support from the church, lest he be denied his reason for boasting (1 Cor 9:15).

In its present literary context, this discussion forms an important excursus in Paul's encouragement for the "enlightened" among the Corinthian believers to forego their "right" (8:9) to consume meat offered to idols out of consideration for the weak (8:1-13): just as Paul is willing to relinquish his apostolic rights by making the gospel available free of charge, so also should those Corinthian believers who possess no qualms about eating meat refrain from this practice due to a concern for "the weak." Yet this excursus also betrays important information about Paul's financial policy of refusing to request or receive compensation for his apostolic activity from a church in which he was actively working to establish a mission. Instead of accepting the patronage of the (relatively) wealthy among the Corinthian congregation, Paul and his associates elected to support themselves by working with their own hands, as he reminds his readers in 1 Cor 4:12 (cf. 1 Thess 2:9). Paul's motivations for this strategy stem from a desire to avoid placing any obstacle in the way of the gospel (1 Cor 9:12), particularly the impediment of appearing to charge for the gospel (9:18).

Confusion about these matters may have played an important role in the dust-up that ensued upon Paul's second and unexpected visit to Corinth, when the apostle asked the Corinthians for a "double benefit" (δευτέραν χάριν, 2 Cor 1:15). By this term Paul likely intended for the Corinthians to contribute twice to the monetary collection that he was presently organizing for the poor among the saints in Jerusalem.[53] Yet this request, particularly if a perception of dishonor was engendered by Paul's earlier refusal to accept financial support from the Corinthians during his residency in their city, sparked flames of dissension between apostle and congregation. Later, in 2 Cor 11:7-12 and 12:13-18, Paul twice defends himself for his decision to proclaim the gospel free of charge, without accepting the support of the Corinthians. We might imagine Paul's opponents in Corinth (those whom he sarcastically calls "super-apostles," 2 Cor 11:5; 12:11) leveling a charge like this against Paul:

> How can you Corinthians entrust your money to a fickle man like Paul? He boasts about proclaiming the good news free of charge, about not becoming your client. Yet he disobeys the command of Jesus that the worker should receive his wages. Moreover, despite the shame you suffered through his denial of your opportunity to support his mission in Corinth, he did become a client of churches in Macedonia by accepting their support. Then he showed up on your doorstep during his second visit asking you to pay for his travels, when he had refused your gracious benefactions while he was living among you. Now, after all this, he has sent representatives from Macedonia to collect money from you! And for his own personal profit!

From his perspective, however, Paul was simply being consistent in his desire not to burden his churches (1 Thess 2:9) and not to cultivate the perception that he was profiting from the gospel (1 Cor 9:18) while working to establish the congregations of his Gentile mission. That his policy also allowed him to avoid becoming a client to wealthy patrons in the Corinthian church is unstated but implied. Thus, Paul's own decisions regarding the financial support of his ministry by the Corinthians appear to have been shaped, at least in part, in response to his desire to minimize vertical relationships of patronage between apostle and church.

---

53. So Gordon Fee, "CHARIS in 2 Corinthians 1:15: Apostolic Parousia and Paul-Corinth Chronology," *NTS* 24 (1977): 533-38.

2.2 *Divisions at the Lord's Supper*

According to Paul in 1 Cor 11:17-34, divisions marked the Corinthian church's celebration of the Lord's Supper. Some members of the community — presumably the wealthier and those with more leisure time — were arriving at the meal earlier, devouring much of the food and drink, and shaming the "have nots" (11:21-22). Gerd Theissen and others have argued that these factions resulted from the practice of celebrating the Lord's Supper in ways consistent with the practices and values of the Greco-Roman patronage system.[54] Often during banquets hosted by patrons, true friends and privileged guests of the patron would receive the choice wine and the most honored seats, whereas the patron's clients would be treated with contempt.[55] Paul challenges these practices in Corinth by refusing to commend the Corinthians (11:22), by reminding them that their celebration of the Lord's Supper is rooted in the narrative of Jesus' self-giving love for others (11:23-26), by warning them that those who eat and drink without discerning "the body" (of believers) risk judgment (11:27-32), and by encouraging them to wait for one another when gathering for the meal (11:33). Paul does not want those observing the Lord's Supper at Corinth to exemplify the practices and values of Roman patronage. Instead, he encourages the Corinthians to recognize that unless the community embodies a concern for others, particularly the poor, modeled on the self-giving love of Jesus Christ, it cannot rightly proclaim the Lord's death. This community should order its dining practices in light of the economy of God — an economy that welcomes the poor to share in the abundance of the table of the Lord.

2.3 *The Collection for the Saints*

One economic endeavor of utmost importance for the apostle Paul was the monetary collection that he organized among the Gentile congregations of his mission for the poor among the believing community in Jerusalem. Paul appears to have spent a considerable amount of time and energy in organiz-

54. Theissen, "Social Integration and Sacramental Activity: An Analysis of 1 Cor. 11:17-34," in *The Social Setting of Pauline Christianity: Essays on Corinth*, ed. John H. Schütz (Philadelphia: Augsburg Fortress, 1982), pp. 145-74.

55. Pliny, *Ep.* 2.6; Martial, *Epig.* 1.20; 3.60; Juvenal, *Sat.* 5. For the practice of members of a voluntary association with higher rank receiving more food at community gatherings, see the Lanuvium inscription at *ILS* II/2, 7212.

ing the relief fund, as is seen in his comments about the project in 1 Cor 16:1-4; 2 Cor 8:1–9:15; and Rom 15:25-32. Gathering the contribution in Corinth was no easy task for Paul and his associates, in large part due to the tensions between Paul and the Corinthians related to the economic matters that were discussed above. In 1 Cor 16:1-4, Paul provides advice on fundraising procedures — advice that reflects his confidence that the Corinthians will continue their support of the fund. Moreover, in 1 Cor 16:2, Paul recommends that each member of the Corinthian congregation (ἕκαστος ὑμῶν) donate to the fund whatever he or she is able to offer, an indication that support of the collection was not merely the responsibility of the few (relatively) wealthy members of the community like an Erastus or a Gaius.

By the time Paul writes 2 Cor 8:1–9:15, however, much water has passed under the bridge: Paul and the church have experienced a serious conflict, probably due in part to disputes about pecuniary matters — although their relationship has been restored by Paul's "letter of tears" and the Corinthians' favorable response to it (see 2 Cor 1:12–2:11; 7:2-16). In 2 Corinthians 8–9, then, Paul undertakes a cautious encouragement for the Corinthians to adopt a reoriented theological conception of the collection and so resume their participation in the offering. In this section, Paul adopts a startling variety of rhetorical appeals to accomplish this aim:

(1) he emphasizes the example of the Macedonians, who have generously contributed to the fund, in spite of their deep poverty (8:1-6);

(2) he highlights the paradigmatic χάρις (grace) of the Lord Jesus Christ, "who became poor for your sakes, although he was rich, so that by his poverty you might become rich" (8:9);

(3) he draws upon the principle of ἰσότης (equality), not merely a philosophical concept for Paul but a notion deeply rooted in the narrative of God's gracious provision of manna to the Israelites in the wilderness (8:13-15);

(4) he suggests that both he and the Corinthians will be shamed if believers come from Macedonia to Corinth and find the undertaking unfinished (9:1-5);

(5) he paints an agricultural metaphor to suggest that giving to the collection is like sowing seed, a metaphor that emphasizes the generative activity of God in the act of human beneficence (9:6-10); and,

(6) he punctuates this appeal by indicating that true generosity results in thanksgiving and praise to God, the one from whom all benefactions ultimately originate (9:11-15).

Moreover, as I have argued elsewhere, a number of linguistic expressions in Paul's rhetoric depict the collection in cultic terms (1 Cor 16:1-2; 2 Cor 8:6, 11-12; 9:12; Rom 15:16, 27-28). In metaphorically framing the activity of collecting money for the poor among the saints as an act of cultic worship, Paul underscores the point that the fulfillment of mutual obligations within the Christian community results in praise, not to human donors, as the dominant ideology of patronage or euergetism would have suggested, but to God, the one from whom all benefactions come. As Paul outlines in 2 Cor 9:14-15, even the very human action of raising money for those in material need originates in ἡ χάρις τοῦ θεοῦ (the grace of God) and will eventuate in χάρις τῷ θεῷ (thanks to God) for his inexpressible gift.[56] Paul's strategy in organizing the collection for Jerusalem, therefore, also bears witness to the apostle's desire to minimize patronal relationships among the various members of his churches and even between the congregations of his mission and the Christ-believing community in Jerusalem.

We might wonder, then, whether the Paul who appears to extend much effort to minimize patronage among his readers would have found patronage to be an appropriate model for divine-human relations. Paul's explicit discussions of pecuniary matters in the Corinthian correspondence unfailingly oppose the institution of exploitative and agonistic economic practices within the community of "those who are being saved" (1 Cor 1:18). Paul's appeals are grounded in a diverse array of theological warrants. Yet we should not abstract the explicit warrants that Paul offers in his considerations of the financial practices of his communities from the larger contexts in which these statements are embedded.

2.4 Fictive Kinship and "God Our Father"

One additional way that Paul encourages the readers of his letters to embody horizontal relationships of reciprocal exchange, as opposed to vertical relationships of patronage and power, is through the rhetoric of fictive kinship. If it is correct that patronage undermines kinship, perhaps we should also interpret the frequent usage of familial metaphors in Paul's letters as an invitation for readers to understand their corporate identity and to structure their common life in ways that challenge the Roman patronage system.

56. David J. Downs, *The Offering of the Gentiles: Paul's Collection for Jerusalem in Its Chronological, Cultural, and Cultic Contexts*, WUNT II/248 (Tübingen: Mohr Siebeck, 2008).

The language of fictive siblingship is a regular feature of the Pauline epistles, though it occurs with more frequency in 1 Corinthians than in any other letter except 1 Thessalonians.[57] In addressing and identifying his readers as "brothers and sisters," Paul draws upon ideals and assumptions about family life in the Greco-Roman world, including goodwill, solidarity, and friendship between siblings.[58] Two recent studies of familial terminology in Paul's writings, however, have suggested that siblingship metaphors do not necessarily suggest an egalitarian perspective, since relationships among siblings (particularly brothers) in the Greco-Roman world were often understood to represent hierarchies of status and seniority.[59] This is a helpful corrective. Yet the fact that sibling relationships *could* be hierarchical does not diminish the claim that Paul's rhetoric of fictive kinship challenges the ideology of patronage. We must attend first to the *function* of the metaphors within their rhetorical contexts, and it does not appear that ἀδελφός (literally "brother," but in the plural often translated "brothers and sisters") is used in 1–2 Corinthians to promote hierarchical relationships within the congregation.[60] In fact, when Paul confronts the church in 1 Cor 6:1-11 for allowing a "brother" to take a "brother" before a court of unbelievers, the familial terminology in that context seems to challenge the Corinthians to view their disputes as internal family matters rather than issues for adjudication in public courts known for serving the interests of the elite.[61] As we have seen, the dangers of the patronage system lie in its potential to exploit the weak and to promote competition in the place of communal solidarity. Paul's siblingship metaphors in 1 Corinthians (and elsewhere; see Phlm 16) have exactly the opposite effect: this community of brothers and sisters is

57. Paul uses the word ἀδελφός 39 times in 1 Corinthians, 20 of which usages occur in the vocative address ἀδελφοί: 1:10, 11, 26; 2:1; 3:1; 4:6; 7:24, 29; 10:1; 11:33; 12:1; 14:6, 20, 26, 39; 15:1, 31, 50, 58; 16:15. The feminine ἀδελφή is found in 1 Cor 7:15 and 9:5. For a statistical summary of this terminology in the NT letters, see Reidar Aasgaard, '*My Beloved Brothers and Sisters!': Christian Siblingship in Paul,* ECC, JSNTSup 265 (London: T&T Clark, 2004), pp. 313-14.

58. Cf. Plutarch, *Frat. Amor.* 484-91.

59. See Trevor Burke, *Family Matters: A Socio-Historical Study of Kinship Metaphors in 1 Thessalonians,* JSNTSup 247 (London: T&T Clark, 2003), pp. 96-127; Aasgaard, '*My Beloved Brothers and Sisters!',* pp. 75-77.

60. Part of the issue stems from the terminology of "hierarchy" and "egalitarian." Paul does not view the church as an egalitarian institution, if that term is intended to connote an absence of structure and leadership. Paul himself uses parental metaphors to remind and convince his readers of his own apostolic authority (1 Cor 3:1-2; 4:15; 2 Cor 12:14).

61. Chow, *Patronage and Power,* pp. 123-30.

called to embody a cruciform gospel by exercising concern for the weak among their number and by eliminating the dissension that stems from an inadequate appreciation of the cross.

Finally, to bring the matter back to Paul's *theo*logy, the fictive siblingship established through Paul's recurrent use of the ἀδελφοί terminology in the Corinthian correspondence finds its meaning only as part of a larger web of familial language in these letters: (1) believers in Corinth as well as those with Paul in Ephesus (1 Cor 16:11, 20), those who work on behalf of the Pauline mission (2 Cor 1:1; 2:13; 8:18, 22), and those in Macedonia (11:9) are all "brothers and sisters"; (2) Paul is both the father of the Corinthian church (1 Cor 4:15; 2 Cor 6:13; 12:14) and its mother, if with Beverly Gaventa we take the reference to the apostle's giving the Corinthians milk to drink in 1 Cor 3:1-2 as a metaphor for nursing;[62] (3) Jesus is the Son of the faithful God (1 Cor 1:9; 15:28; 2 Cor 1:19); (4) and God is called "our Father" (1 Cor 1:3; 2 Cor 1:2), "the Father" (1 Cor 8:6; 15:24), "the Father of our Lord Jesus Christ" (2 Cor 1:3; 11:31), and "the Father of mercies" (2 Cor 1:3). Moreover, Paul's creative citation of 2 Sam 7:14 in 2 Cor 6:18 ("I will be a father to you, and you shall be my sons and daughters") also affirms the notion that believers are sons and daughters of God their Father. Paul's kinship metaphors in 1–2 Corinthians, therefore, create an overlapping network of family relationships, and at the center of this network stands God the Father, the one "from whom all things come" (1 Cor 8:6). This God is also the Father whose eschatological purposes for creation will be fulfilled when all things are put in subjection under him (1 Cor 15:24-28). Indeed, the references to God as Father in 1 Cor 8:6 and 15:24 highlight God's activity at the beginning and end of the story of creation. As Marianne Meye Thompson comments:

> That God is Father and Jesus is the Son of the Father are not abstract statements but, rather, find their proper place in the narrative of God's faithfulness to Israel, which comes to its climax when, "at the right time, God sent forth his Son." Because of the particularity of the biblical narrative, and of Jesus' relationship to God as Father, any abstraction of the language from the narrative itself runs the risk of losing sight of the promise of God's faithfulness and God's mercy. Father will become a dysfunctional metaphor if we insist on the form of the term without lodging it in the biblical narrative of God's faithfulness, care, and provision, and if we ab-

---

62. Beverly Roberts Gaventa, *Our Mother Saint Paul* (Louisville: Westminster John Knox, 2007), pp. 41-50.

stract it from the particular promises made to and through Jesus, the Son, in whom and through whom the faithful have their inheritance.[63]

Indeed, those who would apply a patronage model taken from the fields of anthropology and sociology in order to describe divine-human relations in the Pauline epistles may be off-target precisely because this method leads to the abstraction of Paul's theology from its larger narrative context. Paul's view of God cannot be rightly understood unless it is rooted in the particular story of God's familial action on behalf of a particular people.

3. Summary

Is God Paul's patron? The answer can only be *No.* First, God is not Paul's patron because the sociological model of patronage that is often used to describe divine-human interaction within the Pauline epistles is flawed. Patronage in the Greco-Roman world was a potentially exploitative relationship based on social control and power. Additionally, when understood as a social system (as opposed to a social relation) patronage implies a competition for scarce resources among numerous patrons, brokers, and clients. Yet for Paul there is neither a shortage of resources nor are there any competing patrons within the economy of God, who is the source of all things. Second, God is not Paul's patron because, in spite of the availability of this metaphor in Paul's cultural context, Paul never speaks of God as patron in his extant epistles. The application of social-science models must always be tested against evidence from the texts that they are employed to interpret. God is not Paul's patron but Paul's father — a metaphor that invites readers to conceive of God as the gracious Father of an inclusive family established within and through the narrative of the Father's faithfulness to creation and the Father's mercy to the people of God.[64]

---

63. Marianne Meye Thompson, *The Promise of the Father: Jesus and God in the New Testament* (Louisville: Westminster John Knox, 2000), p. 132.

64. I would like to thank the editors of this volume and several of my colleagues in the New Testament Department at Fuller Theological Seminary (Seyoon Kim, Love Sechrest, David Scholer, and Marianne Meye Thompson) for helpful comments on earlier drafts of this essay. Of course, all shortcomings in the present work are no one's responsibility but my own.

8. The Economics of Humility: The Rich and the Humble in James

Mariam Kamell

In the epistle of James, the intersections of wealth and poverty, humility and humiliation, and the rich and the poor function as key locales for the outworking of salvation. Listing all the verses in James dealing with "wealth and its use," Peter Davids concludes, "If we add these together, we discover that 47 verses out of 105 in the letter, or close to 45%, have an economic theme."[1] Whereas James normally gains notoriety as the epistle about "faith and works," his intensely practical interpretation of "works" reveals his concern that one's relationship to money is a litmus test for one's relationship with God.

In dealing with the topic of James's view on wealth and poverty, two general approaches have been popular. For some, the primary issue to be addressed is whether James accepts or denies that the "rich" (πλούσιοι) can be followers of Jesus.[2] This way of framing the matter results in interpretations that minimize the full scope of James's theology of Christian living. The other approach has been to focus on the apocalyptic or eschatological vision of James and to fit his economic theology within a framework of divine judgment.[3] In this way, James's vision of future judgment creates the moti-

---

1. Peter H. Davids, "The Test of Wealth," in *The Missions of James, Peter, and Paul: Tensions in Early Christianity,* ed. Bruce Chilton and Craig Evans (Leiden: Brill, 2005), p. 355.

2. See, e.g., Pedrito U. Maynard-Reid, *Poverty and Wealth in James* (repr. Eugene, OR: Wipf & Stock, 2004); Davids, "Test of Wealth," p. 357; Steven J. Friesen, "Injustice or God's Will: Explanations of Poverty in Proto-Christian Communities," in *A People's History of Christianity: Christian Origins,* ed. Richard A. Horsley, vol. 1 (Minneapolis: Fortress, 2005), p. 247; George M. Stulac, "Who Are 'The Rich' in James?" *Presbyterion* 16 (1990): 89-102.

3. See, e.g., Patrick A. Tiller, "The Rich and Poor in James: An Apocalyptic Ethic," in

vation for proper behavior toward the poor. This approach has some merit, of course. Clearly it would be futile to argue *against* an eschatological mindset for James, given his statements like "judgment will be without mercy" or "the Judge is standing at the door"! But this approach ultimately does not provide a full explanation of James's theology of Christian living in relation to wealth and poverty, as will be shown.

It is clear throughout the Hebrew Bible that God is one who cares for the poor and the defenseless, and he calls for the same behavior from his people. We can see this in Deut 10:12-22, where God roots his legal require-ments in his own character (10:17-19). As God defines his relationship to the "orphan and widow" as "justice" (מִשְׁפָּט), so James views the treatment of the poor as a justice issue. As in Deuteronomy 10 and other texts that equate caring for the poor with retaining God's favor, so too in James obedience in this area is essential to following Jesus. A close comparison between Deut 10:12-22 and the Epistle of James shows several other common concerns.[4] While I would not argue that James is directly dependent upon Deut 10:12-22, as a part of the Sinai revelation and Exodus narrative it forms a crucial piece of Israel's historical identity formation as the people of God. These narratives undergird later Jewish theology and are reasonably looked to as at least indirect influences on the author of James.

Conflicted Boundaries in Wisdom and Apocalypticism, ed. Benjamin G. Wright III and Law-rence M. Wills, SBLSS 35 (Atlanta: SBL, 2005), pp. 169-79; Todd C. Penner, *The Epistle of James and Eschatology: Re-reading an Ancient Christian Letter,* JSNTSS 121 (Sheffield: Shef-field Academic Press, 1996).

4. For example, James discusses impartiality, even in the face of money (or bribes), in 2:1-11 and 3:17, justice for widows and orphans at least in 1:27, caring for the needy with food and clothes in 2:14-26, and God's grace in electing his people in 1:18. James's term for partial-ity in 2:1, προσωπολημψίαις, is a literal translation of the Hebrew נָשָׂא פָנִים, a standard way of expressing partiality as an act of taking someone by their external appearance. Regarding impartiality, see Ralph P. Martin, *James,* Word Biblical Commentary (Nashville: Thomas Nelson, 1988), p. 68. Alexander Rofé (*Deuteronomy: Issues and Interpretation* [London: T&T Clark, 2002], p. 117) observes that the idea of impartiality largely deals with the character of judges, aptly fitting into the possible law-court setting of Jas 2:1-7. Perceiving the widespread appearance of commands for impartiality across "wisdom literature (Prov 17.23; 18.5; 28.21), and in the descriptions of the divine attributes (Deut 10.17; Job 34.19) [this] seems to repre-sent an ancient legal-wisdom literature describing the desired attributes of the righteous judge and admonishing those who sit in judgment to conform to them." His linking of those two traditions in this imperative helps to explain both why James uses it and why he uses it where he does, as his concern is with setting up a new ethic for this new people identified as Jesus followers, and he uses this within a section that fluidly eludes being pinned either to the individual believer or strictly to judges.

The themes of obedience and concern for the poor, while common to both texts, underscore James's indebtedness to broader Jewish traditions, but Deut 10:12-22 particularly brings out the interplay of election and obedience that is also highlighted in James. This essay, therefore, seeks first to understand the Hebrew Bible's definition of justice, especially as it concerns the wealthy and the poor, since these would be in the background of James's ethical worldview; second, to understand how James interplays humility and humiliation in relation to economic issues and social status; and third, to understand James's concerns and encouragements regarding economic status, charity, and caring for the defenseless.

1. Justice, Wealth, and the Poor in the Hebrew Bible

Guillermo Mendez warns against ideological approaches to the biblical text, especially as demonstrated by liberation theologians, cautioning: "we must go back to the Bible to learn who God is, what his demands are, and the basis from which he judges the human injustices of each and all social systems" before we hope to define justice and injustice.[5] A close reading of the Sinai texts where God is presented as speaking for and concerning himself with the people while issuing commands to them not only helps to form a modern theology of justice but also helps with interpreting other biblical passages such as James. Deut 10:12-22 provides an excellent example, as it consists of Moses' recounted conversation with God immediately following the golden calf incident at Sinai, wherein the people of Israel are informed what the LORD demands of them in order for his presence to remain with them. He states:

> So now, O Israel, what does the LORD your God require of you? Only to fear the LORD your God, to walk in all his ways, to love him, to serve the LORD your God with all your heart and with all your soul, and to keep the commandments of the LORD your God and his decrees that I am commanding you today, for your own well-being.

Having made clear that these commands are for the well-being of the people, the LORD reminds the people both of the extremity of his power ("heaven

5. Guillermo W. Mendez, "Justification and Social Justice," in *Right with God: Justification in the Bible and the World*, ed. D. A. Carson (Carlisle, UK: Paternoster, 1992), pp. 178-96, at 190.

and the heaven of heavens belong to the LORD your God") and of the uniqueness of their election ("the LORD set his heart in love on your ancestors alone and chose you, their descendants after them, out of all the peoples"). Having just reminded them in Deuteronomy 9 about their failure with the golden calf, he instructs them again to practice obedience before God ("circumcise the foreskin of your heart, and do not be stubborn any longer"), reminding them that he alone is God, who is just, generous, and worthy of worship:

> For the LORD your God is God of gods and Lord of lords, the great God, mighty and awesome, who is not partial and takes no bribe, who executes justice for the orphan and the widow, and who loves the strangers, providing them food and clothing. You shall also love the stranger, for you were strangers in the land of Egypt. You shall fear the LORD your God; him alone you shall worship.[6]

Whereas Proverbs 1:7 famously states, "The fear of the LORD is the beginning of wisdom," in Deuteronomy 10 the command to fear the LORD provides an inclusio for God's demands (Deut 10:12, 20). Grammatically, in verse 12 one must ask whether the commands of "walking in his ways," "loving him," "serving him," and "keeping his commandments" are apposite or supplementary to the "fear of the LORD." Put differently, do these actions *comprise* the fear of the LORD or are they *additional* requirements, each one a separate injunction only partially related to the others? It appears better to understand them as the substance: the fear of the LORD is not actualized until obedience happens.[7] Consistently throughout the Hebrew Bible, the "fear of the LORD" is paralleled with some term for obedience, whether in Leviticus in a negative command "do not . . . but fear the LORD" (cf. 19:14; 25:17), or in Joshua or 1 Samuel where "fear the Lord" pairs

---

6. Hebrew Bible translations come from the NRSV; New Testament translations are my own. The conclusion of the passage consists of further injunctions to monotheism and one last reminder of God's work in bringing them out of Egypt.

7. Duane L. Christensen (*Deuteronomy 1:1–21:9*, Word Biblical Commentary 6A, rev. ed. [Nashville: Thomas Nelson, 2001], p. 204) concurs, observing: "Careful prosaic analysis suggests that the term is defined here by means of poetic parallelism: 'to fear YHWH' is 'to walk in all his ways.' This phrase is explained by the words that follow: 'to fear God' means 'to love him and to serve YHWH your God with all your heart and with all your being' (v. 12)." He later suggests that Jonah functions as a midrash on Deut 10:11-12, using the same phrase "arise, go [on your journey]," but Jonah does not act in accordance with the fear of the LORD in his failure to obey.

with "and serve him always" (cf. Josh 24:14; 1 Sam 12:14; 12:24), or in wisdom texts wherein the "fear of the Lord" opposes evil behavior (cf. Job 28:28; Prov 3:7; 16:6; 23:17). It seems legitimate to argue that the "fear of the Lord" is in no way separable from the subsequent commands in Deut 10:12-13, but rather that those commands explain to the people of God what it means for them to "fear the Lord."

In the fourfold list that follows, two commands pair in semantic parallelism to make clear that what God demands from his people is their obedience to his commandments and a lifestyle in accordance with his character, obedience that develops from a desire to serve God because one loves him.[8] In giving substance to the "fear of the Lord," it becomes clear that God does not demand a "legalistic" obedience, but loving service. Christensen explains:

> The people of Israel were to love others because God has loved them. . . . God loves the stranger, the widow, and the orphan; and therefore his people, if they truly love God, must also be concerned for justice and righteousness in relation to their neighbors. In short, God's people are to be known for their concern for those whose social and economic position exposed them to exploitation and oppression. . . . What Moses legislated for the people of Israel is not legalism, or ritual, or the external minutiae of religious observance, or even a creed. What Moses emphasized was simply a vital relationship with God that is worked out in terms of specific responsibilities toward our neighbors.[9]

---

8. The first command, to "walk in his ways," parallels with the last, "to keep the commandments . . . and his decrees," wherein the latter further defines the former. Likewise the middle two also mutually define each other, so that "serve the Lord . . . with all your heart and with all your soul" delineates what it means to "love" the Lord. This becomes even clearer when Jesus combines these two clauses in his summary of the Law, stating, "Love the Lord your God with all your heart and with all your soul and with all your mind" (Matt 22:37; par. Mark 12:30; Luke 10:27). Christensen (*Deuteronomy*, p. 204), in contrast, includes the "fear of the Lord" in the series of commands, thus finding five commands: "In terms of the prosodic analysis presented here, the command 'to love him' stands at the structural center of the rhythmic unit. It is also the central one among the five vocatives used in 10:12-13. . . . The words of the commandment here are essentially a restatement of the great commandment to love God with one's whole being (see 6:5 ad Matt 22:36-38)." Gerhard von Rad (*Deuteronomy: A Commentary* [London: SCM, 1964], p. 83), however, simplifies matters, saying, "The expression 'to fear God', 'the fear of God' simply means obedience, the acceptance of his commandments (cf. Gen. 20.11; 22.12 etc.). He expects a response of love and wholehearted surrender."

9. Christensen, *Deuteronomy*, p. 206.

This love and obedience is said to be both "for your own good" and also a response to God's grace in choosing the Israelites. Rofé observes:

> The ideal relationship that should exist between YHWH and Israel is a relationship of love. YHWH loved the Patriarchs (4.37; 10.15) or Israel (7.8) and for that reason elected the nation. The nation, for its part, must respond to him with complete love (7.5; 10.12; 11.1, 13, 22), which means absolute loyalty to YHWH and acceptance of his service with all one's heart.[10]

Despite God's independence, he chose to love Israel (10:15),[11] ending their independence to act however and worship whomever they might like. Contextually, Deuteronomy 9 repeatedly recounts to the Israelites their stubbornness and rebelliousness, reminding them that "it is not because of your righteousness that the LORD your God is giving you this good land to possess, for you are a stiff-necked people" (Deut 9:6; cf. 9:4-5, 8-24). Their election was not *based* on their righteousness, but it necessarily *leads to* the requirement that they behave according to God's ways.

God goes one step further, however, and declares his own character and the implication this has for the people of Israel. Deut 10:17-19 gives a description of how God interacts with humanity. Preeminent is the statement that God "executes justice," or "does/makes justice" (מִשְׁפַּט), on behalf of the widows and orphans. These people were the most vulnerable, along with the aliens, so this most likely means that God defends them against those who would take advantage of their susceptible state.[12] Throughout all of the He-

---

10. Rofé, *Deuteronomy*, p. 13. Ray Carlton Jones Jr. agrees ("Deuteronomy 10:12-22," *Interpretation* 46 [1992]: 281-85, at 281): "Election and service belong together in the Bible: The consequence of the Lord God's sovereign election of Israel is that Israel must serve the Lord."

11. Christensen (*Deuteronomy*, p. 204) notes: "Though God is presented as a transcendent cosmic power to whom 'belong the heavens and the heaven of heavens [and] the earth and all that is in it,' he is also presented as a personal God who has 'fallen in love' with Israel. . . . That love is the basis of the election of Israel."

12. Harold V. Bennett (*Injustice Made Legal: Deuteronomic Law and the Plight of Widows, Strangers, and Orphans* [Grand Rapids: Eerdmans, 2002], pp. 55-56) notes: "the absence of an adult male protector affected the circumstances of these persons, for it guaranteed that they were a category of socially weak, vulnerable individuals in the biblical communities. This absence limited the access of these persons to commodities in the biblical communities, and it undermined their chances for emancipation from debt slavery and for exculpation in litigation. It is plausible that the inaccessibility to commodities affected the socioeconomic ranking for the [widow, stranger, and orphan] and that this situation cleared

brew Scriptures, "justice" is defined particularly in relation to the poor and
helpless, especially in the legal codes of Exod 23:6: "You shall not pervert the
justice due to your poor in their lawsuits"; Lev 19:15: "You shall not render an
unjust judgment; you shall not be partial to the poor or defer to the great: with
justice you shall judge your neighbor"; or the curse of Deut 27:19: "Cursed be
anyone who deprives the alien, the orphan, and the widow of justice."[13] This
imperative for justice for the helpless can also be seen in later texts, both wisdom and prophetic, such as Prov 31:9: "Speak out, judge righteously, defend
the rights of the poor and needy"; Isa 11:4: "with righteousness he shall judge
the poor, and decide with equity for the meek of the earth"; or Jer 7:5-7: "For if
you truly amend your ways and your doings, if you truly act justly one with another, if you do not oppress the alien, the orphan, and the widow, or shed in-
nocent blood in this place, and if you do not go after other gods to your own
hurt, then I will dwell with you in this place, in the land that I gave of old to
your ancestors forever and ever." The Jeremiah passage bears especial resem-
blance to the Deuteronomy text, for God's demand that his people act justly,
especially in relation to the vulnerable, is a deciding factor in whether God
will, or even can, remain among his people. If the people of Israel act in a manner contrary to God's own nature by oppressing the poor and taking advantage of the powerless, thereby forgetting their own history, then God warns
that he will not remain among them — a warning that started as early as their
initial journey from Sinai and was repeated as they lived in the land.

As God's people on earth, the Israelites are responsible for revealing to
the world the character of the LORD. Because God is the one who "executes
justice [מִשְׁפָּט] for the widow and fatherless," this practice ought to underlie
the economic system of Israel — not one in which the vulnerable are oppressed, but rather one in which "justice" is impartial to wealth, status, or
appearance.[14] In Deut 10:19, God reminds the Israelites of their prior state as

---

the way for the exploitation and oppression of this subgroup by other persons, groups or institutions in ancient Israelite society."

13. Vogt ("Social Justice," p. 39) notes that "in no instance in Deuteronomy do any of
the 7 Hebrew words for 'poor' appear together with the sequence 'alien, orphan, and
widow'. . . . [They] are not to be considered among the poor. . . . They are thought of as being
like the Levites, who also owned no property and who, therefore, relied on an alternative system for provision. . . . By steadfastly refusing to consider aliens, orphans, and widows as
'poor,' Moses in Deuteronomy is insisting that they be integrated fully into the life of the nation, just as the Levites were to be. They, like the Levites, would serve as a barometer for the
obedience of the nation."

14. Christiana van Houten (*The Alien in Israelite Law,* JSOTSS 107 [Sheffield: Sheffield

aliens and oppressed, creating an obligation that they treat people who reside with them differently than they were ultimately treated in Egypt.[15] Preceding their personal and historical obligation, however, the order for justice rests in God's character as the one "who loves the strangers, providing them with food and clothing." As Ray Carleton Jones says, "Aside from the motivating factor that the Israelites themselves were strangers in the land of Egypt . . . the people are to love the stranger because the Lord loves and provides for the stranger (10:18). Just as the Lord's love for Israel is to be reciprocated by Israel's love and service of the Lord . . . , so too the Lord's love of the stranger means that Israel must love the stranger."[16]

2. The Poor in Prophetic Tradition and James

Mimicking God's very nature to care for the oppressed is the culmination of what it means for the Israelites to "walk in his ways" (Deut 10:12, 18-19),[17] a theme consistent through the Hebrew Scriptures and James. The Israelites,

---

Academic Press, 1991], p. 79) subdivides the laws "into laws regulating cultic matters and laws requiring charity and justice. . . . Because the laws do not distinguish between matters of charity and justice, I will not either."

15. Van Houten (*The Alien*, p. 54) analyzes this use of their history: "Depicting the alien as a person who now occupies the position that their forebears had occupied serves to close the gap between the alien and the Israelite. It does not allow the Israelite to hold the alien at arm's length, but causes them to be sympathetic to and identify with the alien. The memory of their stay in Egypt mitigates the apparently universal exclusivism common to all social, political, and religious communities. Using their history in order to motivate obedience contributed to an openness to outsiders which would have far-reaching results."

16. Jones, "Deuteronomy 10:12-22," p. 283. He continues: "In other words, love of the weak — of the stranger and the homeless — is an aspect of the covenant relationship as established by God (see Exod. 22:21-24, which is embedded in the Covenant Code, Exod. 20:22–23:33; see in addition Lev. 19:33-34, which is embedded in the Holiness Code, Lev. 17–26, and is ultimately grounded in the basic presupposition of the covenant relationship: 'I am the Lord')."

17. F. C. Fensham ("Widow, Orphan, and the Poor in Ancient Near Eastern Legal and Wisdom Literature," *JNES* 21 [1962]: 129) notes the commonality of caring for these subgroups, arguing: "The protection of widow, orphan, and the poor was the common policy of the ancient Near East. It was not started by the spirit of Israelite propheticism or by the spirit of propheticism as such. From the earliest times on, a strong king promulgated stipulations in connection with the protection of this group. Such protection was seen as a virtue of god, kings, and judges. It was a policy of virtue, a policy which proved the piety and virtue of a ruler."

as God's people, are meant to resist bribes and partiality while actively caring for the helpless in their midst. James puts these injunctions in two adjacent verses. In 1:27, he observes that the kind of worship that God accepts from his people is "care for *orphans* and *widows* in their affliction" — the same two categories listed in Deut 10:18 as receiving the "justice" of God. Then he offers an immediate warning: "do not hold the faith of our Lord Jesus Christ in *favoritism*" (Jas 2:1). James follows the deuteronomic concern that justice be administered faithfully, especially in caring for the vulnerable and not abusing them. Again, in Deuteronomy the example of the alien depicts God "giv[ing] them food and clothing" (10:18b) — exactly the two necessities that James picks up in 2:15.

The theme of justice for widows and orphans is common throughout all of Scripture. In Zech 7:9-14, God specifies what he desires from his people:

> Thus says the LORD of hosts: Render true judgments, show kindness and mercy to one another; do not oppress the widow, the orphan, the alien, or the poor; and do not devise evil in your hearts against one another. But they refused to listen, and turned a stubborn shoulder. . . . Therefore great wrath came from the LORD of hosts. Just as, when I called, they would not hear, so, when they called, I would not hear, says the LORD of hosts.

Here we find a *lex talionis*[18] within the call to repent, whereby God warns that failure to respond to his call results in a reciprocal form of punishment.[19] Again the command is to "not oppress the widow or the fatherless, the alien or the poor." Failing at *this specific command* in Zechariah brings about the wrath of God.[20]

There are many prophetic echoes of God's original call to his people. For example, Isa 1:16-17 foreshadows the practical concerns of the repentance oracle of Jas 4:7-10, as well as the command to moral cleanliness of Jas

---

18. That is, the "law of retaliation," wherein the punishment fits the crime. At its most basic, it is the "eye for an eye" principle described in Exod 21:23-25, Lev 24:18-20, and Deut 19:21.

19. The *lex talionis* in Zech 7:13 provides an interesting parallel to Jas 2:13: "for judgment will be without mercy to the one not showing mercy." Vogt ("Social Justice," p. 38) also picks out this text from Zechariah as an essential one for understanding the Hebrew Bible's view of the poor, but there he notes that "a single class is being described" of widows, orphans, and aliens *as poor*.

20. Likewise, in Jas 2:13 it is one's failure to live mercifully that brings about one's merciless judgment, not a failure in "righteousness" or "legality." Thus James shares Zechariah's view that failure to care for the truly needy in society results in divine judgment.

1:21, when it states: "Wash yourselves; make yourselves clean; remove the evil of your doings from before my eyes; cease to do evil, learn to do good; seek justice, rescue the oppressed, defend the orphan, plead for the widow." The definition here of learning to "do good" appears to be siding with the helpless in a quest for justice. In another important text, Mic 6:8 ties together the theme of humility with those of justice and mercy. It says: "He has told you, O mortal, what is good; and what does the LORD require of you but to do justice, and to love kindness, and to walk humbly with your God?" Here we see a more abstract triumvirate for behavior, "justice" (מִשְׁפָּט; LXX: ποιεῖν κρίμα), "loving-kindness" or "mercy" (חֶסֶד; LXX: ἔλεος), and "humility" (צָנַע) before God, three traits that James emphasizes heavily. This text therefore helps to shift us to the theology of James more specifically, in which two themes develop in tandem: (1) humility before God, which leads to the practice of true justice and mercy for the helpless, in contrast to (2) the foretold humiliation of the rich who use their security to oppress the powerless.

3. James and the Economics of Humility

The first chapter of James sets up the twin principles of humility and humiliation. Jas 1:9-11 contrasts the fates of the poor and the rich, celebrating the promise of relief to those already humbled by life while calling the prideful to humility before God. Reminiscent of Jesus' promise in Matt 5:7, James enjoins the poor to rejoice: "Let the lowly brother (or sister) boast in their elevation" — a marked contrast between the terms ταπεινός and ὕψος. Ταπεινός indicates someone who is humble or someone humbled by circumstances, lowly and poor, economically speaking. But through its use in the LXX, the term gained additional associations of a person in the theological category of "humble before God."[21] While some argue for an *either/or* between the financial and theological positions, Maynard-Reid, a Latin-American liberation theologian, rightly states: "An absolute either/or position here . . . seems to be

---

21. H.-H. Esser ("Humility," in *NIDNTT,* vol. 2, ed. Colin Brown [Grand Rapids: Zondervan, 1986], p. 260) observes that in the LXX ταπεινός and its cognates "occur in expressions of belief in what Yahweh has done. It is God himself who brings down the proud and arrogant, and chooses and rescues the humiliated." Matthew's Jesus continues this concern with humility before God (cf. especially Matt 11:28-30; 18:1-5; 23:12; see Esser, p. 262), an emphasis that might well have influenced the author of James. See esp. Dean B. Deppe, *The Sayings of Jesus in the Epistle of James* (Chelsea, MI: Bookcrafters, 1989); Patrick J. Hartin, *James and the Q Sayings of Jesus,* JSNT 47 (Sheffield: Sheffield Academic, 1991).

a faulty option. To separate the economically poor and oppressed from the pious in James' community seems to be wrong."[22] He quickly moves, however, to affirm the more basic economic position, arguing that "James's characterization of the poor vis-à-vis the rich throughout his epistle amply demonstrates that his emphasis is on the social station of those classes."[23] It is significant to note that James does not use the term for the economically desolate, πτωχός, that he uses elsewhere to signify the truly destitute (cf. 2:2-3, 5-6). Here he uses this more ambiguous category ταπεινός when foretelling elevation and glory, indicating that perhaps it is not financial poverty that brings about the promised rise. Rather, it is an attitude of humility that characterizes the humble, regardless of their economic status.

In contrast to "the humble," the rich are warned of their imminent downfall. James's language echoes that of Psalm 102, Isaiah 40, or Ecclesiastes, reminding the rich of the transience of life on earth, even when they are at their most secure in making more money. The same root for "humble" from 1:9 appears in 1:10, this time as the noun describing the imminent doom of the rich.[24] Whereas the adjective indicated a sense of stasis, of being humble, or poor, lowly, possibly even "subservient," the noun used in 1:10 indicates the "experience of a reversal of fortunes, humiliation."[25] James thus sets up his basic contrast: those of the less specific category, the humble, will be elevated, whereas the rich, the πλούσιοι, will be humiliated.[26] Because he avoids using the term "poor" (πτωχός), James allows for the possibility that the "humble" could include people with means, in contrast with those who are "rich"

22. Maynard-Reid, *Poverty and Wealth*, p. 40.

23. Maynard-Reid, *Poverty and Wealth*, p. 41.

24. William R. Baker ("James," in *James-Jude: Unlocking the Scriptures for You*, ed. William R. Baker and Paul Carrier [Cincinnati: Standard, 1990], p. 22) comments that "in terms of logic, the irony of suggesting that a person should take pride in what amounts to his own eternal condemnation is too twisted to be taken seriously." Their "humiliation," however, might well be their one chance at salvation, if they can actually learn to rejoice in it and gain a true understanding of their position before God rather than relying on their wealth for their identity and comfort.

25. BDAG, pp. 989-90, emphasis removed.

26. Joseph B. Mayor, *The Epistle of James* (Grand Rapids: Kregel, 1990), p. 42, translates this verse as "Let the rich brother glory in his humiliation as a Christian," understanding ταπεινός as referring to "the loss of position, the scorn which one who became a Christian would have to suffer from his unbelieving fellow-countrymen." In contrast, Davids and Martin understand "James' use of 'rich man' in 1:10 to be polemical and [see] a rich nonbeliever set in contrast over against a poor Christian" (Martin, *James*, p. 26; cf. Peter H. Davids, *The Epistle of James*, NIGTC [Grand Rapids: Eerdmans, 1982], p. 77).

(πλούσιοι), a group specifically demarked by their self-identification through their economic status, not through their status before God. James has left it open for the ἀδελφός to be brought forward from 1:9 to 1:10, so that contrasted here are not the fates of *the poor* and *the rich* but of the more theologically charged categories of *the humble* and *the rich*.[27]

This emphasis on humility appears again in James 4, with its prophetic call to repentance. This passage contains both verbal parallels with 1:9-11 and deeper thematic parallels. Jas 4:1-2 condemns the audience's envy and greed as resulting in metaphorical murder and war. Violence is the practical outcome of the "wisdom from below" of 3:14-16, the result of selfishness and self-serving pride. James condemns this behavior in a wholesale manner. In fact, James's denunciation of these "adulterous people" is nearly as biting as his condemnation of the rich landowners in James 5. While the recipients of this criticism in 4:1-10 are labeled "adulteresses," it is possible that they comprise the poorer members of the congregation fighting for status in the only way and place open to them. Given the upcoming critiques of merchants in 4:13-17 and landowners in 5:1-6, it is likely that Witherington is correct when he concludes that "it is not the have-nots who are praying for more, but the haves, whose thirst for acquisition has not been slacked [*sic*]."[28] Regardless whether the culprits are the richer or poorer of the community, the problem as James sees it is not money itself but the selfish, prideful attitude that goes with wanting and seeking money and status at any cost. To those who fight and scheme for social status and view that as their prime good, James rebukes them as "adulteresses" and "enemies of God"![29] This is not language

---

27. This is in contrast to Davids's comment that "In James' community one would want to be identified as 'poor,' whatever one's financial or social status" ("Test of Wealth," p. 383). I would argue that James would be more concerned that people identify themselves as ταπεινός rather than as "poor." Stulac ("Who are 'The Rich,'" p. 95) adds the grammatical warning that "Understanding *adelphos* in 1:9 to be the referent for both *tapeinos* in 1:9 and *plousios* in 1:10 does seem to be a natural way to read these verses. The important caution in making this argument of 'natural' reading is that it may simply be making the ancient text subject to what seems natural to our modern ears. The difference between the ancient text and our modern thinking is precisely the gap we are trying to cross. The fact is that the grammar of 1:9-10 does not require this reading of *adelphos* as a common referent. Another very possible way to read the passage would be to see *ho adelphos ho tapeinos* standing together as a unit and *ho plousios* as the contrasting subject, with *adelphos* not repeated because the rich here are not brothers, and with *kauchasthō* the verb for both subjects."

28. Ben Witherington III, *Letters and Homilies for Jewish Christians: A Socio-Rhetorical Commentary on Hebrews, James and Jude* (Downers Grove: IVP Academic, 2007), p. 511.

29. F. J. A. Hort (*The Epistle of St James* [London: Macmillan and Co., 1909], pp. 91-92)

to be taken lightly, for James employs Israel's long prophetic history of warning against and condemning idolatry. The only solution James offers is that they return to humility before God, toward which end he quotes Prov 3:34. By means of this quote, James makes one of his clearest assertions of how God relates to his people: pride is condemned, humility is rewarded. Therefore the hearers are urged to "submit themselves" to God, humbling themselves in repentance. Jas 4:10 provides the strongest tie to 1:9-10 — "Be humble before the Lord, and he will lift you up" (ταπεινώθητε ἐνώπιον κυρίου καὶ ὑψώσει ὑμᾶς). Here the first verb is the same root for humility/humiliation as the adjective and noun in 1:9-10, likewise the same verb for the promised elevation in 1:9 recurs here. In many ways, then, 4:10 restates the promise and warning of 1:9-10. James issues this command to his entire audience, thereby indicating that anyone can, *and should,* be among the ταπεινός whom God will raise up. While he does not use the verb ταπεινώθητε here to indicate the person's economic status, 4:10 implies, when paired with 1:10, that everyone must either choose to humble themselves or be humbled by God. As Witherington notes, "James 4:10 clearly indicates that self-humbling leads to God lifting up, but the converse follows if someone exalts themselves."[30] James makes clear that everyone will, at some point or another, be ταπεινός. The question merely is whether this humility is self-chosen (and temporary) or enforced by God (and permanent).

Throughout the epistle, James consistently views humility as a lifestyle that recognizes one's position before God. At the risk of proof-texting, there is ground for building a picture across the entire epistle. Humility does not blame God for one's own failures in the face of temptation (1:13-16). It accepts God's redemptive work and even prepares for it (1:21). It does not boast in one's own "religiousness" (1:26-27). It does not judge others by their looks

---

argues for a literal understanding of adultery here, wherein James addresses sins of pleasure as well as the sins of violence in 4:1-3. In this he stands alone, and Luke Timothy Johnson (*The Letter of James* [New York: Doubleday, 1995], p. 278) reminds the readers that "James is using the symbolism found in Torah for the covenantal relationship between Yahweh as groom and Israel as bride. The covenant was like a marriage (Isa 54:4-8) in which Israel's frequent infidelities could be considered as adultery. . . . In symbolic shorthand, James' epithet accuses the readers of idolatry, which is precisely what their manner of prayer (4:3) revealed." He adds that a Hellenistic understanding of friendship "involved 'sharing all things' in a unity both spiritual and physical. Thus, friends are *mia psychē*" (279), a reality that emphasizes the "double-souled" nature of those attempting friendship both with the world (money, status) and with God (humility). See also Douglas J. Moo, *The Letter of James*, Pillar New Testament Commentary (Grand Rapids: Eerdmans, 2000), p. 187.

30. Witherington, *Letters and Homilies*, p. 516.

(2:1, 4). It cares practically for those worse off (2:14-26). It does not push toward leadership roles (3:1, 16). It is evidence of the "wisdom from above" (3:17-18). It remembers that there is only "one Lawgiver and Judge" and thus refrains from passing judgment on others (4:12). It remembers that our life is nothing but a mist that passes away under the least wind (4:14, in language echoing that of Ecclesiastes).[31] It does not live in self-indulgence at the cost of those poorer (5:1-6). It remembers God's imminence, and as a result it avoids complaining and slandering (5:9). It repents from and confesses sins (5:15-16). In contrast, those who live in selfish comfort and act in arrogance are threatened by their imminent downfall (1:10-11) and with judgment (2:12), warned of possessing a demonic wisdom (3:14-16), charged with being adulterers in their relationship to God (4:4), warned of the Judge's ability to "destroy" them (4:12), reminded of their own transience (4:14), and informed of their coming doom in the "day of slaughter" (5:1-6). Humiliation, in contrast to humility, is a forced upending, the overturning of the life of the proud, and the judgment of God upon those who fail to choose humility before him. Whereas one who is humble remembers that "all flesh is as grass" before God, the proud person attempts to circumvent that reality and live in the now as if their life and lifestyle were something permanent. Thus it is only the ταπεινοί who understand and act on the call to care for the widow, orphan, and alien from Deuteronomy, as they identify with the helpless of society and submit themselves before the God who is "God of gods and Lord of lords, the great God, mighty and awesome" (Deut 10:17), to whom "heaven and the heaven of heavens belong," along with "the earth with all that is in it" (Deut 10:14). By remembering God, the truly humble acknowledge that they are helpless to better their own situation — only God can do that for them (Jas 1:9; 4:11).

31. Jas 4:13-17 illustrates James's concern with humility in his hearers. In this passage, the merchants make plans for their daily and yearly business with no thought beyond their own strategy for making more money. For this they are reminded that they have no control over their future; instead, they are as a "mist." James again pits humility against humiliation. For those who plan their own lives, independent of any other consideration, humiliation comes when they discover their utter lack of control over life. The sheer intangibility of "mist," ἀτμίς, leaves the planners without any firm control, any certainty — to the humiliation and overturning of all their plans. The humble ones, in contrast, being aware of their true nature as mist, consistently remember their position before God and do not boast. Instead, all of their plans remain under the aegis of God's will. Thus, in two verses, James makes the shift from those who pridefully make their own plans without regard to their fleeting nature to those who properly plan and work in humility before God. Humility is the remembrance of who God is in contrast with what humans are.

We thus can see how James's understanding of humility is *not* a wholesale condemnation of those with means but is rather the basis for his economic ethics. His condemnation of the merchants was not that they failed to give their money to the poor but that they failed to be humble before God. The wealthy of 5:1-6 are condemned because they failed to care for the poor, a failure due to their arrogance in ignoring the reality of their own coming "day of slaughter." Compare, then, T. B. Maston on the ethical dimensions of James: "In the field of applied ethics the major emphasis is on personal morality in contrast to social morality. The latter, however, is not entirely lacking."[32] That is an intriguing conclusion, since James appears to work out personal morality in terms of social morality, following the social implications of God's call to his people in Deuteronomy; that is, a correct perspective of God as the only God (Deut 10:14, 17) leads directly to the responsibility to act in accordance with his character toward the helpless in society (Deut 10:18). Interestingly, in all of the Deuteronomy 10 passage, the only specific command comes in the context of caring for the alien, the person with no social recourse.

This leads, perhaps, to another link with Deuteronomy 10 that might help to illumine James's connection between a person's humility before God and a person's economic practices. While the Hebrew Scripture texts cited above were important for understanding how a Jew in James's time might have thought about issues of justice and mercy, wealth and poverty, the Deuteronomy text alone grounds the commands for justice and mercy *in the very character of God,* not merely in demands God has placed upon his people. James does the same thing. In Deuteronomy 10:15, God elects the Israelites to be his representatives in this world, thus empowering them but also holding them liable to living up to God's character as revealed in the rest of the passage. Likewise in James, God's election is emphasized not just in the famous "preferential option for the poor" in 2:5, but also in the reminder to the broader community of their salvation in 1:18, wherein "he chose to give us birth by the word of truth." Describing the "firstfruits" of this new creation, James picks up the theme from the Hebrew Scriptures that election leads to obedience, and in this election to be God's people James grounds his moral imperatives. In 1:5, he calls God the "giving God," a description augmented in 1:17 that "every good gift and perfect giving is from above, from the Father of lights."

James may well have assumed that the jump from God as "giving God"

---

32. T. B. Maston, "Ethical Dimensions in James," *SwJT* 12 (1969): 23-39, at 36.

to the expectation that his people be "giving people" ought to have been made by his audience. Thus his condemnation of the rich in 5:1-6 is scathing — in their actions, they fail on every count.[33] They have hoarded wealth to the point that it has rotted around them (vv. 2-3), and yet in their greed they refuse to pay their workers so that they might hoard the more (v. 4). Their selfishness leads them to live for their own comfort, "fattening themselves in the day of slaughter" (v. 5). This last image is interesting, since it can refer to the basic slaughter day on which people ate fresh meat, but it can also have prophetic overtones from Jeremiah, wherein the "'day of slaughter' can also be when God comes in judgment and slaughters the unrighteous."[34] This double reference to literal and apocalyptic slaughter serves the warning that their deeds have been catalogued and their oppression noted by the Lord Sabaoth, the powerful Lord of Hosts. It must be noted, however, that the condemnation of the rich is not so much that they *are* rich, but that they act in a prideful and selfish way. These sins pit them in direct opposition to the God who both declares himself the most powerful being and yet allies himself with the widow, the orphan, and the defenseless. The crime of the rich, when called the πλούσιοι, is that of arrogance and selfishness (not of being wealthy), and for this arrogance they will be condemned and destroyed.

In the other main passage about money, 2:1-13, James argues against partiality and for mercy. The partiality James condemns is that of catering to a wealthy person while dismissing a poor person, entirely based on each person's appearances.[35] The fault here is not with the "rich" person "with gold rings and in fine clothes" (this character may well be a believer, as James does not use his flagged term πλούσιος in the specific context envisioned in 2:1-

33. Friesen ("Injustice," p. 246) calls this "the author's most caustic critique of the Roman system." On the whole, he sees James as presenting "a relatively simple explanation for economic inequality. Jacob [*sic*] blamed the local elites for economic injustice but also criticizes the general population for complicity. . . . I call the model 'relatively simple' because it reflects primarily on local conditions. It does not address larger issues of empire or social discourse, locating the problems instead in personal desire and temptation" (244). This is intriguing, since Friesen goes on to find James to be criticizing the Roman "status system" (245). Friesen sees James as diagnosing the sickness of participation in and acceptance of a status-driven culture in which the rich are acclaimed *merely because* they are rich, a problem that is both local and empire-wide.

34. Davids, "Test of Wealth," p. 377.

35. Friesen ("Injustice," p. 245) sees James as challenging his audience for their faulty perspective: "how can they honor the rich of the world who use the court system to oppress them but dishonor those who are rich in God's kingdom?" In light of this passage, he concludes, "the courts are not for justice but rather for injustice."

4); instead, the fault lies with the common people who respond to him with notable groveling. They ought to know better, since such behavior was consistently condemned throughout all of the Hebrew Scriptures. Instead James has to remind them of God's self-identification with the needy (2:5). Tiller comments: "The fact that God has chosen the poor and dishonored of this world to be rich in faith and to inherit the kingdom is proof that the conventional criteria for assigning honor are false and in need of reversal."[36] James's use of πτωχός for the elect poor indicates that they are the truly financially helpless, but equally importantly, these poor are also described as those "loving [God]." While the πλούσιοι in 5:1-6 could only be described as loving themselves, here the helpless are characterized by their love of God. It is not merely the fact of their poverty that leads God to choose them, but that their poverty leads them to recognizing their defenselessness and dependence upon God. In this, they are among the ταπεινοί, the humble. Davids warns that "there is no sense in [James's] language that there is some blessedness in this situation of poverty in this world. . . . There is no holy asceticism here,"[37] nor does James "romanticize their present suffering."[38] James does not seek to build up an idealized picture of the poor, but rather to remind his audience that God cares for the helpless and that the humble have a special place in the kingdom. Those who claim to be followers of this God ought to act accordingly.

The rest of 2:1-13 moves to motivating the audience toward charity, and this exhortation comes to its culmination in the "faith and works" debate of 2:14-26. First, in 2:8-13 the crime censured is that of failing to show mercy, a failure that brings about merciless judgment. Davids states, "For James charity is directly related to the quality of one's 'faith' or commitment to Jesus/ God. . . . [T]here is no sense in which charity is optional. It is related to salvation itself."[39] Charity might be seen as the opposite of the selfish lifestyle of the rich, wherein the person acting in mercy acts in the "way of the Lord," following the behavior of the "giving God." As the argument progresses in 2:14-26, mercy toward the poor is the proof of a living faith. Here, however, we see that James *cannot* be said to argue that the rich cannot be saved, for he uses Abraham as the prime exemplar of faith, and Abraham's wealth is repeatedly announced in Genesis. Instead, he uses the example of Abraham's

---

36. Tiller, "The Rich and Poor in James," p. 177.
37. Davids, "Test of Wealth," p. 373.
38. Davids, "Test of Wealth," p. 383.
39. Davids, "Test of Wealth," p. 360.

sacrifice, not merely because of the strength of the 'Aqedah tradition as proving Abraham's faithfulness, but also because Isaac was the embodiment of Abraham's wealth and because this story shows Abraham's willingness to sacrifice even his most precious and most longed for possession to God. Unlike the rich young man of Mark 10:17-23 (par. Luke 18:18-23, where he is said to be πλούσιος σφόδρα [18:23]), Abraham regarded his wealth, even his prized son, as a gift from God, and so for James he functions not merely as an example of hospitality and caring for the poor but as the correct model of a wealthy person's necessary humility before God, the model who stands in opposition not merely to the rich young man from the Gospels but also to the wealthy person in 2:2 or 5:1-6.

4. Conclusion

It appears that, in James, the πλούσιοι stand against the ταπεινοί in salvation language. The πλούσιος in James cannot be followers of Jesus, because they exhibit an independence of spirit that shows their failure to understand both their vapor-like existence before God and also their duty as followers of God toward the oppressed and helpless. By failing in this sort of correct behavior, the πλούσιοι merely prove James's point from 2:14 that faith without "works," and specifically works of mercy toward the oppressed, cannot save. Chrysostom observes the importance of acts of mercy in God's eyes: "We can become more like God if we are merciful and compassionate. If we do not do these things, we have nothing at all to our credit. God does not say if we fast we shall be like God. Rather he wants us to be merciful, as God himself is. 'I desire mercy' he says, 'and not sacrifice.'"[40] The warning of the humiliation of the rich in 5:6 follows as the logical outcome of the promise that God will "execute justice" as he promised in Deut 10:17. The promised justice is the overturning of the social systems of the world — not of the rich versus the poor, but of the prideful versus the humble, of those who trust in being πλούσιοι and care only for themselves versus those who live as ταπεινός and care practically for the πτωχοί.

Both Deuteronomy and James reveal God as acting in solidarity with the poor and the helpless, and it is because of this that Christians ought also to humble themselves before God and act in solidarity with the poor, whether they are poor themselves or not. Indeed, James would argue that

---

40. Chrysostom, *Catena* 9, as quoted in Witherington, *Letters and Homilies*, p. 448.

each person has the choice between the self-chosen humility of acting in accordance with God's character or the divinely inflicted humiliation given to those who live for their own pleasures. James warns his audience in apocalyptic language of judgment, it is true, but this vision of judgment is grounded in the God of Israel's self-revelation that he is both "God of gods and Lord of lords" and one who "executes justice for the orphan and the widow, and who loves the strangers, providing them food and clothing." Ultimately, humility or humiliation will come to every person, whether rich or poor. The question is whether one chooses to humble oneself (4:10) or be humbled (1:10). How one treats the desperately poor, the πτωχοί, is a key indication of one's status as humble or not before the Lord. The truly humble will practice the economics of humility in caring for the helpless rather than flaunting their wealth as their own possession and right, remembering their responsibility to act in accordance with their election and the character of their God. It is thus that the economics of justice will be enacted within the community of God.

9. Aliens and Strangers? The Socioeconomic Location of the Addressees of 1 Peter

David G. Horrell

Recent years have seen a lively discussion of the socioeconomic level of the earliest Christians. A so-called "old consensus" that they came from among the poor, usually attributed to Adolf Deissmann (not entirely accurately), was replaced in the 1970s and '80s with a so-called "new consensus" that they represented a cross-section of urban society and included some individuals of relatively high wealth and status.[1] The initial impetus for this "new consensus" was provided by Edwin Judge,[2] but the main foundations were laid in Gerd Theissen's essay on social stratification in the Corinthian community, first published in 1974.[3] Report of an "emerging consensus" was first announced, and further supported, by Abraham Malherbe in his *Social Aspects of Early Christianity*, published in 1977.[4] A further significant contribution to the establishment of this consensus was a chapter on the social level of the Pauline Christians in Wayne Meeks's classic and wide-ranging treat-

1. For an overview of the discussion to the mid-1990s, see David G. Horrell, *The Social Ethos of the Corinthian Correspondence: Interests and Ideology from 1 Corinthians to 1 Clement*, Studies of the New Testament and Its World (Edinburgh: T & T Clark, 1996), pp. 91-101.

2. Edwin A. Judge, *The Social Pattern of Early Christian Groups in the First Century: Some Prologomena to the Study of the New Testament Ideas of Social Obligation* (London: Tyndale, 1960).

3. Gerd Theissen, "Soziale Schichtung in der korinthischen Gemeinde: Ein Beitrag zur Soziologie des hellenistischen Urchristentums," *ZNW* 65 (1974): 232-72. ET in Gerd Theissen, *The Social Setting of Pauline Christianity* (Edinburgh: T & T Clark, 1982), pp. 69-119.

4. Abraham J. Malherbe, *Social Aspects of Early Christianity*, 2nd ed. (Philadelphia: Fortress Press, 1983 [first ed. 1977]), p. 31.

176

ment of the first urban Christians, published in 1983.[5] Building on Theissen's detailed analysis, Meeks agreed that "[t]he 'emerging consensus' that Malherbe reports seems to be valid: a Pauline congregation generally reflected a fair cross-section of urban society."[6] This consensus then provided the basis for a wide range of further studies, many of which placed a good deal of weight on the conviction that there were wealthy, elite, ruling class members among the early Pauline congregations.[7]

The relatively uncontroversial development of the "new consensus" perspective was brought to an end in 1998 with the publication of Justin Meggitt's *Paul, Poverty and Survival*.[8] This book constitutes a frontal assault on the new consensus, attacking the reading of the evidence on which its reconstruction is based and insisting that Paul and the earliest Christians shared in the absolute material poverty that was the lot of 99 percent of the Roman Empire's inhabitants. Meggitt's book has generated considerable debate, including some vigorous defense of a "new consensus" position. One of the more telling criticisms has been that Meggitt operates with a somewhat crude binary model, which effectively divides the inhabitants of the Roman Empire into two groups: the elite rich and the 99 percent poor.[9] An influen-

---

5. Wayne A. Meeks, *The First Urban Christians* (New Haven: Yale University Press, 1983), pp. 51-73.

6. Meeks, *First Urban Christians*, p. 73.

7. E.g., John K. Chow, *Patronage and Power: A Study of Social Networks in Corinth*, JSNTSup 75 (Sheffield: JSOT Press, 1992); Andrew D. Clarke, *Secular and Christian Leadership in Corinth: A Socio-Historical and Exegetical Study of 1 Corinthians 1–6*, AGAJU 18 (Leiden: Brill, 1993). My own earlier study broadly followed the "new consensus" picture but was more cautious about the socioeconomic level of the members: "we can hardly state with confidence that the most socially prominent members of the Corinthian congregation belong to the 'elite', the 'ruling class', of Corinth. . . . Nevertheless, there do seem to be at least some members of the ἐκκλησία who are relatively well-to-do, who are heads of households which include slaves, the owners of accommodation of some size, and people with some wealth at their disposal" (Horrell, *Social Ethos*, p. 98). I would now be still more cautious, especially regarding wealth and housing (cf. David G. Horrell, "Domestic Space and Christian Meetings at Corinth: Imagining New Contexts and the Buildings East of the Theatre," *NTS* 50 [2004]: 349-69), but would affirm the conclusion that the churches included a range of people from urban society (cf. Horrell, *Social Ethos*, pp. 100-101).

8. Justin J. Meggitt, *Paul, Poverty and Survival*, Studies of the New Testament and Its World (Edinburgh: T & T Clark, 1998).

9. See Dale B. Martin, "Review Essay: Justin J. Meggitt, *Paul, Poverty and Survival*," *JSNT* 84 (2001): 51-64, at 54-57; Gerd Theissen, "The Social Structure of Pauline Communities: Some Critical Remarks on J. J. Meggitt, *Paul, Poverty and Survival*," *JSNT* 84 (2001): 65-84, at 70-75; Steven J. Friesen, "Poverty in Pauline Studies: Beyond the So-called New

tial attempt to develop a more sophisticated and detailed model that avoids this criticism has been made by Steven Friesen, who outlines a "poverty scale" for Roman urban society with seven categories, ranging from the super-wealthy imperial elites (PS1) to those below subsistence level (PS7).[10] It is important to note, though, that Friesen concurs with Meggitt's central arguments: that there is little if any evidence to place any of the Pauline Christians into the category of the wealthy elite (PS1-3); and that the vast majority of the empire's inhabitants, and of the early Christians, were poor, living around or not much above subsistence level.[11]

It is unsurprising that the discussion of the socioeconomic level of the earliest Christians has focused heavily on the Pauline letters. Though even here the evidence is scanty, there are at least snippets of prosopographical and other information to consider within a literary deposit of some size. 1 Peter, on the other hand, in this as in other respects, stands relatively neglected. This, too, is unsurprising: it is one relatively short letter, the authorship and date of which are open to discussion and which provides no significant prosopographical data, at least concerning the addressees of the letter.[12] Yet 1 Peter deserves more careful attention than it has generally received. It is, after all, addressed to Christians across a wide geographical area and constitutes precious early evidence concerning the introduction and spread of

---

Consensus," *JSNT* 26 (2004): 323-61, at 339; Bengt Holmberg, "The Methods of Historical Reconstruction in the Scholarly 'Recovery' of Corinthian Christianity," in *Christianity at Corinth: The Quest for the Pauline Church*, ed. Edward Adams and David G. Horrell (Louisville and London: Westminster John Knox, 2004), pp. 255-71, esp. 261-66; Bruce W. Longenecker, "Exposing the Economic Middle: A Revised Economy Scale for the Study of Early Urban Christianity," *JSNT* 31 (2009): 243-78. Note the criticisms raised of a binary model in the work of ancient historians by Walter Scheidel, "Stratification, Deprivation and Quality of Life," in *Poverty in the Roman World,* ed. Margaret Atkins and Robin Osborne (Cambridge: Cambridge University Press, 2006), pp. 40-59, esp. 40-45. It should be noted, however, that Meggitt does at some points note the significance of differentiations among "the poor" (e.g., p. 5); furthermore, his strategy of stressing the material poverty of the mass of the empire's population is understandable as an attempt to confront the frequent presumption in "new consensus" writing that some members of the churches were wealthy, elite, upper class, etc.

10. Friesen, "Poverty in Pauline Studies."

11. Friesen, "Poverty in Pauline Studies," p. 348.

12. There is, of course, mention of Peter, Silvanus, and Mark (1:1; 5:12-13), but even if these references allow any socioeconomic deductions to be drawn and are not part of what Francis Beare calls "the apparatus of pseudonymity" (Francis W. Beare, *The First Epistle of Peter,* 3rd ed. [Oxford: Blackwell, 1970 (first ed. 1947)], p. 48), they tell us nothing about the Christians to whom the letter was sent.

Christianity in Asia Minor. John Elliott describes it as "one of the most socially significant writings of the early church."[13]

Indeed, the main exception to this general neglect is Elliott's groundbreaking and influential study, *A Home for the Homeless,* the first social-scientific study of the letter, which attempts, among other things, to provide a "social profile" of the addressees of the letter. The starting point for Elliott's analysis of the letter is an argument for the correlation and central importance of two key terms: πάροικος and οἶκος (τοῦ θεοῦ). These terms, Elliott proposes, "are not merely linguistic but also sociological and theological correlates."[14] They therefore invite consideration as to the ways in which they "provide clues to the social condition of the addressees as well as to the socioreligious response offered by the document itself."[15]

After examining the meaning and use of πάροικος and related terms in both secular and biblical texts, Elliott concludes that it refers to those "being or living as a resident alien in a foreign environment or away from home."[16] More specifically, the term πάροικος denotes the "resident alien," while παρεπίδημος refers to the "transient stranger."[17] Furthermore, Elliott argues that in 1 Peter the description of the addressees as πάροικοι and παρεπίδημοι (see 1:1, 17; 2:11) refers to their "actual political and social condition."[18] This

---

13. John H. Elliott, *A Home for the Homeless: A Social-Scientific Criticism of 1 Peter, Its Situation and Strategy,* 2nd ed. (Minneapolis: Fortress, 1990 [first ed. 1981]), p. xxxii. It is curious that 1 Peter does not receive more attention in Stephen Mitchell's massive and magisterial treatment of Anatolia, on which I am dependent for much of the broader information about Asia Minor below. Discussing the origins of Christianity in Anatolia, Mitchell focuses on Paul's mission and letter to the Galatians, while later describing the testimony of Pliny's famous letter (10.96) as "a unique and unparalleled claim that Christianity had established a major hold on northern Asia Minor by the early second century" (*Anatolia: Land, Men, and Gods in Asia Minor,* Volume II: *The Rise of the Church* [Oxford: Clarendon, 1993], p. 37; see pp. 37-38). Mitchell's only substantive comment on 1 Peter is to note that, insofar as there was an early Christian mission in the areas north of the extent of Paul's activity, "the evangelist was surely Peter, who addressed the Jews of Pontus, Galatia, Cappadocia, Asia, and Bithynia in his first epistle" (Mitchell, *Anatolia II,* p. 3).

14. Elliott, *Home,* p. 23.

15. Elliott, *Home,* p. 24.

16. Elliott, *Home,* p. 35.

17. Elliott, *Home,* p. 34.

18. Elliott, *Home,* p. 35. This is somewhat qualified on p. 42, where Elliott notes that "[t]here is neither need nor reason to postulate mutually exclusive literal/figurative options here. . . . [T]hese words in 1 Peter are used to describe religious *as well as* social circumstances," and further in his more recent commentary (John H. Elliott, *1 Peter: A New Translation with Introduction and Commentary,* AB37B [New York: Doubleday, 2000], p. 482):

description thus gives us a concrete indication as to their socioeconomic situation: they are "resident aliens and transient strangers" who "shared the same vulnerable condition of the many thousands of Jewish and other ethnic *paroikoi* of Asia Minor and throughout the Roman empire."[19] Indeed, in summarizing the findings of his opening chapter, Elliott makes clear how fundamentally his conclusions as to the significance of the designation πάροικοι καὶ παρεπίδημοι shape his reflections on the social profile of the addressees:

> In 1 Peter the terms *paroikia, paroikoi* and *parepidēmoi* identify the addressees as a combination of displaced persons who are currently *aliens permanently residing in (paroikia, paroikoi)* or *strangers temporarily visiting or passing through (parepidēmoi)* the four provinces of Asia Minor named in the salutation (1:1). These terms . . . indicate not only the geographical dislocation of the recipients but also the political, legal, social and religious limitations and estrangement which such displacement entails. As *paroikoi* they may well have been numbered among the rural population and villagers who had been relocated to city territories and assigned inferior status to the citizenry. And as both *paroikoi* and *parepidēmoi* they may have been included among the numerous immigrant artisans, craftsmen, traders, merchants residing permanently in or temporarily traveling through the villages, towns and cities of the eastern provinces.[20]

Elliott's next chapter expands many of these observations in offering a "social profile" of the addressees of 1 Peter. For Elliott, the "limited" urbanization of much of Asia Minor combined with the "internal evidence" of 1 Peter "suggest[s] that the letter is directed to a predominantly rural audience."[21]

"The experience of many as actual strangers and resident aliens provided an existential basis for the depiction of all believers as strangers and resident aliens in a metaphorical sense."

19. Elliott, *Home,* p. 37; cf. p. 129.

20. Elliott, *Home,* p. 48.

21. Elliott, *Home,* pp. 62-63. Note, however, that this conclusion is both reiterated and qualified in what follows: most πάροικοι were located in rural areas (p. 68), and this is where most of the addressees were likely to be located (p. 69), but "the letter is intended for Christians in the cities also" (p. 69) and the reference to οἰκέται (2:18-20) suggests an urban location (p. 69). Nonetheless, in his more recent commentary, Elliott reiterates the likely "rural location of the letter's addressees," which "marks 1 Peter as a notable exception to the generalization that early Christianity everywhere constituted an 'urban phenomenon'" (Elliott, *1 Peter,* p. 90).

The Christian communities in view contained a mix of Jews and non-Jews, though mostly the latter.[22] And the conclusion that the addressees were πάροικοι forms the basis for a series of suggestions about their likely legal, economic, and social status: excluded from civic rights, mostly (though not exclusively) in rural areas and involved in agriculture, generally "from the working proletariat of the urban and rural areas" and in "an inferior economic position."[23]

These are the main contours of contemporary scholarship with which this present study must engage. In the examination of the socioeconomic status of the addressees of 1 Peter that follows, the findings will be related to the current "new consensus" debate focused on the Pauline evidence, as sketched above. More specifically, Elliott's influential proposals concerning the recipients of the letter will provide a set of hypotheses to test.

1. The Socioeconomic Structure of the Roman Empire

Before considering the specific evidence from the letter itself, it is important to provide a broader sketch of the Roman economy and of the developments in Asia Minor in the period with which we are concerned.

Moses Finley's *The Ancient Economy,* first published in 1973, remains a landmark study, particularly important for presenting a so-called "primitivist" view of the Roman economy: primarily dependent on agriculture, with land-ownership as the main form of wealth and cities as essentially centers of consumption, dependent on the produce and wealth generated from the land.[24] Trade and industry remained mostly small-scale and rudimentary.[25] The empire itself made significant demands in terms of taxation, both in cash but also, importantly, in kind, with much agricultural produce needed to supply grain to Rome and also to support military presence and activity.

Subsequent studies have challenged and revised aspects of this depiction but have affirmed the essential outlines of Finley's primitivist portrait.[26]

---

22. Elliott, *Home,* pp. 65-67; also pp. 45-46 with pp. 55-56 nn. 76-77.

23. See Elliott, *Home,* pp. 67-70, with quotations from p. 70.

24. Moses I. Finley, *The Ancient Economy,* 2nd ed. (London: Penguin, 1985 [first ed. 1973]); on agriculture, p. 188; on cities, pp. 123-49, 191-96.

25. Cf. also Richard Duncan-Jones, *The Economy of the Roman Empire: Quantitative Studies,* 2nd ed. (Cambridge: Cambridge University Press, 1982 [first ed. 1974]), pp. 1-2.

26. Note Kevin Greene's assessment: "His overall framework has remained intact: gross disparities in wealth, the importance of political power and social status, and the limitations

Richard Duncan-Jones comments that "[t]he Roman economy remained a primitive system which would today qualify the Roman Empire for recognition as a 'developing' country. Almost everywhere a large part of the population was engaged in agriculture at a relatively low level, while industry depended on a backward technology and was rarely organised in large units."[27] Robin Osborne, writing in 2006, characterizes the Roman economy as an "underdeveloped," preindustrial economy based fundamentally on agriculture and with a largely rural population. Life expectancy was very low — estimates suggest around twenty to thirty at birth — and there was widespread malnutrition and periodic famine.[28]

In terms of the overall socioeconomic structure of the empire's population, there is widespread agreement that wealth and power were heavily concentrated in relatively few hands, with the richest elites comprising in total only around 1 percent of the population.[29] The concentration of wealth in few hands in a pre-industrial, agriculturally based economy implies the corollary that the majority of the empire's population did not live comfortably; as Meggitt and Friesen have stressed, "the overwhelming majority of the population under Roman imperialism lived near the subsistence level."[30]

Nonetheless, there is good reason to try to press beyond the binary model — a few very rich, an undifferentiated mass of the poor — found in

of financial systems, are not in dispute. However, most commentators are more positive about the level and nature of economic activity that took place within this framework" (Kevin Greene, "Technological Innovation and Economic Progress in the Ancient World: M. I. Finley Re-Considered," *The Economic History Review,* New Series 53, no. 1 [2000]: 29-59, at p. 52). On the primitivist/modernist debate, see also Meggitt, *Paul,* pp. 41-73, who supports Finley's "primitivist" picture.

27. Duncan-Jones, *Economy,* p. 1. See further pp. 1-2.

28. For all these points, see Robin Osborne, "Roman Poverty in Context," in Atkins and Osborne, eds., *Poverty in the Roman World,* pp. 1-20, at p. 4. See further Geza Alföldy, *The Social History of Rome* (London and Sydney: Croom Helm, 1985), pp. 94-156; Ekkehard W. Stegemann and Wolfgang Stegemann, *The Jesus Movement: A Social History of Its First Century* (Edinburgh: T & T Clark, 1999), pp. 7-95. On life expectancy, see Richard Duncan-Jones, *Structure and Scale in the Roman Economy* (Cambridge: Cambridge University Press, 1990), pp. 93-104.

29. See Alföldy, *Social History,* p. 147; Scheidel, "Stratification," p. 42 with n. 6; Stegemann and Stegemann, *Jesus Movement,* p. 77, who suggest between and 1 and 5 percent for the upper stratum as a whole. For more detailed calculations, leading to the conclusion that "the richest elites made up only about 1.23% of the empire's inhabitants," see Friesen, "Poverty in Pauline Studies," pp. 360-61.

30. Friesen, "Poverty in Pauline Studies," p. 343; Meggitt, *Paul, passim;* Stegemann and Stegemann, *Jesus Movement,* pp. 88-93.

both ancient (elite) depictions and in some modern scholarship.[31] There is insufficient evidence to allow precise, robust conclusions to be drawn about the percentage of people living at various levels of socioeconomic status, but, as Friesen has shown, estimates can be attempted. His chart is as follows:[32]

PS1	Imperial elites	0.04%
PS2	Regional elites	1.00%
PS3	Municipal elites	1.76%
PS4	Moderate surplus	7.00%?
PS5	Stable near subsistence	22.00%?
PS6	At subsistence	40.00%
PS7	Below subsistence	28.00%

It is notable that the figures are most speculative in categories 4 and 5, as Friesen indicates with question marks.[33] This is unfortunate, since, as John Barclay remarks, it is precisely here that the distinctions are crucial: How much is "moderate surplus" and how many of the population (and, more specifically, of the early Christians) might have lived at this level?[34]

However, a recent essay by Walter Scheidel specifically addresses this issue, arguing for a sizeable "middling group" comprising 20-25 percent of Roman society.[35] Drawing on Scheidel's work, Bruce Longenecker argues that the percentages in Friesen's scale should be revised, with the category of moderate surplus (PS4) increased to include around 17 percent of the population, and PS5, 6, and 7 adjusted to 25, 30 and 25 percent respectively. It is

31. For this argument against a binary model, see Scheidel, "Stratification," pp. 40-45; Longenecker, "Exposing the Economic Middle." Among the examples Longenecker cites are Tacitus's contrasts between those who are "virtuous and associated with great houses" and "the dirty plebs" (*plebs sordida, Hist* 1.4) or between "citizens of repute" and "the rabble" (*Ann.* 3.36), though in neither of these instances does Tacitus simply give a binary view of Roman society.

32. See Friesen, "Poverty in Pauline Studies," p. 347.

33. See Friesen, "Poverty in Pauline Studies," pp. 343-45. But the figures in all categories below PS3 are necessarily based on very limited evidence. As Longenecker points out, Friesen's figures for PS6 and PS7 are derived from a 1993 study by C. R. Whittaker of the poor in the city of Rome, with comparisons with cities in pre-industrial Europe, but Friesen takes the top end of Whittaker's percentages for PS6 (30-40%) and PS7 (24-28%) — see Friesen, "Poverty in Pauline Studies," p. 345 n. 69, for his reasons for doing this.

34. John M. G. Barclay, "Poverty in Pauline Studies: A Response to Steven Friesen," *JSNT* 26 (2004): 363-66, at p. 365.

35. Scheidel, "Stratification," p. 54.

important to note that this still leaves 80 percent of the population living near subsistence level, so the picture of a large majority living in poverty remains. Moreover, it remains to be seen how other ancient historians respond to Scheidel's proposals and whether his optimistic view of a sizeable "middle class"[36] turns out to be somewhat too optimistic.

These figures, though they remain highly provisional and open to debate, give us a very broad idea of the socioeconomic structure of the empire's population (albeit, it should be noted, a static snapshot, which does not give any impression of the extent of vulnerability to fluctuation, due, for example, to famine and other changes in circumstance). They do not, of course, tell us anything about where the early Christians fitted into this structure. Nor do they inform us about the particular development of Asia Minor in the period immediately prior to and including the time of 1 Peter's composition.[37] This is a more specific socioeconomic context within which to read and understand the letter.

2. Roman Imperialism and the Development of Asia Minor

Among a number of significant changes that accompanied the development of Roman imperial domination of Asia Minor, one of the most important was urbanization.[38] By deliberate policy and acts of foundation, new cities were established across the provinces of Asia Minor. After surveying the rele-

36. A term Scheidel uses on p. 54, though he generally speaks of a "middling group," or something similar. Many ancient historians have rejected the idea that one can speak of a middle class in antiquity, at least in the sense of a "class" that represents a distinctive socioeconomic group with a particular basis for their economic activity, seeing the socioeconomic structure as essentially divided into two: upper and lower strata.

37. I regard the likely date-range for 1 Peter as approximately 75-95 CE. See David G. Horrell, *The Epistles of Peter and Jude* (London: Epworth, 1998), pp. 8-10. Elliott, *1 Peter*, pp. 134-38, and Paul J. Achtemeier, *1 Peter*, Hermeneia (Philadelphia: Fortress Press, 1996), pp. 43-50, for example, come to broadly similar conclusions (Elliott suggests 73-92 CE, Achtemeier 80-100 CE, probably in the early part of that range).

38. For a brief overview of the development of Roman involvement in Asia Minor, see Richard J. A. Talbert, *Atlas of Classical History* (London and New York: Routledge, 1985), p. 159. For detailed discussion, see T. R. S. Broughton, "Roman Asia Minor," in *An Economic Survey of Ancient Rome,* ed. Tenney Frank, vol. 4 (Baltimore: Johns Hopkins University Press, 1938), pp. 499-916, esp. pp. 505-98; Stephen Mitchell, *Anatolia: Land, Men, and Gods in Asia Minor,* Volume I: *The Celts and the Impact of Roman Rule* (Oxford: Clarendon, 1993); A. N. Sherwin-White, *Roman Foreign Policy in the East 168 B.C. to A.D. 1* (London: Duckworth, 1984).

vant evidence, Stephen Mitchell concludes that "by the end of the Julio-Claudian period most of Pontus, Paphlagonia, north Galatia, Galatian Phrygia, Lycaonia, and Pisidia was divided up between contiguous city territories; only Cappadocia was left outside this pattern of settlement, and remained largely without cities."[39] Moreover, in the period of the Roman Empire, the inscriptional evidence shows "unequivocally that the plateau was densely populated."[40] This change makes clear how important it is to distinguish pre-Roman and Roman Asia Minor, and (without denying that the coastal areas of the province of Asia were more densely populated and heavily urbanized than the interior plateau)[41] should lead us to be cautious about regarding 1 Peter as necessarily addressed to predominantly rural areas, a point to which we shall return.[42]

Another major impact of Roman rule was the development of Asia Minor's network of roads.[43] Facilitating movements of military personnel and supplies, particularly to the Euphrates frontier, was the main reason for this undertaking, but the massive development of the network also, of course, made communications, trade, and travel much easier. The scale of the work should be emphasized: the main highways were, on average, around eight meters wide and covered around 9,000 kilometers.[44] The cost of paying for such an enterprise, which would have been so great as to bankrupt the state and would thus also have been impossible for local communities to bear, leads Mitchell to conclude that the task must have entailed a system of unpaid labor forced upon citizens and slaves, often by the military.[45]

Indeed, military presence — a regular feature of life throughout the region — brought many demands to the communities of Asia Minor. Soldiers were regularly stationed on the roads, protecting routes, collecting fines, and

39. Mitchell, *Anatolia I,* p. 98.
40. Mitchell, *Anatolia I,* p. 148.
41. Cf. Mitchell, *Anatolia I,* p. 80.
42. Cf. Elliott, *1 Peter,* p. 90: "The predominantly *rural* feature of the provinces other than Asia. . . ." Karen H. Jobes, *1 Peter,* BECNT (Grand Rapids: Baker Academic, 2005), describes the area to which 1 Peter was addressed as "a remote and undeveloped region," "a vast geographical area with small cities few and far between" (p. 22), where "Greek or Latin was spoken only by administrative officials" (p. 20). This last assertion (repeated in a similar vein on p. 22) is certainly false, even though it is true that indigenous languages survived especially in rural areas, where knowledge of Greek was less developed; on this point, see nn. 71-72 below.
43. Mitchell, *Anatolia I,* pp. 124-36.
44. Mitchell, *Anatolia I,* pp. 125-26.
45. Mitchell, *Anatolia I,* pp. 126-27.

no doubt taking opportunity to make various demands, legitimate and illegitimate, of the local communities,[46] which had a duty "to feed, clothe, house, and even to provide armour and equipment for the armies."[47] These obligations, Mitchell notes, "were a distinct economic burden."[48] Indeed, much of the agricultural produce, especially grain, paid as tax in kind, was probably used to supply the needs of the military.[49]

As already noted above for the empire generally, so too for Asia Minor, agriculture formed the center of the economy. One of the changes in the Roman period was that — not least due to Roman tax demands forcing people to sell or mortgage their land — "much . . . of the rural territory of central Anatolia was parcelled out into large estates owned by local city gentry, [and] wealthy aristocrats from further afield," often of Roman or Italian origin. Rural villages formed part of such estates.[50] Many country dwellers were thus "effectively serfs, tied to the land with obligations to provide the landowner with labour and produce."[51]

Overall, the detailed picture of Asia Minor's development presented by Mitchell makes clear the impact of Roman rule and the associated economic and population expansion. The establishment of cities (with contiguous territories) and a major road network are key infrastructural developments, with the wealth of the elite conspicuously displayed in public buildings, imperial temples, baths, and so on. The concentration of wealth and landownership in relatively few hands fits with the broader outlines of the poverty scale. Indeed, despite the developments of the imperial period, one should not assume that there was any widespread improvement in the economic position of the majority of the population. On the contrary, the demands for taxes and rents, plus the related responsibilities for sustaining the military presence in the region, would have weighed heavily upon the poor, many of whom labored as peasants on land owned by others.

---

46. See Mitchell, *Anatolia I*, pp. 118-24, 141.

47. Mitchell, *Anatolia I*, p. 134.

48. Mitchell, *Anatolia I*, p. 134.

49. Mitchell, *Anatolia I*, pp. 245-53.

50. See Mitchell, *Anatolia I*, pp. 148-58, with quotation on p. 149. Mitchell includes a third category of landowner here — the Roman emperor himself — though it was only in the second century that emperors began to acquire land in this area (see p. 156).

51. Mitchell, *Anatolia I*, p. 176. On serfdom in the ancient Greek and Roman worlds, see further G. E. M. de Ste. Croix, *The Class Struggle in the Ancient Greek World from the Archaic Age to the Arab Conquests* (London: Duckworth, 1981), pp. 135-36, 147-62.

3. The Addressees of 1 Peter

3.1 Aliens and Strangers?

With the contours of recent debate in mind and the broader context of Roman Asia Minor to inform our investigation, we turn to consider the data in 1 Peter. It is important, first, to assess the implications of the depiction of the addressees as πάροικοι καὶ παρεπίδημοι, since this is central to Elliott's description of their socioeconomic status. Elliott, we recall, took these terms to indicate that the letter's addressees were "resident aliens and transient strangers," identities that had further implications in terms of their inferior social, economic, and political-legal status. It is only fair to note that few have been convinced by this argument.[52]

More recently, Karen Jobes has presented a new variation of this proposal for a literal interpretation of the addressees' identity as πάροικοι καὶ παρεπίδημοι.[53] Noting the lack of evidence for evangelization of northern Asia Minor, Jobes suggests that "the Christians to whom Peter writes had become Christians elsewhere, had some association with Peter prior to his writing to them, and now found themselves foreigners and resident aliens scattered throughout Asia Minor."[54] One possibility is that the first converts in Asia Minor had been Pentecost pilgrims who heard Peter's preaching in Jerusalem (Acts 2:9-11).[55] More likely, according to Jobes, is that they were among those (probably Jews) converted during a visit of Peter to Rome in the 40s, then deported from Rome and made part of the extensive colonization of Asia Minor under Claudius.[56] This intriguing theory is, however, subject to many of the same objections brought against Elliott's proposal, which Jobes does not adequately address,[57] and it suffers from major addi-

---

52. See, e.g., Reinhard Feldmeier, *Die Christen als Fremde*, WUNT 64 (Tübingen: Mohr Siebeck, 1992), esp. pp. 203-10; Steven R. Bechtler, *Following in His Steps: Suffering, Community, and Christology in 1 Peter*, SBLDS 162 (Atlanta: Scholars, 1998), pp. 70-82; Achtemeier, *1 Peter*, pp. 174-75; Torrey Seland, *Strangers in the Night: Philonic Perspectives on Christian Identity in 1 Peter*, Biblical Interpretation Series 76 (Leiden: Brill, 2005), pp. 39-78.

53. Jobes, *1 Peter*, pp. 24-41.

54. Jobes, *1 Peter*, p. 26.

55. Jobes, *1 Peter*, pp. 27-28.

56. Jobes, *1 Peter*, pp. 28-41.

57. It is certainly not the case that "[t]he primary objection to Elliott's specific social reconstruction has been that the relationships between the social and economic classes in first-century Asia Minor are too complex, and the terms that refer to them are understood

tional difficulties: (1) the uncertainty about any visit of Peter to Rome in the 40s and the requirement of an early date for 1 Peter; (2) the lack of any positive evidence to associate Jews expelled from Rome with colonists arriving in Asia Minor in this period (the evidence for the foundation of the Jewish communities of Asia Minor indicates that they were well established from the first century BCE and began earlier still);[58] (3) most crucially, a misunderstanding of the character and development of Roman colonies in Asia Minor. Early on, these were indeed true colonies, involving the settlement of Roman veterans and others from Rome, but increasingly, especially in Claudius's time, entailed the creation of *titular* colonies, that is, the giving of a colonial title to an *existing* city as an honor.[59]

One problem with Elliott's argument has been highlighted by Steven Bechtler, namely, that in extra-biblical Greek the term πάροικος is used to denote a non-citizen, whether native or non-native, rather than a resident alien as such.[60] As Mitchell notes, the rural population of Anatolia was often described as πάροικοι, περίοικοι, κάτοικοι, κωμῆται, or simply as the λαός.[61] As such, the description of the addressees as πάροικοι might still allow a significant deduction to be made about their social, political, and economic status. Yet there are also telling difficulties with Elliott's argument for taking this description in a literal, socio-political sense.

The recipients of the letter are initially addressed, as a group, as παρ-

---

too imprecisely, to validate Elliott's hypothesis" (Jobes, *1 Peter*, p. 31). See below for much more specific and decisive objections, which equally affect Jobes's theory.

58. For a survey of this evidence see Emil Schürer, *The History of the Jewish People in the Age of Jesus Christ (175 B.C.–A.D. 135)*, vol. 3.1 (Edinburgh: T&T Clark, 1986), pp. 17-38; Mitchell, *Anatolia II*, pp. 31-37, and, for an extensive study of the Jewish communities of Asia Minor, Paul R. Trebilco, *Jewish Communities in Asia Minor*, SNTSMS 69 (Cambridge: Cambridge University Press, 1991).

59. See further E. T. Salmon, *Roman Colonization under the Republic* (London: Thames and Hudson, 1969), esp. chap. 10. According to Salmon's list (see p. 160), only three colonies were founded in Asia Minor during the reign of Claudius. Jobes's appeal to the work of David Noy, *Foreigners at Rome: Citizens and Strangers* (London: Duckworth, 2002), and Salmon, *Roman Colonization*, to support her proposals, seems, so far as I can see, entirely misplaced.

60. Bechtler, *Following*, pp. 71-73. Cf. also Elliott, *1 Peter*, pp. 477-78, where the evidence cited indicates that the term πάροικοι stands in distinction to citizens. Elliott recognizes that the term can thus include natives of the locality, such as tenant farmers, but arguably does not take this sufficiently into account.

61. Mitchell, *Anatolia I*, p. 176; see pp. 176-78; Broughton, "Roman Asia Minor," pp. 629-40; cf. Ste. Croix, *Class Struggle*, p. 160, on πάροικοι in Greek texts as those without political rights.

ἐπίδημοι (1:1), while in 1:17 they are said to live out a παροικία, and in 2:11 are exhorted ὡς παροίκους καὶ παρεπιδήμους. The noun παρεπίδημος is rare in Greek literature and occurs only twice in the LXX (Gen 23:4; Ps 38:13).[62] Its pairing with πάροικος in 2:11 suggests that the words function in 1 Peter as a *hendiadys,* both equally appropriate to describe the addressees, which implies that the author is using the terms to convey something about the character of their experience rather than their literal socio-political status (in which case someone would be either a πάροικος or a παρεπίδημος). More crucially still, the use of παρεπίδημος, and the phrase pairing πάροικος with παρεπίδημος, indicates the decisive influence of the LXX on the author's language. Specifically, 2:11 appropriates the language with which Abraham voices the nature of his residence among the Hittites (Gen 23:4). There Abraham describes himself as a "a stranger and an alien" (πάροικος καὶ παρεπίδημος).[63] Further texts in the LXX, echoing this self-description, already indicate a kind of broadening or spiritualizing of the term, beyond a strictly literal or socio-political designation.[64] Perhaps the clearest example is in 1 Chron 29:15: πάροικοί ἐσμεν ἐναντίον σου (i.e., YHWH), clearly spiritualizing to some extent, since the verse ends: "our days on the earth are like a shadow, and there is no abiding" (ESV).[65] This does not deny that the terms, at least in 1 Peter, are used to depict a sense of social alienation or estrangement from the world due to the hostility of the wider society, which seems to me a key point in Elliott's argument.[66] It does, however, strongly suggest that the terms as used in 1 Peter do not reflect their use as socio-political designations in Greco-Roman society but rather their use in Jewish tradition to express the alienation and estrangement of God's people from the world.[67] As such, *pace*

62. See esp. Feldmeier, *Fremde,* pp. 8-12, who notes: "Der . . . Begriff παρεπίδημος begegnet *sowohl im biblisch-jüdischen wie im paganen Schrifttum ausgesprochen selten*" (p. 8).

63. Cited also by Philo, *Conf.* 79.

64. *Pace* Elliott, *Home,* pp. 27-29. See further Feldmeier, *Fremde,* pp. 39-54, 207-8; Reinhard Feldmeier, "The 'Nation' of Strangers: Social Contempt and Its Theological Interpretations in Ancient Judaism and Early Christianity," in *Ethnicity and the Bible,* ed. Mark G. Brett (Leiden: Brill, 1996), pp. 240-70, esp. 244-47, on "self-description as strangers before God" in the post-exilic situation.

65. Cf. also Lev 25:23 (πάροικοι . . . ἐναντίον μου); Ps 39:12 [38:13 LXX] (πάροικος ἐγώ εἰμι παρὰ σοὶ καὶ παρεπίδημος).

66. Cf. Elliott, *Home,* pp. 42-43: "the fundamental contrast in 1 Peter is not a cosmological but a sociological one: the Christian community set apart from and in tension with its social neighbours"; Elliott, *1 Peter,* p. 481: "a condition of *social,* not cosmological, estrangement."

67. See the central arguments of Feldmeier, *Fremde,* and Feldmeier, "The 'Nation' of Strangers."

Elliott, the terms describe not the addressees' socio-legal status *prior* to conversion but their socio-spiritual status *consequent* on their conversion. Unfortunately, therefore, this designation of the addressees can tell us nothing about their concrete socioeconomic status.

If the addressees are not literally πάροικοι, then one major reason to identify them as (mostly) rural dwellers also disappears (see above with n. 21). Other reasons adduced by Elliott — the limited urbanization of much of Asia Minor and the rural metaphors used in the letter (Elliott lists 1:22-24; 2:25; and 5:2-4)[68] — are also questionable. Bechtler has rightly pointed out that the supposedly rural metaphors could just as well be used by urban authors for urbanized audiences (cf. 1 Cor 9:7-10; Gal 6:7-8) and has noted that many of the images in the letter are not especially rural.[69] And, as we have seen, one of the most obvious impacts of Roman rule was the establishment of a network of urban centers, linked by a comprehensive network of roads. While, as elsewhere, the majority of the population remained rural, the character of Asia Minor in the first two centuries CE cannot itself substantially support the hypothesis that 1 Peter was primarily addressed to rural areas. Indeed, there are some reasons to suggest the opposite, beyond the general observation that early Christianity seemed initially to spread through the empire as a primarily urban phenomenon. Since the letter addresses itself to Christians spread across a vast geographical area, it seems likely, *a priori,* that what was envisaged was a distribution (using the road and pathway network) linking urban settlements. More significantly, the facility in Greek one could expect among the population would be higher in the towns than in the countryside. Knowledge of the Greek language was widespread in the country as well as the cities,[70] but the epigraphic evidence shows that the Greek used in the cities was the "orthodox regular language of high culture," while the Greek of the countryside was much more variegated, "deformed" grammatically and orthographically.[71] It is also in the rural areas that indigenous languages persisted most strongly.[72] Questions remain about the precise quality of the Greek of 1 Pe-

68. Elliott, *Home,* p. 63.

69. Bechtler, *Following,* p. 67.

70. Jobes's comment that "Greek or Latin was spoken only by administrative officials" (Jobes, *1 Peter,* p. 20) — cited in n. 42 above — is certainly inaccurate.

71. See Mitchell, *Anatolia I,* pp. 174-75, who notes that "the Greek language was widely if unevenly adopted in the countryside of Anatolia" and that "a majority of the inhabitants of Asia Minor were, in some measure, bilingual in Greek and an indigenous language."

72. Mitchell, *Anatolia I,* p. 50; see further pp. 50-51, 172-75.

ter,[73] but it is clearly a literary text that demands a good level of facility in the language in order to understand it. This does not by any means prove that it was written with urban congregations in mind, but it does make this scenario somewhat more likely than that the addressees were mostly in rural areas.

Pliny makes a relevant comment when he remarks that Christianity has spread through "not only the towns, but villages and rural districts too" (*Ep.* 10.96.9: *Neque civitates tantum, sed vicos etiam atque agros . . .*). While this reveals that Christianity, by the time of Pliny's letter (c. 111-12 CE), was indeed evident in the countryside as well as the cities, the wording also implies that Christianity was initially and most naturally an urban phenomenon that had by this time — the early second century — begun to spread *even* to the rural areas.[74]

3.2 Socioeconomic Status

Elliott's interpretation of the addressees of 1 Peter as πάροικοι and παρεπίδημοι formed the basis, as we have seen, for a clear hypothesis regarding their socioeconomic level: generally, they were "from the working proletariat of the urban and rural areas," mostly the latter, and in "an inferior economic position."[75] If Elliott's interpretation of the terms πάροικος and παρεπίδημος does not in the end convince, then all the associated implications about the status and location of the addressees also fall away. We need then to return to the letter to ask whether there are any other hints concerning the socioeconomic location of the recipients. There are indeed a few points worthy of attention, mostly (though not exclusively) in the so-called domestic code (2:18–3:7), even if the amount of evidence they represent is slim.

---

73. See, e.g., Jobes's recent attempt to demonstrate that the Greek of 1 Peter may well reflect the work of someone for whom Greek was not the first language; Jobes, *1 Peter*, pp. 6-8, 325-38.

74. Cf. Judge, *Social Pattern*, p. 61. "Pliny accepted the fact that Christians represented a broad cross-section of society, from Roman citizens downwards, but reserved his surprise, apart from their numbers, in which he is an alarmist, for the ominous fact that the new religion was infecting not merely the cities, but the countryside. Until then however we may safely regard Christianity as a socially well backed movement of the great Hellenistic cities." Judge's view of Christianity as a movement dominated by the well-to-do of the cities is open to serious question, but his point about the primarily urban focus of early Christianity seems better founded.

75. Elliott, *Home*, p. 70.

It is significant that the first group the writer addresses specifically in this table of ethical instruction is the οἰκέται. This designation, as opposed to the more generic and common δοῦλοι, suggests that these are *domestic* slaves, used in the household rather than in agricultural or industrial activity.[76] This does not exclude the possibility of a rural location, though it is more likely to point to an urban context, where the majority of οἰκέται were used.[77] Given the variety of slave roles and status, and of owners' treatment of their slaves, it would be misleading to imply that the socioeconomic standing of all slaves was identical.[78] Nonetheless, in general slaves were allocated rations, clothing, and living quarters that were basic, amounting to "a fairly bleak material regime for most Roman slaves."[79] This does not mean that slaves' living conditions were necessarily any worse than for many of the empire's free poor; indeed, slaves may have had somewhat greater material security given their owners' duty and incentive to provide for them.[80] But, as Keith Bradley points out, "slaves were especially vulnerable in times of crisis"; Dio, for example, refers to an occasion in 6 CE when, due to a severe famine in Rome, gladiators and the slaves that were for sale "were banished to a distance of one hundred miles."[81] Moreover, Bradley notes, "[e]ven when food was not in short supply it was axiomatic that slaves should eat the poorest and cheapest food in the household."[82] All this implies that, despite the inevitable risk of overgeneralizing, we should place the οἰκέται in PS6, that is, "at subsistence level," with the possibility that some might slip into PS7, especially during times when food was particularly scarce.

76. Cf. Broughton, "Roman Asia Minor," p. 840; Ceslas Spicq, *Theological Lexicon of the New Testament* (Peabody, MA: Hendrickson, 1994), vol. 1, p. 384; *OCD*, p. 1415; Philo, *Spec. Leg.* 1.127.

77. A point also made by Elliott, *Home*, p. 69. An inscription from Sardis detailing the estate of Mnesimachus, which includes villages with their inhabitants, shows that the word οἰκέτης could also be used of slaves in such rural contexts; see Broughton, "Roman Asia Minor," pp. 631-32.

78. Slaves were appointed to a range of positions, with a consequently varied status, both in rural and urban contexts. On the variety of roles, material welfare, and power, see Keith Bradley, *Slavery and Society at Rome* (Cambridge: Cambridge University Press, 1994), pp. 55-80.

79. See Bradley, *Slavery and Society*, pp. 81-106, with quotation on p. 89; also Meggitt, *Paul*, p. 54 n. 65.

80. Bradley, *Slavery and Society*, p. 92.

81. Dio, *Rom. Hist.* 55.26.1; Bradley, *Slavery and Society*, p. 100.

82. Bradley, *Slavery and Society*, p. 101.

It is difficult to know what significance to draw from the fact that slave-owners are not directly addressed in the household code. Elliott takes this to "suggest that pagan masters are assumed,"[83] such that there is no corresponding group of owners/masters within the churches addressed.[84] This is, however, a precarious assumption, given the other New Testament texts where reciprocal teaching is also lacking, but where the existence of household-heads among the believers is explicitly indicated.[85] Indeed, as we shall see below, there are some indications of the presence of male heads of household among the addressees of the letter.

The instruction to wives (3:1-6) supports the view that, in at least some instances, Christian slaves, and certainly Christian wives, were in households where the *paterfamilias* was not a Christian (3:1-2). Given the general view that it was the duty of household members to follow the religion(s) of the head of the household, it is unsurprising if these Christians found themselves in situations of particular difficulty, where suffering for their faith might well occur.[86] It is understandable in such a context that the author's advice to wives is to make their new faith appealing through their pure and quiet demeanor rather than through speaking about it aloud (ἄνευ λόγου; 3:1-2). Nonetheless, despite the arguments of some commentators, the author does not imply that marriage to a non-believer was by any means the norm for wives in the churches.[87] Nor, we might suggest, was it necessarily the norm for Christian slaves to have non-Christian owners. The instruction to "be subject to your own husbands," etc., applies equally to those with believing husbands, as the example of Sarah and Abraham suggests.[88]

---

83. Elliott, *1 Peter,* p. 516.

84. Elliott, *1 Peter,* p. 95.

85. See esp. the instruction to slaves in 1 Tim 6:1-2 and Titus 2:9-10, where it is elsewhere made clear that the leaders of the churches are heads of household (1 Tim 3:1-12; Titus 1:5-7). 1 Tim 3:12 indicates that these households included more than just wife and children. Other NT texts containing household codes do, of course, offer reciprocal instruction to slaves and masters (Col 3:22–4:1; Eph 6:5-9).

86. See Plutarch *Mor.* 140D; David L. Balch, *Let Wives Be Submissive: The Domestic Code in 1 Peter,* SBLMS 26 (Atlanta: Scholars Press, 1981); Elliott, *1 Peter,* pp. 557-58.

87. Beare, *First Epistle of Peter,* p. 153, commenting on εἴ τινες κτλ, asserts: "There is no suggestion that these are exceptional cases; the implication of the whole passage, on the contrary, is that the women whom he is addressing are nearly all married to pagan husbands." Elliott more correctly interprets the force of the phrase: "The conditional formulation 'even if' *(kai ei)* indicates that the author allows for the fact that 'some' *(tines)* of the husbands mentioned in v 1b may be nonbelievers" (Elliott, *1 Peter,* p. 557).

88. *Pace* Achtemeier, *1 Peter,* p. 210: "What is clear is that the conduct of wives with non-

The instruction to wives concerning their proper adornment (κόσμος) — not the external adornment of braided hair, gold, and clothing, but the inner adornment of a gentle and quiet spirit (3:3-4) — picks up a topos common in Jewish, Greek, and Roman moral exhortation. Plutarch expresses the point in a very similar way: "'Adornment' [κόσμος], said Crates, 'is what adorns'; and what adorns a woman is what makes her better ordered [κοσμιώτεραν] — not gold, nor emerald nor scarlet, but whatever gives an impression of dignity [σεμνότης], discipline [εὐταξία], and modesty [αἰδώς]."[89] In early Christian literature there is an especially close parallel in 1 Tim 2:9-10, and, as Elliott notes, the church fathers show considerable interest in this text in 1 Peter, taking it to establish "an authoritative prohibition of external adornment for Christian women."[90]

Bruce Winter has drawn attention to the emergence of so-called "new women" from the first century BCE onwards — women who, at least in the eyes of their critics, adorned themselves elaborately and were sexually promiscuous. He argues that this is a relevant background for understanding the instructions to women and wives in the Pauline communities (especially the Pastoral Epistles).[91] If a similar background is in view in 1 Peter, then this author, too, may be reacting against the (potential) influence of these new values on the wives of the Christian communities. Winter sees the phenomenon of the "new woman" as one originating in upper-class Roman circles, but he notes that the influence of these values filtered down through society.[92]

For Elliott, this echo of "conventional sentiments concerning appropriate attire . . . reveals little or nothing about the actual social status of the

---

Christian husbands is the chief concern of the author here." This emphasis enables Achtemeier to make the implausible claim that this passage (3:1-6) says "nothing . . . about the general status of women within the Christian community, or within Christian marriage" (p. 208), but that 3:7 indicates the "equality between men and women inherent within the Christian community" (p. 219), an "equality . . . enjoined as a Christian duty" (p. 209).

89. *Mor.* 141E (Greek text and ET from Sarah B. Pomeroy, ed., *Plutarch's Advice to the Bride and Groom and A Consolation to His Wife. English Translations, Commentary, Interpretive Essays, and Bibliography* [New York and Oxford: Oxford University Press, 1999]), also cited in Elliott, *1 Peter*, p. 563. Cf. also *Mor.* 144D, 145E-146. For comparable statements from a Pythagorean community, see Elliott, *1 Peter*, pp. 563-64 with n. 174. For critique of women's finery in the Jewish tradition, see Isa 3:16–4:1; *T. Reub.* 5.1-6; Philo, *Sac.* 21; *Virt.* 39-40.

90. Elliott, *1 Peter*, p. 565, and see nn. 175-76.

91. Bruce W. Winter, *Roman Wives, Roman Widows: The Appearance of New Women and the Pauline Communities* (Grand Rapids: Eerdmans, 2003).

92. Winter, *Roman Wives*, p. 8.

wives addressed."[93] Others, however, take a different view. Francis Beare comments on 3:3:

> It is implied that the Christian communities included among their members women of wealth and position. Slave girls and women of the poor might indeed try to make themselves attractive by putting up their hair in braids and by giving some attention to their dress, but they would hardly need the warning against flaunting gold jewellry. Even the ἐμπλοκῆς τριχῶν — "the braiding of hair" — suggests the services of the hairdresser, and the ἐνδύσεως ἱματίων — literally "the putting on of garments" — clearly implies sumptuousness, and perhaps even such elaborate dressing as would require the help of maids.[94]

Beare is probably guilty of reading too much from the text here, just as interpreters influenced later by the so-called "new consensus" have often taken restricted hints in the texts to imply considerable wealth and social position and have rightly been criticized for this.[95] Nonetheless, that the pattern of instruction is an established topos does not mean we should entirely dismiss its socioeconomic relevance. The wives addressed by the author of 1 Peter are instructed not to adorn themselves in this ostentatious way (ὧν ἔστω οὐχ . . .) and are given positive role models of submission and obedience from the Jewish scriptural tradition, the most relevant source of authoritative guidance for the author (3:5-6). This does seem to imply that behaving in such ways is a realistic temptation for the wives in view. A more cautious conclusion, then, is that of Jobes, who comments that "at least some" of those addressed "actually have enough wealth to make this instruction

---

93. Elliott, *1 Peter*, p. 564.

94. Beare, *First Epistle of Peter*, p. 155.

95. E.g., because Gaius is host to the whole church at Corinth, he "is evidently a man of some wealth" (Meeks, *The First Urban Christians*, p. 57); Phoebe functions as a "protector or patroness of many Christians" and so "is an independent woman . . . who has some wealth" (p. 60). Cf. also Theissen, *Social Setting*, pp. 69-119. A striking example is found in Anthony Thiselton's recent comments on Chloe: on the basis solely of the reference to οἱ Χλόης (1 Cor 1:11) and the view that "in its first-century Roman period the city [of Corinth] hummed with wealth" she is seen as a "businesswoman" who has likely sent her "middle managers to Corinth" to conduct her business on her behalf (Anthony C. Thiselton, *First Corinthians: A Shorter Exegetical and Pastoral Commentary* [Grand Rapids: Eerdmans, 2006], pp. 6-7; cf. Thiselton, *The First Epistle to the Corinthians*, NIGTC [Grand Rapids: Eerdmans, 2000], p. 121, where she is termed a "wealthy Asian woman"). For the most extended and penetrating critique of such deductions, see Meggitt, *Paul.*

meaningful."[96] There is precious little information, of course, to enable us to define what "enough wealth" might mean here and where these wives might be placed on the poverty scale. On the one hand, warning against such external adornment by no means requires that the level of wealth is that of the highest social groups (PS1-3), of whose presence there is no hint in the letter. On the other hand, it does suggest that these are people living above bare subsistence (PS5-7), with some surplus resources at least at times.[97] That would suggest PS4.

The instruction to Christian husbands (3:7) — whether their wives are assumed to be Christian or not[98] — yields no relevant information on their likely socioeconomic status, though we can assume that this is the same as (and certainly not lower than) their wives, so, for some at least, probably PS4. There may be a little more information, though still only minimal data, in the later reference to πρεσβύτεροι (5:1-5). Commentators have long debated what exactly this term denotes and whether it refers primarily to age or to a position of leadership. Alastair Campbell has persuasively argued that, at this early period of Christian history, the term refers not to an ecclesiastical office as such, nor simply to age, but rather to a position of seniority, denoting those who are leaders of the early Christian communities by virtue of their social position as heads of households.[99] This helps to explain, on the one hand, why the term has some associations that seem primarily to do with age (cf. 5:5; also 1 Clem 3:3; 57:1-2; Tit 2:2-4), and, on the other hand, why the terms πρεσβύτερος and ἐπίσκοπος (here ἐπισκοπέω)[100] are inter-

---

96. Jobes, 1 Peter, p. 204. In fact, Jobes also refers here to the addressees as being "among the 'foreigners and resident aliens'" of Asia Minor, but for critique of her view on this description of the letter's recipients, see above.

97. Domestic slaves could sometimes be elaborately dressed by their owners, including jewelry, though this was a means to display the wealth and status of their owners, who would be even more sumptuously dressed, and was not something over which slaves had any control (see Bradley, Slavery and Society, pp. 87-88).

98. Cf. Jobes, 1 Peter, pp. 207-8, who makes the point that this instruction may include the situation of a husband with an unbelieving wife.

99. R. Alastair Campbell, The Elders: Seniority within Earliest Christianity, Studies of the New Testament and Its World (Edinburgh: T & T Clark, 1994), with summary on pp. 236-51; followed, for example, by Elliott, 1 Peter, pp. 813-15; Jobes, 1 Peter, pp. 302-3.

100. ἐπισκοποῦντες should probably be accepted here, though it is omitted in ℵ* and B. It is supported by P⁷², ℵ², A, Ψ, 33, 69, 1739. For discussion, see Bruce M. Metzger, A Textual Commentary on the Greek New Testament, 2nd ed. (Stuttgart and New York: United Bible Societies, 1994), p. 625; J. Ramsey Michaels, 1 Peter, WBC 49 (Waco, TX: Word Books, 1988), p. 276 n. b.

changeable.[101] There is evidently also some connection with seniority *in the faith* (cf. 1 Cor 16:15-18; 1 Tim 3:4-6), hence the corresponding instruction here to νεώτεροι, a term Elliott persuasively argues to refer to "the *most recent* converts of the community."[102] The πρεσβύτεροι addressed in 1 Peter, then, may well include some of the masters and husbands whose slaves and wives are also members of the community. These male heads of household have a responsibility as leaders of the churches and are instructed in this role.[103] What one can reasonably deduce from this about their socioeconomic level, however, is rather little, except insofar as the information about wives suggests at least some husbands in PS4. Nothing requires or implies that such senior figures, even if they be heads of households, have wealth or high social status.[104] (Similarly, while the vocabulary of "doing good" [cf. 2:12, 14-15; 3:16-17; 4:19; etc.] could be used to describe the euergetism of wealthy benefactors, it is by no means restricted to such deeds, as 2:20 [and probably 3:6] clearly shows, together with the scriptural texts whose language is quoted in 3:10-11. Thus these references cannot be taken to indicate anything about the socioeconomic standing of the addressees — and particularly the male householders — of the letter.[105]) If some of their households

101. Cf. *1 Clem.* 42:4-5; 44:4-5; Titus 1:5-7. Notably parallel to the use of πρεσβύτερος, ποιμαίνω, and ἐπισκοπέω in 1 Pet 5:1-2 is Acts 20:17, 28, where the same three roots are used to describe the position and calling of the Ephesian church leaders.

102. Elliott, *1 Peter*, p. 840; see pp. 836-40 for the weighing of various scholarly proposals.

103. Cf. David G. Horrell, "Leadership Patterns and the Development of Ideology in Early Christianity," in *Social-Scientific Approaches to New Testament Interpretation,* ed. Horrell (Edinburgh: T&T Clark, 1999), pp. 309-37, at p. 330. Such a pattern of instruction is especially clear in the Pastoral Epistles, where the ἐπίσκοποι, πρεσβύτεροι, and διάκονοι, as leaders of the churches, have responsibilities for respectable citizenship and good household management (1 Tim 3:1-13; Titus 1:5-9).

104. Among the instructions given to them is a warning to fulfill their responsibilities μηδὲ αἰσχροκερδῶς (5:2). Although this adverb appears only here in the NT and LXX, related words and similar warnings are found elsewhere, notably in the Pastorals' instructions to church leaders (see 1 Tim 3:3, 8; 6:10; 2 Tim 3:2; Titus 1:7, 11; also Heb 13:5; *Did.* 3.5; 15.1; etc.). When listing the qualities required of a military general, Onosander mentions that he should be frugal and not given to avarice (*De Imp. Off.* 1.1). Indeed, as Elliott, *1 Peter*, notes, it was "conventional opinion that the gaining *(kerdainō)* of wealth for oneself was highly shameful *(aischros)*" (p. 829, with refs. in n. 679). It is therefore unsurprising that early Christian leaders were warned against such greed, especially given the established obligation of congregations to provide support for leaders (e.g., 1 Cor 9:4-14; *Did.* 11-13). But I do not think the warning in itself says anything significant about the socioeconomic level of the πρεσβύτεροι here.

105. *Pace* Bruce W. Winter, *Seek the Welfare of the City: Christians as Benefactors and*

include οἰκέται, as we may plausibly assume, then they would not appear to be among the most destitute, and, of course, they would have a social status higher than that of the slaves they own, even if they own only one or two.[106] Again, we might very tentatively point to PS4-5 as a plausible but by no means necessary location for such people. The specific data, it is clear, are very limited.

Conclusions

The first conclusion to be drawn from this survey is a negative one. The description of the addressees as πάροικοι and παρεπίδημοι cannot serve as an indication of their socioeconomic status. Elliott's social profile of the addressees — as mostly rural, at the lower end of the economic and social scale — based largely as it is on his conclusions regarding what it meant to be a πάροικος or a παρεπίδημος, does not bear critical scrutiny. This is an unfortunate conclusion, since Elliott's ground-breaking work offered the promise of a more detailed socioeconomic profile than is otherwise possible. But the foundations cannot support the edifice. Without the hypothesis about the socioeconomic location of πάροικοι and παρεπίδημοι, there is much less that can be said about the profile of the letter's recipients. Nonetheless, some tentative conclusions are still possible.

There is little to support the view that the addressees are mostly country dwellers. Indeed, the hints in the letter and the broader evidence suggest the opposite. Instead of 1 Peter being "a notable exception" to the generally urban focus of earliest Christianity,[107] it seems unexceptional insofar as the most likely setting for its addressees is households in urban centers, as we find in the Pauline letters. We should beware of too confident a conclusion here, however, not least due to our ignorance of so much about the location and spread of earliest Christianity. While urban centers emerge most prominently and obviously as the focus of early Christian activity, we can hardly

---

Citizens, First-Century Christians in the Graeco-Roman World (Grand Rapids: Eerdmans, 1994), pp. 25-40, esp. pp. 26, 33, 37, 39.

106. It is also reasonable, therefore, to note that the addressees include both free persons and slaves (Elliott, *1 Peter,* p. 95). Whether it is right to take 2:13-17 as "specific instruction" for "free persons," as Elliott does, on the basis of 2:16 (ὡς ἐλεύθεροι), is more open to question, since the depiction of the addressees as "free" here might express a theological conviction more than a sociological description, as in 1 Cor 7:22.

107. Elliott, *1 Peter,* p. 90.

rule out significant Christian presence in villages and the countryside, as Pliny indicates in the early second century (*Ep.* 10.96.9).

In terms of socioeconomic status, the churches addressed in 1 Peter contained both domestic slaves, relatively low in social status and probably living at subsistence level, and free persons, some of whom may have been male householders and masters whose seniority gave them a position of influence within the community. The women of the communities included at least some with sufficient resources to make elaborate dressing a possibility. While there is clearly insufficient evidence to produce any kind of social profile of the members of these churches, there are at least enough hints to suggest that the addressees of 1 Peter included members from the middle to bottom categories of the poverty scale, PS4-6/7. Allowing for some alarmist exaggeration on Pliny's part, this is broadly congruent with Pliny's depiction of the Christians of Pontus: "a great many individuals, of every age and class, both men and women" (*Multi enim omnis aetatis, omnis ordinis, utriusque sexus etiam* [*Ep.* 10.96.9]). This is also a conclusion congruent with Friesen's analysis of the Christians mentioned in Paul's letters, adding some limited support to that picture of early Christianity's social composition and, importantly, implying that the addressees of 1 Peter were not distinctive or different in socioeconomic location from those we encounter in the Pauline letters, *pace* Elliott. In some respects, though, this is also not too far from a kind of severely chastened "new consensus" picture.[108] Absent, importantly, are the tenuous deductions that take indications of some surplus resources to imply elite status or considerable wealth. In their place is the insistence that the majority of the empire's inhabitants lived at or around subsistence level and that such economic realities must be taken into account.[109] That changes the picture quite considerably from that presented by Theissen, Meeks, and others, where the impression is given that many of the named individuals mentioned in the Pauline correspondence were "wealthy" or "up-

---

108. Cf. Barclay, "Response to Steven Friesen," p. 365, who comments on Friesen's proposals: "To place a few, as Friesen tentatively does, among the 7% in PS 4 is to make a claim for substantial wealth stratification in the Pauline churches — much as claimed by Theissen and Meeks, though with different vocabulary."

109. In commenting that the "extreme top and bottom of the Greco-Roman social scale are missing from the picture," Meeks remarks: "There may well have been members of the Pauline communities who lived at the subsistence level, but we hear nothing of them" (Meeks, *The First Urban Christians*, p. 73). But if the conclusions embodied in the Poverty Scale are even broadly correct, then it is highly likely that many of the groups mentioned — those who go hungry in 1 Cor 11:21, the οἰκέται of 1 Pet 2:18, etc. — are in precisely this position.

per class." But — with those important amendments — to conclude that the early Christian communities encompassed a "fair cross-section of urban society," as Wayne Meeks put it,[110] seems a not unreasonable conclusion to draw from an analysis of the limited evidence in 1 Peter.

Finally, it remains to consider whether this conclusion has consequences for our understanding and interpretation of 1 Peter. Only a few tentative remarks can be offered here. First, without by any means wishing to amalgamate 1 Peter, once again, into the group of later Pauline epistles, the indications concerning its circle of addressees cohere with other aspects of its content to suggest some points of similarity with the Pauline letters and communities.[111] Elliott's depiction of 1 Peter as a distinctive product "of a Petrine tradition transmitted by Petrine tradents of a Petrine circle,"[112] and addressed, distinctively, to a predominantly rural audience, does not seem to match either the content or envisaged recipients of the letter, notwithstanding the value of his efforts to liberate 1 Peter from its "Pauline bondage."[113]

Second, while we must be wary of assuming any deterministic link between social context and theological ideas, such that the latter become merely a reflection of the former, it is entirely reasonable to think that the composition of the early Christian communities had some impact on the kind of teaching that emerged from and was addressed to such communities. Several aspects of the character of 1 Peter's content may perhaps be highlighted in this regard. One is the insertion of the addressees into a (Jewish) narrative of identity that *dislocates* them from the empire and invites them into a self-understanding based on the experience of dispersion and alienation.[114] If this was not, *pace* Elliott, the social experience of the addressees prior to conversion, but rather the consequence of that conversion, then we may understand the letter to be reinforcing and deepening that sense of social dislocation for a group of people many of whom may previ-

110. Meeks, *The First Urban Christians*, p. 73.

111. See further David G. Horrell, "The Product of a Petrine Circle? A Reassessment of the Origin and Character of 1 Peter," *JSNT* 86 (2002): 29-60.

112. John H. Elliott, "The Rehabilitation of an Exegetical Step-Child: 1 Peter in Recent Research," *JBL* 95 (1976): 243-54, at 248.

113. Cf. Elliott, "Rehabilitation," p. 248; Elliott, *1 Peter*, p. 40.

114. See further David G. Horrell, "Between Conformity and Resistance: Beyond the Balch-Elliott Debate Towards a Postcolonial Reading of 1 Peter," in *Reading 1 Peter with New Eyes: Methodological Reassessments of the Letter of First Peter*, ed. Robert L. Webb and Betsy Bauman-Martin, LNTS 364 (London and New York: T&T Clark, 2007), pp. 111-43, esp. 124-33.

ously have been thoroughly integrated into the fabric of urban social life. A second aspect concerns what we may term, following Gerd Theissen, the "love-patriarchal" character of the ethical instruction in the letter.[115] According to Theissen, this ethos, which he saw developing in the Pauline and especially post-Pauline letters, served as a means to integrate and sustain the socially diverse early Christian communities.[116] Similarly, if 1 Peter is addressed to communities containing a "fair cross-section" of urban society, from slaves to householders, then its patterns of community-ethics may reflect the need to hold such a diverse congregation together. A third and final aspect concerns what I have elsewhere called the "polite resistance" that characterizes the author's stance toward the wider world, and specifically the empire.[117] While underscoring the need to worship only God (2:17) and to own the name "Christian" boldly, whatever the cost (4:16), the author of 1 Peter urges the recipients of the letter to honor the emperor (2:13-17) and to do what all will recognize and commend as good (2:12, etc.). This may perhaps, at least in part, reflect the socioeconomic location — and socioeconomic diversity — of the addressees, for whom a nuanced and subtle form of accommodated resistance might seem more realistic, not least as a survival strategy, than a more radical and visible stance, such as is promoted in the book of Revelation.[118]

Given the minimal data on which any socioeconomic profile of the addressees of 1 Peter must be based, it would be foolish to construct on that basis a bold theory concerning the impact of this profile on the content of the

115. Theissen coined the term "love-patriarchalism" *(Liebespatriarchalismus)*, drawing on the work of Ernst Troeltsch, and describes it as follows: "This love-patriarchalism takes social differences for granted but ameliorates them through an obligation of respect and love, an obligation imposed on those who are socially stronger. From the weaker are required subordination, fidelity, and esteem" *(Social Setting, p. 107)*.

116. See Theissen, *Social Setting,* pp. 107-10, 138-40, 163-64. I have previously criticized the suggestion that this term adequately captures the ethos of the early Pauline letters (specifically 1–2 Corinthians), but I have found it appropriate to designate the character of later letters, such as 1 Clement and the Pastorals: see Horrell, *Social Ethos.*

117. Horrell, "Between Conformity and Resistance," p. 143.

118. Such a tentative suggestion raises a host of further questions, which cannot be explored here, such as whether the author of the book of Revelation is addressing very *different* kinds of Christian communities. Here I would just want to note that this need not necessarily be so. John's call to "come out" from the world and resist the Beast may simply represent a more polemical and demanding challenge to his readers, whom he regards as too comfortably assimilated to the world. To echo the terms used by Miroslav Volf, the "difference" John calls for is hard, while that of 1 Peter is softer: see Miroslav Volf, "Soft Difference: Reflections on the Relation Between Church and Culture in 1 Peter," *Ex Auditu* 10 (1994): 15-30.

letter. Nevertheless, when various facets of the letter's character, content, and situation seem together to build a coherent picture, we may cautiously hope that social analysis and theological interpretation can be mutually informative and can further develop our understanding of this fascinating text.[119]

119. Research for the paper has been supported by a British Academy Small Research Grant, for which I would like to record my thanks. An earlier version was presented to the New Testament research seminar at the University of Oxford in February 2008; I am grateful to all at Oxford and St. Andrews who raised valuable questions in discussion.

EARLY CHRISTIAN RECEPTION

10. The Poor of Galatians 2:10: The Interpretative Paradigm of the First Centuries

Bruce W. Longenecker

Not infrequently, scholars see Paul's mention of the poor in Gal 2:10 as peripheral and secondary to the main theological considerations outlined by Paul in 2:1-9. That is the impression, for instance, given by one of the most influential interpreters of Galatians in the late twentieth century, Hans Dieter Betz. He depicts the instruction articulated by the Jerusalem leadership to "remember the poor" as an "additional request" that was "supplementary" and "unrelated to the main points of the debate" in Jerusalem. In Betz's view, "what had been requested and granted was a kind of philanthropic gesture."[1]

Betz and others who hold this view do not see this "philanthropic gesture" as simply a piece of good halakhic advice about how Christians should live in general. If "remember the poor" is simply halakhic advice, Paul should also have listed other pieces of good advice that the Jerusalem apostles might have mentioned in their meeting (which must have lasted several days).[2] But Paul lists no such advice when recalling his discussions with Je-

---

1. Hans Dieter Betz, *Galatians,* Hermeneia (Philadelphia: Fortress Press, 1979), p. 101.

2. So, for instance, the exhortation might have included such things as the appropriation of Scripture within Christian communities, having a good reputation among the populace, avoiding malice and anger, taming the tongue, being humble and merciful, watching out for gluttony and covetousness, honoring the marriage bed, standing fast against adversity and compromise, praying without ceasing, loving one's neighbor, correcting others in love, being submissive to the governing authorities, honoring all people, being patient for and prepared for the Lord's return, and commending the faith to anyone. Judging by texts attributed to leaders of the early Christian movement in the NT, such admonitions were seemingly standard exhortatory fare for them.

rusalem leaders about the essentials of the gospel. So why then did he mention the admonition to remember the poor?[3]

The answer that has pervaded NT scholarship is that the admonition to "remember the poor" fell into a distinct category, being neither "gospel" (as outlined in Gal 2:1-9) nor halakhic advice about Christian living in general. Instead, the admonition to "remember the poor" is thought to fall within the category of what Betz calls "church politics," either as a one-off gesture or as an initiative bound by certain conditions pertaining only to the earliest Christian movement.[4]

This view is ultimately based on the estimate that, in one way or another, the term "the poor" identifies members of the Christian communities *in Jerusalem*. This view, which pervades NT scholarship, is well expressed in Louw and Nida's amplification of Paul's words in Gal 2:10: "all they asked was that we should remember the needy *of their group*."[5] Lou Martyn's commentary is standard in this regard: "by mentioning 'the poor', the Jerusalem leaders refer to their own church, or to a circle of persons within that church."[6] Bengt Holmberg calls this interpretation of the phrase "an *undisputed fact*."[7] Ben Witherington calls it "quite clear."[8] And in his discussion of Galatians 2, Richard Longenecker claims: "All that can be said *with certainty* is that here in v. 10 the Jewish Christians *of Jerusalem* are principally in view."[9] This "certain," "clear," and "undisputed" interpretation is so entrenched that it is legitimate to identify it as commanding the firm consensus within the guild of current NT scholarship, with practically no voices of dissent.

Curiously, however, the first extant interpretations of Gal 2:10 up to the early fifth century testify to the predominance of another interpretation of

---

3. Sam K. Williams (*Galatians,* ANTC [Nashville: Abingdon Press, 1997], p. 55) raises the question this way: "In light of the numerous details about the Jerusalem conference that are missing in Gal 2:1-10, why does Paul include this one, the request to remember the poor?"

4. Betz, *Galatians,* p. 99.

5. Johannes P. Louw and Eugene A. Nida, eds., *Greek-English Lexicon of the New Testament Based on Semantic Domains* (New York: United Bible Society, 1988, 1989), §29.16, emphasis added.

6. J. Louis Martyn, *Galatians,* AB (New York and London: Doubleday, 1997), p. 207.

7. Bengt Holmberg, *Paul and Power: The Structure of Authority in the Primitive Church as Reflected in the Pauline Epistles* (Philadelphia: Fortress Press, 1980), p. 35.

8. Ben Witherington III, *Grace in Galatians: A Commentary on St Paul's Letter to the Galatians* (Edinburgh: T&T Clark, 1998), p. 144.

9. Richard N. Longenecker, *Galatians,* WBC (Dallas: Word Books, 1990), p. 60, emphasis added.

that verse. That the phrase "remember the poor" pertains to exclusively or even primarily to Jewish Christians in Jerusalem has almost no currency in the extant literature from the earliest centuries. What in the current consensus can be hailed "with certainty" as "an undisputed fact" has almost no foothold in the earliest interpretations of Gal 2:10, which testify instead to a different consensus of opinion.[10]

1. Interpreting Gal 2:10 in the Earliest Centuries of Christian Interpretation

As will be shown, at least up to the earliest years of the fifth century, interpretations of Gal 2:10 ran contrary to the consensus held today in NT scholarship. But there is one ancient interpreter who gives the current consensus a foothold toward the end of that period: John Chrysostom (347-407 CE). When amplifying Gal 2:10 in his *Commentary on the Epistle of St. Paul to the Galatians* (written in or after 395 CE), Chrysostom writes: "Who were these poor persons? Many of the believing Jews in Palestine had been deprived of all their goods." Chrysostom makes the point that Paul's efforts on behalf of "the believing Jews in Palestine" were intended precisely to demonstrate the unity within the missions to "the circumcised" and the "uncircumcised." Using Paul's voice, Chrysostom elaborates the verse in this way: "to the sustenance of the poor among the Jews I also contributed my share, which, had there been any dissension between us, they would not have accepted." Chrysostom imagines that Gal 2:10 relates directly to Paul's collection efforts of his later ministry, a notion shared by many who hold the consensus view today but one increasingly disputed among modern commentators.[11]

10. This claim is based on a search of the accordance database of Ante-Nicene, Nicene, and Post-Nicene Fathers. *Church Fathers: The Ante-Nicene Fathers* (ed. Alexander Roberts and James Donaldson); *Church Fathers: The Nicene and Post-Nicene Fathers,* First and Second Series (ed. Philip Schaff); all Edinburgh: T&T Clark, public domain. The electronic text was hypertexted, corrected, and prepared by OakTree Software, Inc. Not discussed here are citations of Gal 2:9-10 in the church fathers that have no relevance to the issue of the identity of "the poor" (e.g., Augustine, *Of the Work of Monks* 24; *Tractates on John,* Tractate 109.5; John Chrysostom, *Homilies on the Acts of the Apostles,* Homily 33, Homily 37; *Homilies on 1 Corinthians,* Homily 39; *Homilies on Ephesians,* Homily 10; Jerome, *Perpetual Virginity of the Blessed Virgin* 15; Gregory Nazianzen, *Orations* 2.51).

11. So, for instance, A. J. M. Wedderburn, "Paul's Collection: Chronology and History," *NTS* 48 (2002): 95-110; James D. G. Dunn, *The Theology of the Apostle Paul* (Grand Rapids: Eerdmans, 1998), p. 706 n. 170.

Chrysostom is of the opinion that Paul's collection for "the poor" (i.e., "the believing Jews in Palestine") was warmly accepted, and he amplifies the point in this way:

> Wherefore he exercises much zeal, as appears in the Epistles to the Romans and Corinthians that these persons should meet with much attention; and Paul not only collects money for them, but himself conveys it, as he says, "But now I go unto Jerusalem ministering unto the saints," for they were without the necessities of life. And he here shows that in this instance having resolved to assist them, he had undertaken and would not abandon it.

Precisely the same interpretation of Gal 2:10 is evident in Chrysostom's *Homilies on the Epistle to the Hebrews,* published after his death in 407 CE.[12] In each of these two cases, Chrysostom links Gal 2:10 with Paul's collection for the poor among the saints in Jerusalem.

But if the consensus view current within NT scholarship has parallels with two of Chrysostom's texts in the late fourth and early fifth centuries, the majority of extant literature from the first centuries CE suggests that Chrysostom's was a minority view. In fact, at best it was a view that came onto the interpretative radar only at a late date in the early centuries. The earliest extant interpretations of Gal 2:10 from the mid-second century right up to the early fifth centuries primarily run along different lines altogether.

This is evident, for instance, from Tertullian's engagement with Marcion in the late second century CE. Paragraph 3 of Tertullian's fifth book in *Against Marcion* discusses Gal 2:9-10. There he writes:

> Rightly, then, did Peter and James and John give their right hand of fellowship to Paul, and agree on such a division of their work, as that Paul should go to the heathen, and themselves to the circumcision. Their agreement, also, "to remember the poor" was in complete conformity with the law of the Creator, which cherished the poor and needy. . . .

Missing from this account is any mention of Barnabas (the same omission marks out Tertullian's discussion of Gal 2:9 in his *Prescription against Heretics* 23).[13] This might look incidental, but it has the (presumably uninten-

---

12. Chrysostom, *Homilies on the Epistle to the Hebrews,* "Argument and Summary of the Epistle," §2.

13. "They accordingly even gave him [Paul only is meant] 'the right hand of fellowship,' as a sign of their agreement with him, and arranged amongst themselves a distribution of

tional) effect of shifting the nuances of the passage into a key different from the one that Paul's own text offers. In Paul's account of the Jerusalem meeting in Gal 2:9-10, "remember the poor" was stipulated by the Jerusalem apostles to the team of Paul and Barnabas, who simply agree (albeit wholeheartedly, 2:10b) to the stipulation: "[the Jerusalem apostles added] only one thing: that we [i.e., Paul and Barnabas] should remember the poor." Those verses are open to the interpretation that Paul and Barnabas were somewhat "inferior" members in the meeting, being the passive recipients of a requirement handed down to them by others. But by omitting Barnabas from the scene, Tertullian's account of the meeting can be interpreted as signaling that the agreement joined together two equal parties — the Jerusalem apostles on the one hand and Paul on the other. In this, all the apostolic figures are yoked together as mutual instigators in a collaborative effort on behalf of the poor. The right hand of fellowship was extended, Tertullian's portrait permits, not simply in relation to respective target audiences (i.e., Jews and gentiles) but also confirming that all parties would "remember the poor." Thus, in Tertullian's account the first-person plural μνημονεύωμεν ("we should remember") can be taken to refer not to Paul and Barnabas but to Paul and the Jerusalem apostles, who took the initiative to "remember the poor" collectively.[14]

And what is it that Tertullian imagines this virtually bilateral agreement to involve? It is notable that he nowhere imagines the agreement to involve support being sent from Paul's communities or from Antioch in order to relieve the hardships of poor Christians *in Jerusalem*. Judging by his comments on the verse, this issue is nowhere in his sights. Tertullian takes the agreement of Gal 2:10 to indicate that both the Jerusalem apostles and Paul unanimously agreed in upholding (a part of) the law given by the creator God to the Jewish people long ago. So the excerpt cited above from *Against Marcion* 5.3 continues in this way: "It is thus certain that the question was one which simply regarded the law, while at the same time it is apparent what portion of the law it was convenient to have observed."

With this claim, Tertullian is attempting to undermine Marcion's charge that the God of redemption in Christ is wholly different from the

---

office, not a diversity of gospel, so that they should severally preach not a different gospel, but (the same), to different persons, Peter to the circumcision, Paul to the Gentiles."

14. Some imagine that Tertullian's handling of Gal 2:9-10 is itself indebted to Marcion's. So Adolf Harnack, *Marcion: Das Evangelium vom fremden Gott* (Leipzig: J. C. Hinrichs, 1921), p. 42.

God of creation who bound himself to Israel. And Tertullian's efforts in this regard gain force from a point that he sought to establish earlier in his text. In *Against Marcion* 4.14, Tertullian argued at length that the Creator God expressed his great concern for the poor in order that he might be recognized as the same God that is proclaimed by Jesus and the apostles. Just as the first recorded word of the Creator God was a "very good" word, so too the first recorded words of Jesus in the Sermon on the Mount are words of goodness: "Blessed are the needy . . . because theirs is the kingdom of heaven."[15] In this way, says Tertullian, the "principle of the New Testament" is initiated "after the example of the Old." Citing eight passages from the Old Testament that demonstrate how entrenched care for the poor and needy is within the heart of the Creator God, Tertullian addresses Marcion directly with these words:

> For even if you suppose that the promises of the Creator were earthly, but that Christ's are heavenly, it is quite clear that heaven has been as yet the property of no other God whatever than Him who owns the earth also; it is quite clear that the Creator has given even the lesser promises (of earthly blessing) in order that I may more readily believe Him concerning His greater promises (of heavenly blessings) also.

According to Tertullian, the Creator God "specially designed that the promise of a similar blessing should serve as a preparation for the gospel, that so men might know it to be His." The implication is that the only god who is concerned with the poor and needy is the creator God who revealed himself to Israel. Tertullian charges that Marcion's own god "has never given proof of his liberality by any preceding bestowal of minor blessings." This, says Tertullian, is in complete contrast to the only true God, the Creator God who has revealed himself both in the Old Testament and in the Christ, and who in each case has revealed himself to be concerned for the poor.

Moreover, Tertullian suggests that it is this concern for the poor that causes the gentile nations to be attracted to Christianity. He finds this demonstrated in passages from Isaiah, who spoke about the gentiles when he wrote, "Behold, they shall come swiftly with speed." And their swift approach to the Creator God is in the knowledge, according to Tertullian, that "'They shall neither hunger nor thirst. Therefore they shall be filled' — a

---

15. Tertullian is clearly aware of the interpretative issue at stake when translating οἱ πτωχοὶ τῷ πνεύματι in Matt 5:3 as "needy," writing in parenthetical tone: "for no less than this is required for interpreting the word in the Greek."

promise which is made to none but those who hunger and thirst." In this way, says Tertullian, "the promise of fullness to the hungry is a provision of God the Creator." Tertullian envisages Isaiah to prophesy about the offsetting of material poverty within the church for the benefit of the poor of the gentile nations. For Tertullian, this is a concrete expression that the God who is operating in the church is one and the same as the Creator God who revealed himself in Scripture.

It is this theological construct that Tertullian draws on when concluding that the agreement to "remember the poor" in Gal 2:10 is about how the law of the Creator is to be apportioned within Christianity. For Tertullian, Paul and the Jerusalem leaders agreed (1) that circumcision is a part of the Creator's law that *is not essential* for Christian observance, and (2) that cherishing the poor and needy is a part of the Creator's law that *is essential* for Christian observance. And in leaving Barnabas out of his discussion of Gal 2:9, Tertullian gives the impression (as perhaps Marcion did as well) that the charge to "remember the poor" is one mutually agreed upon between Paul and the Jerusalem leaders (i.e., "their agreement"), as if the two ministries were linked in a single effort for the poor in different sectors, without any single point of focus or restriction.

If Tertullian asserts that care for the poor fulfills the law of the Creator God (contra Marcion), it is equally important to note what he fails to give consideration to. There are no hints whatsoever that Tertullian considered "the poor" to be Jerusalem Christians; in fact, just the opposite is the case. Tertullian's argument presumes that the poor are not simply Jerusalem Christians. To have restricted the sense of "the poor" to Jerusalem Christians would have significantly weakened Tertullian's argument about fulfilling the law of the Creator. If he assumed that the poor are to be identified with Jerusalem Christians, Tertullian would have needed to expand his argument in order to bolster his overarching concern. He could well have claimed, for instance, that although the agreement to "remember the poor" was initially a matter of benefiting a particular group of people (i.e., Jewish Christians in Jerusalem), the initiative on behalf of the poor in Jerusalem was itself a particular concretization of a more fundamental principle about care for the poor, a principle rooted in the law of the Creator God. But Tertullian does not argue in such a way. The best explanation for this rhetorical road not taken is that Tertullian was unaware of a view that considered "the poor" to be based in Jerusalem alone.

If Tertullian had no cognizance that Gal 2:10 could be interpreted with reference to Jerusalem Christians when writing against Marcion in the beginning of the third century CE (i.e., 207-8 CE), we can extrapolate further that the same was true also for Marcion himself (85-160 CE) when propagating his views in the middle of the second century CE. If Marcion *did* subscribe to the view that the poor of Gal 2:10 were based in Jerusalem, Tertullian seems to have known nothing of it. If either Marcion or any of Tertullian's addressees had interpreted Gal 2:10 in that way, Tertullian would have to be seen as choosing an odd form of rhetoric to construct his case. Instead, there is every reason to think that Gal 2:10 was interpreted without reference to Jerusalem Christians up to the beginning of the third Christian century, at least in the circles of Christianity and its deviations that are known to us from extant literature of that period.

This early interpretation of Gal 2:10 is continued in the only other extant text that interacts with Gal 2:10 up to the beginning of the fifth century. If Chrysostom interprets the verse to refer to Jerusalem Christians (as above), it is also important to note that Chrysostom's contemporary, Jerome (329-420 CE), who like Chrysostom was also frequently based in Syrian Antioch and Constantinople, shows no cognizance of such a reading in his own discussion of Gal 2:10. This is all the more significant in view of Jerome's firsthand connections with Palestine. After a brief pilgrimage to Palestine in 385 CE, Jerome took up residence there in 388, remaining there until his death in 420. But his handling of Gal 2:10 is devoid of a Jerusalem-specific interpretation of "the poor."

So in his letter "To Salvina" (*The Letters of Jerome,* Letter 79; written c. 400 CE), Jerome discusses the advice of the author of 1 Tim 5:11-14 concerning care for widows under 30 years of age, where the advice is that such widows should not receive care from Christian treasuries for the poor but should, instead, seek to remarry. Fearful that the reader of that passage might find Paul to despise youth, Jerome points out that elsewhere Paul is shown to treasure youth and that, in this particular passage, Paul is simply wanting the church to support those in real and poignant need, as opposed to less pressing need. Jerome makes his point by interpreting 1 Tim 5:9-10 in relation to Gal 2:9-10: in 1 Timothy, he says, Paul "is training a church still untaught in Christ, and making provision for people of all stations but especially for the poor, the charge of whom had been committed to himself and Barnabas." In this way, Jerome depicts "remembering the poor" in Gal 2:10 as a general overarching principle that in 1 Timothy is shown to have particular and concrete expression in terms of Christian care for widows.

Like Marcion and Tertullian before him, Jerome shows no cognizance of the poor being based exclusively or even primarily in Jerusalem. If such a view had been entrenched among Jerome's contemporaries, he could not have made his point so easily and in such a streamlined fashion. He would have needed to craft and qualify his discourse much more effectively. It seems, then, that the interpretation of Gal 2:10 with reference to Jerusalem Christians was neither widespread nor significant even at the beginning of the fifth century CE, even within Palestine itself (a point that can hardly be overemphasized). Jerome, evidently in common with the majority of Christians of his day, simply imagined Paul and Barnabas to be those who trained gentile churches to be "taught in Christ," including "provision for people of all stations but especially for the poor."

One further thing needs to be noted from the extant literature up to the early fifth century. We have seen that Chrysostom interprets Gal 2:10 as referring to the poor in Jerusalem in his *Commentary on the Epistle of St. Paul to the Galatians*. But it is also important to note that this interpretation is not exhaustive of Chrysostom's handling of the verse. On occasion, without overthrowing the Judean referent for the term "the poor" in Gal 2:10, Chrysostom nonetheless uses that verse to encourage almsgiving within the church in general. Although Chrysostom imagined Gal 2:10 to make historical reference to the poor Christians of Jerusalem, he is eager to extend the sense of the verse so that it applies more generally to his audience, being a feature of Christian living. So, in Homily 25 of Chrysostom's *Homilies on Acts* the text of Gal 2:9-10 is cited on three occasions. In the first, the phrase "remember the poor" is used to amplify the point that almsgiving and concern for the poor was a marker of Christian living in the apostolic period even at times of hardship.[16] In the second, the almsgiving of gentile Christians to the benefit of Judean churches is used by Chrysostom to indicate how the church universal offsets affliction and difficulty by nature of its essential "fellowship." In the third, Chrysostom highlights various forms of almsgiving as being essential to proper Christian discipleship. Setting out the example of Zacchaeus as one for whom salvation involved giving away one's goods, and showing that a purse was carried among Jesus and his disciples in order to help the poor that they met along the way, and before showing how this concern for the poor coheres with Old Testament Scripture (as Tertullian had done two centuries earlier), Chrysostom simply inserts the example of Paul to demonstrate the point: "And Paul also says, 'Only that we remember the poor.'"

In these cases, Chrysostom does not deter from imagining "the poor" of

---

16. Chrysostom: "Mark how the famine becomes to them the means of salvation, an occasion of alms-giving, a harbinger of many blessings."

Gal 2:10 to have been "the poor in Judaea"; but it is notable that in each case the geographical location of the beneficiaries is a secondary matter, overshadowed by the passage's pertinence in relation to care for the poor in general. In this way we see that Gal 2:10 was used by Chrysostom as an example not simply of a particular ecclesial polity or "church politics" (so Betz), restricted to gentile efforts on behalf of Christian Jews in Jerusalem. Instead, for Chrysostom it came closer to being a feature of (what might today be called) Christian identity.[17]

This is especially evident in Homily 4 of Chrysostom's *Homilies on Philippians*. There, Chrysostom gives no indication whatsoever that he understood "the poor" of Gal 2:10 to have referred in the first instance to Judean Christians in Paul's day. Instead, extolling the virtue of almsgiving as "a great, marvellous light," we hear simply: "Much mention doth Paul, too, make of this mercy. In one place, hear him say, 'Only that we should remember the poor.'" Chrysostom adds two other passages from "Paul" to make the point: "And again, 'And let our people also learn to maintain good works' [Titus 3:14]. And again, 'These things are good and profitable unto men' [Titus 3.8]." In this context, Chrysostom shows how mercy, which results in almsgiving, is an expression of the identity of true humanity and lies at the very heart of reality, the very heart of God: "For this is the true character of man, to be merciful, yea rather the character of God, to show mercy. . . . If you ask why such and such things are, you will always find your answer in Goodness." However he might have imagined the geographical specificity of "the poor" of Gal 2:10 in some of his other writings, in this homily he links the passage to a more general principle of Christian lifestyle, using it to laud the virtue of Christian almsgiving in general. Here again we witness Chrysostom's departure from a view that Gal 2:10 testifies simply to an inci-

---

17. It is also important to note Chrysostom's assumption that early Christianity was united in its commitment to "remember the poor." In his *Homilies on Acts* (Homily 14), when discussing the appointment of the deacons in Acts 6, Chrysostom notes that seven deacons were needed to take in the great sums of money that came to the community. The motivation for the money coming from within the community's own resources is found in Gal 2:10: "Only," it is said, "that we should remember the poor." In Chrysostom's view, remembrance of the poor is something that the Jerusalem community first bound itself to before binding Paul to the same (not surprisingly, in view of the narrative of Acts 2 and 4). This is clear from the sentence that follows immediately, which explains the manner of fund raising: "And how did they bring these [funds] forward? They fasted." Chrysostom does not say, "they charged the Apostle Paul to do it." Even in Chrysostom's reading of Gal 2:10, then, there is the recognition that the two missions are being yoked together in a common cause, even if the common cause was Jerusalem Christianity in the first instance.

dent of "church politics"; for Chrysostom, it seems more the case that concern for the Christian communities in Jerusalem was a specific application of an essential feature of Christian character.

While this is significant, it also might be seen to have the potential to undermine the case made above with regard to Tertullian and Jerome (and presumably Marcion). For instance, if Chrysostom thought that "remember the poor" of Gal 2:10 had a geographically restricted referent in its first instance but also that it had a more general and universal applicability, perhaps the same was also true of Tertullian and Jerome. In essence, then, what we see in their texts is simply the general or universal application of a text that each knew to be more restricted in its primary referent.

In my view, two factors make this unlikely, especially with regard to Tertullian. As noted above, the success of his discursive strategy is wholly dependent on the conviction that Gal 2:10 has general or universal applicability. If a geographically specific interpretation of Gal 2:10 was widespread in Tertullian's day, he would have known that his case could have been weakened by the fact that he by-passes the primary referent of Gal 2:10 — i.e., the Jerusalem church of the first generation of Christianity. In that case, he would have needed to register his interpretative reasoning far more effectively. That he fails to do that suggests that Chrysostom's "two-dimensional" interpretation of Gal 2:10 is not applicable to Tertullian.

The second factor that makes this possibility unlikely pertains to the lack of data suggesting that the term "the poor (ones)" had any currency in the early centuries in relation to Jerusalem-based Christianity — an issue that requires fuller consideration in the next section of this essay.

2. Further Confirmatory Data and an Explanation for the Chrysostom Anomaly

It has been seen that the earliest extant Christian literature is virtually uniform in its interpretation of Gal 2:10, and that most of those who deal with the verse up to the early years of the fifth century CE, whether Christian or "heretical," do so without cognizance of the view that "the poor" referred to therein should be interpreted in relation to the Christian movement in Jerusalem. Seemingly, the sole exception to this monolithic posture up to the early fifth century is John Chrysostom, whose extant texts also include counter-examples to the exception.

These data pertaining to the earliest extant interpretations of Gal 2:10

cohere perfectly with the data assembled by others with regard to how the term "the poor" was used in Christian discourse in the early centuries. In two major articles of the mid-1960s, for instance, Leander Keck forcefully combated a deep-seated view with regard to the Ebionites — i.e., Jewish Christians who came to bear the name "the poor ones" (Aramaic: אביוני; Hebrew: האביונים), and who had a presence within the spectrum of Christianity up through the fourth century, dropping out of our view by the middle of the fifth century.[18] Prior to Keck's work, it was commonly asserted that these Jewish Christian Ebionites or "poor ones" had consciously retained the self-designation of the earliest Jerusalem-based Jewish Christianity (or Christian Judaism). But Keck established that this view is fundamentally flawed. In his work he demonstrates the following:

> [T]here is insufficient reason for thinking that the Ebionite literature, insofar as it is recoverable, reflects the continuous line between the Ebionites and the hypothetical group calling itself "the Poor" in primitive Christianity. . . . The link with the practice of the primitive church in sharing wealth came much later as an apologetic device and cannot be taken at face value.[19]

In 2003, Richard Bauckham confirmed Keck's earlier work, demonstrating that the claim to inherit the name of early Jerusalem Christianity (i.e., "the poor ones") may have been made by "later Ebionites," but it "was not the original significance of their name."[20] Bauckham and Keck argue persuasively that the origins of the name "Ebionite" lie in post-70 CE developments, involving "a sectarian, etiological exegesis of Acts promoted by the Ebionites in defense against the imperial church."[21] Consequently, the self-designation

---

18. Leander E. Keck, "The Poor among the Saints in the New Testament," *ZNW* 56 (1965): 100-129; Keck, "The Poor among the Saints in Jewish Christianity and Qumran," *ZNW* 57 (1966): 54-78.

19. Keck, "The Poor among the Saints in Jewish Christianity and Qumran," pp. 64-66. The quotation continues: "Even if we were to follow Schoeps in saying that these Ebionites are the biological (!) [*sic*] descendants of the radical right wing of Jewish Christianity which Paul opposed, we need not say that their subsequent self-justification has historical merit or that their practices and theories represent the church before 70 A.D."

20. Richard J. Bauckham, "The Origin of the Ebionites," in *The Image of the Judaeo-Christians in Ancient Jewish and Christian Literature*, ed. Peter J. Tomson and Doris Lambers-Petry, WUNT 158 (Tübingen: Mohr Siebeck, 2003), pp. 162-81, esp. p. 178.

21. Keck, "The Poor among the Saints in Jewish Christianity and Qumran," 59; cf. Bauckham, "Origin of the Ebionites," pp. 178-81.

of the Ebionites has little value in determining the technical terms of the Christian movement in its first generation.[22]

Moreover, as Keck shows, of all the ancient historians of earliest Christianity, only Epiphanius of Salamis (d. 403), writing his *Panarion* between 374 and 377 CE, suggests that the Ebionites explicitly claimed to be the inheritors of the name of earliest Christianity in Jerusalem.[23] The usual view within the literature of the early church fathers is that the Ebionites were the followers of a heretic named Ebion. The linking of the Ebionite name to early Jerusalem Christianity has no precedent in the extant discussion of earliest Christianity prior to Epiphanius, even when we would expect it to have arisen in the discourse of second- and third-century discussion of earliest Christianity and/or the Ebionites. So, for instance, in his account of the history of the Jerusalem church, the second-century historian Hegesippus (writing c. 165-75) never uses any special designation such as "the poor" when referring to the Jerusalem church, even when it would have fit his rhetorical purposes perfectly to do so.[24] The same is the case for figures like Justin Martyr (100-165), Irenaeus (130-202), Origen (185-254), and Eusebius (275-339), whose texts provide occasional counter-evidence of one kind or another to the view that Jerusalem Christians were known as "the poor."[25]

The findings of Keck and Bauckham provide the larger context into

22. Moreover, in his article "The Poor among the Saints in Jewish Christianity and Qumran," Keck demonstrated the extent to which religio-historical parallels have been overdrawn in relation to the early Christian community in Jerusalem on the one hand and the Dead Sea community (and Psalms of Solomon) on the other hand, so that the circumlocutionary use of "the poor" in first-century religious communities has been significantly overplayed in scholarship.

23. Epiphanius, *Panar.* 30.17.

24. As Keck notes ("The Poor among the Saints in Jewish Christianity and Qumran," pp. 56-57): "[I]n the story of Domitian's interrogating the descendents of Jesus' family, Hegesippus refers to their extremely limited means: about 9,000 denarii in the land which they worked themselves (Euseb. *H.E.* III 20). Here would have been an obvious occasion to say something about 'the Poor' or the Ebionites. Yet, there is no reference to either the idea or the practice of 'the Poor'. Instead, he reports that the family owned the land on which they paid taxes. Furthermore, when Hegesippus lists the seven heresies of the church, he does not include the Ebionites . . . , nor does he include them in his list of Jewish sects (*H.E.* IV 22). It appears, therefore, that . . . the silence of Hegesippus is not accidental: he does not know of any group which called itself 'the Poor' or 'the Ebionites.'"

25. So, for instance, Origen consistently claims that their name denoted their *theological* poverty, due to their continuing observance of the law and low view of Christ. Never does he entertain the notion that the Ebionites claimed that their name was inherited from the first Jerusalem Christians.

which can be fit the data assembled above regarding the interpretation of Gal 2:10 up to the early fifth century CE. That most interpretations of Gal 2:10 prior to that time show no trace of restricting "the poor" to Jerusalem Christians dovetails perfectly with Keck's more general case that the early church fathers had no cognizance of designating Jerusalem Christianity as "the poor" prior to the late fourth century.

But this data contributes more than just an overarching context into which our findings on Gal 2:10 fit; it also helps to explain the one exception to the prevalent interpretation of Gal 2:10 noted above: that is, Chrysostom's interpretation of "the poor" as Jerusalem Christians. It is noteworthy, and arguably more than a simple coincidence, that the earliest extant identification of "the poor" of Gal 2:10 with Jerusalem Christians arises only as the fourth century was giving way to the fifth, in the work of Chrysostom, who himself was writing in the wake of Epiphanius's spurious linking of Ebionism with early Jewish Christians in Jerusalem. Epiphanius made that link in 374-77 CE, whereas Chrysostom wrote his *Commentary on the Epistle of St. Paul to the Galatians* no earlier than 395 CE, with his *Homilies on the Epistle to the Hebrews* being written late in his life and published only after his death in 407 CE. It is not difficult to imagine that the spurious linking of the Ebionite "poor ones" and earliest Jerusalem Christianity arose in the second half of the fourth century[26] and that, once made, that linkage then influenced Chrysostom's reading of Gal 2:10 at the end of the fourth century and early fifth century CE. That the link was not uniformly definitive is testified to by Jerome, who continues to read Gal 2:10 in the manner that characterized its interpretation in earlier centuries.

3. Conclusions

The earliest extant Christian literature is virtually monolithic in its interpretation of "the poor" in Gal 2:10. Most of those who engaged with that verse up to the early years of the fifth century CE, whether orthodox or "heretical," show no cognizance of the view that the term "the poor" should be interpreted as signaling the Christian movement in Jerusalem. The sole exception to this ubiquitous posture up to the early fifth century is John Chrysostom.

26. Whether or not this link was first made by Epiphanius is of no concern for our purposes. The point is that it is first testified to in the late fourth century in Epiphanius's work, and not before that date.

But we have seen reason to believe that Chrysostom's interpretation resulted from the unfounded view, first evidenced in the final quarter of the fourth century, that the Ebionite "poor ones" had retained the name of the earliest Jerusalem Christians. And at times Chrysostom peripheralizes the issue of the geographical location of "the poor" of Gal 2:10, using that verse instead to reinforce his conviction that "remembering the poor" is (to be) an essential component of what today might be called "Judeo-Christian identity." In this, Chrysostom's discussion of Gal 2:10 differs significantly from most articulations of the current scholarly consensus view of that verse.

Of course, it might be that the earliest extant consensus on the identity of "the poor" in Gal 2:10 was ultimately ill-founded and should defer to the modern consensus. Clearly, when judged in strict historical-critical terms, the early fathers often interpreted texts "incorrectly," and perhaps the same is true of their nearly monolithic interpretation of "the poor" in Gal 2:10.[27] But for this to be the case, we must imagine that the term "the poor" had initially designated (a part of) the community of Jewish Christians in Jerusalem early on, that the designation had quickly lost its geographical specificity, that it continued to bear a non-specific application for centuries, and that its original specificity was reintroduced in the late fourth century through a spurious connection made by Epiphanius in the final quarter of that century.

In my view, it is simpler to imagine that the term "the poor" of Gal 2:10 was ubiquitously interpreted throughout the earliest centuries without geographical specificity for good reason, and that the specious linkage of the Ebionite name with the earliest Christian communities in Jerusalem has thereby had a disproportionate and misleading effect on the interpretation of that verse ever since. The first to be misled by the link was, evidently, John Chrysostom. The modern guild of NT scholarship seems also to have been under the heavy influence of Epiphanius's specious linkage. Estimates about "the poor" of Gal 2:10 being "undisputedly" and "certainly" based in Jerusalem are ultimately founded on the conviction that "the poor" was "a religious title which the earliest community adopted and which is preserved in the later designation of the Palestinian Jewish Christians as 'Ebionites.'"[28]

27. Tertullian's tendency to remove Barnabas from the socio-religious dynamics of Gal 2:9-10 is obviously not a live exegetical option. But neither is that feature of Tertullian's interpretation foundational for his view that "the poor" has a general rather than specific referent.

28. Martin Hengel, *Acts and the History of Earliest Christianity,* trans. John Bowden (London: SCM, 1979), p. 118. Cf. H. Chadwick, *The Early Church* (Harmondsworth: Penguin,

Unfortunately there is no trace of this view within the literary record of the first centuries until the middle of the fourth century.

It is arguable, then, that, in contrast to the current "undisputed" and "certain" consensus of NT scholarship, the consensus of the early church fathers is founded on a better interpretative premise, precisely because it is unaffected (and uninfected) by the historically illegitimate view that the Ebionites perpetuated the self-designation of early Jewish Christians based in Jerusalem.[29] Although the claim would require a robust analysis of Gal 2:1-10, that passage is best read as indicating that remembrance of the poor is something that would (continue to) characterize the emergent Christian movement in its mission both to the circumcised and to the uncircumcised. Assuming that such remembrance would inevitably characterize the Jewish mission, the Jerusalem apostles were nonetheless concerned that Jewish traditions about caring for the poor could be lost in Paul's mission to the pagan world. Paul was quick to offer assurances that such would not be the case on his watch.[30]

1967), p. 23: "The Jewish Christians [of the second through fourth centuries CE] called themselves Ebionites, a name derived from the Hebrew word meaning 'the poor'; it was probably a conscious reminiscence of a very early term which is attested by St Paul's letters as an almost technical name for the Christians in Jerusalem and Judaea."

29. It is notable, then, that in the past few decades New Testament scholars are increasingly sitting lightly to the view that the Ebionites inherited and promulgated the name of the first followers of Jesus in Jerusalem (doing so, I suspect, largely because of Keck's argument of the mid-1960s). One might expect this to result in a consequent sitting lightly to a geographically restrictive interpretation of Gal 2:10. Instead, scholars are beginning to construct other ways of arriving at a geographically specific interpretation of Gal 2:10, but often only by resorting to "system-dependent" argumentation or by failing to consider all the interpretative options. These claims cannot be developed here, but if they have merit (as I will seek to show elsewhere), they are indicative of the extent to which scholars are intent on retaining the paradigmatic consensus by taking paths around its data anomalies.

30. See chapter 8 of my forthcoming book, *Remember the Poor: Paul, Poverty, and the Greco-Roman World* (Grand Rapids: Eerdmans). It falls beyond the scope of this essay to consider whether those whom Pauline communities targeted for support were "the poor" in general or the Christian poor in particular, requiring some adjudication of passages like Gal 6:10 on the one hand and 1 Thess 5:15 on the other. While the ideal might have been for care to have been given to the poor in general, in practice Paul's communities would have had a primary duty of care to those within their membership. Such were the realities for the earliest urban Christian movement. But the ideal was often lauded in early Christianity, as in Shepherd of Hermas, *Sim* 10.4.2-4: "Every person [*omnem hominem*] must be helped out of his need. For whoever starves and suffers want of the most necessary things of daily life endures great pain. . . . Whoever knows of the need of such a person and does not help him out commits a great sin."

Throughout the nineteenth and twentieth centuries, almost all interpretations of "the poor" in Gal 2:10 assume that the Galatian Christians whom Paul addressed would have understood "the poor" to be a geographically specific group. But the extant literary database from the first four centuries suggests that this assumption is founded on an extremely weak evidential base. Perhaps it is time to consider the structure, rhetorical force, and theological implications of Gal 2:6-10 in an interpretative paradigm that shows closer affinity to the paradigm of the early church fathers.

11. Tertullian on Widows: A North African Appropriation of Pauline Household Economics

David E. Wilhite

Should a widow remarry? This is the central concern of Tertullian's letters to his wife, *Ad uxorem* 1 and 2 (c. 200). In what purports to be a last will and testament, Tertullian requests that his wife not remarry after his death. In book 1 Tertullian champions the practice of *uniuira*, the life-long commitment to one spouse that includes celibacy after the death of the spouse.[1] In *Ad uxorem* 2 Tertullian concedes that remarriage is permitted but clamors to ensure that Christian widows who insist on remarrying should do so only "in the Lord" (ref. 1 Cor. 7:39).[2] In his argumentation against widow remarriage Tertullian displays a reliance on 1 Timothy particularly, but the affective nature of this reliance is problematic: Tertullian rejects remarriage for *all* widows, while 1 Timothy stipulates that widows under the age of sixty should in fact remarry.

In order to analyze the difference between Tertullianic and Pauline stances on widows, I will put forward an economic reading, derived from a postmodern and interdisciplinary approach: insights from social and cultural anthropology will help guide the interpretive steps when encountering Tertullian's works, while both patristic and Pauline scholarship will inform

1. On the ideal of *uniuira,* see J. Gardner and T. Wiedemann, *The Roman Household: A Sourcebook* (London: Routledge, 1991), p. 57; and see Geoffrey S. Nathan, *The Family in Late Antiquity: The Rise of Christianity and the Endurance of Tradition* (London: Routledge, 2000), p. 22 n. 60, for *uniuira* as "an ideal espoused by the imperial poets" but rarely practiced by Tertullian's day.

2. For Tertullian's use of Scripture, see bibliography in Charles Kannengiesser, *Handbook of Patristic Exegesis: The Bible in Ancient Christianity* (Leiden: Brill, 2006), pp. 593-622.

the critical engagement with the primary texts. To state my thesis plainly, I believe Tertullian's views on widows are a kind of theo-economics, which fluidly and creatively negotiates our modernist categories of doctrine, practice, politics, and domestics. In order to present such a reading of Tertullian, I will first invoke the postmodern philosophy of John D. Caputo, who provides a means of speaking about "economics" while avoiding essentialist tendencies. In turn I will then utilize theories from social and cultural anthropology, which on the whole are currently post-foundationalist in practice, in order to appreciate the overlap of categories that will arise in Tertullian's reading of Paul — namely, the categories of religion, kinship, and economics. The works of Tertullian and Paul will then be explored, not merely from an "economic" standpoint, nor solely through a "theological" framework, but in terms of theo-economics.

1. Theology and Economics

The term "theo-economics" used here is adapted from the postmodern notion of theo-poetics, as formulated by John D. Caputo. In a popularized account of theo-poetics, Caputo answers the rhetorical question, "Have we not learned by now to keep theology out of politics?"[3] Caputo insists that theology cannot be kept out of such matters, because "theology goes all the way down" — that is, all the way down into things like politics and economics. In an earlier monograph Caputo applied a postmodern deconstruction, or "radical hermeneutic," to all foundational paradigms, including those related to metaphysics, ethics, and politics.[4] The key notion of theo-poetics for Caputo is the interpretative aspect, the burden on the interpreter to apply creatively rather than rely on a prescribed formula, logic, or paradigm.[5]

---

3. John D. Caputo and Catherine Keller, "Theopoetic/Theopolitic," *Cross Currents* 57, no. 1 (2007): 103.

4. Caputo, *Radical Hermeneutics: Repetition, Deconstruction, and the Hermeneutic Project* (Bloomington: Indiana University Press, 1987), see esp. p. 224.

5. See another of Caputo's recent works for non-specialists (*What Would Jesus Deconstruct?* [Grand Rapids: Baker, 2007], p. 134), where he contends, "theo-poetics — not of a politics or an ethics or a 'church dogmatics' — in which the task of converting that poetics into reality falls squarely on our shoulders." Caputo defines his use of "theo-poetics" in *The Weakness of God: A Theology of the Event* (Bloomington: Indiana University Press, 2006), pp. 102-24, which is his "poetics of the kingdom." His earlier "poetics of obligation" is found in Caputo, *Against Ethics: Contributions to a Poetics of Obligation with Constant Reference to Deconstruction* (Bloomington: Indiana University Press, 1993), p. 20, where he credits his

Reading Tertullian in light of Caputo's poststructuralist concerns helps to highlight the way in which the ancient writer employed a theo-economics, which is less a set of rules than a creative interpretation of doctrine and ethics applied to his own concrete situation. Tertullian's theology "goes all the way down."

Theo-poetics, and my adaptation, theo-economics, resists any modernist dichotomies — such as the dichotomy between religion and economics. A historian who segments society into separate spheres creates a false construct and skews the data. While we often like to believe the apostles and early church writers were "above" such menial matters as money,[6] I wish to read Tertullian as very much concerned with both economic issues and religious ones — the line between the two often being imperceptible.[7]

Precedence for this approach has been established in the various fields of discipline drawn upon for this study.[8] With the "linguistic turn" (i.e., the focus on the relationship between philosophy and language), many patristic scholars have embraced social theory, including economic theory.[9] Moreover, economic issues arose in the "new consensus" debate, which viewed early Christian communities through the lens of socioeconomic status.

The current essay will in no way diminish any religious, spiritual, ethical, or theological matters inherent in Tertullian's works — in fact, I believe they will be made explicit in this study. Nevertheless, I will proceed with an economic question at the forefront. This essay aims not toward economic reductionism but toward its opposite. I will assume economics to be inextricably entangled with religion, while also assuming that the economic aspects need to be highlighted because we can be blinded to economic mat-

---

turn toward a *poetice* approach to Johannes de Silentio (ref. Søren Kierkegaard, *Kierkegaard's Writings*, vol. 6, *"Fear and Trembling" and "Repetition,"* trans. H. Hong and E. Hong [Princeton: Princeton University Press, 1983], p. 7). Cf. Caputo, *More Radical Hermeneutics: On Not Knowing Who We Are* (Bloomington: Indiana University Press, 2000), p. 257; and Caputo, *Weakness of God,* p. 107.

6. Similarly, see David Konstan, "The Classics and Class Conflict," *Arethusa* 27, no. 1 (1994): 48, who comments on classical studies in general.

7. On this point more broadly, see recent trends toward "history from below," e.g., *The People's History of Christianity* series by Fortress Press (2005-).

8. Generally, see Walter Scheidel, Ian Morris, and Richard Saller, eds., *The Cambridge Economic History of the Greco-Roman World* (Cambridge: Cambridge University Press, 2007). Older studies include Michael Ivanovitch Rostovtzeff, *The Social and Economic History of the Hellenistic World,* 3 vols. (Oxford: Clarendon Press, 1941).

9. For discussion, see Elizabeth A. Clark, *History, Theory, Text: Historians and the Linguistic Turn* (Cambridge, MA: Harvard University Press, 2004).

ters if preoccupied with other supposedly "more religious" concerns. Postmodern, and especially poststructuralist, thinking aids the historian on this point, for any approach that claims that the early Christian writers addressed "nothing but" religion, or "nothing but" doctrine, or "nothing but" ethics is unconvincing.[10]

2. Problematic Theology in *Ad uxorem* 1

In *Ad uxorem* 1 Tertullian speaks to his wife with the stated request that she "reject [any future] marriages" (1.1.4) and instead embrace "the wisdom of widowhood" (1.1.6).[11] This "wisdom," Tertullian claims, will be "profitable" (*proficiat*, 1.1.6), but profitable in a way that is not readily apparent without further elaboration.

Tertullian's *Ad uxorem* is an open letter, addressed to his wife but written with a wider audience in mind — namely Christians in Carthage. Tertullian's discourses to women invoke the complicated problem of Tertullian's views on gender. Tertullian infamously appears in feminist discussions of early Christian history as a quintessential example of misogyny and patriarchy in the guise of authoritative doctrine.[12] Against this trend, however, many scholars have returned to Tertullian's views on women to find this kind of reading to be superficial.[13] Even if Tertullian might rightly be regarded as suspect on this issue, I contend that his gender biases should

10. Following Jean-François Lyotard, *The Postmodern Condition: A Report on Knowledge,* trans. Geoffrey Bennington and Brian Massumi (Minneapolis: University of Minnesota Press, 1984 [1979]). Caputo interacts with Lyotard throughout his works, but for a helpful introduction see Caputo, *Philosophy and Theology* (Nashville: Abingdon Press, 2006).

11. The text of *Ad uxorem* used here is that of Charles Munier, Sources Chrétiennes 273 (1980). All translations are my own.

12. For a general introduction and bibliography to feminist readings of Christian origins up to Tertullian's period, see Elizabeth A. Castelli, "Heteroglossia, Hermeneutics, and History: A Review Essay of Recent Feminist Studies of Early Christianity," *Journal of Feminist Studies in Religion* 10 (1994): 73-98.

13. Defenses (or at least nuanced readings) of Tertullian include F. Forrester Church, "Sex and Salvation in Tertullian," *Harvard Theological Review* 68 (1975): 83-101; Suzanne Heine, *Women and Early Christianity* (London: SCM Press, 1987), p. 28; Karen Jo Torjesen, "Tertullian's 'Political Ecclesiology' and Women's Leadership," *Studia patristica* 21 (Louvain: Peeters, 1989): 277-82; Elizabeth Carnelly, "Tertullian and Feminism," *Theology* 92 (1989): 31-35; Marie Turcan, "Être femme selon Tertullien," *Vita Latina* 119 (September 1990): 15-21; and Daniel L. Hoffman, *The Status of Women and Gnosticism in Irenaeus and Tertullian,* Studies in Women and Religion 36 (Lewiston, NY: E. Mellen Press, 1995), p. 148.

at least be viewed alongside his other concerns, such as economic ones, which surface in his reading of the Scriptures.

Tertullian explicates marriage as "permitted, but only once, because Adam was the only husband [*unus . . . maritus*] of Eve, and Eve his only wife [*una uxor*]" (1.2.1). Tertullian then concedes that the patriarchs were granted license in their polygamy, but explains that after the "spiritual circumcision" (1.2.4) such practice was "cut off" (*amputari*, 1.2.3). Old Testament polygamy was abrogated by Jesus and Paul, both of whom agreed on two points: (a) that marriage should be permitted and recognized as "good," and (b) that celibacy is "preferred" (*praeferente*, 1.3.2; ref. Matt 19:11-12 and 1 Corinthians 7).

Tertullian then shifts to a different Pauline text for his next point: 1 Tim 5:9-10.[14] According to Tertullian, Paul "would not agree to appoint a widow into the order unless she had been *uniuira*" (1.7.4; ref. 1 Tim 5:9-10).[15]

Here, Tertullian's argumentation seems shaky at best. Does not the pastoral advice of 1 Timothy *require* widows under the age of sixty to remarry and have children (5:14)?[16] In *Ad uxorem*, however, Tertullian makes no stipulation to age but instead flattens the category of widowhood, insisting that the Christian ideal is single marriage or *uniuira*, which he applies not (only) to divorce but to widowhood.[17] But when the pastoralist limits the episcopate to "the husband of one wife" (μιᾶς γυναικὸς ἄνδρα [*unius uxoris uirum*], 1 Tim 3:2), and likewise when limiting enrollment of widows to one who has been the "wife of one husband" (ἑνὸς ἀνδρὸς γυνή [*unius uiri uxor*], 1 Tim 5:9), is not this an injunction against polygamy or perhaps even divorce?[18] It

---

14. The authorship of disputed Pauline texts is irrelevant to the present discussion. Tertullian read both 1 Corinthians and 1 Timothy, and he heard the voice of Paul. I will refer to these texts and to "Paul" without arguing for or against Pauline authorship. The focus will be on Tertullian's Paul, who prefers celibacy.

15. Tertullian is widely read by scholars as referring to a quasi-clerical order of widows — the widows are seated near and honored like the priests and deacons, but they do not perform sacerdotal functions. See, e.g., B. B. Thurston, *The Widows: A Women's Ministry in the Early Church* (Minneapolis: Fortress, 1989), p. 88. Cf. Tertullian, *De pudicitia* 13.

16. Consider Deborah Krause's claim (*1 Timothy* [London: T&T Clark, 2004], p. 100): "the letter writer's ideal ('real') widow is really a dead widow, or a nonexistent widow."

17. Clement of Alexandria, *Stromateis* 3.4, prefers *uniuira* but concedes that Paul (ref. 1 Corinthians 7) permits second marriages. The *Didascalia Apostolorum* (see esp. 14), which curiously lowers the age to fifty years old, seems to strike a balance by forbidding second marriages but prohibiting young widows from being appointed to the order of widows. Cf. *Constitutio Apostolica* 3.

18. See I. H. Marshall, *The Pastoral Epistles*, International Critical Commentary (Edin-

is certainly not a prohibition of remarriage for widows; after all, in the broader context of 1 Timothy 5, the preference of Paul is explicitly for "younger widows to get married and have children" (1 Tim 5:14).[19] Has Tertullian simply proof-texted the Pastoral guidelines to suit his purpose? It seems that he has.[20] What reason, then, should we attribute to Tertullian that would explain his turning a blind eye to the Pauline stipulation?[21] One possibility is that Tertullian became a Montanist.

Montanism has been understood as the heretical movement begun under the prophet Montanus and his fellow prophetesses, Prisca and Maximilla, and it has been conjectured that Montanism spread to North Africa around the turn of the third century, at which time Tertullian joined the sect. Tertullian then would have rejected the traditional Christian and Pauline teaching that second marriages are acceptable because of the rigorist tendencies essential to Montanism. Unfortunately, this outdated caricature still haunts Tertullian studies.

Tertullian was not a schismatic Montanist. The term "Montanism" itself is now widely acknowledged by scholars to be anachronistic — a more appropriate appellation for Tertullian's era being "New Prophecy" or even "new prophecies."[22] Moreover, there is no evidence that he ever "left" his Christian church in Carthage to "join" the Montanists.[23] The understand-

---

burgh: T&T Clark, 1999). Cf. Judith 8:4-8; 16:22. All NT texts come from NA[27], the *Biblia Sacra Vulgata* 5th ed., and the New Revised Standard Version.

19. M. Dibelius and Hans Conzelmann, *The Pastoral Epistles* (Philadelphia: Fortress Press, 1972), p. 75. Tertullian apparently knows the age stipulation of 1 Tim 5:9, since he uses it as an argument against the "virgin" who was admitted to the order in a certain church (*De uirginibus velandis* 9.2-3); he also singles out the fact that the gluttonous and twice-marrying psychics are "young" (*De ieiunio* 17; generally dated later). Admittedly, both of these references are somewhat oblique in regard to age.

20. For the early Christian writers' tendency to do this in regard to asceticism generally, see Elizabeth Clark, *Reading Renunciation: Asceticism and Scripture in Early Christianity* (Princeton, NJ: Princeton University Press, 1999), p. 3; and for Tertullian's tendency specifically, see Peter Brown, *The Body and Society: Men, Women and Sexual Renunciation in Early Christianity* (New York: Columbia University Press, 1988), pp. 76-82 (note that Brown's insightful reading does not comment on *Ad ux.*).

21. While "motive" can at times be a helpful heuristic device, I have elsewhere argued that it should be used tenuously: Wilhite, "Identity, Psychology, and the *Psychici*: Tertullian's 'Bishop of Bishops,'" forthcoming. We are not here attempting to conjecture what Tertullian's motive was, but we are instead trying to read his *stated* reasons with this question in mind.

22. For discussion and bibliography, see Nicola Denzey, "What Did the Montanists Read?" *Harvard Theological Review* 94, no. 4 (2001): 427-48.

23. Instead, he embraced "new prophecies," as did many (if not most or even all) Chris-

ing of Tertullian as in full communion with the North African church is now a consensus among Tertullian scholars (even if it has still not trickled down into many reference works). Accordingly, any attempt to trace an original Pauline teaching through an institutionalization in the Pastoral Epistles finally resulting in a rigorized version in Tertullian's so-called Montanist period is problematic.[24] *Ad uxorem* 1 and 2 are generally dated earlier than this supposed shift in his thinking.[25] Even if they were later, laying Tertullian's decisions at the feet of Montanus would in no way help the discussion, since few, if any, "uncorrupted Montanist teachings" can be surgically extricated from Tertullian's works.[26] He does argue for the ascetic option of *uniuira*, but not because of any Montanist tendency toward asceticism. Instead, we must look to his own explicit rhetorical construc-

---

tians in Carthage; see especially Douglas Powell, "Tertullianists and Cataphrygians," *Vigiliae christianae* 29 (1975): 33-54; L. J. van der Lof, "The Plebs of the Psychici: Are the Psychici of De Monogomia Fellow-Catholics of Tertullian?" in *Eulogia: Mélanges offerts à Antoon A. R. Bastiaensen à l'occasion de son soixante-cinquième anniversaire,* ed. G. J. M. Bartelink, A. Hilhorst, and C. H. Kneepkens (Steenbrugis: In Abbatia S. Petri, 1991), pp. 353-63; David Rankin, *Tertullian and the Church* (Cambridge: Cambridge University Press, 1995); and William Tabbernee, "Perpetua, Montanism, and Christian Ministry in Carthage c. 203 C.E.," *Perspectives in Religious Studies* 32 (2005): 430.

24. Clark, *Reading Renunciation,* pp. 267-68 n. 34. Such a narrative could more plausibly be plotted for Tertullian's later work *De monogomia,* wherein he seems to forbid all second marriages. His stance in that work is usually attributed to the influence of Montanism, a notion now problematized. For my treatment of *De monogomia,* see Wilhite, *Tertullian the African: A Social Anthropological Reading of Tertullian's Context and Identities,* Millennium Studies 14 (Berlin: Walter De Gruyter, 2007), pp. 167-76. Cf. also Tertullian, *De exhortatione castitatis.* Again, Clark (*Reading Renunciation,* p. 291) is helpful in recognizing how Tertullian rhetorically constructs his arguments in opposition to specific viewpoints — his rhetoric, however, does not necessarily represent his own preferences.

25. See René Braun, *Deus Christianorum* (Paris: Études augustiniennes, 1977 [1962]), pp. 567-77, who places the works within Tertullian's "Période catholique" at circa 206. Jean-Claude Fredouille, *Tertullien et la Conversion de la Culture Antique* (Paris: Études Augustiniennes, 1972), pp. 487-88, agrees. T. D. Barnes, *Tertullian: An Historical and Literary Study* (Oxford: Clarendon Press, 1971), esp. pp. 54-56, and his "Postscript" in the revised edition of the work (1985), offers the "conjecture" that the work be dated between 198 and 203, prior to "the earliest precisely datable trace of Montanism" (first ed., p. 46).

26. Hans von Campenhausen (*The Fathers of the Latin Church,* trans. Manfred Hoffmann [London: Adam & Charles Black, 1964], p. 31) concludes, "As a Montanist, Tertullian did not become other than he had always been." Similarly, William Tabbernee, *Montanist Inscriptions and Testimonia: Epigraphic Sources Illustrating the History of Montanism* (Macon, GA: Mercer University Press, 1997), p. 234; and Geoffrey D. Dunn, *Tertullian* (London: Routledge, 2004), p. 6.

tion for why widows must not remarry, which is laced with economic considerations.

3. Economic Rhetoric in *Ad uxorem* 1

Turning back to Tertullian's *Ad uxorem,* one can find an economic theme that runs throughout that would explain the author's willingness to forgo the Pauline injunction for widows to remarry. In order to "find" this theme, however, we must blur the categorical distinctions between economics and kinship — to name but two.

The dichotomy between kinship and economics was unknown in the Roman Empire and should not skew our reading of Tertullian.[27] When writers from the Roman era spoke of things we could classify as familial or domestic (such as marriage, the termination of marriage, children, households, and patrons and clients), these matters entailed a much larger set of meanings, including those under the rubric of kinship, but also those under the rubric of economics. These two categories fuse together neatly under the helpful notion of *Haustafel* in New Testament studies, and work on this concept proves especially instructive in reading Tertullian's appropriation of Pauline household codes from 1 Timothy.[28]

The destabilization of "economics" and "kinship" is homologous to Caputo's deconstructing of economics and religion. But here I am relying on theories from social and cultural anthropology. Anthropological studies of kinship once entailed elaborate kinship charts that traced patrilineal and/or matrilineal relationships with an eye to translate indigenous kinship terms into the given European language. Scholars began to argue, however, that this approach was in fact ethnocentric, because it assumed that indigenous constructions of kinship were intellectually inferior to the

27. For Roman kinship as fluid and dynamic, see Janet Huskinson, "Looking for Culture, Identity and Power," in *Experiencing Rome: Culture, Identity and Power in the Roman Empire,* ed. Janet Huskinson (London: Routledge, 2000), pp. 10-11. Recent Roman historians typically emphasize the complex interconnections of kinship, economics, religion, etc.; e.g., Shelley Hales, *The Roman House and Social Identity* (Cambridge: Cambridge University Press, 2003), pp. 1-3. Caputo himself has touched on this point for classics (*Radical Hermeneutics,* pp. 248-58).

28. For an introduction and bibliography, see Roger W. Gehring, *House Church and Mission: The Importance of Household Structures in Early Christianity* (Peabody, MA: Hendrickson Publishers, 2004 [2000]).

Western scientific mind — evidenced in anthropological descriptions of "fictive kinship" (i.e., kinship that does not fit the scientific/biological model).[29]

Anthropologist David M. Schneider, who rejected the "virtual unanimity in defining kinship in terms of human reproduction,"[30] advocated a "cultural" approach to kinship.[31] In so doing, Schneider called into question the fundamental presuppositions of kinship theory: by recognizing biological kinship as a Western cultural explanation, Schneider destabilizes the entire notion of "kinship" itself. Schneider asserted, "In my view, 'kinship' is like totemism, matriarchy and the 'matrilineal complex.' It is a non-subject. It exists in the minds of anthropologists but not in the cultures they study."[32] Although Schneider's assertions sent shock waves through the discourse of anthropology, many scholars incorporated his critique while continuing their research on kinship, only insisting that the ethnographers not force the data into preconceived assumptions about what kinship "is."[33] A lengthy quote from Schneider helps illustrate the problem with preconceived models, categories, and paradigms:

> The division of the sociocultural world into institutions, domains, or rubrics of kinship, economics, politics, and religion which are presumed to be universally vital, distinct functions and the major building blocks out of which all cultures or societies are made assumes a priori what should be the question: of what blocks is *this* particular culture built? . . . We then approach a particular culture and describe it first in terms of one, then another of these institutional entities. And then comes the great discov-

29. See the debate between Rodney Needham, "Descent Systems and Ideal Language," *Philosophy of Science* 27 (1960): 96-101, and Ernest Gellner, "The Concept of Kinship," *Philosophy of Science* 27 (1960): 187-204.

30. David M. Schneider, *A Critique of the Study of Kinship* (Ann Arbor: University of Michigan Press, 1984), p. 193.

31. See especially Schneider, *American Kinship: A Cultural Account* (Chicago: University of Chicago Press, 1980 [1968]); Schneider, "What Is Kinship All About?" in *Kinship Studies in the Morgan Centennial Year,* ed. P. Reining (Washington, DC: The Anthropological Society of Washington, 1972), pp. 32-63; repr. in *Kinship and Family: An Anthropological Reader,* ed. Robert Parkin and Linda Stone (Malden, MA: Blackwell, 2004), pp. 257-74; and Schneider, *A Critique.*

32. Schneider, "What Is Kinship All About?" p. 269.

33. The school of thought that disagrees with Schneider is known as "biological anthropology," and it has increasingly become peripheral to studies on kinship; for a review, see Parkin and Stone, eds., "General Introduction," in *Kinship and Family,* pp. 1-23.

ery! All of these institutions are inextricably interrelated and intertwined so that in any particular case they cannot be distinguished![34]

Anthropologists who follow in the wake of Schneider tend to highlight the complexity and interconnectedness of these rubrics, and they insist on the fluidity between what were once hard-and-fast theoretical distinctions.[35] Such an approach is incorporated in this reading of Tertullian (and for that matter Paul), whose writings rarely distinguish between matters of kinship (i.e., to which household widows belong) and economics (i.e., on whom does the widows' financial responsibility fall).

To return to Tertullian's argument, we find him interweaving matters of kinship (widows' marriage) and economics (widows' greed), for (as Schneider would insist) the two inhabit the same sphere for Tertullian. After outlining the scriptural rationale and claiming Paul as the champion of *uniuira,* Tertullian answers the diatribal objection that the "flesh is weak" (ref. Matt 26:41) — an excuse we would label religious. Tertullian refutes this objection by juxtaposing the fleshly temptation, or what he calls "fleshly lusts" (*concupiscentia carnis,* 1.4.2 and *passim*) with another kind of temptation widows face, "worldly lusts" (*concupiscentia saeculi,* 1.4.3 and *passim*) — a reason we would deem economic. The religious excuse Tertullian swiftly dismisses as irrelevant for a Christian widow whose "spirit is stronger than the flesh" (1.4.2). The religious excuse is unmasked as a red herring for the economic reasons, which include:

> glory, greed, ambition, lack of self-sufficiency, which provides a [supposed] necessity for marriage . . . : to be matron of an alien inheritance, to roost on alien resources, to extort an alien plantation [*gloriam, cupiditatem, ambitionem, insufficientiam, per quas necessitatem nubendi subornat . . . dominari in aliena familia, alienis opibus incubare, cultum de alieno extorquere,* 1.4.6].

Tertullian answers that Christians should not lust after "heavy jewelry, a tedious wardrobe, or exotic caravans" (*monilium pondera, non uestium taedia, non Gallicos mulos, nec Germanicos baiulos,* 1.4.7). He sees the temptation to

---

34. Schneider, *A Critique,* p. 197; emphasis original.

35. For a general review of kinship theory in recent decades, see Linda Stone, "Introduction: Theoretical Implications of New Directions in Anthropological Kinship," in *New Directions in Anthropological Kinship,* ed. Linda Stone (Lanham, MD: Rowman & Littlefield Publishers, 2001).

remarry one of monetary greed, and this will be seen to fit within Tertullian's overall economic framework in this treatise.

In chapter 5 of *Ad uxorem* 1, Tertullian acknowledges another objection to *uniuira:* "an anxiousness for a posterity [*posteritates*] and the bitter-sweet desire for children [*liberorum amarissima*]" (1.5.1). Like his response to "fleshly lusts" in chapter 4, Tertullian curtly dismisses this for Christians, who expect the imminent *parousia.*[36] This objection, he argues, pertains more to "Gentiles [*gentilium*], who are forced to bear children by laws" (1.5.3) — a reference to the imperial edicts of Augustus that required widows who were Roman citizens to remarry ten months after the death of their husband in order to bear children.[37] Tertullian's reference to Augustan laws again demonstrates how he, like most in the Mediterranean region of his day, linked kinship with economics: in other words, one's marriage entailed one's class status and inheritance *(familia).*[38]

The Roman *domus* or household into which a bride entered represented a microcosm of the broader socioeconomic and political values of the empire: the *dominus* in the household functioned as the emperor, to whom the children, clients, and slaves paid homage.[39] All of these were classified under

36. Cf. Tertullian, *De resurrectione carnis* 36.

37. See Tacitus, *Annales* 3.25; and discussion in R. Saller, *Patriarchy, Property and Death in the Roman Family* (Cambridge: Cambridge University Press, 1994), p. 1; Susan Treggiari, *Roman Marriage: Iusti Coniuges from the Time of Cicero to the Time of Ulpian* (Oxford: Clarendon Press, 1991), pp. 493-94; and Suzanne Dixon, *The Roman Family* (Baltimore: Johns Hopkins University Press, 1992), p. 120, but Dixon also argues (pp. 160-61) that only legal changes took place, not "significant" societal shifts. For the relevance of these laws to 1 Timothy, see Lilian Portefaix, "'Good Citizenship' in the Household of God: Women's Position in the Pastorals Reconsidered in the Light of Roman Rule," in *A Feminist Companion to the Deutero-Pauline Epistles,* ed. Amy-Jill Levine and Marianne Blickenstaff, Feminist Companion to the New Testament and Early Christian Writings 7 (London: T&T Clark, 2003), pp. 147-58.

38. See Jane F. Gardner, "Legal Stumbling-Blocks for Lower-Class Families in Rome," in *The Roman Family: Status, Sentiment, Space,* ed. Beryl Rawson and Paul Weaver (Oxford: Clarendon Press, 1997), pp. 35-36; Dixon, *The Roman Family,* p. 11; Nathan, *The Family,* pp. 3, 27; and Paul Weaver, "Children of Junian Latins," in Rawson and Weaver, eds., *The Roman Family,* pp. 55-72.

39. For the *domus* as a microcosm of Roman society, see Nathan, *The Family,* p. 15; Gardner and Wiedemann, *The Roman Household,* p. 2; and Saller, *Patriarchy,* p. 102. For women and the Greek οἶκος see L. Schottroff, *Lydia's Impatient Sisters: A Feminist Social History of Early Christianity* [*Lydias ungeduldige Schwestern*], trans. Barbara and Martin Rumscheidt (Louisville: Westminster/John Knox Press, 1995 [1994]), esp. p. 30. For recent bibliography, see Kate Cooper, "Approaching the Holy Household," *Journal of Early Christian Studies* 15, no. 2 (2007), esp. pp. 131-38.

the Roman term *familia;* the bride was necessary for producing heirs, and so she was symbolically elevated in status during this period of the principate. All notions of romance, emotion, and/or love aside,[40] the Roman household functioned as the foundation of the Roman economy, and therefore Tertullian's advice to widows pertains to both "worldly" and "fleshly" impulses.[41] He again unmasks the objection about posterity and portrays the root of the temptation as monetary greed: invoking the Lukan Jesus' commentary on Sodom and Gomorrah and on the flood, the conjunct sins are said to be both "marrying and purchasing" (1.5.4; ref. Luke 17:27-28).

Returning to the first objection of "fleshly lusts" in chapter 4, one can see the internal logic of Tertullian's response, which is in terms of both kinship and economics. In opposition to the "fleshly lusts," Tertullian promotes "the examples of our sisters" (1.4.3); he lauds their "marriage to God" *(Deo nubere),* which includes the reciprocation of "prayers as dowries" (*orationes . . . uelut dotes,* 1.4.4) from the widows to God, and "wedding gifts" (*munera maritalia,* 1.4.4) from God to the widows.[42] The status of enrolled widows emerges both in domestic terms, for the widows are now "counted as part of the angelic *familia*" (*de familia angelica deputantur,* 1.4.4), and in economic terms, for the widows are "compensated with imperishable goods" (*immortalium bonorum compensatione,* 1.4.6). This intertwining of familial and economic spheres leads Tertullian into the discussion of greed, which was surveyed above.

Tertullian then turns to proofs of reason, or nature, looking to "gentile" (*gentilium,* 1.5) examples where non-Christian priests and priestesses remain celibate in widowhood, which should shame the Christian widows into surpassing their non-Christian counterparts in the virtue of *uniuira.*[43] He con-

---

40. For an example of an attempt to read emotion into ancient Roman kinship, see M. Golden, "Did the Ancients Care When Their Children Died?" *Greece & Rome* 35 (1988): 159-60.

41. Cf. Tertullian, *De ex. cast.* 8-10; and commentary by Thurston, *The Widows,* pp. 83-85. Also see Philip Rouseau, "The Pious Household and the Virgin Chorus: Reflections on Gregory of Nyssa's Life of Macrina," *Journal of Early Christian Studies* 13 (2005), esp. p. 183.

42. On dowry in Roman marriages, see Dixon, *The Roman Family;* and Treggiari, *Roman Marriage,* chap. 10. For dowry in Roman Africa, see the conflict of Apuleius and his new in-laws *(apud Apologia),* discussed in Mireille Corbier, "Family and Kinship in Roman Africa," *The Roman Family in the Empire: Rome, Italy and Beyond,* ed. Michele George (Oxford: Oxford University Press, 2005), pp. 255-85.

43. The ideal of *uniuira* continued into the principate almost exclusively in the offices of religious cults, in that *uniuira* symbolized one's purity. See discussion in I. C. Mantle, "The Roles of Children in Roman Religion," *Greece & Rome* 49 (2002): 85-106.

cludes with Paul's ideal of single marriage for widows (1.6, cited above), claiming that "the discipline of the Church" (1.7.4) deems "second marriages" untenable.[44]

So far in *Ad uxorem* 1 we see Tertullian selectively invoking the Pastoral Epistles to ban second marriages for widows. We have also seen the overlap of religion, kinship, and economics in Tertullian's rhetoric, for he believes the motivation of the widows who wish to remarry to be driven by "worldly lust" for wealth. We may tentatively hypothesize from this that Tertullian's concern is in regard to the widows' wealth: if the widows remarry, their "dowries" will be paid to new husbands and not to God via the church.

Admittedly, the evidence for wealthy widows sponsoring the church is still slim in Tertullian's *Ad uxorem* 1; after all, while the widows may desire wealth, there is little evidence that they personally own wealth. Perhaps we could look to other witnesses of second- and third-century North African Christianity in order to establish the plausibility of such a reading. One such example is found in the *Martyrdom of Perpetua and Felicitas*.[45]

Perpetua is said to be of noble birth (2.1) and recently married (*matronaliter nupta*, 2.1), but the absence of her husband has led many scholars to conjecture that she is a widow.[46] She is a recent convert and so does not function as a wealthy sponsor of the church. The account does, however, celebrate her as a "matron" (*Domina*, 4.1; 5.5),[47] who has now been

---

44. Except perhaps "spiritual marriages" (*uxorem spiritalem*, *De ex. cast.* 12). It is noteworthy, in light of the argument and conclusion of this present study, that in *De ex. cast.* Tertullian addresses wealthy men and recommends that they marry one of the poor widows. Hoffman, *The Status of Women*, p. 165, comments, "Tertullian may have been concerned that church resources would be depleted. . . ."

45. Tertullian certainly knew of Perpetua and her death, if not of the *passio* itself (see *De anima* 55). The text and translation of the *Passio sanctarum Perpetuae et Felicitatis* come from Herbert Musurillo, *The Acts of the Christian Martyrs: Introduction, Text and Translation* (Oxford: Clarendon Press, 1972), pp. 106-31.

46. Although there is no consensus among scholars, Maureen A. Tilley conjectures that *matronaliter nupta* (2.1) should be interpreted in light of her title "wife of Christ" (*matrona Christi*, 18.2); see Tilley, "One Woman's Body: Repression and Expression in the *Passio Perpetuae*," in *Ethnicity, Nationality and Religious Experience*, ed. Peter C. Phan (New York: University Press of America, 1991), p. 62; Tilley, "The Passion of Perpetua and Felicity," in *Searching the Scriptures*, vol. 2: *A Feminist Commentary*, ed. Elisabeth Schüssler Fiorenza (New York: Crossroad, 1994), p. 844.

47. For the translation as "lady/goddess" in Greco-Roman prayers, see Tilley, "One Woman's Body," p. 60; and as one of "utmost respect," see Tilley, "The Passion," p. 838. Similarly, William Tabbernee argues that *domina* was generally applied to women martyrs in North Africa; see Tabbernee, *Montanist Inscriptions and Testimonia*, pp. 448-49, and

"married to Christ" (*matrona Christi*, 18.2).[48]

Another account that may shed light on Tertullian's context is the *Acts of Paul and Thecla*.[49] Thecla has no wealth of her own, nor is she a widow (she remains a virgin throughout her life). The account does, however, mention a Trifina, "a certain very rich widow" (8.2).[50] The account also narrates how "Trifina had sent large sums of money to Paul, and also clothing . . . for the relief of the poor" (10.5).[51] While this account is set in the context of Asia, the narrative was known by Tertullian and his fellow Christians in North Africa (see *De bapt.* 17).[52] And while Tertullian reproved the *acta* for its depiction of a woman baptizing, the portrayal of the matron Trifina is unaddressed and must have been a plausible phenomenon to the North African church.[53]

Later examples from North Africa proximate to Tertullian's period include wealthy matrons in Cyprian's day (c. 200-258) whom the bishop implored to give in the work of almsgiving.[54] From these accounts, we have the plausibility of wealthy matrons sponsoring the church in North Africa,[55]

Tabbernee, "Perpetua," p. 433. It should be noted, however, that other African martyrdoms are modeled on Perpetua's (barring that of the earlier *Passio sanctorum Scillitanorum* in which *domina* is not used).

48. For a recent discussion of this motif in early Christian writers, see Elizabeth Clark, "The Celibate Bridegroom and His Virginal Brides: Metaphor and the Marriage of Jesus in Early Christian Ascetic Exegesis," *Church History* 77 (2008): 1-25.

49. Schottroff, *Lydia's Impatient Sisters*, pp. 105-10. Text in Oscar von Gebhardt, *Passio S. Theclae Virginis*, Texte und Untersuchungen zur Geschichte der altchristlichen Literatur 22 (1902); and M. R. James, trans., *The Apocryphal New Testament* (Oxford: Clarendon Press, 1924).

50. For full discussion of Tryphaena as "patroness," see Magda Misset-van de Weg, "A Wealthy Woman Named Tryphaena: Patroness of Thecla of Iconium," in *The Apocryphal Acts of Paul and Thecla*, ed. Jan N. Bremmer (Kampen: Kok Pharos, 1996), pp. 16-35.

51. See also 10.15, on other "certain gentlewomen" who "abandoned this world and led a monastic life with [Thecla]."

52. A. Hilhorst, "Tertullian on the Acts of Paul," in Bremmer, ed., *The Apocryphal Acts of Paul and Thecla*, pp. 150-63.

53. Schüssler Fiorenza, "Word, Spirit and Power: Women in Early Christian Communities," in *Women of Spirit: Female Leadership in the Jewish and Christian Traditions*, ed. Rosemary Ruether and Eleanor McLaughlin (New York: Simon and Schuster, 1979), pp. 32-39.

54. *De opera et eleemosynis*; see discussion in Dunn, "The White Crown of Works: Cyprian's Early Pastoral Ministry of Almsgiving in Carthage," *Church History* 73 (2004): 734; and James Dunn, "Widows and Other Women in the Pastoral Ministry of Cyprian of Carthage," *Augustinianum* 45 (2005): 306.

55. See Stephen Davies, *The Revolt of the Widows: The Social World of the Apocryphal Acts* (Carbondale, IL: Southern Illinois University Press, 1980), pp. 70-94, for other apocry-

and from *Ad uxorem* 1 we have Tertullian's concern with widows' relation to wealth. In the latter instance Tertullian seems to fear widow remarriage because it will inevitably result in the loss of the widows' dowries that fund the church's programs. In order to find specific references to wealthy widows in Tertullian's audience, we must turn to *Ad uxorem* 2.

4. Theology and Economics, Take Two (*Ad uxorem* 2)

The relationship between books 1 and 2 of *Ad uxorem* is ambiguous at best.[56] In his preface to the second book, Tertullian references the first book as having been written "recently" (2.1.1), and he declares the purpose of the sequel to offer "follow up advice" or "second-best wisdom" *(secunda consilia)* on widowhood. For some, the opportunity for *uniuira* has arisen from either "divorce or the demise of their husbands." However, there has been at least one instance of a widow remarrying against the "authority" *(potestate)* of the apostle Paul, and against the "advice" (*consilio*, 2.1.4) of book 1. Moreover, someone has even married a non-Christian. In response, Tertullian's voice becomes more shrill, returning to 1 Corinthians 7 and expositing it both more fully and more forcefully (2.2).

Strengthening his point with the theologism that "we are not our own, but we have been bought with a price" (2.3.1; ref. 1 Cor 6:19-20), Tertullian insists on the indebtedness inherent in such a claim by pressing the patronage motif.[57] Jesus acknowledged that "no one can serve two patrons [*duobus dominis*]" (2.3.4; ref. Matt 6:24/Luke 16:13). So how could the widow owned by God marry a non-Christian husband? Such a widow will serve her new patron, mammon: "beauty, fashion, worldly elegance, unclean flatteries" (2.3.4). Moreover, the non-Christian husband is himself a "client of the

---

phal *acta* (notably from non-African contexts) in which widows are dependent on the church rather than being matron sponsors.

56. See Robert Dick Sider, *Ancient Rhetoric and the Art of Tertullian* (Oxford: Oxford University Press, 1971), p. 118.

57. For patronage in social anthropology, see Eric R. Wolf, "Kinship, Friendship, and Patron-Client Relations in Complex Societies," in *The Social Anthropology of Complex Societies,* ed. Michael Banton (New York: Frederick A. Praeger, 1966), pp. 1-22; and Howard F. Stein, "A Note on Patron-Client Theory," *Ethos* 12, no. 1 (1984): 30-36. For Greco-Roman studies, see A. Wallace-Hadrill, ed., *Patronage in Ancient Society* (London: Routledge, 1989). For early Christian studies, see Zeba A. Crook, *Reconceptualising Conversion: Patronage, Loyalty, and Conversion in the Religions of the Ancient Mediterranean* (Berlin: Walter de Gruyter, 2004).

devil" (*diaboli serui*, 2.4.1). The tension between these two patrons is seen in their competing summons:

> If there was to be a prayer day, the husband would make reservations at the spa on that day. If they should be keeping a fast, the husband hosts a feast on the same day. If she should go out on visitation, he must meet for a family engagement [*familiae occupatio*] — nothing else being more important. For who would allow his wife, given to visiting the brothers, to go around street-to-street to certain strange huts — especially in the slums? Who would allow his wife to go to the late-night prayer meetings, if it should be necessary from such late-night lurking that he would willingly have to bear his own deprivation? In sum, what husband will tolerate without anxiety the all-night Easter ceremonies? What husband would send out his own wife to the Patron's Feast [*dominicum*] without any suspicion? What husband would allow his wife to crawl into a prison to kiss the chains of the martyrs?[58] In truth, to kiss any of the brothers? Or provide water for the feet of the saints? Or a cup? Or take food? To yearn for them? To keep them in mind? If a foreign brother arrives, what guest room is there in the strange household [*in aliena domo hospitium*]?[59] If there needs to be an endowment [*largiendum*] made, the barn [*horreum*] and the storeroom [*proma*] are shut tight. (2.4.1-3)[60]

Throughout this paragraph Tertullian contrasts the interests of husbands (i.e., the non-Christian husband and Christ). It must be kept in mind that these are not simply husbands in terms of kinship for Tertullian, but they are also heads of households in terms of economics; they are "dueling *domini*." Or to translate the concept more clearly, they are each a *patronus* at odds with the other; they cannot be honored simultaneously.

The motif of patronage in this paragraph also underscores the economic language Tertullian emphasizes: the non-Christian husband thrusts

---

58. Cf. Lucian, *De morte Peregrini* 12.

59. For a review of the practice of hospitality in the ancient Mediterranean and its import for early Christian studies (esp. New Testament), see Andrew E. Arterbury, *Entertaining Angels: Early Christian Hospitality in Its Mediterranean Setting* (Sheffield: Sheffield Phoenix Press, 2005).

60. Cf. *Didascalia Apostolorum* 15, and the comments of Georg Schöllgen, *Die Anfänge der Profesionalisierung des Klerus und das Kirchliche Amt in der Syrischen Didaskalie*, Jahrbuch für Antike und Christentum 26 (Münster: Aschendorffsche Verlagsbuchhandlung, 1998), on the economics entailed in this document. (I am indebted to Rev. Harold Sikorski of Saginaw, MI, for this last source and for his helpful notes.)

the baths, the feasts, and the storehouses upon the wife, which is in stark contrast to Christ as *Patronus,* who summons her to the slums, the prisoners, and the aliens.[61] Both wish her to invest her dowry, only they do so in much different ways. The non-Christian husband, in fact, will use extortion if necessary: "They keep Christian wives, whose dowries [*dotes*] they make into bribes for silence about the condemnable Christian name" (2.5.4).[62]

As in book 1, Tertullian expands his argument to find proofs from general revelation or natural theology, *per exemplum negativum.* For "even among the nations [*nationes*]" (2.8.1), patrons *(domini)* strictly monitor the marriages of their clients *(seruis)* in order to prevent "handing out the patron's assets [*dominica*] to outsiders." For Christians to hold themselves to a lesser standard, Tertullian declares, is "insanity" (*amentiae,* 2.8.2), the cause of which is "worldly lusts" *(concupiscentias saecularium)* or greed. This greed, Tertullian insists, is found among the "more wealthy" (*plurimum,* 2.8.3) who have "the title of matron" *(nomine matronae).*

The widows in Tertullian's purview are "wealthy," and while Tertullian would prefer them to remain *uniuira* and give their dowry to God (i.e., *Ad uxorem* 1), he contends that it is not beneath these widowed matrons who insist on remarrying to give their dowry to a Christian man, even if he be poor (*Ad uxorem* 2.8.5). The married couple can still carry out the services of widowhood, a list comparable to those of other early Christian writers of this era,[63] which include "relieving the poor" and "giving alms" (2.8.8).[64] His final sentence is another echo of Paul: Tertullian says that to abandon these practices is neither "lawful nor expedient" (*non licet . . . non expediret,* 2.8.9). Or should we translate this punch line "neither legal nor profitable"?

The underlying concern with the remarriage of widows in book 1 is accentuated in book 2, where the widows' "dowries" are not only at risk of being pulled out of the church's funds but are at risk of being placed in the ac-

---

61. Cf. *De baptismo* 18.6.

62. See this undertone carried throughout 2.6-7, where from a Christian perspective, such marriages cannot be "prosperous" (*prospere,* 2.7.3).

63. E.g. Hippolytus, *Traditio Apostolica* 10.1-4; 23.1 (and see commentary in U. E. Eisen, *Women Officeholders in Early Christianity,* trans. Linda M. Maloney [Collegeville, MN: Liturgical Press, 2000]); and Clement of Alexandria, *Stromateis* 3.12.86: "Perhaps the Saviour did not refer to begetting children, but was exhorting those who wished only to possess large wealth and not to help the needy to share their goods with others" (trans. John Ernest Leonard Oulton and Henry Chadwick, in *Alexandrian Christianity* [Philadelphia: Westminster Press, 1954], p. 81; ref. Matt 6:19 and Isa 50:9).

64. Contra *Constitutio apostolica.* 3.1.6.

counts of non-Christians and being lost entirely. In light of this, Tertullian grudgingly grants that widows may remarry, but he insists with Paul that this be a marriage "in the Lord," or "under Christ's patronage."

5. The Voice of Paul

We may now return to the question as to why Tertullian ignored the fuller context of Paul's counsel on widow remarriage, for not only does 1 Timothy "permit" remarriage, but it requires it for widows under the age of sixty.[65] It needs to be clarified that there was no uniform view of widows among early Christians. Whether there is diversity within the biblical or even Pauline corpus on this subject is beyond the scope of this essay. Whether there is diversity within Tertullian's oeuvre is a question that has been kept in view, but mostly relegated to footnotes. Nevertheless, when speaking of widows in 1 Timothy or Hippolytus or Tertullian, we must admit that each writer is contextualized and, therefore, may or may not be speaking of the same phenomenon and praxis. This assumption, which is underscored here in my reading of Tertullian, helps us to see how Tertullian's theology "goes all the way down" in that his own contextual situation requires a creative application of previous Christian discourse on widows, or in a Caputoan framework, a theo-economics.

When we move from the context of 1 Timothy to that of North Africa, Paul's stipulation for widows below the age of sixty to remarry has been ignored, if not contradicted, by Tertullian. Tertullian's motivation can now be seen as a concern with the economic implications for the church: if the wealthy matrons remarry, their dowries/endowments no longer fund the church. It needs to be noted here that Tertullian was not an ordained priest. This point has become a consensus since Timothy David Barnes's seminal work in 1971, but it bears repeating in order to remind us that no evidence exists that suggests Tertullian was on the payroll of his church.[66] Any discus-

---

65. The problems inherent in 1 Timothy itself, what Bruce Winter has called an "exegetical headache" ("Providentia for the Widows of 1 Timothy 5:3-16," *Tyndale Bulletin* 39 [1988]: 83), will not be resolved here. Winter's article provides a helpful bibliography on these matters. For a feminist study of 1 Timothy, see Krause, *1 Timothy*; Jouette M. Bassler, "The Widow's Tale: A Fresh Look at 1 Tim 5:3-16," *Journal of Biblical Literature* 103 (1984): 23-41; and essays in Levine and Blickenstaff, eds., *A Feminist Companion to the Deutero-Pauline Epistles* (cited in n. 37 above).

66. The financial remuneration for clerics at this time is debated; see Schöllgen, *Die*

sion of economic matters (i.e., church finances) in Tertullian's works should not be immediately dismissed as self-serving.[67] Moreover, his explicit concern, which I think can largely be taken at face value, is with the church's distribution of alms to the poor.

With this understanding of Tertullian, we may also look closer into 1 Timothy, for there we hear the voice of Paul — who, like Tertullian, was not on the payroll of the church (cf. 1 Corinthians 9), and who, like Tertullian, discusses the household of God in economic terms. On widowhood Paul implicitly, if not explicitly, shares the same concern as Tertullian about the financial risk to the church.

The first mention of women in 1 Timothy comes as an injunction against "expensive clothes" (2:9). There is, however, no reason for conflating the "women" or even "wives" of 2:9-10 who appear wealthy with the women who are "really widows" of 5:3-16 who appear destitute. In fact, the women of chapter 2 may be taking advantage of the widow system in that they are enrolling their widowed relatives in the church's care, which frees up additional expendable income for themselves for things such as "expensive clothes"; therefore, they are "not providing for their family members" (5:8).

In the description of a deaconess, economic factors are not directly mentioned, but the deaconesses are to be "like" (ὡσαύτως, 3:11) the deacons, who not only must be good household managers (3:12) but also must "not [be] greedy for money" (3:8). The epistolary purpose statement at the end of 1 Timothy 3 is expressly concerned with divine household-economics (οἶκος θεοῦ, 3:15; cf. 6:9-10, 6:17-18), which is expatiated first in terms of doctrine (3:16–4:16) and then in terms of praxis (5:1ff.).

Within the latter section on praxis comes the first mention of widows, and the church is given a command: to "honor widows who are really widows [ὄντως χήραι]" (5:3). The first part of this command, "honoring," is a phenomenon that in the Pastoral Epistles includes the notion of remuneration.[68] This understanding of "honor" coincides with the second part of the

---

Anfänge, pp. 56-57, for bishops' wages during Tertullian's time. The point made here is more apophatic than kataphatic: rather than assuming that any presbyters were paid, I am insisting that church funds in no way flowed into Tertullian's pockets.

67. This point is meant to avoid a hasty dismissal of the problem of Tertullian's reading of Paul without hearing out his stated concerns. As to Tertullian's role in his church, I have elsewhere argued (Wilhite, *Tertullian the African*, p. 178) that Tertullian was one of the African church's lay elders *(seniori laici)*. At the time I did not know of the same conclusion of Tabbernee ("Perpetua," p. 441).

68. Reggie M. Kidd, *Wealth and Beneficence in the Pastoral Epistles: A "Bourgeois" Form*

command — i.e., "really widows," which in the following verses is explained to mean those women who have no children, grandchildren, or any other persons who can give a "repayment" (5:4), such the wealthy women/wives of 2:9 would be able to give.[69] The "real widow" who depends on God alone for sustenance (5:5) is contrasted with a woman "who lives for pleasure" (5:6). At this point, the rule is given that only widows of at least age sixty can be enrolled (5:9), because any that are younger could marry (and perhaps generate more funds for the church), rather than drain funds from the church.

It is interesting to note that the list of additional qualifications for ecclesial widowhood matches up very closely with Tertullian's list of widows' services, both of which include having "shown hospitality, washed the saints' feet, [and] helped the afflicted" (1 Tim 5:10).[70] In *Ad uxorem* 2.4.1-4 (cited above), Tertullian's list suggests additional dependence on and application of Paul's words from 1 Timothy. Tertullian's close reading of Paul becomes apparent again in his accommodation of the underlying economic concerns about widow remarriage.

Beyond all of the spiritual concerns, which are in no way diminished in this theo-economic reading, the "bottom line" seems to be found in the maxim of 1 Tim 5:16: "let the church not be burdened, so that it can assist those who are real widows."[71] Paul and Tertullian both share this maxim, only the resulting injunctions are opposed. In 1 Timothy, in order "not to burden the church" young widows are forbidden from being enlisted, which would bleed funds away from those who truly need them. However, in the

---

of Early Christianity? (Atlanta: Scholars Press, 1990), p. 103. See esp. 1 Tim 5:17-18; 6:1; and 2 Tim 2:20.

69. Cf. *Const. app.* 3.1.7.

70. See the widows as making "pastoral house calls" in Dibelius and Conzelmann, *Pastoral Epistles*, p. 75.

71. A point noted by some scholars: e.g., Francis C. Synge, "Studies in Texts: 1 Timothy 5:3-16," *Theology* 68 (1965): 200-201; Thomas C. Oden, *First and Second Timothy and Titus*, Interpretation (Louisville: John Knox Press, 1989), p. 153; Johnson, *Letters*, p. 139; Justin T. Meggitt, *Paul, Poverty, and Survival* (Edinburgh: T&T Clark, 1998), p. 70; and Portefaix, "'Good Citizenship,'" p. 156; see also Osiek, "The Widow as Altar," p. 166; Bassler, "The Widow's Tale," p. 34; and Manabu Tsuji, "Zwischen Ideal und Realität: Zu den Witwen in 1 Tim 5.3-16," *New Testament Studies* 47 (2001): 92-104. Kidd (*Wealth and Beneficence*, pp. 103-6) also concludes that 1 Timothy 5 is concerned with church funds expended on "destitute widows." However, he segments vv. 9-15 out from vv. 3-8 and 16, which allows for two kinds of widows in the passage: "destitute" and "enrolled." Kidd's segmentation is an attempt to resolve the problems of this passage by conflating the women/wives of chapter 2 with (some of) the widows of chapter 5. Cf. Hermas, *Sim.* 1.8; 5.3; Ignatius, *Polyc.* 4; 1 *Clem.* 8.

context of Tertullian's *Ad uxorem* 1, wherein the widows are wealthy matrons, in order not to bleed funds from those who truly need them widows are forbidden from remarrying, which would result in their dowries being unavailable to the church.

Both actions stem from the same theo-economic concern: "let not the church be burdened so that it can assist those" in need.[72] Tertullian, it seems, has profoundly heard the voice of Paul. In other words, rather than inaccurately proof-texting the Scriptures, Tertullian had to contradict Paul semantically in order to be faithful to Paul theologically.[73] Tertullian clearly knows of Paul's economics, but to Tertullian they represent more of a theo-economics, which must be creatively interpreted and faithfully appropriated to his own North African context.

---

72. This may be the passage's "hermeneutic-phenomenological content" or "the event of appeal or claim or call that issues from" this passage (see Caputo, *Weakness of God,* p. 117, on Scripture).

73. My study of 1 Timothy is largely indebted to the expertise and guidance of David Garland and Todd Still, my senior colleagues at George W. Truett Seminary of Baylor University, both of whom read an early draft of this essay and — independently of each other — insightfully commented that Tertullian could have learned this hermeneutic from Paul's texts. See, too, the theological reading of Luke Timothy Johnson, *1 Timothy, 2 Timothy, Titus* (Atlanta: John Knox Press, 1987), pp. 71-74.

12. Critiquing Rome's Economy: Revelation and Its Reception in the Apostolic Fathers

Grant Macaskill

It is almost universally acknowledged within scholarly circles that John's Apocalypse, the Book of Revelation, contains a polemic against Roman imperial power and that an important aspect of this polemic concerns the economic and mercantile dimensions of the empire.[1] Given the concern with economics and charity in the writings of the early church fathers, discussed elsewhere in this volume, we might expect this polemic to gain a prominence in the patristic reception of Revelation. Surprisingly, however, we find that for the most part this is not the case. With the notable exception of Tertullian, the economic aspect of Revelation's critique of Rome is largely eclipsed by other moral issues or by a millenarian preoccupation with the identity of the Antichrist, the beast. Neglectful of the text of Revelation as it is, this tendency may reflect the ideological adjustments that were necessary for the church to make as it became an established part of the imperial system in the fourth century: to benefit from the imperial economy may not have been as troubling to the church's conscience as we — or John — might expect, providing that more obvious idolatries had been transformed by the presence of the gospel.

This, then, is what I will explore in this essay, which will fall into two parts. The first part will outline the economic aspect of the polemic against Roman imperial power in Revelation, locating this polemic within wider

---

1. This statement is not, of course, intended to obscure the range of scholarly positions taken on the precise details or significance of this polemic. The following discussion will reference some of the key works and will note some of the points of variance.

theological contexts in Revelation and noting connections that can often be overlooked in modern biblical scholarship. The second part will then examine the reception of the economic texts in Revelation in the church fathers.

1. The Economic Critique of Rome in Revelation

The economic critique of Rome in Revelation is one aspect of a much broader negative portrayal of Roman imperial power that becomes prominent in the visions cycle from Revelation 12 onward. The economic aspect of this is anticipated in the letter to the church in Laodicea, whose self-perception as rich is deemed to be a glamour (Rev 3:17-18), but it is only with the development of the symbolism of the beasts and the harlot in Revelation 12, themselves earthly manifestations of the power of the dragon, that we encounter the full force of Revelation's polemical symbolism.

Revelation 12 describes the hurling down of Satan to the earth within the context of Satan's ongoing cosmic conflict with the people of God, depicted as a woman with child.[2] The importance of this for our purposes lies in its narrative connection to the appearance of the beasts in Revelation 13. In 13:1-2 we read,

> And [the dragon] stood on the sand of the seashore. And I saw a beast coming up out of the sea, having ten horns and seven heads, and on his horns were ten diadems, and on his heads were blasphemous names. And the beast which I saw was like a leopard, and his feet were like those of a bear, and his mouth like the mouth of a lion. And the dragon gave him his power and his throne and great authority.[3]

The power of this first beast, then, is fundamentally evil, derived from his Satanic patron. It is also fundamentally blasphemous: Rev 13:3-4 speaks of the

2. For the background of Revelation 12 in ancient conflict myths, see A. Yarbro Collins, *The Combat Myth in the Book of Revelation*, HDR 9 (Missoula: Scholars Press, 1976). For the identification of the woman as the people of God, see G. K. Beale, *The Book of Revelation: A Commentary on the Greek Text*, New International Commentary on the Greek New Testament (Grand Rapids: Eerdmans; Carlisle: Paternoster, 1999), pp. 621-43. Beale's discussion covers the various interpretative options and presents a helpful critique of approaches that understand the woman as being symbolic of Mary.

3. Unless otherwise noted, all biblical quotations are taken from the Revised Standard Version.

mock resurrection of the head that appeared to have been slain[4] (ὡς ἐσφαγμένην; the phrase parallels that used of the Lamb in 5:6), an event that causes the nations to worship him, saying, "Who is like the beast? Who can make war against him?"[5] The beast himself continues to utter blasphemies in 13:6 and is given power to overcome (νικῆσαι) the saints. His rule, it is stressed, is global, and he is worshiped by all who live on earth whose names are not in the Lamb's Book of Life (13:8), so that a basic dichotomy is established between those in the Lamb's following and those in the beast's following.

From 13:11-18 we find the account of a second beast, this time rising from the earth. Essentially, his ministry is to bring glory to the first beast, from which his own authority is derived (13:12). Part of his responsibility is the enforcement of the worship of the beast from the sea (13:15), and connected to this is his branding of all with a mark, which is "the name of the beast or the number of his name," 666. It is here that the first clear trace of economic concern appears, for in the vision no one is permitted to trade unless they bear the mark of the beast.

While popular millennial literature doubtless will continue to seek to identify the beasts with contemporary figures, scholarship is all but united in seeing the two beasts as symbolic of the Roman imperial power,[6] with the second beast representing the propaganda machine of the imperial

4. This may refer to the *Nero Redivivus* myth or to the recovery of the empire after the suicide of Nero. See G. B. Caird, *A Commentary on the Revelation of St. John the Divine* (New York: Harper & Row, 1966), pp. 164-65. For discussion of the *Nero Redivivus* myth, see R. J. Bauckham, *The Climax of Prophecy* (Edinburgh: T&T Clark, 1993), pp. 384-452, especially 415-50. Arguments against the consensus identifying the beast with Nero may be found in the older article by P. S. Minear, "The Wounded Beast," *JBL* 72 (1953): 96-101. He is critiqued, in turn, by J. M. Court, *Myth and History in the Book of Revelation* (London: SPCK, 1979), pp. 122-53, esp. 130.

5. Rev 13:4. Compare Exod 15:11; Ps 71:19; 89:6; 113:5; Isa 44:6-7.

6. Reflecting such a consensus, see P. Prigent, *L'Apocalypse de Saint Jean*, CNT 14 (Lausanne and Paris: Delachaux et Niestlé, 1981), p. 201, or more recently R. J. Bauckham, *The Theology of the Book of Revelation* (Cambridge: Cambridge University Press, 1993), pp. 35-39, which does not even mention other views. It is worth noting here also the work of Elisabeth Schüssler Fiorenza. For example, in "Religion und Politik in der Offenbarung des Johannes," in *Biblische Randbemerkungen: Schülerfestschrift für Rudolph Schnackenburg zum 60. Geburstag*, ed. Helmut Merklein and Joachim Lange (Würzburg: Echter, 1974), pp. 261-72, and later in *Revelation: Vision of a Just World* (Edinburgh: T&T Clark, 1993), she relates the portrayal of the beast to wider polemical themes in Revelation concerning Christian participation in Roman imperial power. While some scholars take issue with her work (notably David Barr, *Tales of the End* [Santa Rosa: Polebridge, 1998]) they do not question the fundamental centrality of Roman imperial power to the symbolism of Revelation.

cult.[7] The probable significance of the mark of the beast as constituting gematria on the name of Nero (represented as *Kaiser Nerōn*)[8] or even on the title *Lateinos*[9] would confirm this, but even those who dismiss the idea that this is gematria (such as Beale, who prefers to see 666 as a trinity that falls always short of Revelation's "perfect" number seven)[10] see the symbolism of the beasts as unmistakably pointing toward the Roman imperial power, in its military, religious, and economic aspects, not least because in a first- or second-century context the image of global military authority would unavoidably have Roman imperial connotations.[11] The objections raised against such a view have often arisen from an overly simplistic concept of symbolism that has failed to recognize the subtle ways in which images may represent discrete aspects of the empire.[12]

Revelation 14–16 returns to themes introduced earlier in the book. The 144,000-strong army (first encountered in 7:4-8) reappears in 14:1-5, following the Lamb wherever he goes. Placed after the account of the beasts, this mention of the 144,000 foregrounds the basic enmity between this army and the bestial power, mentioned again in 14:9-10, where it is stressed that anyone receiving the mark of the beast will share its destiny in the judgment of God. This warning is preceded (14:8) by the statement that Babylon has fallen. This is the first occurrence of the name Babylon in Revelation and would be intrusive on the flow of the narrative unless there was some implicit connection or identification between Babylon and the bestial power. The juxtaposition suggests that the two are to be correlated, and, as the narrative comes to focus on the symbol of Babylon in Revelation 17–18, such an identification is further legitimated, though with an important measure of differentiation. The symbols represent different aspects of the empire, leaving room for one aspect to attack another, as in 17:16.

7. Bauckham, *The Theology of the Book of Revelation*, pp. 37-38.

8. Bauckham, *The Climax of Prophecy*, pp. 384-417, argues the case with mathematical brilliance.

9. Irenaeus, *Adversus haereses* book 5, chapter 30, notes this as a possibility, though he prefers to see "Titan" as the name represented by the gematria.

10. Beale, *The Book of Revelation*, pp. 718-28.

11. This is precisely why Rick van de Water's assertion that the beasts in fact refer to Palestinian and Diaspora Judaism ("Reconsidering the Beast from the Sea (Rev 13)," *NTS* 46 [2000]: 245-61) must be deemed implausible. Van de Water remarkably neglects Bauckham's work on the mark of the beast (*The Climax of Prophecy*, pp. 384-452) and fails to adequately account for the military honor so central to the portrayal of the beast from the sea.

12. See Court, *Myth and History*, p. 130, criticizing Minear, "The Wounded Beast."

Revelation 17–18 contains the most overtly economic material in the book, describing the downfall of Babylon the harlot and the laments of the merchants who have depended upon her for their trade.[13] There are elements that further support the identification of Babylon with Rome: the harlot sits upon seven hills (17:9), as does Rome, and rides upon the back of a scarlet beast (17:3), rehearsing the imagery of Revelation 13 but with a technicolor dimension that calls to mind the Roman army. These features point us in the direction of seeing Babylon as a further symbol of the Roman Empire and not, as has been suggested, as a cipher for Jerusalem and its destruction in 70 CE.[14] She sits not only upon seven hills, but also upon the waters (17:15), implying naval power,[15] and is the great city that rules over the kings of the earth (17:18);[16] neither of these would be applicable to Jerusalem, but both accord with a Rome referent. Surely fatal for the idea that Jerusalem is in view is the fact that Babylon is depicted as the center of world trade in Revelation 18, a fact that brings us to the core of Revelation's economic polemic. While Revelation 17–18 presents Babylon as a prostitute (an image that connotes seductiveness and immorality more generally), and while this imagery introduces the description of Revelation 18 (thus retaining its importance therein), it is the city aspect of Babylon that comes to the fore much more in Revelation 18. Babylon is a city, and that city is economically powerful. Mercantile imagery runs through this chapter, but it is the list of goods in 18:11-13 that most obviously develops the polemical themes of the book.[17]

13. See Elisabeth Schüssler Fiorenza, *The Power of the Word: Scripture and the Rhetoric of Empire* (Minneapolis: Fortress Press, 2007), pp. 130-47, for the argument that the use of feminine imagery is not misogynistic in Revelation when understood in the context of the book's polemical and theological structures. Instead, the emphasis falls on the imperial (not feminine) qualities of this city.

14. See D. C. Chilton, *Days of Vengeance* (Fort Worth: Dominion, 1987), p. 443; J. M. Ford, *Revelation,* Anchor Bible (Garden City, NY: Doubleday, 1975), p. 285; R. van de Water, "Reconsidering the Beast from the Sea," pp. 256-57.

15. Van de Water, "Reconsidering the Beast from the Sea," takes this to be a reference to the Jewish Diaspora rather than naval power, but this surely neglects the rulership implied by sitting upon the waters.

16. Beale (*The Book of Revelation,* p. 889) describes the texts adduced by Ford in support of Jerusalem's economic and political influence (*Revelation,* p. 285) as "unpersuasive," noting further that "it is also fatal to the preterist view that the influence of Jerusalem was at its lowest in the two centuries immediately preceding A.D. 70, whereas Babylon's demise in Revelation 17–18 is an immediate fall from great power and prosperity."

17. References to merchants, ἔμποροι, are found in 18:3, 11, 15, and 23 — the first and last of these, coming at the opening and closing of the description of fallen Babylon, must be re-

And the merchants of the earth weep and mourn for her, since no one buys their cargo any more, cargo of gold, silver, jewels and pearls, fine linen, purple, silk and scarlet, all kinds of scented wood, all articles of ivory, all articles of costly wood, bronze, iron and marble, cinnamon, spice, incense, myrrh, frankincense, wine, oil, fine flour and wheat, cattle and sheep, horses and chariots, and slaves, that is, human souls.

The list of goods is generally seen to draw upon Ezek 27:7-25, with which it shares fifteen out of its twenty-nine items.[18] This allows Bauckham to note that the depiction of Rome in Revelation 17–18 conflates passages about Babylon (Isa 13:1–14:23; 21:1-10; 47:1-15; Jer 50–51) with a passage about Tyre, since that city is the referent of Ezekiel 26–28.[19] This point is significant to Bauckham: to portray Rome as another Babylon is inadequate since its economic and mercantile power requires comparison also with a city such as Tyre.[20] Moreover, it is precisely the city associated in the OT with economic activity, Tyre, that in all probability supplies the imagery of the harlot: "The Old Testament prophets do not portray Babylon as a harlot, but Isa 23:15-18 uses the image of the harlot for Tyre."[21] Thus, while we have already noted the connotations of seductiveness and immorality carried by the image of the prostitute, this central image also connotes economic wantonness, a point we can easily overlook.

While Ezek 27:7-25 may supply us with a textual background for Revelation 18, it cannot be regarded as the sole source for this list, since a further fourteen items in Rev 18:11-13 are not found there. Bauckham argues that, while Ezekiel may be in the narrator's mind, in constructing his list the author was also influenced by concrete realities of his day. Consequently, the list outlines the most expensive goods that were being imported into the households of Rome's wealthy citizens.[22] Such imports, of course, were essentially drawn from the territories occupied by Rome, the nations it had conquered, and represented the movement of limited goods into the city, as

---

garded as structurally important, perhaps even forming a loose *inclusio* that implies the centrality of economics to the passage.

18. Beale, *The Book of Revelation*, p. 909.

19. Bauckham, *The Climax of Prophecy*, p. 345.

20. "If Rome was the heir of Babylon in political and religious activity, she was also the heir of Tyre in economic activity" (Bauckham, *Climax of Prophecy*, p. 346).

21. Bauckham, *The Climax of Prophecy*, p. 346.

22. Bauckham, *The Climax of Prophecy*, pp. 350-71. Cf. John S. Perry, "Critiquing the Excess of Empire: A Synkrisis of John of Patmos and Dio of Prusa," *JSNT* 29 (2007): 473-96.

Roman householders maintained their luxurious lifestyle at the expense of others. The fact that the list climaxes (perhaps we should say that it rhetorically *anti*-climaxes) with the mention of the trading of human lives (καὶ σωμάτων, καὶ ψυχὰς ἀνθρώπων) last upon the list is indicative of Rome's heedlessness of the human cost of its lifestyle. Viewed from the perspective of modern discussions of globalization, this perhaps ought to prompt us to recognize the human cost implicit in every item on the list, as limited goods were lost to the peripheries and as the various industries maintained themselves through the labor of the poor. It is perhaps noteworthy that many of the items were associated with Asia Minor — the specific localities to which Revelation is addressed. Consequently, the list would have carried additional resonance with such an audience.

As significant and effective as this portrayal of Rome's economy may be, it would be a serious mistake to see it as primarily an attack on Rome, as an expression of anti-Roman sentiment, though some commentators fail to move beyond this. The truth is that it is part of a complex theological parenesis in Revelation. The parenetic dimension emerges in 18:4, where, immediately after the pronouncement of Babylon's destruction but preceding the description of its economics, another voice from heaven cries, "Come out of her, my people, lest you take part in her sins, lest you share in her plagues." Taken alone, the significance of this would be limited. When, however, we read this exhortation through the lens of the letters to the seven churches, which within Revelation form a vestibule that we must pass through before we approach the visionary material of 4–22, this exhortation becomes powerful. As is widely acknowledged, the letters present a generally negative picture of the churches. Beale, for example, detects an *a b c c c b′ a′* chiastic structure:

The first and last [churches] are in danger of losing their very identity as a Christian church. Therefore, they are exhorted to repent in order to prevent their judgment and to inherit the promises that genuine faith deserves. The churches addressed in the three central letters have to varying degrees some who have remained faithful and others who are compromising with pagan culture. . . . The second and fifth letters are written to churches which have proved themselves faithful to Christ's "name" in the face of persecution from both Jews and pagans. . . . The significance of this is that the Christian church *as a whole* is perceived as being in a poor condition, since not only are the healthy churches in a minority but the literary pattern points to this emphasis because the churches in the worst condition form the literary boundaries of the letters and the churches with serious problems form the very core of the presentation.[23]

With this impression of the state of the church registered at the start,[24] the exhortation to "come out from among her" becomes much more forceful and challenging. There is a real sense that Christians are often part of the economic problem being challenged, or potentially complicit with it. (This, of course, would require us to accept that the churches in Asia Minor were not comprised only of those at or below subsistence level, as indicated already by Rev 3:17).[25] The probability that some Christians were caught up in this sinful economy, then, is a real one.

The problem, though, rests on deeper theological foundations. It is easily overlooked that Revelation is framed by references to the church's union with Christ or to its participation in the divine life. Revelation 1:9 is the first of these references:

> I John, your brother, who share with you [ὁ ἀδελφὸς ὑμῶν καὶ συγκοινωνὸς] in Jesus [ἐν Ἰησοῦ] the tribulation and the kingdom and the patient endurance, was on the island called Patmos on account of the word of God and the testimony of Jesus.

Striking here are the corporate language and the fact that what is shared corporately, whether good (kingdom) or bad (tribulation), is shared "in Jesus." This is, nevertheless, addressed to the members of the flawed churches of Revelation 2–3, so the union with Jesus, while actual, is clearly not yet perfected — a fact demanded by Revelation's own theo-logic. At the other end of Revelation we have the depiction of the church enjoying perfect, unspoiled fellowship with the divine life, symbolized as the river flowing from the throne of

---

23. Beale, *The Book of Revelation*, p. 227. Cf. M. R. Mulholland, *Revelation* (Grand Rapids: Zondervan, 1990), p. 112.

24. This assumes that the churches addressed in Revelation 2–3 are intended to be seen as representative of the church as a whole, a fact surely required by their numerical value of 7, especially when this is understood in connection with the vision of Jesus standing in the midst of the 7 lampstands (1:12-13). See further Steve Moyise, *The Old Testament in the Book of Revelation*, JSNTS 115 (Sheffield: Sheffield Academic Press, 1995), p. 24, who notes that after Revelation 3 "it is the universal church that is centre stage, with no further mention of congregations."

25. Bauckham (*The Theology of the Book of Revelation*, p. 15) notes that the depiction of the churches undermines the generalization that Revelation is primarily consolatory in character.

God and the Lamb (and implicitly an image of the Spirit).[26] This is, of course, the heart of the New Jerusalem described in Revelation 21–22. It is vital that we recognize that the New Jerusalem is not the place where the church will dwell eschatologically: the New Jerusalem *is* the church, the Bride (21:9-10). In fact, it is an image of the church in its perfected, not its present, state: "Let us rejoice and exult and give him the glory, for the marriage of the Lamb has come, and his Bride has made herself ready" (19:7). Specifically, for this perfected church in the new world order (21:1) there will be "no more curse" (22:3), for the cursed, sinful world order of the present world will have passed away.

The presentation of the New Jerusalem, the Bride, in perfect marital union with Jesus forms the essential counterpoint to the presentation of Babylon the harlot, riding upon the back of the beast and through him in fellowship with the dragon. Indeed, we find a counterpoint to Babylon's wanton luxury in the description of the bejeweled splendor of the Bride in 21:11, 18-21. This splendor is, of course, eschatological, but it is also christological: it proceeds from union with God through Jesus. Thus, we also find a counterpoint to the mark of the beast on the foreheads of those complicit with the Roman economy: the saints will have the name of God and of the Lamb on their foreheads (22:4; cf. 7:3; 14:1; and 3:12, where the name of Christ and the Father are accompanied by the name of the New Jerusalem).

The economic critique of Rome in Revelation must be read within this rhetorical, moral, and theological complex if we are not to misconstrue it. The problem with the economics of Rome is that it is part of the present, cursed world order. As such, it is caught up in the web of sin from which the church is being delivered. Within this matrix of sin and its consequences, the impact of the worldly economy on human life is often itself evil, mindless of human cost. Christians are called to recognize this web of sinfulness and their own potential complicity with it. They are also challenged to regard the present economy from the point of view of their union with Christ and their participation in an inaugurated eschatological reality; the riches of Rome are less valuable than the heavenly treasure that will be realized only in the eschaton. Proper appreciation of this theological context allows us to move beyond simplistic characterizations of John's economic polemic as Marxist[27] or anti-globalized and to

26. The blessing of 1:4 is best understood as Trinitarian (see Bauckham, *The Climax of Prophecy,* pp. 162-66). Once this is noted, the absence of an explicit mention of the Spirit in 22:4 is intentionally surprising; the parallels between this verse and John 7:38-39 suggest that the river is to be seen as a symbol of the Spirit.

27. On this point see R. M. Royalty, *The Streets of Heaven: The Ideology of Wealth in the Apocalypse of John* (Macon: Mercer University Press, 1998), especially pp. 244-46, where he

see it as an outworking of a nuanced Christian eschatology, with the changed values and social responsibilities that ought to proceed from it.[28]

It is perhaps worth noting, as we draw this section to a close, the suggestion that John himself was of relatively significant social standing. Ben Witherington III has suggested this to be an implication of John's exile to Patmos (1:9), which would presumably have been a form of *relegatio,* a punishment appropriate only to those of relatively high social standing.[29] The relevance of this to our study is that John's critique, while that of an exile, is not to be seen as the grumbling of the poor against the rich, but rather the insight of someone who himself has participated in the Roman world.

2. The Reception of Revelation's Economic Critique in the Early Church Fathers

We turn now to the question of how this moral and theological polemic was received by the early church. Some limits need to be set from the outset on which texts will be examined. While Revelation is not as widely cited as many other books from the New Testament, it is still popular enough for us to run the risk of retrieving information too general to be of use. Moreover, a good deal of the material that we encounter in the later reception of Revelation simply repeats the findings of earlier commentators. For this reason, I will focus primarily on the ante-Nicene fathers — those writing prior to the establishment of Christianity under Constantine. This inevitably means that we are confined to Western fathers, since the first of the Eastern fathers whose commentaries survive are Oecumenicus and Andrew of Caesarea, both from the sixth century.

In the Western tradition, the earliest of the fathers to make any substantial use of Revelation is Irenaeus in *Adversus haereses* (c. 180). Irenaeus refers

---

brings his conclusions to bear on Marxist interpretations. I do not agree with all of Royalty's conclusions or argumentation, but his refutation of such approaches is helpful.

28. This dimension is explored in a more theological context by Jürgen Moltmann, *Theology of Hope: On the Ground and the Implications of a Christian Eschatology,* trans. J. W. Leitch (London: SCM, 1962; originally published as *Theologie der Hoffnung* [Munich: Chr. Kaiser, 1964]). A multitude of works have critically engaged with Moltmann's thought, often scathingly. Nevertheless, I cite it because of its importance in exploring the question of how Christian eschatology impacts upon social action.

29. Ben Witherington III, *Revelation,* New Cambridge Bible Commentary (Cambridge: Cambridge University Press, 2003), pp. 9, 79-80. Note Witherington's arguments (pp. 79-80) against the idea that John was consigned to mine labor on Patmos.

to Revelation a number of times, but only in book 5, chapters 28–30, does he touch upon any of the texts that constitute the economic critique of Rome, and even then attention is paid only to Revelation 13. In paragraphs 2-3 of chapter 28, Irenaeus quotes Rev 13:17-18 in full, the quotation leading without pause into his interpretation of the number 666:

> that is, six times a hundred, six times ten, and six units. [The author gives this] as a summing up of the whole of that apostasy which has taken place during six thousand years. For in as many days as this world was made, in so many thousand years shall it be concluded. And for this reason the Scripture says: "Thus the heaven and the earth were finished, and all their adornment. And God brought to a conclusion upon the sixth day the works that He had made; and God rested upon the seventh day from all His works." This is an account of the things formerly created, as also it is a prophecy of what is to come. For the day of the Lord is as a thousand years; and in six days created things were completed: it is evident, therefore, that they will come to an end at the sixth thousand year.[30]

Nothing is said here of the economic or mercantile dimension of the text; this is eclipsed by the significance of the numerical value of the mark. Similarly, as he expands his interpretation in chapter 29, his concern is with the way in which Antichrist will be a kind of representation of all evil as he is consigned to destruction:

> And there is therefore in this beast, when he comes, a recapitulation made of all sorts of iniquity and of every deceit, in order that all apostate power, flowing into and being shut up in him, may be sent into the furnace of fire. Fittingly, therefore, shall his name possess the number six hundred and sixty-six, since he sums up in his own person all the commixture of wickedness which took place previous to the deluge, due to the apostasy of the angels.[31]

In chapter 30, Irenaeus explores the various possibilities of what the name actually is (understanding the number as gematria). While, however, he is

---

30. Alexander Roberts and James Donaldson, eds., *The Ante-Nicene Fathers: Translations of the Writings of the Fathers down to* A.D. *325* (American reprint of the Edinburgh edition. Revised and chronologically arranged, with brief prefaces and occasional notes, by A. Cleveland Coxe; 1st edition, Edinburgh: T&T Clark; this edition, Grand Rapids: Hendricksen, 1995), vol. 1, p. 557. For consistency, all quotations of the fathers are taken from this edition of *The Ante-Nicene Fathers (ANF)*.

31. *ANF* 1, p. 558.

aware of the possible connection of the number with Rome (as gematria on *Lateinos*),[32] he again fails to make any comment on the mercantile dimension of the Antichrist's work.

Very similar conclusions can be drawn regarding the work of Hippolytus of Rome (170-236 CE), unsurprisingly perhaps, given his connection with Irenaeus and his shared preoccupation with speculation on the Antichrist. It is worth pointing out, however, that despite quoting Revelation 17–18 in full, he makes no further comment on the economic aspects of the Antichrist's rule (*Treatise on Christ and Antichrist* 36-42).[33] The extended quotation is followed simply by his statement of intent to explore the question of when the judgment of Babylon will take place:

> With respect, then, to the particular judgment in the torments that are to come upon it in the last times by the hand of the tyrants who shall arise then, the clearest statement has been given in these passages. But it becomes us further diligently to examine and set forth the period at which these things shall come to pass, and how the little horn shall spring up in their midst.[34]

Similarly, when Hippolytus discusses the mark of the beast in paragraphs 48-50, while arguing that the number refers to a Roman figure (seeing 666 as gematria on *Lateinos*) and suggesting that the Antichrist will establish his reign "after the manner of the law of Augustus, by whom the Empire of Rome was established,"[35] the extent of his comment on the economic aspect of the mark is to suggest that it refers to the requirement to sacrifice:

> For, being full of guile, and exalting himself against the servants of God, with the wish to afflict them and persecute them out of the world, because they give not glory to him, he will order incense-pans to be set up by all everywhere, that no man among the saints may be able to buy or sell without first sacrificing; for this is what is meant by the mark received upon the right hand.[36]

---

32. This must be compared with his earlier suggestion in *Adv. haer.* 25 that the Antichrist will be a Jew of the tribe of Dan.

33. See *ANF* 5, pp. 211-12.

34. *ANF* 5, p. 212.

35. *ANF* 5, p. 214.

36. *ANF* 5, p. 214. Hippolytus suggests this on the basis of parallels with the activity of Antiochus Epiphanes.

It is important to recognize that both Irenaeus and Hippolytus equate the numerical value of the mark of the beast with a Roman figure, but not necessarily with the Roman Empire of their day. This may be the crucial insight to allow us to understand why they overlook or marginalize the economic dimensions of the polemic: they associate this economy with a future rather than a contemporary period or order.

Roughly contemporary with Hippolytus is Clement of Alexandria (who died c. 220 CE). Clement cites Revelation a number of times, but it is in book 2 of his *Paedagogus* that he makes his only reference to a text of economic character. The reference is made in chapter 13 of book 2, where he discusses fondness for jewels. The *Paedagogus* is widely concerned with the question of possessions and wealth, and Clement generally promotes a modest (though not ascetic) lifestyle, urging readers to eschew worldly preoccupation with wealth and luxury. He frequently quotes the teaching of Jesus in support of this,[37] but in chapter 13 it is Rev 21:18-21 that Clement draws upon:

> We have heard, too, that the Jerusalem above is walled with sacred stones; and we allow that the twelve gates of the celestial city, by being made like precious stones, indicate the transcendent grace of the apostolic voice. For the colours are laid on in precious stones, and these colours are precious; while the other parts remain of earthy material. With these symbolically, as is meet, the city of the saints, which is spiritually built, is walled. By that brilliancy of stones, therefore, is meant the inimitable brilliancy of the spirit, the immortality and sanctity of being. But these women, who comprehend not the symbolism of Scripture, gape all they can for jewels, adducing the astounding apology, "Why may I not use what God hath exhibited?" and, "I have it by me, why may I not enjoy it?" and, "For whom were these things made, then, if not for us?" Such are the utterances of those who are totally ignorant of the will of God.[38]

Striking here is the sensitivity to the theological underpinnings of the Christian appraisal of wealth. It is the presence of the Spirit, uniting us to Christ, that constitutes true wealth, and this is the fundamental viewpoint from which worldly wealth is to be regarded. The text also seems to require (as does all of the *Paedagogus*) that many within the church of Clement's day are wealthy enough to have such preoccupations. There is, however, no criticism

---

37. See, for example, chapters 3 and 7 of this work.
38. *ANF* 2, p. 268.

of the economy of the day *as a system;* rather, economic responsibility is a matter of individual conduct. Revelation's critique of Rome, relevant as it is to Clement's purpose, is largely sidelined.[39]

Almost identical comments could be made concerning Cyprian, who draws upon Revelation 3 in paragraph 14 of his treatise *On Works and Alms:*

> You are mistaken, and are deceived, whosoever you are, that think yourself rich in this world. Listen to the voice of your Lord in the Apocalypse, rebuking men of your stamp with righteous reproaches: "Thou sayest," says He, "I am rich, and increased with goods, and have need of nothing; and knowest not that thou art wretched, and miserable, and poor, and blind, and naked. I counsel thee to buy of me gold tried in the fire, that thou mayest be rich; and white raiment, that thou mayest be clothed, and that the shame of thy nakedness may not appear in thee; and anoint thine eyes with eye-salve, that thou mayest see." You therefore, who are rich and wealthy, buy for yourself of Christ gold tried by fire; that you may be pure gold, with your filth burnt out as if by fire, if you are purged by almsgiving and righteous works. Buy for yourself white raiment, that you who had been naked according to Adam, and were before frightful and unseemly, may be clothed with the white garment of Christ. And you who are a wealthy and rich matron in Christ's Church anoint your eyes, not with the collyrium [eyewash] of the devil but with Christ's eye-salve, that you may be able to attain to see God, by deserving well of God, both by good works and character.[40]

Again, this is underpinned by an awareness of the connection between earthly wealth and the corrupted world order from which Christians are being delivered, with fellowship with God being seen as true wealth. But there is no clear sense of the systemic evil or corruption of Rome's economy: earthly wealth is simply considered to be valueless, rather than being seen as part of an evil system.

The next of the fathers to make substantial use of Revelation is Tertullian (c. 160-225 CE, although the precise dates of Tertullian's life are difficult to establish). As with Clement, he frequently cites or alludes to Revelation, though mostly in ways that are irrelevant to our purposes here. In one text, however, he cites Revelation in relation to the luxuries of his day,

---

39. This may be said also of subsequent paragraphs in this chapter, which continue to devalue earthly wealth and to exhort Christians to charity but neglect to develop any kind of critique of Rome as a system.

40. *ANF* 5, p. 480.

understood as status markers within the Roman system. This text is striking because it seems to appreciate that the force of Revelation's polemic is directed not at a future political order but at the present one. The reference in question is found in *De Capula,* a text in which Tertullian reflects on self-lauding and luxury. The text is inspired by an incident in which a single Christian soldier in a military victory celebration goes bareheaded, refusing to wear the laurel-leaf crown of Roman conquest, and is consequently arrested. Tertullian's defense of the soldier's actions becomes an extended reflection on whether floral crowns ought to be worn by believers, touching also upon the subject of submission within marriage and the wearing of veils. The inspirational starting point, however, also establishes the imperial context within which so much of this takes place. As he draws toward his conclusion, Tertullian says the following:

> For state reasons, the various orders of the citizens also are crowned with laurel crowns; but the magistrates besides with golden ones, as at Athens, and at Rome. Even to those are preferred the Etruscan. This appellation is given to the crowns which, distinguished by their gems and oak leaves of gold, they put on, with mantles having an embroidery of palm branches, to conduct the chariots containing the images of the gods to the circus. There are also provincial crowns of gold, needing now the larger heads of images instead of those of men. But your orders, and your magistracies, and your very place of meeting, the church, are Christ's. You belong to Him, for you have been enrolled in the books of life.[41]

This, of course, is a reference to the Roman system as set over against the kingdom of God. As Tertullian continues, however, the link to Revelation is made explicit and the crowns are given a certain significance: they represent the luxury and self-worship of Babylon.

> From so much as a dwelling in that Babylon of John's Revelation we are called away; much more then from its pomp. The rabble, too, are crowned, at one time because of some great rejoicing for the success of the emperors; at another, on account of some custom belonging to municipal festivals. For luxury strives to make her own every occasion of public gladness. But as for you, you are a foreigner in this world, a citizen of Jerusalem, the city above. Our citizenship, the apostle says, is in heaven.[42]

---

41. *ANF* 3, p. 101.
42. *ANF* 3, p. 101.

The interweaving of the crown question with participation in civic life construed in economic terms through the near-personification of "luxury" seems to reflect the same kind of integrated evaluation of economics and worldliness that we observed in Revelation. While not an extended study of Revelation, this does appear to be a rare instance of the full significance of John's polemic being appreciated by the church fathers. Of course, Tertullian's attitude to Rome is famously complex: here, and in *Adversus Iudaeos*,[43] he equates Rome with Babylon, though not with the figure of the Antichrist. As such, believers are not to participate in its systemic evils. Yet elsewhere, believing that the Antichrist will appear only once Rome has fallen, Tertullian supports Rome: "We have no desire, then, to be overtaken by these dire events; and in praying that their coming may be delayed, we are lending our aid to Rome's duration."[44] Despite this complexity, Tertullian is nevertheless the only one of the fathers studied here to make this thorough connection between the Roman imperial system, its economy, and the contrastive life of those whose citizenship is in heaven.

I will pass over Origen, who makes extensive use of Revelation in his work but makes no comment on the economic aspects of the text. This brings us to the commentary of Victorinus of Pettau (Ptuj in modern Slovenia), written in the late third century, possibly between 258 and 260 CE, during the reign of Gallienus. Any discussion of the reception of Revelation must, at some stage, discuss this work. Yet for our purposes it turns out to be largely irrelevant. Victorinus's discussion of Revelation 13 is almost exclusively concerned with identifying the person of the beast and pays no attention to the economic aspect of his reign. His discussion of Revelation 17 recognizes that Babylon is a cipher for Rome (the key being the reference to the seven hills),[45] but he is largely concerned with the significance of the *Nero Redivivus* myth in relation to this, arguing that "him therefore, when raised up, God will send as a worthy king, but worthy in such a way as the Jews merited."[46] This becomes a platform for his conviction that the risen Nero will be a Judaizing figure: "he will recall the saints, not to the worship of idols, but to undertake circumcision, and, if he is able, to seduce any; for he shall so conduct himself as to be called Christ by

43. *Adv. Iud.*, chapter 9.

44. *Apologia*, chapter 32.

45. The same is true of the seven heads of the dragon in Revelation 12, of which Victorinus writes: "His seven heads were the seven kings of the Romans, of whom also is Antichrist" (*ANF* 7, p. 355).

46. *ANF* 7, p. 358.

them."[47] The interpretation is of historic interest, but it is hardly mindful of any economic aspects to the Antichrist's regime.

This brings us to the end of our study of the fathers. Of the remaining ante-Nicene fathers, the reconstructed commentary of Tyconius is the only work worthy of consideration. Tyconius was a Donatist whose interpretation of Revelation was essentially mystical. Again, however, despite the huge influence of this commentary on figures such as Jerome and Augustine, there is no evidence that this work took notice of the economic aspects of John's polemic.

3. Conclusions

The economic aspect of Revelation's critique of Roman imperial power is a vital part of the work as a whole. It is, moreover, an integrated aspect of John's theology of the church in union with Christ. For this reason it is not to be judged primarily as an attack on Rome so much as a challenge to a potentially complicit church. The reception of this polemic among the ante-Nicene fathers is mixed. One definite tendency, displayed by Irenaeus, Hippolytus of Rome, and Victorinus, is for the economic aspects of the text to be eclipsed by the interest in the identity of the Antichrist. Another, seen in Clement of Alexandria, is for the economic aspects to be acknowledged, but only in terms of personal morality. Only Tertullian seems to recognize the systemic dimension of the economic problem and the implications that this has for believers in their engagement with Rome.

This essay may serve as a platform for the study of the reception of this theme in the Nicene and post-Nicene fathers (notably in Jerome, who draws on the work of Victorinus and Tyconius but corrects aspects of their millenarianism). The establishment of the church under Constantine created a situation radically different from the one reflected by John's Apocalypse. The trajectories of interpretation of Revelation among the early church fathers, however, suggest that full integration into the Roman economic system may not have been as troubling for the church as other aspects of Roman life, notably idolatry. With the single exception of Tertullian, the evidence suggests a general tendency by the fathers to overlook the systemic importance of economics.

---

47. *ANF 7*, p. 358.

13. By Almsgiving and Faith Sins Are Purged? The Theological Underpinnings of Early Christian Care for the Poor

Christopher M. Hays

"It is impossible, though we perform ten thousand other good deeds, to enter the portals of the kingdom without almsgiving."[1] Thus spake the "golden-tongued" John in his commentary on the Fourth Gospel at the very end of the fourth century. Some might ask how such a statement could be made in discussion of the same Gospel that affirms that Jesus is the Way, the Truth, and the Life and that nobody comes to the Father except through him. Yet Chrysostom comes by this seemingly hyperbolic statement honestly. He had imbibed the theological streams on alms or charitable giving that had flowed forth from the previous three centuries, diverse rivulets from Scripture and philosophy whose confluence produced a massive current, driving the Christian to good works and alms.

The present essay aims to describe some of the most prominent theological tributaries in the development of early Christian almsgiving and briefly to assess to what degree we might assent to and endorse these ethical exhortations of the earliest churches.[2] The themes considered will be (1) appeals to charitable giving that are not based on warrants of self-interest and (2) appeals that highlight the benefits accrued to the giver. This latter category examines how almsgiving (a) was construed as a mechanism of purg-

1. John Chrysostom, *Hom. Jo.* 23.
2. This essay will address only the teachings of the church from the late first to third centuries; for treatments of later Christian teaching on almsgiving, see Walter Shewring, *Rich and Poor in the Christian Tradition* (London: Burns, Oates and Washbourne, 1947), pp. 17-42; Boniface Ramsey, "Almsgiving in the Latin Church: The Late Fourth and Early Fifth Centuries," *Theological Studies* 43, no. 2 (1982): 226-59.

ing of the passions, (b) was highlighted as a mechanism for remitting sins, and (c) was encouraged under the threat of eschatological judgment.[3]

1. Almsgiving as an Expression of Love

It is of no small import in a study such as this to affirm that, from the beginning, love formed the backbone of early Christian charitable paranesis.[4] The earliest church documents make it abundantly clear that almsgiving was to be an expression of love.[5] To underscore the most obvious evidence that this was an intentional theological move, it warrants note that the love commands ("You shall love the Lord your God . . . you shall love your neighbor as yourself"; Matt 22:37-39//Mark 12:30//Luke 10:27, combining Deut 6:5 and Lev 19:18) appear repeatedly in patristic exhortations to charitable giving.[6]

3. It is interesting that patristic exhortations to generosity seldom appeal to the Holy Spirit.

4. See also Adolf von Harnack, *The Mission and Expansion of Christianity in the First Three Centuries*, trans. James Moffatt, vol. 1 (London: Williams and Norgate, 1908), pp. 147-52; Étienne Chastel, *Étude historique sur l'influence de la charité durant les premiers siècles chrétiens, et considérations sur son rôle dans les sociétés modernes* (Paris: Capelle, 1853), pp. 80-83. Love is also one of the major grounds on which usury is forbidden in the fathers; Robert P. Maloney, "The Teaching of the Fathers on Usury: An Historical Study on the Development of Christian Thinking," *Vigiliae Christianae* 27, no. 4 (1973): 242, 62; Ignaz Seipel, *Die wirtschaftsethischen Lehren der Kirchenväter*, Theologische Studien der Leo-Gesellschaft, vol. 18 (Vienna: Verlag von Mayer, 1907), p. 181.

5. *2 Clem.* 4.3; Tertullian, *Apol.* 39; Clement of Alexandria, *Strom.* 2.18; 4.18; *Quis div.* 38. Ps-Clement, *Epistle to James* 9, similarly claims that hospitality to the poor and hungry and strangers is "the only fit means" of fixing love in one's mind. Almsgiving also occurs in apposition with 1 Pet 4:8, "but [δέ] love covers a multitude of sins" in *2 Clem.* 16.4; Clement of Alexandria, *Quis div.* 38. Particularly important among these is the *Didache*'s opening salvo, which declares the existence of Two Ways, one of life and one of death (*Did.* 1.2), the former of which is primarily characterized by the double command to love God and one's neighbor. The *Didache* exposits the manner in which one loves God and neighbor by cobbling together citations from the Gospels endorsing almsgiving and generosity (*Did.* 1.4-6, citing Matt 5:40-41; Luke 6:29-30). On the textual history of the Two Ways teaching, see F. E. Vokes, "Life and Order in the Early Church: The Didache," in *Aufstieg und Niedergang der römischen Welt*, ed. Wolfgang Haase and Hildegard Temporini (Berlin: Walter de Gruyter, 1993), pp. 213-16.

6. I.e. Clement of Alexandria, *Strom.* 2.15; *Paed.* 2.13; Tertullian, *Marc.* 4.28 citing Deut 6:5 alongside Luke 11:42; Irenaeus, *Haer.* 4.12.2-5, couples the commands with warnings against the covetousness of the rich ruler and exhortations to generosity like that of Zacchaeus.

In one such passage, Clement of Alexandria exposits Mark 10:17-31, expanding the account so that Jesus accuses the rich young ruler of not fulfilling all the commandments from his youth. Why? Because the ruler's refusal to share his possessions with the poor proved that he did not love his neighbor.[7] In other texts, authors take a cue from the parable of the sheep and the goats (Matt 25:31-46),[8] construing almsgiving as an expression of love for the Creator, as mediated through his people, the poor.[9] Others rework Paul's rapturous exposition of love in 1 Corinthians 13. For example, Cyprian of Carthage demonstrated his exegetical prowess by translating 1 Cor 13:4 *"caritas magnanima est, caritas benigna est, caritas non zelat,"* claiming that love is "generous" *(magnanima)* rather than "patient" (μακροθυμεῖ), and translating χρηστεύεται ("to be kind") with *benigna*, which could be read as "bounteous."[10] In a variety of ways, then, theologians of the second and third centuries exposited the biblical text in order to highlight that almsgiving was fundamentally an expression of love. In contrast, certain heretics[11] were said to "have no concern for love, none for the widow, none for the orphan, none for the oppressed, none for the prisoner or the one released, none for the hungry or thirsty."[12]

What can we say of the logistics of this process? In the first place, many alms were cast into the church treasure chest[13] on a weekly or monthly basis to be distributed by the bishop.[14] For that reason, descriptions of clerical offices require that bishops be "lovers" of the widow and the stranger.[15] In addition, the Eucharistic celebration, called the *agapē* even in Latin-speaking circles, was intended especially to provide a regular meal for the

---

7. Clement of Alexandria, *Strom.* 3.6; in this passage Clement draws also on the Matthean version of the pericope, which appends the love command to the abbreviated Decalogue, which the ruler claimed to have observed (Matt 19:20).

8. Cyprian, *Eleem.* 23; Clement of Alexandria, *Quis div.* 30 (cf. 13); *Apos. Con.* 5.1; *Didascalia Apostolorum* 5.1.

9. Clement of Alexandria, *Strom.* 2.18; Cyprian, *Eleem.* 16; cf. Clement of Alexandria, *Quis div.* 26-27.

10. Cyprian, *Zel. liv.* 13; see also Clement of Alexandria, *Strom.* 4.18.

11. See *Gos. Thom.* 14, cf. 6; Ignatius, *Smyrn.* 6.2; cf. Robert M. Grant, *Early Christianity and Society: Seven Studies* (London: Collins, 1978), pp. 128-29.

12. Ign. *Smyrn.* 6.2.

13. Tertullian, *Apol.* 39.16; Justin, *1 Apol.* 67.

14. *Acts John* 12–13; *Const. ap.* 2.4; 3.1.13; 4.1.2; *Didascalia Apostolorum* 2.27; Pontius, *Vita Cypriani* 6; cf. Ign. *Pol.* 4.1. Alms were also distributed by the presbyters and deacons in the bishop's stead: Justin, *1 Apol.* 67; Herm. *Sim.* 9.26.2; Pol. *Phil.* 6.1; Herm. *Sim.* 9.27.

15. *Apos. Con.* 2.3.

poor.[16] Thus, in light of the exegeses that pervade early Christian teachings on alms, as well as the very descriptions of their clerical offices and shared meals, we need not doubt that love, not self-interest, was at least ideally construed as the primary motivation of almsgiving.

2. Almsgiving and *Koinonia*

Another theme disconnected from personal gain undergirds Christian exhortations to almsgiving: the motif of κοινωνία (i.e., corporate fellowship, community). The most prominent New Testament example of this evocation is Luke's description of the Jerusalem community as sharing all things in common (Acts 2:44; 4:32). Scholars have often opined that the language of holding all things in common must refer to an idealized socialist practice, implying thereby that Luke has romanticized his portrayal of the community. For example, William Countryman claimed that Luke advocates a love socialism in which there is no formal requirement for sacrifice of goods, but strong religious pressure resulting in a "voluntary communism."[17] That Luke makes no such claim, however, is manifest from his use of imperfect verbs to describe the sale of property for the benefit of the poor (ἐπίπρασκον, διεμέριζον, εἶχεν [Acts 2:45], ἐτίθουν, διεδίδετο, εἶχεν [Acts 4:35]), implying that people were regularly liquidating assets as necessary to care for the needy. Furthermore, the Jerusalem Christians continued to meet in the houses of wealthy benefactors (Acts 5:42; 12:12), and it would make little sense to laud Barnabas for selling a single field if others were completely divesting themselves in order to draw on a common treasury.[18] Luke depicts the Jerusalem community as maintaining private property, but

16. Tertullian, *Apol.* 39.16; cf. Minucius Felix, *Oct.* 31; Clement of Alexandria, *Paed.* 2.1, citing Luke 14. These communion meals were later supplemented by more extravagant "parties for the poor"; see Paulinus, *Ep.* 13; *Carm.* 18.44-51; Lucy Grig, "Throwing Parties for the Poor: Poverty and Splendour in the Late Antique Church," in *Poverty in the Roman World*, ed. Margaret Atkins and Robin Osborne (Cambridge: Cambridge University Press, 2006), pp. 146-48.

17. L. W. Countryman, *The Rich Christian in the Church of the Early Empire: Contradictions and Accommodations,* Texts and Studies in Religion (New York: Edwin Mellen, 1980), p. 80; see also Brian Capper, "The Palestinian Cultural Context of the Earliest Christian Community of Goods," in *The Book of Acts in Its Palestinian Setting,* ed. Richard Bauckham, The Book of Acts in Its First Century Setting (Grand Rapids: Eerdmans, 1995), pp. 323-56.

18. David Peter Seccombe, *Possessions and the Poor in Luke-Acts,* vol. 6, SNTU Series B (Linz: A. Fuchs, 1982), p. 207.

subordinating concerns for ownership and affluence to the basic needs of the community.

Moreover, the language of commonality need not imply the dissolution of private property and, indeed, seldom did so in the first-century world. Scholars routinely observe that the notion of κοινωνία as espoused by Plato advocated a society in which private property was abolished in favor of communal property.[19] However, Aristotle used the same language to advocate a practice of private property that assumed generous sharing.[20] The prevalent understanding of κοινωνία was that expressed in the friendship maxim "friends' possessions are shared" (κοινὰ τὰ φίλων), which was widely disseminated through the Greek- and Latin-speaking world, referring to the practice of freely sharing one's belongings with one's friend, while maintaining personal ownership over those possessions.[21]

The vast majority of the early church espoused a form of sharing just like that endorsed by Luke and implied by the κοινωνία topos.[22] The *Epistle of Barnabas* and the *Didache* exhorted their readers to share all things (κοινωνήσεις ἐν πᾶσιν) and to call nothing their own (οὐκ ἐρεῖς ἴδια εἶναι), evoking Acts 4:32,[23] on the grounds that "if you are sharers [κοινωνοί ἐστε] in incorruptible things, how much more so in corruptible things?"[24] The same rhetoric persisted in later fathers,[25] is echoed in the ascetic *Sentences of Sextus*,[26] and was known even to the Syrian satirist Lucian.[27] Yet in invoking κοινωνία language, the early fathers did not enjoin "socialist" behavior, but rather generous sharing of one's own private possessions, as is explicitly and

---

19. Plato, *Resp.* 416B-417B; 458C-D; 462B-464A; *Laws* 679B-C.

20. Aristotle, *Pol.* 2.2.1-9.

21. Aristotle, *Eth. Nic.* 8.9.1; 9.8.2; Euripides, *Orest.* 1046; *Andr.* 367f; *Phoen.* 243f; Plato, *Resp.* 424a; 449c; Philo, *Mos.* 1.156; Cic., *Off.* 1.16.51 [*amicorum esse communia omnia*]; Martial, 2.43 [2x]; Sen. *Ben.* 7.4.1.

22. Cf. Stanislas Giet, "La doctrine de l'appropriation des biens chez quelques-uns des pères," *Recherches de Science Religieuse* 35 (1948): 86; argued thoroughly by Justo González, *Faith and Wealth: A History of Early Christian Ideas on the Origin, Significance, and Use of Money* (Eugene, OR: Wipf & Stock, 2002).

23. *Const. ap.* 7.12: "you shall share in all . . . you shall not say anything is your own, for the common participation has been prepared for all men by God" (translation mine); so also in *Sent. Sextus* 227.

24. *Barn.* 19.8; *Did.* 4.8.

25. Clement of Alexandria, *Paed.* 2.13; Cyprian, *Eleem.* 25; cf. Tertullian, *Pat.* 7.

26. *Sent. Sext.* 228: "It is impious for those who share God in common, and indeed as Father, not to share possessions in common."

27. Lucian, *Peregr.* 13.

pervasively entreated throughout patristic literature.[28] The voluntary nature of giving is emphasized,[29] much in contrast to the compulsory fees and tithes for Hellenistic associations.[30] In most Christian circles, private property persisted, while Christians were exhorted to extend to the poor whatever they possessed in excess of providing for their own basic needs.[31] As such, we ought to resist the stock opinion, argued at length by Countryman, that "the language of communism is simply part of an argument for almsgiving";[32] in reality, the invocation of κοινωνία language called for nothing more than sharing.

3. Almsgiving and the Purgation of the Passions

This survey of the theological substructure of early Christian charitable paranesis turns now toward more self-interested motivations, exhortations that point out the personal benefit of almsgiving.

One major concern of the philosophical life, and, by extension, of Christians who incorporated philosophical preoccupations in their theology, was that of subduing the passions.[33] A wide range of patristic literature with various philosophical preferences exhibits the traditional conviction

28. Justin, *1 Apol.* 14.2; 15.10; *Sent. Sextus* 82b; Clement of Alexandria, *Paed.* 3.7; *Strom.* 4.18; *Quis div.* 31.

29. 2 Cor 9:7; Justin, *1 Apol.* 67.6; Tertullian, *Apol.* 39.5; cf. Grant, *Early Christianity,* pp. 134-36.

30. F. Sokolowski, "Fees and Taxes in the Greek Cults," *Harvard Theological Review* 47, no. 3 (1954): 153-64. On early Christian organizations as close analogues of Hellenistic *collegia,* see J. Paul Sampley, "Societas Christi: Roman Law and Paul's Conception of the Christian Community," in *God's Christ and His People: Studies in Honour of Nils Alstrup Dahl,* ed. Jacob Jervell and Wayne A. Meeks (Oslo: Universitetsforlaget, 1977), pp. 158-74; Robert L. Wilken, "Collegia, Philosophical Schools, and Theology," in *Early Church History: The Roman Empire as the Setting of Primitive Christianity,* ed. Stephen Benko and John J. O'Rourke (London: Oliphants, 1971), pp. 268-91.

31. Herm. *Vis.* 3.9.3-4; Clement of Alexandria, *Paed.* 2.13; 3.7; *Strom.* 3.7; *Sent. Sextus* 115; Hippolytus, *Frag. Comm. Matt.* 6.11; Ernst Troeltsch, *The Social Teaching of the Christian Churches,* trans. Olive Wyon, vol. 1, Sir Halley Stewart Publications (London: George Allen & Unwin, 1931), p. 116; González, *Faith and Wealth,* pp. 102-3.

32. Countryman, *Rich Christian,* p. 77; see also Troeltsch, *Social Teaching,* p. 115.

33. See, for example, Clement of Alexandria's Stoic definition of passions in *Strom.* 2.13; similarly *Sent. Sextus,* 74-75b, cf. 71a; note the similarity to Diogenes Laertius 7.110; cf. S. R. Lilla, *Clement of Alexandria: A Study in Christian Platonism and Gnosticism* (London: Oxford University Press, 1971), pp. 84-92.

that good works discipline the soul, helping expunge it of passions or inordinate desires.[34] So also, deprivation of possessions can contribute to subduing one's passionate impulses,[35] since possessions can blind a person or make one susceptible to apostasy.[36] Clement of Alexandria affirmed that riches interfere with virtues[37] and that deprivation of possessions can help extinguish one's passions,[38] though being quick to add that merely removing possessions, if the soul remains vicious, avails for nothing.[39] From this vantage point, then, it was only a short step for Clement to commend almsgiving to his congregation as a key means of purging themselves of passions.[40] Similarly, Cyprian and Tertullian exposit Jesus' dialogue with the Pharisees about purity, tithing, and almsgiving (Luke 11:41) by saying that giving alms cleanses a person internally.[41] As such, almsgiving served as one of the good works by which Christians could resist their internal passions. But the benefits of this spiritual wonder-drug could do more than inoculate a person against vicious impulse; indeed, it could even restore to health persons whose sinful infection had so spread as to bring them to peril of spiritual death. It is to this latter function of almsgiving we now turn.

4. Almsgiving and the Remission of Post-Baptismal Sins

4.1 Survey

Many patristic authors went beyond the assertion that almsgiving might be a mechanism of ameliorating sinful impulses to contend that almsgiving might also remit sins themselves. While mainline early church writers never explicitly contested the New Testament conviction that repentance and faith, exemplified in baptism, forgave sins,[42] they were less unanimous on whether

---

34. Irenaeus, *Haer.* 4.12.5; Herm. *Sim.* 10.1.3; *Sent. Sextus,* 70-72; Clement of Alexandria, *Paed.* 2.1; compare Gal 5:23-24.

35. *Ps-Clementine Homilies* 15.9; Clement of Alexandria, *Strom.* 4.6.

36. Origen, *Cels.* 7.18, 21; Cyprian, *Laps.* 11.

37. Clement of Alexandria, *Strom.* 3.5.

38. Clement of Alexandria, *Quis div.* 16, 18; cf. Irenaeus, *Haer.* 4.12.5.

39. Clement of Alexandria, *Quis div.* 11-12, 14-15; this notion grows in popularity in subsequent centuries; see Augustine, *Enarrat. Ps.* 51.4, 83; Grig, "Throwing Parties," pp. 153-54.

40. Clement of Alexandria, *Strom.* 4.6, 18.

41. Cyprian, *Eleem.* 2; Tertullian, *Marc.* 4.27.

42. Acts 2:38; 22:16; Rom 6:4; Col 2:12; 1 Pet 3:21.

or not baptism remitted all sins[43] or only those committed *prior to* baptism. This concern emerged in the earliest days of the sub-apostolic church. It is the central theme of the *Shepherd of Hermas*.[44] Similarly, *2 Clem.* 6.9 inquires, "what assurance do we have of entering the kingdom of God if we fail to keep our baptism pure and undefiled?" The author offers no advocate except "holy and righteous works."

Preeminent among these righteous works was almsgiving.[45] So continues *2 Clement:*

> Charitable giving, therefore, is good, as is repentance from sin. Fasting is better than prayer, while charitable giving is better than both. . . . Blessed is everyone who is found full of these, for charitable giving relieves the burden of sin.[46]

This runs conceptually parallel to (or perhaps partially depends upon) the long-standing Jewish notion of a treasury of merits,[47] which itself issued in a robust rabbinic conviction that God forgave sins because of almsgiving.[48]

Nonetheless, advocates of redemptive almsgiving take pains not to displace the atonement of Christ. Cyprian cautiously distinguishes between two periods of sin, saying, "Alms do deliver from death, and not, assuredly, from that death which once the blood of Christ extinguished, and from which the saving grace of baptism and of our Redeemer has delivered us, but from that which subsequently creeps in through sins [*sed ab ea quae per delicta postmodum serpit*]" (Cyprian, *Laps.* 35).[49]

---

43. So probably *Diogn.* 9.3-5.

44. See Herm. *Vis.* 1.2.1; cf. H. B. Swete, "Penitential Discipline in the First Three Centuries," in *Christian Life: Ethics, Morality, and Discipline in the Early Church*, ed. Everett Ferguson, Studies in Early Christianity (New York: Garland, 1993), p. 251.

45. Herm. *Sim.* 10.2.4; *De Doctrina* 4.4-8 (on this document, see Roman Garrison, *Redemptive Almsgiving in Early Christianity*, JSNTS vol. 77 [Sheffield: JSOT, 1993], pp. 74-75); Origen, *Hom. in Lev.* 2.4; *Didascalia Apostolorum* 2.26; see also Garrison, *Redemptive Almsgiving*, pp. 86-107.

46. *2 Clem.* 16.4; contrast *b. Ber.* 32b.

47. *2 Bar.* 14.12; Tob 4:5-11; Sir 29:9-13; *Lev. Rab.* 34.7; Gary Anderson, "Redeem Your Sins by the Giving of Alms: Sin, Debt, and the 'Treasury of Merit' in Jewish and Early Christian Tradition," *Letter and Spirit* 3 (2007): 49-52. Interestingly, though the idea of a treasury of merits became prominent later in church history, it is seldom appealed to in second- and third-century Christian literature.

48. *t. Pe'ah* 4:21; *b. Git.* 7a; *B. Bat.* 9a-10a; *Shab.* 156b; *Suk.* 49b; *Midr. Ps.* on 50.8; see also Abraham Cronbach, "The Me'il Zedakah," *Hebrew Union College Annual* 11 (1936): 528; Garrison, *Redemptive Almsgiving*, pp. 56-59.

49. It is clear that sins committed after one's baptism are in view in *2 Clement* 16, since

This discussion raises the question of the place of almsgiving relative to the development of the sacrament of penance, though it is not my task at present to summarize all the contours of this debate.[50] Suffice it to say that, while second-century literature does not appear to have developed a sophisticated account of second repentance, by the third century most "orthodox" theologians came to a consensus in affirming that, for grave post-baptismal sins, one event of penance and reconciliation remained available to Christians.[51] The Council of Nicea loosened this limitation.[52] Origen noted that sins that were not "unto death" could be repaired by confession (Origen, *Hom. in Lev.* 15.2)[53] and elsewhere gives a list of the seven manners in which sins might be forgiven. On this list, Origen places almsgivings in third place, after baptism and martyrdom; the last means mentioned is penitence.[54] As such, it seems that the list was intended to describe all the means available for the remission of sins: baptism for pre-conversion sins, penitence for grave sins, and then four other means for lesser sins. Augustine later claimed that almsgiving suffices to remit only venial sins, but not grave ones.[55]

4.2 Scriptural Foundations

All evidence indicates that the early fathers understood these doctrines to be derived from Scripture.[56] The most frequent expository port of call was to

---

it addresses a Christian congregation in the first plural throughout, and 17.2 specifies a concern for the restoration of the weak. So also Cyprian, *Ep.* 51.22; *Eleem.* 1.

50. For an extended discussion of penance for post-baptismal sins, see Bernard Poschmann, *Paenitentia Secunda: Die kirchliche Busse im ältesten Christentum bis Cyprian und Origen: Eine dogmengeschichtliche Untersuchung,* vol. 1, Theophania (Bonn: P. Hanstein, 1940). See also Swete, "Penitential Discipline," pp. 249-65; G. H. Joyce, "Private Penance in the Early Church," *Journal of Theological Studies* 42 (1941): 18-42.

51. Cyprian, *Laps.* 16; *Ep.* 61.3; Clement of Alexandria, *Strom.* 2.13; Origen, *Hom. in Lev.* 15.2; even in Tertullian's Catholic period he agreed (Tertullian, *Paen.* 6-7), though his views on penance grew more rigorous as he turned toward Montanism (see *de Pudicitia*). Later, Novatian, the opponent of Cyprian, followed in Tertullian's footsteps, denying the capacity of the bishops to remit mortal sins (*Ep.* 30, 36). See further Swete, "Penitential Discipline," pp. 254-64.

52. *First Council of Nicaea,* Canon 13 (ND 1602).

53. On the existence of private penance in the second and third centuries, see Joyce, "Private Penance," pp. 18-42.

54. Origen, *Hom. in Lev.* 2.4; cf. Swete, "Penitential Discipline," pp. 332-33.

55. Augustine, *Serm.* 9.19.

56. See also Sir 3:30; 7:10; Tob 4:7; 12:8-9. I will not trace the development of this doc-

the Septuagint reading of Prov 15:27,[57] which slightly modifies the Hebrew text of Prov 16:6.[58] The reading of the MT, "by loyalty and faithfulness iniquity is atoned for" (בְּחֶסֶד וֶאֱמֶת יְכֻפַּר עָוֹן), is shifted in the Septuagint to say "by almsgiving and faith sins are purged" (ἐλεημοσύναις καὶ πίστεσιν ἀποκαθαίρονται ἁμαρτίαι). We should also note that the Septuagint has rendered "faithfulness" (אֱמֶת) with the dative plural form of πίστις, thus indicating that "deeds [plural] of faithfulness" cleanse an individual from sins, not simply faith in abstraction.[59]

Similarly, the *Apostolic Constitutions* (3.1.4) cite Dan 4:27, in which Daniel counsels Nebuchadnezzar to "atone for your sins with righteousness [בְּצִדְקָה], and your iniquities with mercy to the oppressed, so that your prosperity may be prolonged."[60] The Septuagint, though, translates the term צְדָקָה ("righteousness") with ἐλεημοσύναις ("almsgiving"). This translation might not be so arbitrary as it may seem at first. Gary Anderson has argued that "almsgiving" was in fact the intended significance of בְּצִדְקָה from the time of the composition of the document.[61] The rabbis came to pervasively understand "righteousness" as a concrete deed, almsgiving,[62] which was to function in tandem with הֶסָדִים גְּמִילוּת/חֶסֶד ("doing the deeds of kindness"), actions that required one's time or energy.[63] So it seems that the fathers were following a well-established Septuagint translation, analogous to contemporaneous Jewish readings, in understanding Dan 4:27 to refer to almsgiving as the means by which Nebuchadnezzar was to atone for his sins. Indeed, צְדָקָה was the term used for alms in the Hebrew *Vorlage* of Sir 3:30

---

trine in the Old Testament or Judaism, except insofar as the fathers explicitly appeal to certain passages or concepts; on the development of this idea, see Garrison, *Redemptive Almsgiving,* pp. 46-59; Anderson, "Redeem Your Sins," pp. 40-54.

57. Ps-Ign. *Hero* 5; Clement of Alexandria, *Strom.* 2.15; Cyprian, *Laps.* 35; *Eleem.* 2; *Apos. Con.* 2.35; 3.1.4; 7.12.

58. Interestingly, the Septuagint of Prov 16:6 adds that righteous deeds are more acceptable to God than sacrifices, similar to Hos 6:6.

59. I am grateful to Bruce Longenecker for drawing this to my attention.

60. So also Cyprian, *Eleem.* 5, and later, Aquinas, *ST* 2-2 q. 32 a. 5.

61. Anderson, "Redeem Your Sins," pp. 40-43; cf. John J. Collins, *Daniel: A Commentary on the Book of Daniel,* Hermeneia (Minneapolis: Fortress Press, 1993), p. 230.

62. Though in time it acquired other related referents that in earlier stages would have been more properly construed as חֶסֶד; see Cronbach, "The Me'il Zedakah," pp. 505-6.

63. See *t. Pe'ah* 4:19; *y. Pe'ah* 1:1; 4:19; *b. Sukkah* 49a-b; Frederick B. Bird, "A Comparative Study of the Work of Charity in Christianity and Judaism," *Journal of Religious Ethics* 10, no. 1 (1982): 152; *Enc. Jud.* V: 340; George Foot Moore, *Judaism in the First Centuries of the Christian Era: The Age of the Tannaim,* vol. 2 (Cambridge, MA: Harvard University Press, 1927), p. 171.

("As water extinguishes a blazing fire, so almsgiving atones for sin"),[64] a passage cited by Cyprian (*Eleem.* 2) in support of redemptive almsgiving.[65] Another crucial New Testament text appealed to in this vein was 1 Pet 4:8-9, which noted that "love covers a multitude of sins" before proceeding to enjoin its audience to practice hospitality.[66]

In addition, the notion that by giving alms one lent to God bolstered the belief in the redemptive properties of almsgiving.[67] The theme of lending to God derives particularly from Prov 19:17: "Whoever is kind to the poor lends to the Lord, and will be repaid in full" (δανίζει θεῷ ὁ ἐλεῶν πτωχόν, κατὰ δὲ τὸ δόμα αὐτοῦ ἀνταποδώσει αὐτῷ; cf. Luke 6:38). Clement and Cyprian repeatedly evoked this passage to goad their readers toward almsgiving,[68] not in the avaricious expectation that they would regain or augment their wealth as a consequence of almsgiving, but rather that they would be repaid in celestial currency, the forgiveness of sins.[69] Thus, when Cyprian exhorts his congregation, "let us lend of our wealth and our means to the Lord, who shall judge concerning us" (*Laps.* 35), the matter at hand is the remission of sins in fear of the final judgment.[70] This type of proposal persisted well into the fourth and fifth centuries.[71]

The belief that almsgiving delivered from death also buttressed confidence in the redemptive potential of almsgiving.[72] This conviction arose in

---

64. Also in Sir 7:10; 12:3; 16:14; 40:24, and probably in 29:8, 12; 35:4, where no Hebrew texts are extant; Patrick W. Skehan and Alexander A. Di Lella, *The Wisdom of Ben Sira: A New Translation with Notes, Introduction, and Commentary,* The Anchor Bible (New York: Doubleday, 1987), p. 165.

65. Cyprian (*Eleem.* 18) also appeals to Job 1:5 (Septuagint), arguing that almsgiving can also remit the sins of one's children; John Chrysostom, *Hom. 1 Cor.* 41.5 (cf. CCC §1032), applies this passage to almsgiving for the dead in purgatory.

66. 2 *Clem.* 16.4; Clement of Alexandria, *Quis div.* 38; cf. Clement of Alexandria, *Strom.* 4.18.

67. On the Old Testament background to "lending to the Lord," see Anderson, "Redeem Your Sins," pp. 45-48.

68. Cyprian, *Eleem.* 15-16, 26; *Const. Ap.* 3.1.4; 7.1.12; Clement of Alexandria, *Paed.* 2.13; 3.4; *Strom.* 3.6.

69. This idea is prevalent in the rabbis as well; Cronbach, "The Me'il Zedakah," pp. 525-26.

70. See also Cyprian, *Quis div.* 16, 26; *Dom. or.* 33; *Apos. Con.* 7.1.12.

71. Augustine, *Serm.* 38.8; 42.2; 123.5; 357.5; Jerome, *Hom. Eph.* 5.1; *Ep.* 120.1; Ambrose, *Tob.* 16.55; see further Ramsey, "Latin Church," p. 229 nn. 15-21; Seipel, *Wirtschaftsethischen Lehren,* pp. 222-27.

72. Cyprian, *Eleem.* 6; see the rabbinic material as well; Cronbach, "The Me'il Zedakah," pp. 532-37.

Proverbs (10:2; 11:4)[73] and then was stated more forcefully in Tobit (4:10; 12:9), to which patristic authors often referred in their expositions on almsgiving.[74] But the paranetic potential of affirming that almsgiving delivered one from physical death paled in comparison to the possibilities contained in the contention that almsgiving protected from spiritual death. Thus, the church fathers most frequently dangled eternal salvation through alms in front of their recalcitrant or ungenerous audiences, like the proverbial carrot in front of a mule.[75] Similar to the negative appeal that almsgiving could remove sins, the positive rhetoric of accruing "reward" through charity occurs frequently in patristic literature,[76] owing to the Gospel teachings about storing up treasure in heaven.[77] But it merits emphasizing that the rewards seem not to consist in an ever-increasing accumulation of heavenly capital (for example, "crowns");[78] rather, the reward seems to be heaven itself and the blessings entailed thereby.[79]

It was often asserted in the service of this doctrine that God heard better the prayers of those who give alms,[80] a not unfounded claim considering the examples of Tobit (12:8)[81] and Cornelius (Acts 10:31).[82] By extension, the re-

---

73. Anderson, "Redeem Your Sins," pp. 48-49.

74. Pol. *Phil.* 10.2; Cyprian, *Ep.* 51.22; *Laps.* 35; *Dom. or.* 32-33; *Eleem.* 5, 20. On the acceptance of Tobit by many early Christians, see Origen, *Ep. Afr.* 13.

75. Cyprian, *Eleem.* 5; Tertullian, *Pat.* 7.13; cf. Herm. *Vis.* 3.9.5-6; *Sim.* 10.4.4. Also see Peter of Alexandria's homily *On Riches,* which dates to the very beginning of the fourth century; Birger A. Pearson, "A Coptic Homily *On Riches* Attributed to St. Peter of Alexandria," *Studia Patristica* 26 (1993): 300.

76. 2 *Clem.* 11.6-7; *Barn.* 19.11; Clement of Alexandria, *Fragments from the Hypotyposes* 3.3; Pope Pontianus, *Ep.* 1; Cyprian, *Eleem.* 24, 26; Clement of Alexandria, *Strom.* 4.6; *Quis div.* 32; 1 *Clem.* 34.2-3; Lactantius, *Inst.* 6.11-12; cf. *Sent. Sextus* 52.

77. Matt 6:19-21; Luke 12:32-34; Clement of Alexandria, *Quis div.* 19; Lactantius, *Ep.* 65; *Apos. Con.* 2.36.

78. Contemporary Catholic teaching has gone a slightly different direction, claiming that good deeds done in this life will permit a more profound enjoyment of God in heaven: "Our charity on earth will be the measure of our sharing in God's glory in heaven"; *Letter of the S. Congregation for the Doctrine of the Faith on Certain Questions Concerning Eschatology,* 7 (ND 2317); see also *General Council of Florence, Decree for the Greeks* (ND 2309).

79. See, for example, *1 Clem.* 34.2–35.2; *2 Clem.* 11.6-7; *Barn.* 19.11; Cyprian, *Eleem.* 26; Clement of Alexandria, *Quis div.* 32; *Strom.* 3.6; though see Pope Pontianus, *Ep.* 1.

80. Cyprian, *Dom. or.* 32-33; *Eleem.* 5-6; Peter of Alexandria, *Canonical Epistle* 11; *Gos. Bir. Mary* 4.

81. Cyprian, *Dom. or.* 32; *Eleem.* 5. Conversely, consider Sextus: "God does not heed the prayer of a man who does not listen to the needy" (*Sent. Sextus* 217, cf. 378).

82. Cyprian, *Dom. or.* 32.

cipients of alms were to pray for their benefactors,[83] thus constituting an exception (*Const. Ap.* 3.1.4; 3.1.13-14) to the general rule that one should give alms secretly.[84]

Another natural entrée into this teaching was the conventional association of alms with sacrifices, as in the letter to the Hebrews: "Do not neglect to do good and share what you have, for such sacrifices are pleasing to God" (Heb 13:16; so also Sir 35:1-2). Thus, widows came to be called "God's altar,"[85] because caring for them is Christian worship (Jas 1:27) and because widows were among the primary and perpetual recipients of alms.[86] The image of alms as sacrifices was utilized all the more vigorously after the fall of the Temple,[87] and one cannot help but recognize that one function of certain sacrifices — indeed, the primary function of sacrifice — is to gain forgiveness of sins. Such a development was also paralleled in Judaism, according to traditions recounted in rabbinic literature. Simeon the Righteous (ca. 200 BCE)[88] claimed that the world was sustained by Torah, Temple worship, and charity (*m. 'Abot* 1:2). After the Temple fell, Rabbi Joshua cried out, "Woe to us, for this house that lies in ruins, the place where atonement was made." But Rabbi Johanan ben Zakkai responded to him, "My son, do not be grieved; we have another means of atonement which is as effective, and that is, the practice of loving-kindness, as it is stated, *For I desire loving-kindness and not sacrifice.*"[89] The passage Rabbi Johanan invokes from Hosea (6:6) is

83. Herm. *Sim.* 2.5-6; 5.2.10; see also Cyprian, *Eleem.* 5, citing Prov 21:13 and Sir 29:12, and Cyprian, *Eleem.* 6 with the widows praying for Tabitha; Clement of Alexandria, *Quis div.* 34-35; and later Aquinas, *ST* 2-2 q. 32 a. 9 ad. 2; cf. Rebecca H. Weaver, "Wealth and Poverty in the Early Church," *Interpretation* 41, no. 4 (1987): 371. This concept may also be incipient in the story of St. John and the robber in *Quis Div.* 42; Countryman, *Rich Christian*, pp. 56-57. Conversely, if one were not to give, the groans of the poor might reach the ears of God against them (Herm. *Vis.* 3.9.6).

84. Matt 6:4-6; Clement of Alexandria, *Strom.* 4.22; Origen, *Comm. Matt.* 11.15; *Sent. Sextus* 342.

85. Pol. *Phil.* 4.3; Tertullian, *Ux.* 1.7; Ps-Ign. *Tars.* 9; *Apos. Con.* 2.26.

86. Ign. *Pol.* 4.1; *Smyrn.* 6.2; Herm. *Mand.* 8.10; Acts Thom. 19; *Const. Ap.* 3.1.13; 4.1.1; 4.2.8; *Divine Liturgy of the Holy Apostle and Evangelist Mark* 14; Lactantius, *Inst.* 6.12; Aristides, *Apol.* 15.6; Eusebius, *Mart. Pal.* 11.22; Ps-Clement, *First Epistle Concerning Virginity* 12.

87. Justin, *Apol.* 1.13; Irenaeus, *Adv. Haer.* 4.17.1-4.18.2; Clement of Alexandria, *Strom.* 7.6; 7.7; Cyprian, *Eleem.* 15; Lactantius, *Inst.* 6.12; *Epit.* 6.21; *Apos. Con.* 2.35.

88. Hermann L. Strack and G. Stemberger, *Introduction to the Talmud and Midrash,* trans. Markus Bockmuehl (Edinburgh: T&T Clark, 1991), p. 70.

89. *Abot R. Nat.* 4:5 [20a]; quoted from A. Cohen, ed., *The Minor Tractates of the Talmud: Massektoth Ketannoth* (London: Soncino, 1965).

adopted by Tertullian and Clement in the same vein.[90] So, almsgiving became sacrifice *redivivus.*

Previous scholarship has contrasted representation of almsgiving as a sacrifice (thank offering?) with that of almsgiving as a meritorious deed,[91] claiming that the "biblical" idea of good deeds as a response to God's grace was progressively "choked" out as the church slid toward Catholicism.[92] But the reality is that the language of sacrifice persisted right alongside the notion that almsgiving acquired merit for the giver and, indeed, was not itself (at least for long) rhetoric expressive of purely "disinterested" giving.

4.3 Assessment

It is arguable that the biblical passages on which the fathers grounded the doctrine of redemptive almsgiving remain insufficient to support the weight of that doctrine. The appeal to Dan 4:27 ("atone for your sins with alms, and your iniquities with mercy to the oppressed") could be seen as misguided since the passage refers to attaining freedom from the temporal consequences for sins and garnering earthly prosperity,[93] as is clear from the punishment that Nebuchadnezzar received. So also, at that point the notion of almsgiving as saving from physical death had not yet been transmuted into an expectation of escaping spiritual death. Similarly, Prov 16:6 (or 15:27 in the Septuagint), "by almsgiving and faith sins are purged," contextually promises salvation only from the temporal consequences for sin, as is clear from the parallel phrase "by fear of the Lord one avoids evil."[94] Furthermore, the MT of Prov 16:6 does not even mention almsgiving in this connection, but only "loyalty" (NRSV rendering of בְּחֶסֶד).[95] So also Tob 4:10 (setting

---

90. Tertullian, *Marc.* 4.27; Clement of Alexandria, *Strom.* 4.6.

91. Origen, *Comm. in Lev.* 2.4; and Cyprian, *Eleem.* 5.

92. G. Uhlhorn, *Christian Charity and the Ancient Church,* trans. Sophia Taylor (Edinburgh: T&T Clark, 1883), p. 153; cf. C. S. Phillips, *The New Commandment: An Inquiry into the Social Precept and Practice of the Ancient Church* (New York: Macmillan, 1930), pp. 88-89.

93. John E. Goldingay, *Daniel,* Word Biblical Commentary (Dallas: Word Books, 1989), p. 95; Collins, *Daniel,* p. 230.

94. William McKane, *Proverbs,* Old Testament Library (London: SCM, 1970), p. 498.

95. Though the MT of Prov 16:6 is certainly derived from much later manuscript evidence than that of the LXX, it remains likely that the MT preserves earlier tradition, in which the more ambiguous חֶסֶד had not yet been disambiguated as referring to almsgiving. While temporal priority does not necessarily make the MT preferable, there is precedent to give more theological weight to this reading. While Septuagintal text forms certainly pre-

aside the issue of its canonical status) merely promises temporal protection and recompense for almsgiving. Sirach 3:30 in the Septuagint may well be a source of the doctrine that almsgiving remits eternal consequences of sins, since atonement through almsgiving is likened to water extinguishing a fire. However, Sirach, at least in the early Hebrew traditions, is generally recognized as lacking an expectation of an afterlife,[96] making it unlikely that 3:30 should be construed as originally referring to any type of postmortem salvation. Finally, 1 Pet 4:8 ("love covers a multitude of sins") quotes Prov 10:12, which contrasts love that covers or overlooks offenses[97] with hatred that stirs up strife, thus referring to social relations.[98] In a context addressing the expressions of unity in the church (1 Pet 4:9-10), 1 Peter refers to forgiving or overlooking each other's offenses[99] and thus ameliorating the interpersonal consequences of sins.[100] It concerns the relations within the Christian community, not salvation from eternal punishment, and it does not even explic-

---

dominated in church use in the second and third centuries, as early as Jerome the Christian tradition began to favor the Hebrew canonical forms. Catholic scholars generally prefer the MT to the LXX text form for non-apocryphal books, and the Protestant tradition has historically also favored the MT. Septuagint text forms do often offer more original readings than the MT and theologically insightful expansions; however, in this case the LXX text cited seems to be functioning as an interpretive translation. It is entirely proper to think of almsgiving as an expression of חֶסֶד, and in this respect the translation is appropriate, if a bit narrow; but even in the LXX form quoted by the fathers, the text need not refer to anything more than an avoidance of the temporal consequences of sin. When the early fathers applied this text to the issue of post-baptismal sin, they made a theological extrapolation, which needs to be evaluated in relation to the theological issues of justification and perseverance, since the text alone does not support the weight of their conclusions.

96. So see Sir 7:17. The Greek says, "the punishment of the ungodly is fire and worms" but the Hebrew says, "what awaits man is worms" (Skehan and Di Lella, *Ben Sira*, pp. 201-21; Josef Schreiner, *Jesus Sirach 1-24*, Die neue echter Bibel [Würzburg: Echter, 2002], p. 50). The addition of "fire" in the Greek text probably reveals the influence of Isa 66:24, cf. Jdt 16:17.

97. Roland E. Murphy, *Proverbs*, Word Biblical Commentary (Nashville: Thomas Nelson, 1998), p. 74.

98. McKane, *Proverbs*, pp. 418-19.

99. Following the precedent of the Septuagint of Ps 31:1 "Happy are those whose transgression is forgiven, whose sin is covered [ἐπεκαλύφθησαν]," the verb καλύπτει refers to forgiving sins. John H. Elliott, *1 Peter: A New Translation with Introduction and Commentary*, Anchor Bible (New York: Doubleday, 2000), p. 751. Also, Psalm 31 sees this forgiveness as issuing in help in time of trouble (Ps 31:5-7), not eternal salvation.

100. J. Ramsey Michaels, *1 Peter*, Word Biblical Commentary (Waco, TX: Word Books, 1988), p. 247; Elliott, *1 Peter*, p. 751; Donald P. Senior, *1 Peter*, Sacra Pagina (Collegeville, MN: Liturgical, 2003), p. 120; Paul Achtemeier, *1 Peter: A Commentary on First Peter*, Hermeneia (Minneapolis: Fortress, 1996), p. 296.

itly mention almsgiving. None of these texts can substantiate a claim that almsgiving can remit the eternal consequences of sins.

With that said, however, when the fathers appealed to almsgiving as the basis of heavenly rewards, they had good grounds to do so in the Gospels, which promised treasures in heaven for those who gave alms.[101] Additionally, in the narrative of Acts, though Tabitha was only resurrected from the dead for her piety toward widows (Acts 9:36-42), Cornelius's generosity garnered him the opportunity to become the first Gentile Christian, complete with personal evangelism by the apostle Peter (Acts 10:1-4, 31). So also 1 Tim 6:18-19[102] counsels the rich to "do good, to be rich in good deeds, liberal and generous, thus laying up for themselves a good foundation for the future, so that [ἵνα] they may take hold of the life which is life indeed." This passage clearly indicates that munificence will somehow be directly beneficial for attaining eternal life.[103]

By far the most conceptually multifaceted (and potentially objectionable) theological conception used to motivate early Christian charity was the notion that almsgiving served even to remit the eternal consequences of post-baptismal sin.

5. Almsgiving and the Expectation of Judgment

The anxiety over post-baptismal sins raises the specter of eschatological judgment into view, and we might briefly inquire as to what role this played

101. See esp. Luke 6:38; Matt 6:19-21//Luke 12:32-34; compare Rom 2:6-7. See also Luke 11:41; cf. Tertullian, *Marc.* 4.36.4-5; J. Ramsey Michaels, "Almsgiving and the Kingdom Within: Tertullian on Luke 17:21," *Catholic Biblical Quarterly* 60, no. 1 (1998): 475-83.

102. Which Luke Timothy Johnson rightly relates to the Gospel discussions of treasures in heaven; Luke Timothy Johnson, *The First and Second Letters to Timothy: A New Translation with Introduction and Commentary,* Anchor Bible (New York: Doubleday, 2001), p. 311.

103. Garrison, *Redemptive Almsgiving,* p. 71. Though commentators often simplistically aver that the language is not about "earning heaven" but about "demonstrating" godliness, they do not account for the fact that the purpose clause (ἵνα ἐπιλάβωνται τῆς ὄντως ζωῆς) indicates a more robust relationship between the generosity and the attainment of eternal life; see, for example, William D. Mounce, *Pastoral Epistles,* Word Biblical Commentary (Nashville: Thomas Nelson, 2000), pp. 367-68; Philip H. Towner, *The Letters to Timothy and Titus,* New International Commentary on the New Testament (Grand Rapids: Eerdmans, 2006), pp. 427-28. To imply that the only alternative to "demonstrating" is "earning" evinces a lack of theological reflection on the manner in which works could be involved in attaining eternal life.

in second- and third-century charitable paranesis. Luke regularly appealed to the eschatological judgment in his ethical endorsements,[104] as do numerous other New Testament authors.[105] The strategy was not lost on certain patristic writers. Hermas describes the kingdom of God as a tower whose constituent blocks represented the saints. In this connection, the elderly woman of his visions, who fills the role of the apocalyptic messenger, exhorts the wealthy, saying, "you who have more than enough, seek out those who are hungry, until the tower is finished. For after the tower is finished, you may want to do good, but you will not have the chance."[106]

In 2 Clement, the sins of the rich owe in some degree to their conviction that the parousia is distant, so the homilist consistently affirms, indeed, at times threatens, its nearness.[107] He ties this menacing judgment directly to an exhortation to almsgiving:

> Seeing there, brethren, inasmuch as we have received no small opportunity to repent, let us, while we still have time, turn again to God. . . . You know that "the day" of judgment is already "coming as a blazing furnace," and "some of the heavens will dissolve," and the whole earth will be like lead melting in a fire, and the works of men, the secret and the public will appear. *Therefore almsgiving is good as repentance from sin.*[108]

So also, Cyprian's exhortations to almsgiving often appealed to the final judgment.[109] This comes as little surprise, since he was convinced that the end of the world was upon him, owing to the plagues, kidnappings, barbarian invasions, divisions in the church, and persecutions that characterized the period of his episcopacy.[110] Nonetheless, as the years after Christ's death piled up without a hint of the parousia, the frequency with which Christians appealed to the last judgment in support of almsgiving diminished as well.

---

104. Luke 12:35-48; 17:20-37; 19:11-27; cf. 16:19-31.

105. I.e., Rom 13:11-13; 1 Thess 5:2-8; Jas 5:1-6; 2 Pet 3:1-15.

106. Herm. *Vis.* 3.9.5; see also the conclusion of the document in *Sim.* 10.4.4.

107. See especially 16.1-4; and also 8.1-3; 9.7-8; 12.1; 17.1-4; Garrison, *Redemptive Almsgiving*, p. 127.

108. 2 *Clem.* 16.1-4, italics my translation. Note that Clement here combines attention to the themes of eschatology and remission of sins.

109. Cyprian, *Laps.* 35; *Quis div.* 15, 21-23, 26; Weaver, "Wealth and Poverty," p. 374.

110. Géza Alföldy, "Der heilige Cyprian und die Krise des römischen Reiches," *Historia* 22 (1973): 479-501.

6. Other Stimuli to Almsgiving: An Encomium

And what more should I say than this? For time would fail me to recount the appeals to John the Baptist, Elijah, and Jeremiah, who in simplicity wore rags and loincloths.[111] Or what of those who ministered both to prisoners[112] and to people forced into the mines,[113] those who ransomed captives,[114] buried the dead,[115] showed hospitality,[116] gave relief in plagues,[117] and extended aid to other churches?[118] What of those who knew that true riches reside in virtue or wisdom,[119] and that stinginess results in punishment?[120] Widowed women received support and responded in ecclesial service.[121] Others refused wealth in this age in order to obtain riches at the resurrection.[122] Some invoked Isaiah (58:1-9), who was sawn in two.[123] Rich theologians sold all

---

111. Clement of Alexandria, *Paed.* 2.11; 3.6.

112. *1 Clem.* 59.4; Ign. *Smyrn.* 6.2; Clement *Ep. ad Jacob.* 9; Cyprian, *Ep.* 4.1; 76.1-6; 79; Aristides, *Apol.* 15.7; Tertullian, *Mart.* 1; *Apos. Con.* 4.1.2, 9; 5.1.1; Lucian, *Peregr.* 12-13.

113. Eusebius, *Hist. eccl.* 4.23.10, quoting Dionysius of Corinth (cf. Basil, *Ep.* 70); Cyprian *Ep.* 76-79; *Apos. Con.* 5.1; *Didascalia Apostolorum* 5.1.

114. *1 Clem.* 55.2; 59.4; Ign. *Rom.* 1.2; Herm. *Sim.* 1; *Man.* 8.10; *Apos. Con.* 4.9; Cyprian, *Ep.* 42; Hippolytus, *Ref.* 9.12; Basil, *Ep.* 70; Lactantius, *Ep.* 65; *Inst.* 6.12 approvingly quotes Cicero *Off.* 2.18 saying that it is a better type of benefaction than putting on games; *Apos. Con.* 4.9. See especially Carolyn Osiek, "The Ransom of Captives: The Evolution of Tradition," *Harvard Theological Review* 74, no. 4 (1981): 365-86.

115. Sozomen, *Hist. eccl.* 5.15; Tertullian, *Apol.* 39; Aristides, *Apol.* 15.7; *Apos. Con.* 3.7; Lactantius, *Inst.* 6.12; *Ep.* 65.

116. Heb 13:2; Justin, *Apol.* 1.67; *1 Clem.* 1.2; 35.5 (cf. Henry Chadwick, "Justification by Faith and Hospitality," *Studia Patristica* 4, no. 2 (1961): 280-85; Herm. *Man.* 8.10; *Sim.* 9.27.2; *Apos. Con.* 2.3; Cyprian, *Ep.* 7-8; Lactantius, *Inst.* 6.12, though not just to be bestowed on "worthy" recipients; Lactantius, *Epit.* 65; Ps-Clement, *First Epistle Concerning Virginity* 12; *Second Epistle Concerning Virginity* 2-4; Aristides, *Apol.* 15.6; Eusebius, *Hist. eccl.* 4.23.10; Melito of Sardis wrote a treatise on it, now lost, acc. to Eusebius, *Hist. eccl.* 4.26.2. Christian hospitality was well known to Julian the Apostate (Sozomen, *Hist. eccl.* 5.16.3).

117. Eusebius, *Hist. eccl.* 7.22.7-9; 9.8.14; Cyprian, *Demetr.* 10; Pontius, *Vita Cypriani* 9.

118. Acts 11:27-30; 2 Corinthians 8–9; Rom 15:26-27; Cyprian, *Ep.* 62; Dionysius of Corinth in Eusebius, *Hist. eccl.* 4.23.10; Tertullian, *Jejun.* 13; cf. Countryman, *Rich Christian*, pp. 118-19.

119. Clement of Alexandria, *Quis div.* 19; *Paed.* 2.13; 3.6-7; *Strom.* 5.4.

120. Cyprian, *Eleem.* 9; Archelaus, *Disputation with Manes* 9.

121. On widows as an office of service in the church, see Clement of Alexandria, *Paed.* 3.12; Tertullian, *Ux.* 1.7; *Virg.* 9; *Mon.* 11; *Pud.* 13; cf. 1 Timothy 5; Ign. *Smyrn.* 13; Herm. *Vis.* 2.4.

122. On changing temporal riches for those in the age to come see Herm. *Sim.* 1.8-10; *Sent. Sext.* 127-28, cf. 118.

123. Irenaeus, *Adv. Haer.* 4.17.3; Cyprian, *Eleem.* 4; *Dom. or.* 33; *Const. Ap.* 3.1.4.

their goods;[124] poor laity fasted to provide meals for the needy[125] and sold themselves into slavery to redeem their brethren.[126] Men and women of whom the world was not worthy, they lived in deserts and cities and on poles in the ground, yet all these, though they were commended for their faith, are outside the scope of the present essay.

7. Appropriating Patristic Argumentation

Since we are surrounded by such a great cloud of theological impetuses to almsgiving, let us cast off the scholarly detachment that so easily dulls praxis, and in closing let us ask with perspicuity how these theological propositions might yet bear upon us.

While modern apprehension of global structures and economics might well incline the contemporary Christian to diversify the manners in which she expresses charity beyond mere almsgiving, we ought not assume that the theological argumentation utilized by the early fathers cannot yet serve to inform our contemporary reflection and exhortations on caring for the poor.

The rhetoric of κοινωνία has faded from use, in its application both to ancient socialist theory and friendship practice; "sharing" is a lesson we teach our children but, strangely enough, seldom practice as adults. Yet the example of the Jerusalem community still calls into question any presuppositions of absolute rights to private property; as the 1967 encyclical *Populorum Progressio* asserts, "Private property does not constitute for anyone an absolute and unconditioned right. No one is justified in keeping for his exclusive use what he does not need, when others lack necessities."[127]

The rhetoric of "passions" also has obsolesced over the centuries, as even the language of "virtue" has grown *passé*. Nonetheless, the role of concrete deeds in resisting sinful impulses can hardly be eschewed by popular Christianity, and in this capacity, endorsements of generosity might yet be advanced in part as a means to resisting avarice and anemic faith. So also in the Roman Catholic Church, acts of penance serve in part as "an aid to a new

---

124. Origen: Eusebius, *Hist. eccl.* 6.3.9; Cyprian: *Vita Cypriani*, 2.

125. Herm. *Sim.* 5.3.7; *Apos. Con.* 5.1; Aristides, *Apol.* 15.7; *Sent. Sextus* 267; cf. Tertullian, *Jejun.* 13; Countryman, *Rich Christian*, p. 114.

126. *1 Clem.* 55.2.

127. *Populorum Progressio*, 23.

life and an antidote for weakness,"[128] much akin to Clement's and Sextus's discussion of almsgiving as a mechanism of purging one's passions.

Nonetheless, neither Protestants nor Catholics would ever go so far as to contend that almsgiving, or any other righteous deed, serves as a substitute for divine grace in Christ in remitting sins, post-baptismal or otherwise. The biblical text in no way envisages almsgiving as a mechanism of forgiveness alternative to the work of God in Christ. Closer examination of this theme may suggest, however, that deeds like almsgiving function in the soteriological economy as more than mere "evidence" of our salvation (i.e., 1 Tim 6:18-19).[129]

Living 1700 years after Hermas and Cyprian played on the expectation of eschatological judgment to move their congregations to almsgiving, the delayed parousia might seem of meager hortatory potential for the modern church. Evangelicalism in particular has, however, received a major boost from conservative emphases upon the return of Christ (leaving aside the details on the expectation of a "rapture"). It stands to reason that if conservative evangelicalism were to develop a more robust concern for issues of justice, so also the expectation of the return of Christ might well motivate social action.

Of course, the most obvious and crucial goad toward generosity must be love, love for God and love for neighbor. In recent years, the notion of brotherly love as the cement of human solidarity has grown into the bulwark of Catholic social teaching[130] and has issued into a robust recognition that Christian ethics must develop a global character.[131] In light of the modern apprehension of the global socioeconomic factors that birth and sustain poverty and oppression, the Catholic Church has been right to begin to reroute the patristic theological reflections on almsgiving into discussions of

128. *Rite of Penance* 18; cf. 6, 7, 10, and the *Counsel of Trent,* Session 14, Chapter 8 (ND §1631).

129. On more recent Protestant and Catholic reflection on the issue of justification, see in particular Michael Root, "Aquinas, Merit, and Reformation Theology after the *Joint Declaration on the Doctrine of Justification,*" *Modern Theology* 20, no. 1 (2004): 5-22; Joseph Wawrykow, "John Calvin and Condign Merit," *Archiv für Reformationsgeschichte* 83 (1992): 73-90.

130. *Rerum Novarum* 22, 29, 63; *Mater et Magistra* 23; *Gaudium et Spes* 24; *Populorum Progressio* 3, 43, 66, 71, 74; *Octagesima Adveniens* 17; *Centesimus Annus* 10, 58. Alongside justice, love is the crucial criterion of economic ethical reflection: *Quadragesimo Anno* 137; *Mater et Magistra* 39, 43.

131. *Mater et Magistra* 71, 121, 160-74, 183, 192; *Pacem in Terris* 121-45; *Gaudium et Spes* 27; *Populorum Progressio* 3, 13, 40-79.

integral mission and sustainable development. As has been the case for two millennia, Christ and the poor stand poised before the Church. Pointing toward our wealth, comforts, and security, Christ still asks, "Lovest thou us more than these?"

14. Zacchaeus's Half: Ascetical Economy in the Syriac *Book of Steps*

Robert A. Kitchen

1. *The Book of Steps,* Briefly

"You are not able to serve both God and mammon" (Matt 6:24; Luke 16:13) is the quintessential biblical maxim regarding the engagement of the committed Christian with economic activity. The mid-to-late-fourth-century Syriac *Book of Steps* provides a case study of an isolated Christian community that attempted to work out this conundrum.[1] A collection of thirty *mēmrē* or discourses, the *Book of Steps* depicts a rare portrait of a Christian community over a significant, though undetermined, length of time. Situated in the Adiabene region (contemporary northeast Iraq) in the Sassanian Empire, the Christian community in the fourth century was periodically under duress from the Zoroastrian majority, being suspected to be Roman sympathizers. The book's author hints at periods of persecution in the church's

---

1. Syriac critical edition and Latin translation: *Liber Graduum,* ed. M. Kmosko, Patrologia Syriaca 3 (Paris, 1926); English translation and introduction: *The Book of Steps: The Syriac Liber Graduum,* trans. Robert A. Kitchen and Martien F. G. Parmentier, Cistercian Studies 196 (Kalamazoo, MI: Cistercian Publications, 2004). Other works focusing on *The Book of Steps* include: Columba Stewart, *Working the Earth of the Heart: The Messalian Controversy in History, Texts, and Language to* A.D. *431* (Oxford: Oxford University Press, 1991); Daniel Caner, *Wandering, Begging Monks: Spiritual Authority and the Promotion of Monasticism in Late Antiquity,* The Transformation of the Classical Heritage 33 (Berkeley: University of California Press, 2002); *Breaking the Mind: New Studies in the Syriac Book of Steps,* ed. K. S. Heal and R. A. Kitchen, Studies in Early Christianity (Washington, DC: Catholic University of America Press, forthcoming).

memory, but recent scholarship believes that a peaceful coexistence was in order at the time when *The Book of Steps* was written.[2] This community was apparently untouched by the various doctrinal controversies of the early fourth century in the West. No other authors are cited or doctrinal issues alluded to, only the biblical record and its characters, in its endeavor to construct and exhort its members to a vibrant Christian ascetical way of life.

The Book of Steps is unique in portraying how a pre-monastic asceticism constructed its economic behavior, indeed, perhaps the last authentic glimpse of how a segment of the early church dealt with asceticism in the secular world before monasticism emerged to provide its own economic strategies.

The Book of Steps is a lengthy complex work by a single author who did not wish to make his name known. The author's anonymity evinces his principles of deep humility and determination to renounce the world — its possessions, one's family, and personal identity. While his single voice is discernible throughout the work, he does not limit himself to one literary genre, offering discourses on the structure, rules, and theology of the ascetical life, extended biblical expositions, sermons on particular occasions and conflicted issues, pithy Evagrian-like sentences illustrating the contrast between different levels of the Christian life. This is neither a systematic theology in the Western tradition nor an attempt at a historical chronicle of this ascetical experiment; instead, it appears to be the collected occasional writings of the spiritual leader of this isolated church.

The collection is untitled, the *"Book of Steps" (ktābā dmasqātā)* having been bestowed upon the work by its editors and cataloguers. The "steps" are mentioned only in *mēmrē* 19 and 20, referring to the steep road and steps one must climb to the city of the king our Lord. As effective as the term is, it does not reappear as a theme in the rest of the collection.

There is, nonetheless, a narrative laced throughout *The Book of Steps.* The anonymous author did not intend to chronicle his journey and efforts, but his engagement with particular developments within the community (i.e., specific situations, practical and theological dilemmas, crises, bad ideas, and backsliding) enables us to create an outline of the history of the community over what might have been decades.

---

2. Cf. Geoffrey Greatrex, "The Romano-Persian Frontier and the Context of the *Book of Steps,"* in Heal and Kitchen, eds., *Breaking the Mind;* also, Joel Thomas Walker, *The Legend of Mar Qardagh: Narrative and Christian Heroism in Late Antique Iraq,* The Transformation of the Classical Heritage 41 (Berkeley: University of California Press, 2006), esp. pp. 1-13, 87-120.

The object of the work is to describe the optimum spiritual way of life, to admonish those who have fallen away from its correct practice, and to exhort all to a higher and more faithful performance. The subject of his *mēmrē* is clearly the two levels of Christians living under his spiritual direction and pastoral care, the Upright ones *(kēnē)* and the Perfect ones *(gmīrē)*.

The Upright live in the town or village, are married, have secular jobs, and possess property and income by which they support the Perfect ones and perform the traditional acts of charity to the poor and sick. The Perfect, while not yet considered monks, are committed ascetics living within or on the edge of the community. They are celibate and have renounced all possessions, including family and home. They pray unceasingly, teach and mediate conflicts in their wandering lifestyle, and pointedly do not work.

These are not static descriptions, for over the time span of these *mēmrē* situations and people change. Initially, the author promotes the Perfect way of life as the model and goal for all Christians eventually to attain, but, disappointed and perhaps disillusioned in their failings, the author shifts at the end of the discourses to favor and encourage the Upright, who, except for their non-celibacy, have shown more evidence of the fully lived Christian life. A virtually unprecedented shift in the Christian ascetical literature of late antiquity, this is the consequence of a document that does not merely present a cameo of ideal expectations, but records their development and decline over a significant period of time.

How the committed Christian deals with money, possessions, work, and property is a theme submerged in the more public displays of the Upright and the Perfect in *The Book of Steps,* yet economic behavior is at the very root of the Christian and biblical paradigm for the author. Possessions and money are mentioned periodically in describing how the Upright may operate within the secular world and still maintain a consecrated life of Christian service, hopefully progressing toward Perfection. Predictably, biblical characters are promoted as types for both the Perfect and, especially, the Upright. Abraham and Zacchaeus emerge as the patron saints of the Uprights' economic and spiritual way of life, which the author will illustrate in extended exegeses in the concluding *mēmrā.*

2. The Economy of Uprightness

Asceticism in the early Syriac Christian church of the third through sixth centuries readily developed standard roles and institutions. The sons and daughters of the covenant (an ascetic order of consecrated Christians, *bnay* and *bnāt qyāmā*) and the solitaries *(īḥīdāyē)* are well attested in the works of Aphrahat (d. 355) and Ephrem (d. 373) and are mentioned on a few occasions in *The Book of Steps*. Itself written in the mid-to-late fourth century, *The Book of Steps* appears to share a common understanding of these ascetical categories rather than to have borrowed or received them from previous writers. If there is a historical antecedent for the Upright, particularly as the lower member of a two-tiered system, it would be the Manichaean system of the spiritually superior Elect who were served by the lower status Hearers. While the analogy is close, most scholars believe that there is not a direct borrowing, although the structure of this hierarchy might well have survived in the collective institutional memory.[3]

Uprightness *(kēnūtā)* is depicted by the author as the lower level or step in his conception of the Christian life. While one might label Uprightness as the faith of the laity, in itself it is a committed, if not consecrated, choice of discipleship. On a number of occasions, the author cautions his listeners not to fall below Uprightness through lax behavior. The most notable people who did fall were the Old Testament prophets who committed acts of violence, even slaying their opponents, under the command of God. These prophets, languishing in a spiritual no-man's-land, were eventually promised to be ushered into salvation and perfection, but only after the apostles were received.[4]

The first Upright ones were Adam and Eve, who had been Perfect, but whose sin had been to attempt to become God. Following their fall from the Perfection of Eden, God did not destroy them but offered them the possibility of being Upright ones. This involved a life that permitted marriage, required labor, and involved the love of the world and its possessions. Most human beings have had the opportunity to continue in this way of life, while a few have striven for Perfection. The primary and problematic characteristic of the Upright is that they can be married and are allowed to participate in sexual relationships. They must work and labor as a consequence of the expulsion from Eden, and they accumulate possessions and wealth. If they use their possessions to help others in need, do not do unto others what they would hate having done to them, and treat all people well, then they will be

---

3. Cf. Timothy Pettipiece, "Parallel Paths: Tracing Manichaean Footprints Along the Syriac *Book of Steps*," in Heal and Kitchen, eds., *Breaking the Mind*.

4. Cf. Memra Nine, "On Uprightness and the Love of the Upright and the Prophets," in Kitchen and Parmentier, eds., *The Book of Steps*, pp. 87-103.

able to enter the salvation of the kingdom of heaven, although their reward will be of a lesser nature than that of the Perfect.

The author goes into more detail regarding the mechanics of how the Upright should operate with regard to their possessions and how to deal financially with others. In the thirteenth *mēmrā*, "On the Ways of the Upright," the most nuanced regarding the behavior of the Upright, the author stresses their obligations regarding loans to others and their contribution to the church and community.

> [Uprightness] claims what belongs to it according to its [fair] measure, but does not get involved in usury or approach a bribe. [Uprightness] possesses wealth righteously and buys and sells as is appropriate before God. [Uprightness] neither deceives nor borrows something it lacks, but claims only what it has loaned without interest, even if it will be one hundred years [before it is repaid]. (13.1; 127)[5]

The Upright one may be involved in business, yet his purpose is not to make money but only to serve God and the needs of others without taking advantage of their poverty and powerlessness. When it comes to supporting the local church, however, antipathies and conflicts sometimes need to be overcome.

> [Uprightness] honors the priests, heeds their words, and goes to them. It gives the best of all its crops to its priests and the best of its dough and the first-born of whatever it possesses and it brings [all of that] to the house of the Lord, without being envious of the tranquil life of the priests, who bury its dead, visit its sick, teach and edify its living. On Sunday, [Uprightness] places in the Lord's house some of [the fruit of] its labors for the needy because [the latter] visit the house of our Lord. During the observances of fasting, [Uprightness] brings to the house of the Lord whatever it saves. [Uprightness] is concerned to go and pray at the right time and to see whether there are [any] needy there it could help so that it might receive a reward from our Lord. (13.2; 128-29)

There is such a burden and pressure upon the Upright to enable the institution to continue that the author's prescriptions encourage the Upright to keep in mind the provenance of their possessions. The possessions of the

---

5. References to the text are from Kitchen and Parmentier, eds., *The Book of Steps*, in the following order: Mēmrā number + section; + page number.

Upright are not precisely "their" possessions, for they are caretakers and distributors for the community.

The Upright ones, therefore, can never be ordinary church members living in the workaday world. They are something quite alien. "The Upright build and possess, not as [if] forever, but live in the world as strangers" (14.1; 136). "Stranger" *(nūkrāyā)* is a common term in Syriac ascetical literature to describe the individual who no longer belongs to the worldly pursuits of marriage, family, and possessions. Eventually, a "stranger" will indicate a monk or hermit, and the term shares close affinity with the term "solitary" *(īḥīdāyā)*, for both kind of individuals are alone, not receiving support from society.

A requisite function of the Upright is to provide sustenance and support for the Perfect, which is a "good work" reckoned to their own salvation. "Since the Perfect lack clothing and food, and God sends no manna at all down to them, the Upright can give [them] alms in order to be saved in this way" (28.11; 319). The author is explicit concerning division between the biblical age and the contemporary age. There is no more manna; indeed, the biblical era has expired. In particular, God no longer gives license to prophets or others to slay God's opponents (9.15; 99). A different ethos and ethic are now in effect than during the biblical era; now one must rely upon an intimate acquaintance with God's commandments in order to live righteously and not to expect miracles. The Upright are part of God's new economy, as one can observe in a passage addressed to the Perfect. "Our Lord commanded them, 'Your Father knows that you require food and clothing.[6] Do not be anxious, because I will tell the Upright who work the earth to nourish and clothe you and they will live the life of the new world on account of you, and will do for you these things by their labor while not treating anyone badly'" (25.3; 293).

The eighth *mēmrā,* "On One Who Gives All He Has to Feed the Poor," addressed primarily to the Upright, chastises those who give aid to those in need but do not also have love for their enemies, an exposition of Paul's admonition in 1 Corinthians 13.

> He who gives all he has to feed the poor on account of God and renounces — as [the Lord] said to him — all he possesses, but does not have in him that humble love that loves his murderers and washes the feet of his enemies and considers everyone better than himself, giving heed to heaven and not to earth, his mind serving there in the heavenly Jerusalem, bound there to our Lord, [then, without this, he is nothing]. (8.2; 82)

6. Matt 6:32.

Nancy Khalek has pointed out insightfully that in this *mēmrā* the author does not indicate that it is the traditional poor who are being helped. Instead, the author categorizes the Perfect as "the poor" to whom assistance needs to be given.[7]

Evidently, the burden these responsibilities exacted created difficulties on occasion for the Upright, to whom the author makes some practical suggestions. While the Upright worked and earned income, all were not necessarily wealthy, so sometimes a communal effort was advised. "Everyone is 'a son of Adam,' indeed, our neighbor and our fellow human being. If it is difficult for a single individual to clothe a naked person on account of his poverty, five or ten should join together and clothe the flesh of their neighbors" (7.2; 66). In addition, the author mentions the existence of a "steward of the poor" in the community whose special calling is to minister to the needs of the poor: "Well, a steward of the poor is such a man who *in our Lord* takes care of all sorts of miserable people, such as the sick, the naked and the foreigners, receiving from those who have and giving to those who have not" (3.6; 27). The implication is that such a steward functions as a member of the church, though the author is quick to emphasize that he still belongs to the level of Uprightness, even if he seeks to be a Perfect one.

> This is a good and honorable thing to do, and yet someone who does this does not empty himself in accordance with what the word of our Lord says, "Do not be anxious in any way for your life in minding about food and clothing, but give away all you have to the poor, in a day or in a month, and then take up your cross and follow me."[8] No, someone who does not possess anything himself, but receives from one person and gives to another, still stands in a relation of taking and giving, of accepting and providing with this world, and still does not empty himself in accordance with what our Lord said, "Raise yourselves up from the earth and do not be anxious,"[9] and in accordance with what the Apostle said, "Seek the things that are above and set your mind on them."[10] (3.6; 27-28)

---

7. Nancy A. Khalek, "Methods of Instructing Syriac-Speaking Christians to Care for the Poor: A Brief Comparison of the Eighth *Mēmrā* of the *Book of Steps* and the Story of the Man of God of Edessa," *Hugoye Journal of Syriac Studies* 8, no. 1 (January 2005), available at http://syrcom.cua.edu/Hugoye/Vol8No1/HV8N1Khalek.html.

8. Cf. Matt 6:25.

9. This is an apocryphal saying.

10. Col 3:1.

It is not surprising that the author identifies the ministry of the Upright with Martha, the sister who, while diligent, chose the lesser portion. "At the same time [as Mary], Martha served our Lord with clothing and food, for himself and for the crowd that was with him, as she had a house and possessions, like Abraham, and she led an Upright life. But she did not go so far as to take up the Cross" (3.13; 34). The most anticipated rewards of the spiritual life are not accessible to the Upright simply because, being enmeshed in the world's business, their spiritual faculties are clouded. "Those who do conduct business with this world and who use it to take care of the hungry and the naked, while doing evil to no one, will be saved; although they cannot receive the Paraclete, yet the pledge of the Holy Spirit will grow in them" (3.14; 35). The full gift of the Holy Spirit is not yet attainable, though the portion or pledge of the Spirit increases as they spiritually progress.

Not everyone in the faith community buys into this calling, however. At least a few members have fallen below Uprightness as a result of a business perspective. So, one passage speaks their voice with a remarkably modern refrain: "But when Sunday comes, in order that we do not learn about righteousness, sin directs us to say, 'Our business has suffered loss.' When the time for prayer comes, in order that we do not worship our Creator, we say that 'our profits have perished'" (7.20; 79).

Throughout the early *mēmrē*, the author has a clear role and status envisioned for the Upright. They are the critical people in the faith community who keep the worldly side of things functioning, not only fulfilling the so-called "minor commandments" to minister to the poor, needy, and ill, but also providing the basic necessities for the higher status of the Perfect ones so that the latter may carry out the corresponding "major commandments." But by being involved with worldly affairs, especially money, possessions, and their business dealings, the Upright are contaminated and inhibited from attaining the higher levels of the kingdom of heaven. The author has an exalted conception of the Perfect life and does not seem aware of the irony that it is only by the "giving and taking" of the Upright that the Perfect can ever hope to live their irenic lifestyle. In time, perhaps after decades of experience, the author comes to recognize that the most committed of the Upright have recorded much more in their spiritual ledger than he initially thought possible.

3. The Uneconomical Perfect

The problem with the Perfect ones, initially the heroes of *The Book of Steps,* though never its saints, is that their status defies definitive description. Whereas the Upright are told precisely how often to pray and what to do in certain situations, the Perfect are never confined to a quantitative measure for any activity. A concise description is found in the fifteenth *mēmrā:* "The Perfect do not take wives, nor do they work in the field, nor acquire possessions, nor have a place to lay their heads on earth like their teacher" (15.13; 150).[11] Celibacy is a persistent feature of Syriac asceticism, previewing the monastic state about to appear on the horizon.[12]

The command that the Perfect do not work will be examined below, but significantly for the modern study of *The Book of Steps* this requirement has been linked to the fourth- and fifth-century movement of Messalianism. The label derives from the Syriac word *maṣallāyē* or "those who pray." Their history is cloudy, and what is known about them derives largely from those who condemned them as heretics. Messalians reputedly disdained the sacraments as ineffective for salvation, relying solely upon unceasing prayer. Work, therefore, was also rejected, and the various bands of Messalians wandered throughout the region, characterized wonderfully by Antoine Guillaumont as a "kind of hippies."[13] On the surface this seems to fit *The Book of Steps,* so the editor of the critical edition, Michael Kmosko, was convinced this work was the missing "asketikon" of the Messalians alluded to at the Council of Ephesus.[14] As a result, a generation of scholars held *The Book of Steps* at arm's length until Arthur Vööbus refuted these aspersions and others followed his lead.[15] Most scholars today recognize Messalian elements

11. Matt 8:20.

12. The tradition that the early Syriac church required celibacy for baptism, as described by A. Vööbus, *Celibacy, a Requirement for Admittance to Baptism in the Early Syrian Church,* Papers of the Estonian Theological Society in Exile 1 (Stockholm, 1951), has now been greatly amended. Cf. George Nedungatt, "The Covenanters of the Early Syriac-Speaking Church," *OCP* 49 (1973): 191-215, 419-44; Robert Murray, "The Exhortation to Candidates for Ascetical Vows at Baptism in the Ancient Syriac Church," *NTS* 21 (1974): 59-80.

13. A. Guillaumont, "Un Mouvement de 'Spirituels' dans l'Orient chrétien," *Revue de l'Histoire des Religions* 189 (1975): 126.

14. Kmosko's extensive introduction (*Praefatio,* i-cccvii) assembles all the major Greek texts regarding the Messalian controversy.

15. A. Vööbus, *Liber Graduum: Some Aspects of Its Significance for the History of Early Syrian Asceticism,* Papers of the Estonian Theological Society in Exile 7 (Stockholm, 1954), pp. 108-28.

in *The Book of Steps* but do not interpret this to mean that the book or its author was consciously Messalian.[16] Nevertheless, the renunciation of work by the Perfect is a singular characteristic that deserves further attention, both for its theological rationale and its economic ramifications.

The author understands that Perfection is the status in which Adam and Eve lived in the Garden of Eden before Adam sinned, and that Perfection is the angelic status. Therefore, the Perfect ones are angels living upon the earth.

> The Perfect are like angels, as our Lord said, "Those who are worthy of that resurrection are not able to die, but are like the angels."[17] From then on they become like angels. Whoever wishes to be perfected should imitate the angels. Let us see, what is the work of the angels? The angels do not cultivate the earth, nor do they clothe the naked, nor feed the hungry, nor does their mind remain on earth, but with the word of our Lord they admonish everyone as he is capable. As they are continually in [God's] presence and minister to his majesty, they are not anxious for their food, because our Lord is concerned for them and for everyone. It is fitting for these who would become like angels that they should imitate angels and preach the word of our Lord, as he had commanded them, "Do not be anxious about food or clothing,"[18] nor about themselves, nor about their brothers, because our Lord cares for them and for everyone, and he is concerned about his creation so that he might guide it. (25.8; 298)

The active function of the Perfect is to be teachers and pastors to all whom they meet in their wanderings, and as the need arises to be disinterested mediators of conflicts they encounter, an important function in ancient society. Earlier in the twelfth *mēmrā*, the author pointed to Jesus' command to Simeon as programmatic for the Perfect.

> Because of this conduct and profit our Lord did not allow this person, who is a helper for all people, to work on the land, because he said to him

---

16. The best recent analyses of the Messalian connections are in Stewart, *Working the Earth of the Heart*; Klaus Fitschen, *Messalianisimus und Antimessalianisimus: Ein Beispiel ostkirchlicher Ketzergeschichte*, Forschungen zur Kirchen- und Dogmengeschichte 71 (Göttingen: Vandenhoeck & Ruprecht, 1998), esp. pp. 108-19; and Marcus Plested, *The Macarian Legacy: The Place of Macarius-Symeon in the Eastern Christian Tradition* (Oxford: Oxford University Press, 2004), pp. 16-27.

17. Luke 20:35-36.

18. Matt 6:25.

as [he had said] to Simeon, "If you love me, feed for me my flock and my sheep, my ewes and my lambs."[19] This one who feeds the sheep of Christ is not able to go guide the plow and work the visible land, but gathers, feeds, and reconciles the sheep who were delivered to him, and his face will be revealed on that day before the one who commanded him, "Feed my flock and my ewes and my lambs."[20] (12.6; 124-25)

The distinction of the teaching role of the Perfect from the physical ministry of the Upright is epitomized by the author in the martyrdom of Stephen, an Upright one who grows to Perfection.

In the same way the apostles appointed seven deacons to take care of food and supplies, while they occupied themselves with teaching the word of God.[21] But even from these stewards, whoever wants to make the effort and empty himself will reach the major commandments and stand fast in Perfection, as for example Stephen did, who was one of them. He emptied himself and received the Paraclete. *He was killed while teaching the word and not while giving material alms.* (3.15; 35-36)

The Perfect are summoned to actualize Jesus' commandment to live in the world but not be of the world by delineating a clear boundary between physical and spiritual ministries. They do not participate in the economy except as passive consumers of the labor of others. Sometimes, the situation may arise in which it would be easier for the Perfect one to give aid directly to someone in need, but the author cautions him to maintain his separation from any kind of physical ministry and seek the aid of those whose specific calling is to support Christian charity.

It is better if such a person teaches his wealthy sponsors to become doers of good works personally and to give away out of their riches with their own hands to all the needy and afflicted, as the Apostle said, "As for the rich who are in this world, teach them to be ready for good works and to store up treasures in heaven, and not to put their trust in transient riches."[22] So the person who has been put in charge of taking and giving should act as follows: he should teach the wealthy to give from their possessions to the poor with their own hands. He himself should be constant

19. John 21:15-17.
20. John 21:15-17.
21. Acts 6:4.
22. 1 Tim 6:17-19; Matt 6:19-20.

in prayer and intercession, in ministering and studying, in applying himself to the word of God's truth and to have it interpreted, in conformity with what our Lord himself and his apostles practiced when they appointed deacons for the sick, the naked, the strangers, the captives and all others in need, while they themselves attended to the word of God and prayer.[23] (3.7; 28)

The author not only advocates that the Perfect should teach the wealthy citizens of the church regarding social justice and ministry, but goes one step further in order to preserve the integrity of the Perfect one's status and enable him to avoid getting into troublesome conflict.

In case the rich do not see where the afflicted are, the person who wants to be Perfect should just show them where they are, and not take them himself into his house, thus involving himself in a great deal of distraction. Many will grumble at him, aggravate his spirit, and not allow him to become Perfect. For this is what happens: the person who has been helped grumbles and complains, "You've got it [wealth], but you won't give it to us," and then they inflict harm on him who came too close to things visible. (3.7; 29)

It is obvious here that the author and the Perfect ones are well experienced in the ambiguities of living the fully ascetical way of life in the midst of the non-ascetical world. Some who are poor and destitute become so frustrated that they assume the Perfect are quite wealthy but lack generosity, due to their calm and assured demeanor.

The author depicts the Perfect as those who "neither build nor possess, nor does their mind abide on the earth" (14.1; 136). The Perfect one may have his feet planted upon earthly soil, but his mind and vision are peering into the kingdom of heaven at all times. How this is to be achieved, the author never details.

4. God Would Have Provided

As is probably evident by now, attaining Perfection for the author of *The Book of Steps* is a reentry into the Garden of Eden before Adam had sinned, a common theme in early Syriac Christianity.[24] The reentry into Eden or Par-

---

23. Acts 6:4.
24. Cf. Gary A. Anderson, *The Genesis of Perfection: Adam and Eve in Jewish and Chris-*

adise through baptism required a certain exegesis that saw Adam and Eve living in a state between mortality/humanity and immortality/divinity.[25] That God assigned Adam to till or cultivate and keep the garden (Gen 2:15) is generally overlooked because the original couple were understood still to be living in sacred time and had not yet been caught in the grasp of historical time and geographical space. This grasp is marked by the condemnation of fallen humanity (Gen 3:16-17) to the difficulties of sexuality and childbirth and to the sweat of labor.[26] The Perfect one, therefore, is recapturing the spirituality of the pre-fallen Adam and Eve, a primary characteristic of which is that one does not work. Work, the foundation of economic activity, appears suddenly just like the first couple's awareness of their nakedness and sexuality. Work is assigned to the banished couple as the consequence of their disobedience and inappropriate aspirations to divinity (Gen 3:17-19). Possessing things is natural, things given to them by God, but work is neither natural nor obvious. "Did not the first couple — who did not work — also [possess] goods like you?" (7.19; 78).

Reviewing the human condition, one wonders how we could have survived without some measure of work, but the author insists that if Adam and Eve had remained obedient and faithful, God would have provided for them, and for us, the necessities of life.

> God, in fact, wanted these things to be this way: [God] wanted all humanity to praise him without having to work. It would have been so if Adam had only remained straight. But he did not, and neither did his sons; and we too exacerbate our Creator continually — our wickedness goes on increasing. (3.15; 36)

Indeed, God could have transformed human social structure if God had so desired, but as things worked out, a different strategy was implemented for the benefit of one's salvation.

---

tian Imagination (Louisville: Westminster John Knox Press, 2001); also Robert A. Kitchen, "Syriac Additions to Anderson: The Garden of Eden in the Book of Steps and Philoxenus of Mabbug," *Hugoye Journal of Syriac Studies* 6, no. 1 (2003), available at http://syrcom.cua.edu/Hugoye/Vol6No1/HV6N1kitchen.html.

25. Sebastian Brock, *The Luminous Eye: The Spiritual World Vision of Saint Ephrem the Syrian,* Cistercian Studies 124 (Kalamazoo, MI: Cistercian Publications, 1992), pp. 31-34, 100-101, 139-40.

26. And as noted above, the affinities of *The Book of Steps* to the purported ideas of the Messalian controversy perhaps indicate the prejudices of the author toward the renunciation of work.

God could have made all the world rich and healthy and life-long residents,[27] and not needy people; but he made some rich and some poor and
some strangers and some sick ones. He tempts those who have by those
who have not [in order to see] if their affections are for their fellow human beings. If the rich take care of the poor and the healthy [take care of]
the sick and the clothed [take care of] the naked and the life-long residents [are hospitable to] the strangers; and if they will do this and have
compassion upon those who are worse off than them, those worse off will
be able to find relief with the powerful ones and the powerful will be justified through those worse off.

But if they do not do as our Lord commanded — to have compassion
on those who are worse off than they — [the Lord] will provide for the
poor according to his mercies and will have pity "like a poor person" on
this world. These who have not been compassionate will be without fruits
and without righteousness on the Day of our Lord. For Lazarus was ill-
treated and lived in this world, but he went to that [other] world and was
given rest.[28] But woe to that rich person who has gone without [spiritual]
provisions, because his stomach will not be full with the rich food of the
new world. (10.6; 109)

An intriguing note is the inclusion of "life-long residents" among the
privileged rich and healthy. Literally, "the sons of the household of the father," this term refers to the locally entrenched residents who traditionally
control most aspects of town life, including access to its economic dimensions. The author refers to them several times as the counterparts to "strangers," who presumably are not granted access to much of anything. Recognizing the problems created by such life-long residents, the author gives
evidence of living in an actual community, not just relying upon the traditional types of the rich and wealthy. The provisions of God extend as well to
the more specific human needs.

And so our Lord would have made them children as he had made Eve from
Adam, without lust and without marriage, or if he had wanted he could
have made children by the hairs of their heads or by their finger nails, and
the people would have become the images of angels. He who created them
would have prepared food for them if he had wanted without labor. He

---

27. Lit. *bnay bēt ābā*, "sons of the household of the father" — i.e., "local natives" belonging to the patriarchal establishment of the community.
28. Luke 16:19ff.

would have carried their burden, as our Lord said, "Do not be anxious for your body or for your soul, because that one who created you is greatly concerned about you."[29] Therefore, "Cast down your anxiety upon the Lord and he will nourish, comfort, and keep you."[30] (21.7; 238)

The author takes Jesus' assurance about non-anxiety as a pastoral warrant for the Perfect ones to avoid working.

Our Lord commanded them, "Your Father knows that you require food and clothing.[31] Do not be anxious, because I will say to the Upright who work the earth to nourish and clothe you and they will live the life of the new world on account of you, and will do for you these things by their labor while not treating anyone badly. If it were not for your sake that [the Perfect] were to live among you, I would have rained food and clothing upon you from heaven. If all the earth had practiced Perfection and holiness without having worked or having possessed, I would have fed all without toil as in the beginning. (25.3; 293)

5. The Decline of the Perfect

In the last six *mēmrē,* the author expresses concern over the increasing imperfection of the Perfect. Their fault was not moral, but in being confused and seduced by Satan to relax their Perfect discipline and unwittingly take on the tasks and work of Uprightness.

[The evil one,] deluding the Perfect one, says the following, "It is virtuous that you should acquire a little [wealth] through Uprightness, sufficient for your own comfort and for whoever comes to you. Build for yourself a dwelling that is just adequate for strangers to come and rest in it. Plant a little crop and make for yourself a vegetable garden that will be for the healthy and the sick." Under the pretext of the comfort of the afflicted [the evil one] schemes to make [a Perfect] one fall from that major commandment which [Jesus] directs to the Perfect, "Do not be anxious even about yourself,"[32] and from that [other] commandment,

29. Matt 6:25.
30. Ps 55:22; 1 Pet 5:7.
31. Matt 6:32.
32. Matt 6:25.

"Think about what is above and not of what is on the earth."[33] (25.5; 294-95)

The spiritual dilemma for the Perfect is that under the seductive suggestions of the evil one they are thinking too much, generating anxiety about their former worldly concerns. Notably, all these concerns involve economic prosperity and production.

> Therefore, once the evil one has made a person turn away from heavenly matters and beset him with the toil of Uprightness and he has acquired gardens and earthly Paradises, properties and buildings, then the evil one begins to pull him down also from Uprightness. Once [the evil one] had gone to encourage others to treat him badly, he went on to attack the Upright one who had fallen short of Perfection while not knowing that the evil one would trouble him and make him do [evil]. He begins by saying to him, "They have plundered your house that you have built with great effort"; then the person will go quarrel and fight [against them]. Here is one profit he has gained. Again he says to him, "Grasping people who are not satisfied have picked through [your] plants and vegetable garden," and the person goes off to struggle [against them]. Here is another profit that the evil one advised him to do. Once more he says to him, "They have struck and killed and led away your flock[34] while it was feeding on your mountain," and then he wrings his hands and is disturbed. Here is another profit that the evil one advised the heavenly ones that they should own and build. (25.6; 296-97)

Nevertheless, the Upright are never to shirk their calling to help other people. The author recognizes that they may not be wealthy and may even be considered poor, but that can never be an excuse for lack of compassion for their fellow human beings. He is now eager to encourage the Upright to greater achievement and holiness, expanding the path of salvation for the Upright in the twenty-ninth *mēmrā*, demonstrating that even those who perform a small service to someone in need will reap a significant reward.

> When is a person so poor that he cannot afford a cup of water and morsel of bread, nor afford the washing of feet, nor the bandaging of [the wounds of] the sick, nor hosting strangers [for the night], [if] he has a

33. Col 3:2.
34. Literally, "your possession."

house? No one is too poor to [be able to give] compliments and a loving greeting, unless he wishes to become an evil one. But God, who sees the diligence of those who wish to make the weary live despite their poverty and are afflicted in order to keep his commandments, will treat them well with these visible things, and will give them these things that are promised, but not visible.[35] (29.14; 334)

Celibacy is often identified as the boundary line between the two levels, but economic characteristics equally distinguish how one dispenses wealth, devotes oneself in service to others, and consequently works. At first the Upright are granted grudging permission to participate in the physical economy, expecting that such participation will always be directed for the benefit of the community as a whole, and in particular for the Perfect. The Perfect do not participate actively in the economic functions of society and strive to become "a-economical," so that the primary challenge of the author is how to direct the higher level to survive physically and spiritually outside the boundaries of economic life.

6. Poverty and the Poor in *The Book of Steps*

A couple of words used sparingly by the author witness to a perception of poverty in that society. These are not necessarily Christian definitions but belong to a deeper substratum of language and culture.

The author uses a rare adverbial expression *mēskānāīt*, literally "like a poor [person]." "[The Lord] will provide for the poor according to his mercies and will have pity 'like a poor person' on this world" (10.6; 109), implying positively that those who are poor instinctively are more merciful and compassionate toward the needs of others. In the twentieth *mēmrā*, the author describes the persistence of the Perfect one as he climbs up the steep road to the city of our Lord.

Then a person may ascend that [second] step in which one should not be anxious or work, trusting in our Lord [and saying], "If I climb up, good; if I remain [on the same step], so be it." That is, [we receive sustenance] from our Lord as well as from begging food and clothing *like a poor person.* "If I die, I will die; and if I live, I will live," as long as I do not abandon

35. Heb 6:1.

the journey of that great road on account of nourishment and clothing. (20.2; 212)

Acting like a poor person does not appear to be a fully positive status. One who is poor is necessarily humbled, humiliated. But this is precisely what the Perfect one should strive to become. The second word indicates the social location of poverty in the language and thought-world of fourth-century Syriac culture.

The tenth *mēmrā* is a sermon delivered directly to the community, denouncing those who believe that after becoming "spiritual" beings they no longer have to engage in any discipline of physical asceticism, such as fasting. The author observes that no one would think of going on a long journey without ample supplies and resources, and he extends the analogy to which spiritual resources one must take on the long journey into the next world of death. "Because if a person does not take anything with him here [in this world], no one will give him [anything] there [in that other/next world], for they will call him a *poor man*" (10.3; 106). This label appears to bear a pejorative sense, and what is interesting is the Syriac word itself, *bāyšā*. While this adjective/substantive means "poor" (economically) along with "unfortunate, sad, unlucky," it is a relatively rare use of the root "*b-y-š*," which typically means "evil, bad" *(bīšā)*. In a non-vocalized text there would be no distinction. To be poor meant to be essentially evil.

However, for the author and for the Perfect this prejudice carries powerful weight for the vitality of the spiritual life. The author persistently urges the development of a deep and authentic humility among his most advanced charges. The fact that no names, except those of biblical characters, are mentioned in *The Book of Steps* and that the author does not want to make his name known is literary evidence of this humility. His favorite maxim is Philippians 2:3b: "Consider everyone better than yourselves." The Perfect one is meant to perceive himself, not as a lofty spiritual being, but as lowly a sinful human being as imaginable. To understand oneself and to be perceived as a poor man, yes, evil and wicked, is exactly what his soul needs to be prepared for the journey.

7. Good Money

The Book of Steps is virtually unique in its presentation over a period of time of the development of an author, a community, and its ascetic ideals. Individual *mēmrē* can be read as univocal descriptions of what the Upright and the Perfect should be at a particular time; but to see how this community's efforts toward an ascetical life change, one must examine the whole work as an organic unit. The most significant development and surprising change is the author's shift in sympathy from the contemplative Perfect ones in the earlier *mēmrē* to the worldly active Upright ones in the concluding *mēmrē*.[36] The arena in which this shift takes place is primarily in the involvement and non-involvement of the Upright and Perfect in economic activities. There is no mistaking that *The Book of Steps* is about the construction and mainte-nance of an ascetical community, a way of life that typically looks askance at business and property concerns. Predictably, the majority of the *mēmrē* treat economic life in precisely this way; one could say the Perfect are being called to an "a-economic" existence, as much as that is possible. At some point, the author's frustrations with backsliding Perfect ones collided with his delight and amazement at the genuine spiritual progress of the Upright ones, and he comes to realize that his observations must change his theology.

The author's exposition of biblical narratives and personalities unveils his ascetical and theological directions. Most of the expositions portray either the righteous behavior of a Perfect one or one's fall from the grace of Perfec-tion down to Uprightness, or even the descent from Uprightness into the darkness of the violent world (as in the case of those Old Testament proph-ets). The only instance of an Upright one graduating up to Perfection is that of Stephen, 3.15; 35-36). In the thirtieth and final *mēmrā* the author presents two biblical persona, Abraham and Zacchaeus, whom he squeezes into role models for the Upright ones, neither of whom makes it to Perfection. Their behavior — not always exemplary — demonstrates how one should deal with money and wealth to assist others and earn a measure of salvation for oneself.

The author appears to be countering criticism of the Upright that they are acquiring a more exalted status than they have earned. He does this by reminding his readers of the biblical occasions in which individuals were granted salvation through simple means, first by simply doing what they are commanded as in the case of Zacchaeus (Luke 19:8-9).

---

36. A major problem created by the anonymity of *The Book of Steps* and corresponding lack of chronological and geographical detail is that we are not able definitively to settle upon a chronological order of the *mēmrē*. Most of the references to the "shift" away from the primacy of the Perfect toward the Upright do occur in *mēmrē* 25-30; yet there are a scattered few, particularly in *mēmrē* 9 and 10, which seem too "early." For the time being, the received order of the *mēmrē* should not be equated with chronological sequence but should be con-sidered an approximation of the sequence.

Understand from this that people are saved if they do as they were commanded: [following] that precept that is lower than that perfect and superior precept, [even] while they are married and possessing wealth. [This is clear] by that demonstration when our Lord entered the house of Zacchaeus, a sinner and an extortionist and doer of evil things, and admonishing him made him a disciple with these commandments which are inferior to Perfection. [Jesus] did not say to him, "Unless you leave your wife and your house and your children and empty yourself from everything you own, you will not be saved." Look, the response of Zacchaeus makes it clear that our Lord admonished him in such a way that he need not empty himself, because he knew that he could not reach the power of that great portion. Zacchaeus said, "Everyone whom I have cheated I will repay four-fold, and half of my wealth *only* I will give to the poor." See, while he did not say to our Lord, "I will abandon everything I have," our Lord did say the following to him, "Today salvation has come into this house." Zacchaeus shall be called a son of Abraham, he who when he promised to repay their lords what he had extorted had said, "Half of my wealth *only* I will give." But whoever gives to the poor half of his wealth while not defrauding anyone, look, is he not greater than Zacchaeus, who was called righteous? When he gave two portions of his wealth, look, does not he grow greater still? Whoever gives all he possesses to the poor and the strangers, look, is [that person] not better and greater? (30.27; 361)

Half of my wealth *only*. Eisegesis needs only one word to alter a universe. Needless to say, the word "only" is non-canonical, but as far as the author was concerned, its use was legitimate and clearly understood in the context. Craig Morrison has pointed out that such additions to the text were usually intentional in order to emphasize a particular exegesis.[37] The congregation upon hearing such a canonical aberration would recognize the innovation and instinctively pick up on the intended emphasis. The author shifts the focus away from Zacchaeus's sinful extortions of the citizenry through his tax collecting to the more narrow issue of how he uses his money and possessions. He is not renouncing the world, and he will keep half of his wealth for himself, which is something most church members could and would like to do. Still, he can have his cake and eat it too, for Jesus hears what he offers and

37. Craig Morrison, O. Carm., "The Bible in the Hands of Aphrahat the Persian Sage," in *Syriac and Antiochean Exegesis and Biblical Theology for the Third Millennium*, ed. Robert D. Miller, Gorgias Eastern Christian Studies 6 (Piscataway, NJ: Gorgias Press, 2008), pp. 1-25, esp. 10-23.

grants him immediate salvation. The author continues, however, to call his Upright to a higher renunciation. Zacchaeus is just the minimum.

While Zacchaeus is an unlikely and probably contentious saint, he is nevertheless identified by both Jesus and the author as a "son of Abraham." The author concludes the entire work by presenting the universally accepted model of the first patriarch, Abraham.

> Therefore, let no one say that whoever does not empty everything he has and follow our Lord is not saved. If people then desire to become sons of Abraham while being wealthy, as Zacchaeus had become, they will grow in abundance and receive whatever is better in the kingdom, as our Lord said to the Jews, "But if you had been sons of Abraham, you would have done the deeds of Abraham,[38] and you would have become the sons of Abraham through the deeds of Abraham, while you are with your wives and your children and your wealth as when Abraham was with his wife and children, with his servants and all of his possession."
>
> [Abraham] did not treat anyone badly and he removed from them many evil things. He did good things with his wealth for all the people who were in need and encountered him. He walked among them and treated well [equally] the good [people] and the evil, those who treated him badly, and those who treated him well. With these he became an heir in heaven and an excellent example for all the generations after him so that they might imitate him. Because of this he became great and was glorified and called the ruler of the feast[39] so that all the Upright and the righteous might be comforted in the bosom of his righteousness.[40] (30.28; 362)

The author's assessment of Abraham is ingenious, for he has sifted out of Abraham's wide range of qualities, achievements, piety, and faith the reality that the patriarch does not fit the typical model of the ascetic Christian — and yet he is the archetype for all Christians. Abraham's possessions mark him as much as his faith, but no one will argue with his holiness and generosity. The Upright cannot ignore this combination of characteristics — they are called to increase in faith and sanctity, as well as to dispense with their wealth generously for the benefit of others in need. Just as the author had insisted that the Lord would have made provisions for humanity without working, if Adam had only not sinned, now he adjusts the formula.

---

38. John 8:39.
39. Matt 8:11.
40. Luke 16:23.

If the Lord had said to them, "Renounce your wives and let go of your property," as he had said to the Apostles, they would have done his will, just as when he had said to them, "Go out from your land and from your family, and go where I tell you."[41] Because they loved him and loved [fellow] human beings, they went gladly even while they knew that they had been plundered and cheated and had their wives taken, in order that they might fulfill the commandment of him whom they loved, and in order to continue honoring those whom they loved. Also, whenever he asked them to sacrifice their sons, they gladly sacrificed, because his love was fixed in their heart and they did His will in all He commanded them.

But had [God] said to them, "Give up your wives and your sons and your possessions, and go proclaim me wherever I will tell you," it would have been easier for them to leave their wives in celibacy and their living children in their homes and their wealth and everything that belonged to them with their families and go wherever the Lord sent them; much more easily than what he did say to them, "Go with everything you have with you," because their women were carried away by force to be dishonored before their very eyes, and their sons to be sacrificed in the face of [their sense of] compassion, and their possessions were to be plundered every day as they looked on with their own eyes and endured it — because of the hope of truth which is to come. But all whom the Lord held back from renunciation and from physical celibacy were to become an example to all who are married in this world, so that they might live like them. (9.19; 101-2)

The author insists that Abraham could have lived the ascetic and celibate life if God had called him to do so, but instead he lived the Upright existence to the full with wives and family, possessions and wealth. It is remarkable for an ascetical work to make this shift, but even more so is the declaration that staying in the world is the more difficult route — and presumably the more spiritually beneficial.

Has the author completely changed his understanding of asceticism and moved away from an a-economic model to one in which the committed disciples of Christ are immersed in the human economy as well as the divine economy? Never hearing the end of the story, either from the author or from later witnesses and chroniclers, one cannot render a definitive answer. Certainly, subsequent ascetical literature did not follow this lead, but continued to promote a rigorous physical asceticism that eschewed the worldly ways of marriage, possessions, and business. The emergence of coe-

41. Gen 12:1.

nobitic monasticism[42] would present a new economic model, with each monastery striving for self-sufficiency in production of food, clothing, furniture, and necessary equipment as work became an essential part of the ascetical regimen. Nevertheless, it would be hard to imagine that there were not a number of communities in the next era that would live out the faithful commitment of the Upright ones working in their world toward Perfection in a manner similar to *The Book of Steps*. But no one seems to have written about them.

42. A community-based type of monasticism established by Pachomius in the third century.

EDITORIAL AFTERWORD

15. Afterword

Bruce W. Longenecker

Running throughout this volume are two predominant threads, demonstrating the following points: (1) deeply embedded within the theology of many New Testament texts is an economic dimension with regard to care for those in economic need, and (2) the economic dimension of New Testament theology often provided the basis for further theological reflection in literature from the patristic period. Along the way, a few other important issues pertaining to economic aspects of the New Testament have also been explored (i.e., essays by Oakes, Kloppenborg, and Horrell). But the majority of the essays in this book gravitate toward demonstrating that an economic component is inherent within the theology of the New Testament texts examined (i.e., essays by Barton, Capper, Kuecker, Downs, Kammell), and that the earliest interpreters often read those texts in that light (i.e., most of the essays in the section "Early Christian Reception").

It is arguable that focusing not simply on New Testament texts themselves but also on their reception within the early centuries of the common era enables contemporary interpreters to consider their own reading strategies in a better light. Noticing how the earliest interpreters utilized New Testament texts offers a rough taxonomy of reception history from which to gauge interpretative merits and weaknesses. So, we have seen occasions when early interpretations challenge the paradigms that have long been established within the contemporary academy (e.g., Longenecker's case about the interpretation of Gal 2:10). Occasions when early interpreters seem largely to have "got it wrong" have also been noted (e.g., Macaskill's case about patristic interpretations of the Johannine Apocalypse); potential deficiencies in patristic readings might correspond with similar deficiencies in some twenty-first-century readings. More complicated are occasions in which the fathers "got it wrong precisely in order to get it right" — to brashly summarize Wilhite's case regarding Tertullian's position vis-à-vis Paul. But what emerges from the essays of Hays and Kitchen is the notable extent to which the New Testament's earliest interpreters employed its texts in vigorous reflection on the economic dimension of what it means to be a follower of Jesus in their respective contexts.

Theological reflection of that kind is unlikely to result in uniformity of conviction or practice among contemporary followers of Jesus — not least because the New Testament texts themselves are marked out by a diversity of views with regard to the legitimacy of financial gain. If we follow Kammell's argument regarding James, for instance, the Jacobite author imagined those who benefited from the economic system of the Greco-Roman world not to be at risk before God, as long as they maintained an attitude of humility with regard to their wealth and its usage (an attitude to be fostered within communities of Jesus followers). If we follow Macaskill's argument regarding the Johannine Apocalypse, however, John imagined those who benefited from the economic system of the Greco-Roman world to be participating in a demonic system. If these two contributors are correct, we might imagine this intermingling of views within New Testament texts to correspond to diversity within the twenty-first century with regard to the legitimacy of financial gain in today's globalized economic system. But regardless of the mix of views that the New Testament "canonizes" on this score, it is arguably the case that giving for the benefit of those in need runs like a spine throughout the New Testament, intertwined with the conviction that this self-giving narrative is to inform the corporate ethos of the followers of Jesus even in their economic relationships with each other and beyond. In effect, care for the economically vulnerable seems to have been non-negotiable within early Christian reflection and practice, even when theological convictions may have diverged on other scores.[1]

In fact, many historians have seen in this "non-negotiable" feature of

---

1. Even Paul needs to be recognized as affirming this non-negotiable aspect of Christian identity. See my *Remember the Poor: Paul, Poverty, and the Greco-Roman World* (Grand Rapids: Eerdmans, forthcoming). Cf. Neil Elliott (*Liberating Paul: The Justice of God and the Politics of the Apostle* [Maryknoll, NY: Orbis Books, 1994; reprinted, Sheffield: Sheffield Academic Press, 1995], p. 87): "Any interpretation that excludes the possibility of Paul's awareness of the poor, and his reflection on the situation of the poor in the light of the gospel he proclaimed, ought to be considered doubtful."

early Christian communities the most compelling explanation for the rise and spread of the early Jesus movement within the Greco-Roman world. Toward the end of his book *The Origins of Christian Morality*, Wayne Meeks writes:

> Perhaps . . . it was in certain of their social practices that the Christian groups most effectively distinguished themselves from other cult associations, clubs, or philosophical schools — [1] their special rituals of initiation and communion, [2] their practice of communal admonition and discipline, [and 3] the organization of aid for widows, orphans, prisoners, and other weaker members of the movement.[2]

If such corporate features distinguished early groups of Jesus followers from other Greco-Roman associations, the historian Henry Chadwick suggests that the "practical application" of charity was probably the most potent single cause of Christian success."[3] Classicists have repeatedly made the point that Christian care for the destitute was "a new form of charity" in the ancient world that "exercised a powerful attraction within the cities of the later Empire" and offers the historian "one explanation for the success of Christianity."[4]

The evidence for this view of the historical development of Christianity cannot be assembled here.[5] But unless we are blind to the economic dimension of New Testament theology, it is not hard to see how such a view is arrived at. In light of the economic dimension of the founding documents of Christianity, assessments such as the following might look slightly curious: "What is remarkable is that the poor became a very important part of Christian thought and practice, in a world having little or no concern for them."[6] That the poor became a "very important part of Christian thought and practice" can only be thought of as "remarkable" in relation to the historical

2. Wayne A. Meeks, *The Origins of Christian Morality: The First Two Centuries* (New Haven and London: Yale University Press, 1993), p. 213.

3. H. Chadwick, *The Early Church* (Harmondsworth: Penguin, 1967), p. 56, with examples on pp. 56-58. On this, see esp. Richard Finn, *Almsgiving in the Later Roman Empire: Christian Promotion and Practice, 313-450* (Oxford: Oxford University Press, 2006).

4. C. R. Whittaker, "The Poor in the City of Rome," in *Land, City and Trade in the Roman Empire* (Aldershot: Variorum Ashgate, 1993), article 7 [there is no sequential pagination throughout the book; internally the article's pagination is from 1-25], p. 4.

5. I engage with this view in my *Remember the Poor*.

6. Gildas Hamel, *Poverty and Charity in Roman Palestine, First Three Centuries C.E.* (Berkeley: University of California Press, 1990), p. 236.

context of the emergent Christian movement, not in relation to the theological interests of that movement's founding documents.

The quotations used in a preceding paragraph have twice made use of the word "charity" in relation to Christian identity — a word that has received some bad press, and not without reason. We will all have heard that charitable initiatives should have little place in the rectification of economic injustice; countering poverty requires measures that operate at the level of deep economic structures, rather than at the surface level. Charity is the strategy of the pseudo-satanic, it might be said, because it leaves the benefactor feeling justified while the fundamental problem goes unaddressed. Charity cannot plumb the depths of economic injustice, but it can all too easily distract us from the urgent task of implementing essential solutions. Only the reconfiguration of economic structures has any real hope of introducing equity into economic social relations.

Clearly there is quite a lot to this. And it is not only modern wisdom, but ancient wisdom as well. "You do no service to a beggar by giving him food or drink, for two reasons: you lose what you give him, and you prolong his life for misery" are the words of the Greco-Roman playwright Plautus.[7] The primary disservice against the poor man arises from the fact that nothing of significance really happens in benevolent gestures of charitable action; the poor man continues to be poor and is perpetuated in his situation of poverty. Addressing the issues of entrenched poverty requires structural change that transcends short-term forms of charity.[8]

The curious thing is that the pertinent texts of the New Testament show no cognizance of this dichotomizing of charity and structural reform. But then, the charitable initiatives of the earliest followers of Jesus were not comprised simply of the tossing of a coin to the needy while passing them by on the street. For all that we can tell, those early communities of Jesus followers did not simply keep the poor at arm's length through a charitable gesture. Instead, the poor were welcomed into the very heart of those communities of fellowship and were "gifted" as contributing members within it. That, at least, is the impression that Paul gives, in his discussion of the interworking of the corporate "body" of Christ (1 Cor 12:4-26; Rom 12:4-8). No different from

7. *Trinummus* 339, slightly paraphrased.

8. Moreover, however well-intentioned the giver of charity might be, charity can often be degrading to its intended recipient(s). Compare the lyrics of the song "I Don't Want Nobody to Give Me Nothing" by Phil Upchurch (from the 1997 album *Whatever Happened to the Blues* [Go Jazz Records]): "I don't want nobody to give me nothing, just open up the door, I'll get it myself."

anyone else, the poor were expected to contribute their own "gifts" and to participate in the nurturing of a group of fictive kin who supported each other and bore the "burdens" of each other. Whatever charitable initiatives flowed within such contexts were not seen as an ineffectual part of the problem but as part of the solution. The corporate meals of urban Jesus followers were not intended as a mean of simply filling stomachs; instead, they were seen as incarnations of the kingdom or empire of God. In that empire (in contrast to the empires of this age, including that of Rome), the rich do not accumulate resources at the expense of the poor and furnish their tables with food that the poor have no access to (unlike the parable of the rich man and Lazarus). Instead, in the empire of Israel's God, the poor "are welcomed to the messianic banquet alongside the rich, where they find not only a place but a voice"[9] — or better, perhaps, a place where their voice is heard and a place where their needs are met, as they themselves help to contribute to an empire in which the various needs of all are met, as the people of a generous God give expression to their "faith working practically through love" (Gal 5:6).

It seems, then, that some of the earliest Jesus followers imagined charitable initiatives within their communities to be incarnations of a divine order that was invading the very structures of this world, advertising a "kingdom" that rested on foundations contrary to the structures of "this age," an empire empowered by the sovereign creator and loving redeemer. In this way, they imagined even their low-grade charitable initiatives to advertise and participate in the structural rectification inherent in the reign of God that was invading the world in and through their communities. Accordingly, they seem often to have imagined their miniature acts of generosity to be part of a much grander narrative of the structural reform that would eventually change things forever, through the power of God. We might hope that they were not altogether wrong about that.

9. Michael S. Northcott, *A Moral Climate: The Ethics of Global Warming* (London: Darton, Longman and Todd, 2007), p. 251.

Contributors

STEPHEN C. BARTON is Reader in New Testament in the Department of Theology and Religion, Durham University, and a priest of the Church of England. His publications include *Discipleship and Family Ties in Mark and Matthew* (1994), *Life Together: Family, Sexuality and Community in the New Testament and Today* (2001) and, as editor, *Holiness Past and Present* (2003), *The Cambridge Companion to the Gospels* (2006), and *Idolatry: False Worship in the Bible, Early Judaism and Christianity* (2007).

BRIAN CAPPER is Reader in Christian Origins at Canterbury Christ Church University. He taught previously at the universities of Edinburgh, Oxford, and St. Andrews. He holds his doctorate from Cambridge University, held a research fellowship at Tübingen University, and was more recently *Gastdozent* for two years in Tübingen. His research focuses on the social context of early Christianity, including apocalyptic and the Dead Sea Scrolls, the roles of women, the beginnings of the Johannine tradition, and the realities of wealth and poverty in the ancient world. He is presently writing a book, *Jesus and the Poor*, on agrarian economics and the piety of poverty.

DAVID J. DOWNS is Assistant Professor of New Testament Studies at Fuller Theological Seminary in Pasadena, CA. He is the author of *The Offering of the Gentiles: Paul's Collection for Jerusalem in Its Chronological, Cultural, and Cultic Contexts* (2008). He has also published articles in journals such as *Catholic Biblical Quarterly, Horizons in Biblical Theology, Journal for the Study of the New Testament,* and *New Testament Studies.*

CHRISTOPHER M. HAYS is doing doctoral research under the supervision of Professor Markus Bockmuehl at the University of Oxford. His thesis examines Lukan wealth ethics and their impact on second- and third-century Christian ideology and praxis.

DAVID G. HORRELL is Professor of New Testament Studies at the University of Exeter, UK. He is the author of a number of books, including *The Epistles of Peter and Jude* (1998), *Solidarity and Difference: A Contemporary Reading of Paul's Ethics* (2005), and *1 Peter* (New Testament Guides, 2008). He is currently leading a project on Uses of the Bible in Environmental Ethics and continuing work on 1 Peter.

MARIAM KAMELL is finishing her doctoral research under the supervision of Professor Richard Bauckham and Dr. Grant Macaskill at the University of St. Andrews. Her publications include: a co-authored commentary on James (with Craig Blomberg); an essay, "Faith in Hebrews and James" (2008), as well as exegetical essays on selected passages from Luke for a lectionary commentary series.

ROBERT A. KITCHEN is minister at Knox-Metropolitan United Church in Regina, Saskatchewan. He read for the D. Phil. in Syriac patristics at the University of Oxford, and has translated (with Martien F. G. Parmentier) *The Book of Steps: The Syriac Liber Graduum* (2004). With Kristian S. Heal he is the co-editor of a volume of essays, *Breaking the Mind: New Essays on the Syriac Book of Steps* (forthcoming); and is preparing a new translation and introduction to *The Discourses of Philoxenus of Mabbug* for Cistercian Publications.

JOHN S. KLOPPENBORG (Ph.D., University of St. Michael's College, 1984) is Chair of the Department and Centre for the Study of Religion at the University of Toronto. His most recent publications are *Q, the Earliest Gospel* (2008); *The Tenants in the Vineyard: Ideology, Economics, and Agrarian Conflict in Jewish Palestine* (2006), *Excavating Q: The History and Setting of the Sayings Gospel* (2000); *The Critical Edition of Q*, with James M. Robinson and Paul Hoffmann (2000); and *Voluntary Associations in the Graeco-Roman World*, with S. G. Wilson (1996).

AARON J. KUECKER is Assistant Professor of Theology at Trinity Christian College in Palos Heights, IL. He recently completed his doctoral research at the University of St. Andrews under the supervision of Philip Esler, Richard Bauckham, and Ben Witherington, III. His research interests lie in the relationship between the Holy Spirit and identity formation, especially as it relates to ethnic identity and intergroup reconciliation in Luke-Acts.

KELLY D. LIEBENGOOD is Assistant Professor of Biblical Studies at Le Tourneau University in Longview, Texas. He is currently finishing his doctoral thesis, "Zechariah 9–14 and 1 Peter's Theology of Suffering," at the University of St. Andrews under the supervision of Bruce W. Longenecker. Prior to his doctoral studies, he was Assistant Professor of New Testament at Seminario ESEPA (San José, Costa Rica), and Seminario Las Palmas (Cuba).

BRUCE W. LONGENECKER, the W. W. Melton Chair of Religion in the Department of Religion, Baylor University, is the author of five books, including *Rhetoric at the Boundaries* (2005), *The Lost Letters of Pergamum* (2003), and *The Triumph of Abraham's God* (1998). He has edited or co-edited three earlier volumes: *Narrative Dynamics in Paul* (2002), *Luke, Paul and the Graeco-Roman World* (2002), and *The Holy Spirit and Christian Origins* (2004).

GRANT MACASKILL is Lecturer in New Testament in the Faculty of Divinity at the University of St. Andrews. His publications include: *Revealed Wisdom and Inaugurated Eschatology in Ancient Judaism and Early Christianity* (2007), "Creation, Eschatology and Ethics in 4QInstruction" (2007), and "No Monuments in Heaven: Miroslav Volf and the Forgetting of Suffering" (2007).

PETER OAKES is Greenwood Lecturer in the New Testament in the School of Arts, Histories, and Cultures at the University of Manchester. His publications include *Philippians: From People to Letter* (2001) and *Rome in the Bible and the Early Church* (2002). He is the editor of the *Journal for the Study of the New Testament Booklist*.

DAVID E. WILHITE is Assistant Professor of Theology at George W. Truett Theological Seminary, Baylor University. He is the author of *Tertullian the African: An Anthropological Reading of Tertullian's Context and Identities* (2007), and he is currently co-authoring *The Doctrine of the Church: A Guide for the Perplexed* with Matt R. Jenson (forthcoming).

Index of Modern Authors

Index of Ancient Sources